MW01097389

THE RAINBOW ROUTE

AN ILLUSTRATED HISTORY

of

THE SILVERTON RAILROAD
THE SILVERTON NORTHERN RAILROAD
and
THE SILVERTON, GLADSTONE & NORTHERLY
RAILROAD

The First Printing of the First Edition
is limited to 3,000 copies, each of which is
numbered and signed by the authors

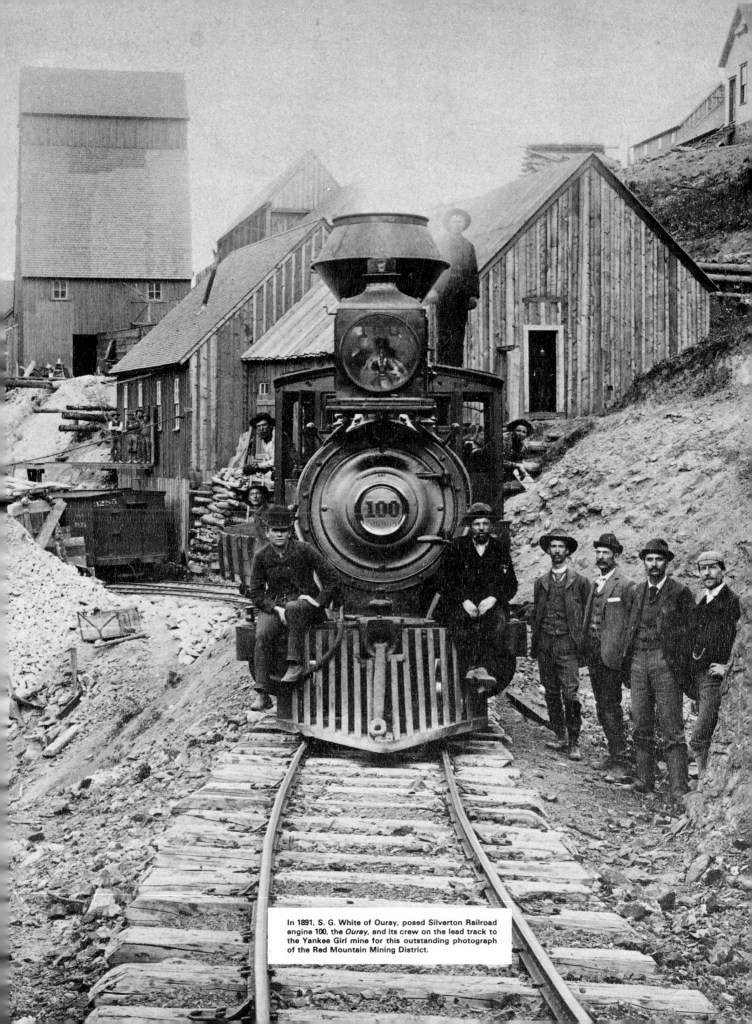

In 1891, S. G. White of Ouray, posed Silverton Railroad engine 100, the *Ouray*, and its crew on the lead track to the Yankee Girl mine for this outstanding photograph of the Red Mountain Mining District.

THE RAINBOW ROUTE

AN ILLUSTRATED HISTORY

of

THE SILVERTON RAILROAD
THE SILVERTON NORTHERN RAILROAD
and
THE SILVERTON, GLADSTONE & NORTHERLY RAILROAD

By

Robert E. Sloan
and
Carl A. Skowronski

SUNDANCE PUBLICATIONS *Limited*

THE RAINBOW ROUTE

By

Robert E. Sloan
and
Carl A. Skowronski

A DELUXE ILLUSTRATED HISTORY OF THE THREE LITTLE NARROW-GAUGE RAILROADS WHICH OPERATED OUT OF SILVERTON, COLORADO: THE SILVERTON RAILROAD; THE SILVERTON NORTHERN RAILROAD; AND THE SILVERTON, GLADSTONE AND NORTHERLY RAILROAD

PUBLISHED BY
SUNDANCE PUBLICATIONS LIMITED

Russ Collman, *Editor-in-Chief*
Dell McCoy, *Production Manager*
Peter E. Voorheis, *Business Manager*

Jackson C. Thode, *Editor-Writer*

Fritz Klinke, *Editorial Consultant*

Printing by
Sundance Publications Limited
Denver, Colorado, U.S.A.

Copyright © 1975 by Sundance Publications Limited
250 Broadway, Denver, Colorado, U.S.A. 80203
All Rights Reserved
Reproduction of the whole or any part of the contents
without written permission is prohibited
ISBN 0-913582-12-3

4

CHAPTER

I

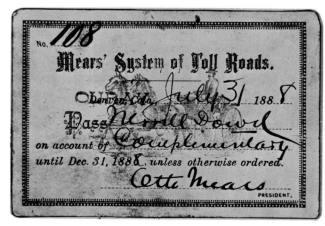

MORRIS W. ABBOTT COLLECTION

Before the Railroad

THE SILVERTON Railroad; the Silverton Northern; and the Silverton, Gladstone & Northerly were organized and built for the prime purpose of turning marginal mines into lucrative big producers. That success was achieved in the goals of this assemblage of three-foot-gauge railroads, venturing where even the almighty Denver and Rio Grande feared to tread, there can be no dispute; in the process, they created a lore not surpassed by any other narrow-gauge mountain railroad.

To perceive and understand the problems posed to the people, the mines and the railroads of the region covered by this book, it is necessary to review the elements of the setting which led to their development. Up to the end of the Age of Dinosaurs—about 65-million years ago—the region that now comprises the San Juan Mountains of Colorado and New Mexico was a flat-lying sea-bottom and coastal plain. Vegetation along the shores of the sea was formed into massive deposits of coal and oil in the neighboring rocks as they accumulated. Then, four major volcanoes erupted in a line extending southwestwardly from Ouray to Rico and LaPlata, all in Colorado, on to the Carrizo Mountains in northeastern Arizona—introducing gold and silver ores into the older rocks, ores that in large part were responsible ultimately for the creation of the Rio Grande Southern Railroad.

Some 10-million years later, about 55-million years ago, the Needle Mountains between Silverton and Durango, Colorado, were raised above sea level—the rivers from them carrying sediment both to the north and to the south. Then again, in the era between 34-million years ago and 24-million years ago, most of southwestern Colorado became an area of awesome volcanoes of monstrous proportions. The volcanoes belched forth at least 12,000 *cubic miles* of lava and volcanic ash from at least 13 major volcanic centers. Two of these centers were located on a line from Silverton to Lake City, and most of the exposed rocks in this area today came from this cataclysmic volcanic activity.

The final stage of this volcanic activity was the production of gold, silver, copper, zinc and lead ores in the fractures in the rocks of the San Juan Mountains. Following this volcanic episode, the mountains were cut down and eroded into sharp peaks and steep-sided valleys, at first by stream erosion, then by the development of mountain glaciers during the last million years. All the happenings recorded in this book came about as a result of these natural events, particularly of the most recent ones in this abbreviated geologic history.

The first humans in the San Juans were the ancestors of the North American Indians who originated in Asia and migrated to this continent about 24,000 years ago. They came as a wandering people, without dogs or any other domestic animals (none had yet been domesticated anywhere)—with only spears and knives as weapons. These people were primarily big game hunters. The comings and goings of the various tribes of these Indians through the area are not known, however, until the last 3,000 years.

SUNDANCE PHOTO BY DELL A. McCOY

In this view you are looking down on the road Otto Mears built, former Ouray & Red Mountain Toll Road — now U.S. Highway 550, often referred to as the Million Dollar Highway. The toll gate was located to the left, at Bear Creek Falls, along the cliffside above the Uncompahgre River.

10

RONALD F. RUHOFF PHOTO

Red Mountain Number 1 shows off her colors in this spectacular panoramic view. The camera was aimed directly at the peak and the Corkscrew Gulch turntable site. A portion of the abandoned grade of the Silverton Railway can be seen, cutting through the trees above the gulch. Out of sight, to the left and below, is the ghost town of Ironton. Many aspen and evergreen trees have grown up along the old grade.

From about 3,000 years ago until about 450 A.D., the Indians in the present Four Corners area (including the San Juans) were the group called the Basketmakers, or the *Anasazi*—the ancient ones. Basketmaker Indians grew corn and squash, and hunted and fished to supplement their diet. Their basketry is famous for its beauty and design—the Indians even using their own hair in the weaving process. They lived in caves or rock shelters, and for hunting and defense used spears, spear throwers, called *atlatl,* and clubs.

By about 500 A.D., newcomers arrived on the scene and apparently settled with the Basketmakers. These people became the ancestors of today's Pueblo Indians. Eventually, these enterprising Indians learned to make pottery, and began using the bow and arrow as their principal weapon. They also learned how to make underground roofed pithouses to help ward off the cold

of winter. They clothed themselves with yucca-fiber sandals, breechclouts and robes of turkey feathers or rabbit skins. By 700 A.D. these industrious people began to replace their pithouses with structures built entirely above ground. At first the walls were constructed of adobe—sun-baked mud, reinforced with sticks or straw. However, later the walls came to be made almost entirely of stone, with the pithouses—known as *kivas*—used only for ceremonial occasions. Subsequently, cotton was added to their crops, the cotton being woven into fabrics. Like corn, cotton cultivation was introduced from Mexico.

From 1100 A.D. to 1400 A.D. the Anasazi culture reached its Golden Age. Large multi-story pueblos were built at Mesa Verde, Colorado; Chaco Canon, New Mexico; and Kayenta, Arizona. These towns contained hundreds of rooms and were as high as four and five stories; it is not

11

STATE HISTORICAL SOCIETY OF COLORADO COLLECTION

The Cliff dwellings pictured here were photographed by Jackson during the Hayden survey.

unreasonable to suppose these settlements contained as many as 3,000 souls. The snowcapped San Juan Mountains nearby were regarded as sources of timber and game, but were not places in which to live the year around.

The great Anasazi pueblo period came to a close with a prolonged interval of drought, which is well-recorded in the growth rings of trees in the Southwest. Beginning about 1276, the drought continued for almost a quarter of a century—to about 1300. With a generation of crop failures, it is not surprising that these people became reduced in numbers and gradually migrated from the region. Many moved to the Rio Grande Valley in New Mexico, where small villages—such as those at Bandelier National Monument near Los Alamos—developed. The Hopi Indians of New Mexico are among the descendants of these early inhabitants of the San Juans.

In the late Fifteenth Century—about the time Columbus made the New World known to Western civilization—a group of Indians from the Canadian mountains migrated south into the Four Corners area. These were the ancestors of both the Navajos, who became herdsmen and agriculturists, and their relatives, the Apaches. The latter became Plains Indians, who in adapting themselves to the horses introduced by the Spanish, became the

finest light cavalry in the world. Still later, in the early 1500's, relatives of the Aztec Hopi—originally from Nevada, and now known as the Utes—migrated into and settled in and around the San Juan Mountains.

In 1540 the entire Four Corners area was claimed for Spain by Francisco Vasquez de Coronado. At first the effects were minor, but as Spanish colonization continued, more and more cultural changes ensued.

The first sign of mining interest in the region came in 1765 when Don Juan Mira de Rivera led an expedition from Mexico up the Rio San Juan to the Sierra La Plata (freely translated to mean, "The Silver Mountains"), and around the San Juans to the Black Cañon of the Gunnison, to investigate rumors of gold and silver. Since he did not go up into the San Juans, he found only minor amounts of placer gold. By 1776, when Escalante and Dominguez brought a 12-man expedition to the San Juans from Santa Fe, many of the mountains and rivers already had been named by the Spaniards.

In 1821 Mexico finally won her independence from Spain, and the San Juans became part of Mexico. Ten years later, a party of 60 fur trappers

STATE HISTORICAL SOCIETY OF COLORADO COLLECTION

The Hayden survey campsite near Eureka was a scene of activity as the crew prepared their work as breakfast was prepared.

RICHARD A. RONZIO COLLECTION

Situated high above Silverton, 13,000 feet above sea level, Baker's cabin kept the hardy miners going. Its hand-hewn logs provided adequate protection against the elements of Nature. Bakers Park was named for Charles Baker — the builder of this cabin — who explored and prospected in the area shortly after 1869.

Miners living in the camp associated with the Mountaineer and North Star lodes had this view — looking down Cunningham Gulch, 1,000 feet above the valley floor. At the left is King Solomon Mountain, in the center is Tower Mountain, while at the right is Galena Mountain.

WILLIAM H. JACKSON PHOTO — U.S. GEOLOGICAL SURVEY

from the St. Louis Fur Company, headed by William G. Walten, left St. Louis during the spring—heading for the Southwest. They reached Taos, New Mexico, by the fall of that year, and spent the next 12 months trapping beaver and pelting on the Rio San Juan and its tributaries. During the summer of 1833 they spent their time in the valley of the Rio Dolores and around the present site of Trout Lake.

The Treaty of Guadalupe Hidalgo ceded the San Juan area, among other Mexican territory, to the United States in 1848. John C. Fremont went up the Rio Grande, trying to find a route for a railroad across the San Juans, but failed miserably. Snow, cold and conflicts between Fremont and his guide, mountain man "Preacher Bill" Williams, wrecked this expedition and only 22 of the 33 escaped alive. No one was able to re-locate the site where they had panned gold near Lake City.

In 1851 the San Juans became part of Utah Territory, named for the Ute Indians. In 1853 Captain John W. Gunnison skirted the northern end of the San Juan Mountains in following the Gunnison River. In 1859 Lieutenant James Simpson led a geologic party into the San Juan Basin, south of the San Juan Mountains, and Captain J. N. Macomb led a party up the river north of Mesa Verde. The Colorado gold rush began in 1859 on Cherry Creek in present-day Denver, and opened up what was to become Colorado Territory in 1861.

Captain Charles Baker—by some sources known as John or Jim Baker—a veteran of the 1860 gold campaign in California Gulch near Leadville, obtained the financial support of his employers to pay for an expedition along the San Juan River. He left California Gulch with seven men in July of 1860. His letters to his employer, S. B. Kellogg, described placer deposits paying 25 cents per pan. Kellogg and his family left Denver on December 14, 1860, accompanied or rather followed by 150 treasure-seekers from the 1859 diggings along Cherry Creek and Clear Creek between Golden and Denver. Among the pioneers were Abner French, "Noisy Tom" Pollock (Denver's executioner at the time) and his new wife, Sarah, daughter of Reverend (later Major) John M. Chivington. Other parties joined up, for a total of 300 people—and the San Juan gold rush was on.

The route followed was south to Pueblo, thence westward over Sangre de Cristo Pass. Winter road building took 14 days before the entourage could cross the pass and drop down into the San Luis Valley. By March, 1861, they reached the town of Conejos, one of the oldest towns in Colorado, and proceeded on west by way of Pagosa Springs. The first day of April found the party at the mouth of Cascade Creek along the Rio de las Animas Perdidas (River of Lost Souls—later Americanized to the "Las Animas River" and colloquially referred to as "the Animas"). Advance scouts met the members of the Baker party who had lived the winter through in a broad, beautiful, sheltered valley 18 miles north—up the cañon of the Las Animas. This protected spot became known as Bakers Park and is the present-day townsite of Silverton. Baker's party had built brush lean-to shanties for wintering, while the actual "diggings" were at the site of what ultimately was to become Eureka, nine miles farther up the cañon.

By June of 1861, when rumors about the outbreak of the American Civil War reached the camp, sluice boxes along the Las Animas were netting no more than 50 cents per day. The Cascade Creek camp had broken up about May 1 —the people moving south to found the town of Animas City, just north of present-day Durango. However, they abandoned their townsite in July, thus giving this settlement the dubious honor of becoming the first ghost town in the San Juans.

Baker and a few of his original party stayed at Eureka Gulch until fall, searching for gold and not suspecting the presence of vast quantities of silver. They left the region by way of Fort Garland, where the rumors about the war were found to be true. Baker, who was from Virginia, went home and fought with the Confederacy until the surrender at Appomattox. His departure was typical of the general exodus of prospectors and miners from Colorado resulting from the outbreak of the Civil War.

About one-fourth of the people in Colorado at the time were Confederate sympathizers, with an even higher proportion in Denver. The South was short of money, and several abortive attempts to capture the Colorado gold fields for the Confederate States were made during the conflict. The first one consisted of guerrilla raids in southern Colorado by a Captain Madison in 1862. The second was a full-blown attempt by the Second Texas Cavalry under General Henry H. Sibley— more remarked for inventing the small portable tent stove (still in use) than for his generalship— to capture the mines of Colorado, Nevada and California. The Texans left El Paso in February, 1862, proceeding up the Rio Grande Valley. They took Albuquerque and Santa Fe, and were advancing on Fort Union when they met and were repulsed by the First Colorado Volunteers at Apache Pass, New Mexico, on March 26. Two days later, a major battle was fought in a broad meadow near the crest of La Glorieta Pass. During the fight

Major John M. Chivington, whose son-in-law and daughter had been among the San Juan miners the previous year, crossed the mountains over trail-less areas and burned all the Confederate supplies behind the lines. This stopped the Southern campaign cold and the Texans beat a hasty retreat, thus assuring that the First California Volunteers —and in particular a young private therein named Otto Mears—would have no major part in fighting the Civil War. In later years—as a result of building most of the roads and railways in the Silverton area—Otto Mears was to become known as the *Pathfinder of the San Juan.*

In 1863 Alexander C. Hunt and Kit Carson began negotiations with the Ute Indian nation for a treaty giving the San Luis Valley to the whites. The Utes, however, were reluctant to give up any of their land, and were not persuaded until 1868. They were guaranteed all lands west of the 107th meridian and south of a line 15 miles north of the 40th parallel.

With the San Luis Valley open to settlement and the Civil War ended, prospectors began poking around in the San Juans in greater numbers. As early as 1869, there was an encampment of prospectors near the present site of Lake City.

About the time the treaty was signed, Charles Baker returned to Colorado and started an exploring party near Buena Vista. They headed southwest, exploring the country and being harassed by the Utes as they went. Ironically, Baker— who had survived the hazards of active participation in the War Between the States, was killed by the Utes at this time; in fact, they allowed only two members of the party to escape.

Another party of 50 men, under Calvin Jackson and Captain C. E. Cooley, tried to reach the San Juans from Prescott, Arizona, starting in 1869. The Apaches stopped them, allowing only eight of the men to continue under the proviso that they would dig no holes nor search for gold in any way. By October, the small party had reached the Mancos Valley, where an early five-day snowstorm forced them to retreat. They struggled to the log houses of the 1861 Kellogg-Pollock expedition at Animas City ten days later, and got provisions from Santa Fe, but found the Utes also were aware of their presence. Ute chiefs Ignacio and Sopath extracted promises from the prospectors that they would not plow or build fences, or cabins, and would remember that the land belonged to the Utes. They wintered at Tierra Amarilla, New Mexico, where they were joined by four others from the original party, and in April of 1870 they resumed the journey north. One group went up the Rio Dolores, while the other group prospected around Bakers

Park and wintered there.

By following some placer gold upstream, Dempsey Reese, Adnah French and Miles Johnson discovered a gold-bearing quartz vein on the north side of Arrastra Gulch in 1871. Naming their find the "Little Giant Mine," they began extracting the ore and built a crude *arrastra* to process it, giving the name to the gulch. The arrastra, an old Spanish device for crushing gold and other consisted of a circular enclosed stone bed v centerpost and rotating horizontal arm to w burro was hitched. The burro—walking arou centerpost—pulled heavy stones which gro ore to small fragments against the stone was slow and rather inefficient, but ver The arrastra used at the Little Giant $4,000 in gold for its owners in the first of operation.

Word of their strike traveled quickly ing the remoteness of the location, b more prospectors and miners. Late i Little Giant was bought by a Ma Hamilton, who ordered the machiner mill to process the ore. The machinery Fe for quite some time, awaiting son it to Arrastra Gulch. Finally, late in a retired Union Army major by Martin Van Buren Wasson took delivered the "Little Giant Quartz Hamilton. Erection of the mill was ately, but bad weather closed in a not completed until July 19, consisted of a 115-horsepower Dodge five-stamp crusher, and Located about 1,000 feet below was connected to the mine with The Little Giant produced $1 the few cabins clustered arour as Bullion City.

When word of the gold and Saguache, Colorado, Enos Mears, who had moved to Colorado mustered out of the Union Army, decided to cash in on the impending stampede to the San Juan mining districts, and formed the "Saguache and San Juan Toll Road Company" late in 1871. They projected their toll road from Saguache, in the northern end of the San Luis Valley, through the tiny mining camp of Lake City (then consisting of

Following page — "When will this trip end?" Not even the hand-hewn rock or the spectacular fall of water, or the deep gorge and towering mountains, could make this woman look into the canyon. This is the way the Bear Creek Falls toll gate house looked in 1894.

WILLIAM H. JACKSON PHOTO — JACKSON C. THODE COLLECTION

STATE HISTORICAL SOCIETY OF COLORADO COLLECTION

A. D. Wilson took a breather and enjoyed the view from atop Sultan Mountain, as Rhoda triangulated.

WILLIAM H. JACKSON PHOTO — | U.S. GEOLOGICAL SURVEY

Howardsville was but a cluster of tent cabins and log structures in 1875, as prospectors began to arrive. The view is looking northwest across the Rio de las Animas Perdidas, taken from the Stony Pass trail which went from Del Norte to Howardsville.

STATE HISTORICAL SOCIETY OF COLORADO COLLECTION

Topographer A. D. Wilson was mounted on his horse, ready for business, while mapping the Howardsville area in 1874.

only 13 windowless cabins), on across the San Juan Range to the Rio de las Animas. (Incidentally, the name, *Saguache*, is Indian in origin and is pronounced "Sawatch"—generally translated to mean "blue earth.") The 96 miles between Saguache and Lake City were completed; however, the road ended there for a time. In 1872, the Blue Mesa road was built from the Lake Fork of the Gunnison westward for 25 miles to Cimarron.

With the apparent success of the Little Giant operation, it soon became clear that neither the Federal government nor the Ute Indians were going to be able to keep the miners out of the San Juans. In 1872, new negotiations were begun with the Utes to sell the mining region, and when the treaty was finally signed on September 13, 1873, the Ute nation had relinquished all of what was to become the counties of Hinsdale, San Juan, Ouray, San Miguel, Dolores, Montezuma and La Plata.

When word got around that the Utes were going to give up the San Juan mining districts, the rush was on! Between 1,000 and 1,500 claims were staked out during the season of 1873, one yielding $15,000 by the end of the year, a fortune in those days.

The town of Howardsville sprang up around George Howard's cabin at the mouth of Cunningham Gulch. Since it was at the terminus of the Stony Pass trail, the route used most frequently to gain access to the district, Howardsville grew rapidly and soon boasted many firsts. Among these were the first brewery, the first post office, the first assay office, the first public blacksmith shop, and eventually, four saloons.

Some of the newcomers followed the Rio de las Animas south and settled around F. M. Snowden's cabin in Bakers Park. The season of 1873 saw the first woman in the new camps, always a welcomed sight in young mining towns.

In mid-1873, 6,000 pounds of machinery arrived from Denver for the first sawmill in the area. It was set up on Mineral Creek, on the south side of Bakers Park, and went into production immediately. With the availability of building materials assured, a townsite was selected and named *Silverton*. Reportedly, the name came from a local miner who exclaimed, "We ain't got much gold, but we've got silver by the ton!" Silverton was platted in 1874, and by early spring of that year, surveys for the streets had been completed—the new town containing about 25 cabins, with a population of approximately 100 souls. Two years later, in 1876, Silverton was incorporated.

In April of 1874, Congress approved the Brunot treaty and issued the proclamation that the San Juans were open to prospecting and settlement. With this, the Silverton boom began in earnest.

George and William Greene owned the largest store in Silverton at this time. In 1874 they hired John A. Porter to design the new 30-ton smelter they intended to build on the north side of Cement Creek in Bakers Park. The smelter made one run on ore from Arrastra Gulch, but the process was a failure. Porter then remodeled the furnace into a water-siphon-tap type, based on those he had seen at Eureka, Nevada, in 1873. The remodeled smelter was blown-in again in August of 1875, and ran until November, producing about $35,000 in refined ore.

Until 1874, the entire San Juan mining district had been part of Conejos County, but on February 10, 1874, La Plata County was organized, with Howardsville as county seat. La Plata County then included Howardsville and Silverton, and extended south as far as the new town of Parrott City (near present-day Durango)—and beyond, to the New Mexico border.

In 1875, the Silverton area mining activities spread rapidly from Arrastra Gulch to Sultan Mountain south of Bakers Park, where the North Star, Jennie Parker, Hercules and Little Dora quickly became producing properties. The activity

THE SILVERTON MINER, 1907 — MORRIS W. ABBOTT COLLECTION

The first cabin in Silverton was built by Colonel F. M. Snowden in 1874.

also spread up the Rio de las Animas to Cunningham Gulch, where the Pride of the West and Highland Mary became the leading mines, followed by the Dives, Shenandoah, and North Star. From Cunningham Gulch the excitement spread farther up the Animas to Maggie, Minnie, Eureka and Placer gulches. By 1876, the total output was estimated at over $1-million.

With the discovery of the Hotchkiss mine near Lake City in August of 1874, the boom in that area was off and running almost simultaneously with the Silverton boom. As new mines were opened, small camps and towns sprang up all over the San Juans. Mineral Point dates back to 1873, as does

RICHARD A. RONZIO COLLECTION

Above is a view of the first courthouse in San Juan County — which included all of southwestern Colorado at the time it was built. The log cabin sat at the mouth of Cunningham Gulch at Howardsville and later became a schoolhouse.

19

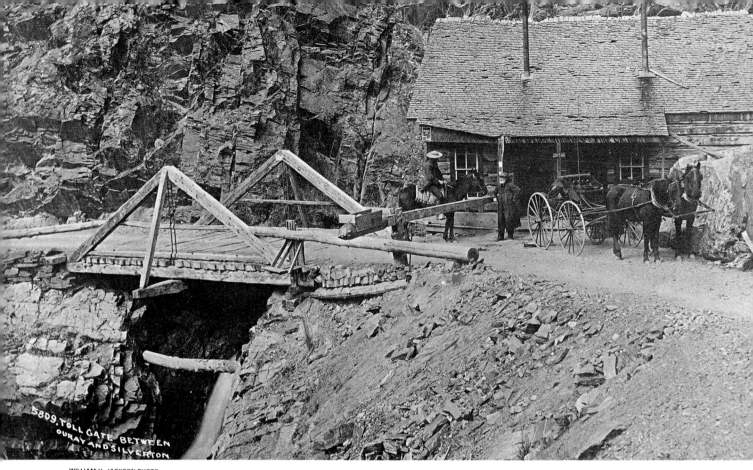

WILLIAM H. JACKSON PHOTO —
RICHARD A. RONZIO COLLECTION

The view above shows the toll gate on Mears' and Walsen's Ouray & Red Mountain Toll Road, which afforded travelers a rest stop at Bear Creek Falls. The toll house offered the finest in ginger ale, pear cidor, whiskeys and fine cigars, and even provided packed lunches "to go." This scene was photographed in 1885.

MOORE PHOTO — JACKSON C. THODE COLLECTION

Animas Forks. Eureka was laid out in 1874 at the mouth of Eureka Gulch. Between Animas Forks and Lake City three settlements—Rose's Cabin, Galena City (later called Capitol City) and Henson —were formed along Henson Creek.

On July 5, 1875, the commissioners of La Plata County authorized $600 for construction of a road between Silverton and Animas Forks, and by July 14, Otto Mears had arrived in Silverton to begin construction.

The same year, rich ores were discovered near present-day Ouray and soon after, a new rush started near Telluride.

In 1876 Colorado became the thirty-eighth state of the Union, and La Plata County was split; the southern portion retained the name, Parrott City being made county seat. The northern portion became San Juan County, with Howardsville as county seat. Popular legend has it that certain Silverton citizens, displeased with this arrangement, one night got the officials in Howardsville drunk and stole the county records, thereby establishing Silverton as the county seat. However, the facts are that an election was held in the new county to decide the matter. The outcome was that the new county seat was Silverton.

Wightman and Wallace built the toll road between Silverton and Animas City, near Durango, during 1876 and 1877; Mears connected Animas Forks and Lake City with a road. This not only permitted travel and transport of ores between the two major mining centers of Silverton and Lake City, but the increased traffic also assured continuing growth to the smaller communities along the route.

Animas Forks then contained 30 houses as well as the smelting and refining works of the Dakota and San Juan Mining Company, the San Juan Smelting Company, and later, in 1879, the Mineral Mountain Mining Company's dry concentrator. A judge declared there was no appeal from a verdict in Animas Forks since it was "the Highest Court in the Land"—11,300 feet above sea level.

A wagon road was completed in 1879 from Silverton up Cement Creek to Gladstone, extending on to the head of Poughkeepsie Gulch, where there was great activity on the Old Lout, Alabama, Poughkeepsie, Red Roger, Saxton, Alaska, Bonanza and other claims. A chlorination works was established that year in Gladstone to handle these ores.

MRS. MARVIN GREGORY COLLECTION

Rose's Cabin was a stagecoach stop between Lake City and Animas Forks, and was a welcome sight for trail-weary travelers.

While the Gladstone road was being built in 1878 the Rico rush began, and this, too, increased in 1879.

In Silverton the San Juan and New York Mining and Smelting Company had purchased the old Greene smelter, which had been operating unprofitably for four years, together with the Aspen mine and other properties on Hazelton Mountain. In 1879, under the management of John A. Porter, the Greene smelter was dismantled, the machinery moved south 45 miles and re-erection was started at the base of Smelter Hill, across the Rio de las Animas from the eventual site of Durango. This site was better suited for a smelter as it was closer to extensive supplies of good coal. The smelter was a ready customer when the Denver and Rio Grande Railway arrived on July 27, 1881.

Since the signing of the Brunot treaty in 1873, tension had been growing between the Utes and the settlers, culminating in the Meeker Massacre in 1879. This unfortunate event gave the State and U.S. governments the excuse they needed to force the northern Utes out of Colorado completely. A new treaty was signed on March 6, 1880, and the last band of northern Utes left Colorado for their new reservation in Utah on September 1, 1881.

During the summer of 1881 John Robinson discovered the metallic lode that became the Guston mine near Red Mountain. By autumn he had located the Yankee Girl, and immediately sold it for $125,000—then staked the Orphan Boy and Robinson claims adjacent to the Yankee Girl. This was the start of the incredibly rich Red Mountain mining district.

The Denver and Rio Grande's tracks reached Silverton in July, 1882—at last providing a rapid

Opposite page — a six-horse team and Concord coach added to the rugged grandeur of the scenery found along the Ouray & Red Mountain Toll Road.

SUNDANCE PHOTO BY DELL A. McCOY

Abrams Mountain rises to an elevation of 12, 801 feet, providing a most attractive scene. You are looking south, near the site of Otto Mears' Bear Creek Falls toll gate. In 1892, plans were drawn up to build a combination electric - rack-and-pinion railway up this extremely steep, narrow canyon — from Ouray to Albany, in Ironton Park. However, economic conditions put an end to this project.

SUNDANCE PHOTO BY DELL A. McCOY

When the photographer recorded this golden autumn scene, he was looking at the bucket-tramway house that once served the Buffalo Boy mill. This cableway climbed Green Mountain, crossed the Stony Pass road and continued over the ridge to the Buffalo Boy mine — on the slope of Canby Mountain. The Stony Pass trail was the original route used by early-day prospectors venturing over the hills into the Bakers Park area.

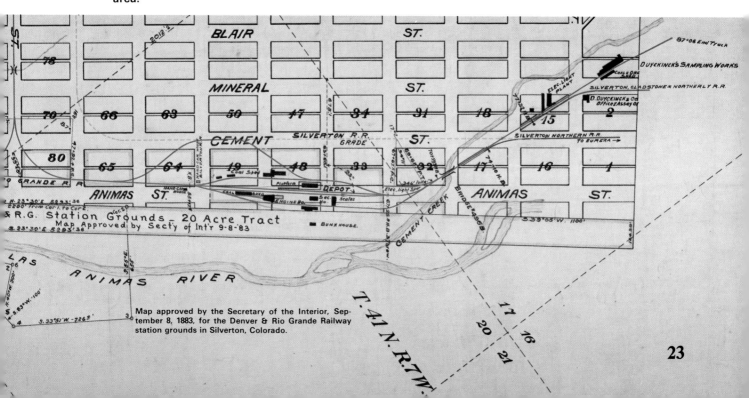

Map approved by the Secretary of the Interior, September 8, 1883, for the Denver & Rio Grande Railway station grounds in Silverton, Colorado.

23

connection with the outside world. Lower-grade ores could now be transported economically to the smelters at Durango, Pueblo, Denver, and even as far away as New York. The Denver and Rio Grande promptly initiated through narrow-gauge Pullman service between Denver and Silverton, and newcomers poured into the wide-open town.

After the arrival of the Denver and Rio Grande in Silverton, the Martha Rose smelter was built in the southwestern corner of the park on Mineral Creek, primarily to process ores from the Red Mountain district. The smelter operated from 1882 until the Silver Panic of 1893, producing only 11 tons of bullion during those years.

Late in the winter of 1882-1883, the twin towns of Red Mountain and Congress were built in six feet of snow on opposite sides of Red Mountain Pass. Red Mountain town was built in a glen right next to *the Knob,* a high hill of silicified rock, full of caves lined with crystals of silver-bearing lead carbonate. The National Belle mine, which had been staked earlier, seriously began development that winter. On January 19, David F. Day, the intrepid editor of *The Solid Muldoon* of Ouray, published the following blast:

> The *Red Mt. Pilot* and *Red Mt. Review* are both published in Silverton and are a tissue of falsehoods.
>
> There is but one tent and three bunches of shingles in Red Mt. City, they blow so much about, and the miners of Red Mt. refuse to patronize or tolerate such frauds. Both the enterprising editors have been ordered out of camp. Red Mt. needs neither gush nor exaggeration. We have ore enough in sight to attract capitalists and insure permanency and do not desire the services of journalists who are willing to do an unlimited amount of lying for a certain number of town lots. Curry and Raymond would kill any camp. —

Seven weeks later, on March 9, 1883, *The Solid Muldoon* was singing a different song:

> Five weeks ago the site where Red Mt. now stands was woodland mesa, covered with heavy spruce timber. Today, hotels, printing offices, groceries, meat markets, . . . a telephone office, saloons, dance houses are up and booming; the blast is heard on every side and prospectors can be seen snowshoeing in every direction.
>
> Everything has been packed or sledded over or under three feet of snow. . . We predict that by Sept. 1, Red Mt. will have a population of nearly ten thousand and a daily output surpassed by Leadville only.

* * * * *

MRS. MARVIN GREGORY COLLECTION

The Vanderbilt mine was 450 feet above the track level of the Silverton Railroad, and in 1888, was renamed the Genessee-Vanderbilt when it merged with the Genessee mine, and drove a tunnel 820 feet long into the mountainside from track level to drain the mine. This sketch shows the original mine as it appeared in 1882.

At about the same time, the town of Ironton was established at the head of Ironton Park, at the other end of the Red Mountain mining district.

With the opening of the Red Mountain mines in 1882, Otto Mears and Fred Walsen built 12 miles of toll road between Red Mountain and Ouray. Half of this distance was blasted into the hard rock of Uncompahgre Canon, portions of the work costing as much as $1,000 per foot. In 1883 they extended the Red Mountain road—the first *Rainbow Route* and predecessor of the *Million Dollar Highway*—12 miles south from Red Mountain to Silverton to meet the Denver and Rio Grande. Upon reaching Silverton in 1883, Mears then turned north up the Rio de las Animas and rebuilt the nine miles of road to Eureka.

Opposite page — just a short distance out of Ouray, passengers could take their first look into the deep gorge of Uncompahgre Canyon, and pose for photographs on the Ouray & Red Mountain Toll Road.

JACKSON C. THODE COLLECTION

24

competitions over their later rivals.

In 1882 an Englishman, W. S. Thompson, built the large and impressive Grand Hotel in Silverton — later renamed the Imperial — and now the Grand Imperial. The building's outside appearance has not changed significantly since it was built. For years the Hub Saloon in the Grand Imperial never closed its doors, and was the birthplace of the song, *There'll Be a Hot Time in the Old Town Tonight!*

Three sampling works were established in Silverton in 1883, by E. T. Sweet, T. B. Comstock, and Gus and Edward G. Stoiber.

In 1882 Rasmus Hansen discovered the Sunnyside Extension in Placer Gulch, southwest of Animas Forks, and in 1883 great strikes were announced at the Ben Franklin and Sampson claims near Gladstone. During the mid-1880's the Sunnyside mine near Eureka was a steady pro-

SAN JUAN COUNTY HISTORICAL SOCIETY

Here we see Edward G. Stoiber, mining engineer and developer of the famed Silver Lake mine and mill.

SAN JUAN COUNTY HISTORICAL SOCIETY

Helen "Lena" Allen-Webster-Stoiber-Rood-Ellis, wife of Edward G. Stoiber, and personnel manager of the Silver Lake mine, east of Silverton.

ducer, as were the North Star on Sultan Mountain, the Belcher, Aspen, Gray Eagle and North Star located on Solomon Mountain near Silverton, and the Red Mountain district mines. During this period, too, the Stoiber brothers gathered a group of 200 claims at the head of Arrastra Gulch at 12,000 feet and established the Silver Lake mine.

Ed Stoiber married a very liberated divorcee named Helen "Lena" Allen Webster in 1884. She assisted in the operation of the Silver Lake mine. In 1887—perhaps egged on by their wives—Ed and Gus had a disagreement, and the partnership was dissolved. Gus took the sampling works on Mineral Creek and Ed took the mine. Ed and Lena moved to near the base of the tramway from the Silver Lake mine to the mill, and there they built the biggest combination mansion and office in the whole San Juan region, calling it *Waldheim* (forest home). Ed ran the engineering aspects of the mine, while Lena—as the entire personnel department— bossed all the miners and managed the company boarding house up at Silver Lake, where the miners lived. Pay day for the miners was twice a year—Christmas and the Fourth of July!

By 1889, Ed and Lena were greatly increasing their profits by processing large amounts of low-grade ore. They hung on after the 1893 panic, finally selling out for $1,300,000 in 1903 to the Guggenheim brothers, Simon and Daniel, who owned the American Smelting and Refining Com-

MRS. MARVIN GREGORY COLLECTION

The shafthouse and outbuildings of the Robinson mine were sketched by an unknown artist in 1888. The hoist was in the tall structure, while the blacksmith shop and ore-sorting sheds surrounded the main building.

Freshly discharged from the Union Army, Otto Mears — only 24 years old — posed smartly in August of 1864, ready to start his pioneer life in Colorado.

Burros laden with 20-foot lengths of 20-pound rails destined for the mines, rested on Thirteenth Street in Silverton during 1887.

NARROW GAUGE RAILWAYS IN AMERICA
BY HOWARD FLEMING

STATE HISTORICAL SOCIETY OF COLORADO

WILLIAM H. JACKSON PHOTO —
STATE HISTORICAL SOCIETY OF COLORADO

Chief Ouray of the Utes and Otto Mears, interpreter, C. 1872.

31

PATTISON & FRINK.
MINERS SUPPLIES.

354 CON CRESS

347. EUREKA

RICHARD A. RONZIO COLLECTION

Chattanooga was a sizable settlement of store buildings and canvas-roofed cabins in 1883 — before the arrival of the Silverton Railroad. In this view, you are looking down the valley of Mineral Creek.

pany. Thus rewarded for their long years of effort, Ed and Lena Stoiber left the San Juans for good. They became world travelers, built a large mansion in Denver (which still stands). After Ed's death, Lena had two other husbands, and when she died, she was a very rich woman. Waldheim then became a home for the managers of the Silver Lake mine. It was torn down in 1945.

Opposite page, above — the town of Congress, located about one mile south of Red Mountain Pass, existed from 1883 until 1886. When the Silverton Railroad was built, it by-passed the town and the residents moved their dwellings to Red Mountain town.

JOSEPH COLLIER PHOTO — RICHARD A. RONZIO COLLECTION

Opposite page, below — this 1880 view shows Eureka before the Silverton Northern was built into town. Eureka merchants served the needs of the miners of the region.

JOSEPH COLLIER PHOTO — RICHARD A. RONZIO COLLECTION

Meanwhile, Silverton had gained prominence as the vice and lust center of the region. The town had 30 saloons, most of them featuring gambling, and two dance halls where the "Daughters of Eros" could be found. Most of these establishments were located along Blair Street, one block east of the town's main street. Counteracting these nefarious influences, the Congregational Church was built in 1881 and St. Patricks Catholic Church was built in 1883.

The city of Silverton devised a novel way of eliminating the necessity for property taxes by charging a $500 annual license fee on each of the saloons and dance halls. Also, supposedly as a means of identification, each "lady of the evening" was required to pay a monthly "fine" of $5.00 to the city treasurer. The largest amount collected by this means in a single month was $300.00.

By 1885, all the towns of the region had increased in size. Silverton had a population of 1,500, with a newspaper, the *Miner*, founded in July of 1875, a smelter, three sampling works, a chlorination works, three sawmills, a bank, and

SAN JUAN COUNTY HISTORICAL SOCIETY

The Riverside Slide — below Ironton on the Ouray & Red Mountain Toll Road — killed the mail carrier and his 16 mules at this spot, July 6, 1888. Even in recent times, this slide has taken lives, and bodies have not been located until after the spring thaw.

Masonic and Odd Fellows halls—to say nothing of the baser institutions. Howardsville had a year-round population of 100, 30 buildings, several saloons and a reduction works. Eureka had a store, a hotel, a smelter and a year-round population of 200. Animas Forks had two stores, a hotel, several shops, a saloon and 170 hardy people. Gladstone had a general store, two quartz mills, a sawmill and 100 permanent residents. Chattanooga had a postoffice, an inn, a store and saloon, with 60 year-round residents. Congress, on the southeast side of Sheridan Pass (Red Mountain Pass), named for Jim Sheridan, innkeeper, storekeeper and postmaster at Chattanooga, had a population of 300 in winter and 1,000 in summer. Ironton had a population of 125.

Ouray was the biggest town in the region, with 1,800 people; 2 hotels, the Delmonico and the Sanderson; two newspapers, the *Ouray Times,* and terrible-tempered David F. Day's famous publication, *The Solid Muldoon;* 10 stamp mills; a sampling works; 3 churches; and schools. In 1886, Red Mountain town had its own municipal water works, and the famous U. S. Geological Survey geologist, S. F. Emmons, made the first detailed technical study of the area. All the ores at this time were the early bonanza ores and none of the mines were very deep as yet.

It was in this exuberant setting that the irrepressible Otto Mears originated the idea of, and raised the capital to build, his *Rainbow Route*— the Silverton Railroad.

CHAPTER II

Those Who Did!

ITH THE RAPID buildup of mining in the Silverton area, good transportation was a necessity. Profitability of the mines depended on the economic transportation of large volumes of low-grade ore. During the early *bonanza* days—which can be classified as the rich shallow-ore stage of mining development—wagons could freight out a ton or two of rich ore on each trip. Wagon roads thus were necessary first, and it was that remarkable Russian immigrant by the name of Otto Mears who undertook their construction.

But as the mines went deeper, costs escalated, and the volume of ore needed to make a profit increased. Wagons and primitive roads were no longer sufficient; railroads were needed. The Eastern and European stockholders of General William J. Palmer's Denver and Rio Grande Railway, however, no longer were in any mood to invest more money in branch lines; they wanted returns on their old investments.

The time was ripe for a railroad in the San Juans; however, since no outside investors would tackle it, the business society of the area—headed by Otto Mears—filled the gap and built the Silverton Railroad with local money. Biographies of these men will show the character of this society and the sources of funds.

Otto Mears, *Pathfinder of the San Juan*, devoted much of his life to building and operating the roads and railways which were so vital to the development of the mines and human resources of the area. He also incidentally became a millionaire, and a state and national figure. Unlike most fortunes based in Colorado, the one accumulated

by Mears was largely reinvested in the regional economy to benefit the citizens of the Centennial State.

Mears was a pioneer in the true sense—the very personification of the Horatio Alger story, come true. Arthur Ridgway, a one-time Mears employee who became chief engineer of the Denver and Rio Grande Western Railroad, knew him well and after transcribing a biographical interview with him in 1926, characterized him as follows:

> Eccentric, visionary, impetuous, indefatigable, generous, human, sympathetic, charitable—all combined in one personality made it impossible to say that as a man he was this or that or the other. You will observe from the story in *Pioneers of the San Juan Country* that of his varied activities and accomplishments, Mr. Mears has little to say. I doubt if he knew himself all of the things in which he was interested and even had an active part. He, through his energy, had many fortunes and lost as many through his generosity and good will to others. It is difficult to say to just how many activities and projects he devoted his time and money. The number is legion.

Mears built the Silverton Railroad in the years from 1887 to 1889, the Rio Grande Southern Railroad from 1890 to 1892, the Silverton Northern Railroad in 1895, and then moved to Washington, D.C., where he built the Chesapeake Beach Railroad during the three-year period from 1897 to 1899. Moving to New York City, he was a director of the Mack Brothers Company and then was the president of the Mack Brothers Manufacturing Company for the first year of its founding in 1906. He returned to his old stamping grounds at Silver-

EARLY DAYS ON THE WESTERN SLOPE OF COLORADO —
RICHARD A. RONZIO COLLECTION

Otto Mears, *Pathfinder of the San Juan,* photographed in 1880 while he was dressed for bitter winter weather.

running condition. Mears often wandered down to the enginehouse, where he just could not keep his hands off the work in progress. When the job was done, he would wash up in the cold water at the enginehouse sink, then pull on his coat, and replace his tie and hat before he stepped outside to return to other tasks.

Mears was born in Kurland, Russia, on May 3, 1840, of an English father and a Russian mother, both of whom died while Otto was still a tot. His maternal uncle took the orphaned boy into a large family of ten boys and two girls. As the thirteenth member, Otto did not get along with his cousins, and when he was nine, his uncle sent him to an English relative. At the age of ten he was sent to Ireland, where he was placed aboard a ship and sailed off to yet another relative in New York City.

ton in January of 1907 to operate his Colorado properties, and there he remained for the next five years. When he decided to retire in November, 1911, he moved to California where he purchased stock in the Maryland Hotel at Pasadena. Otto Mears' wife of 54 years, Mary, died in Pasadena in 1924; while he died there on June 24, 1931, a month past his ninety-first birthday.

Otto Mears was a man of small stature, and despite his many years in the United States, always spoke with a thick Russian accent. In his youth he wore a beard, but by 1905, when he was 65, he was clean shaven. Although he consistently wore a business suit, tie and hat, he remained a jack-of-all-trades, and expected his employees to perform in the same manner. The many minor infractions of his employees he would forgive, but abuse of his locomotives was not to be tolerated; engineers were expected to keep their engines in good repair and

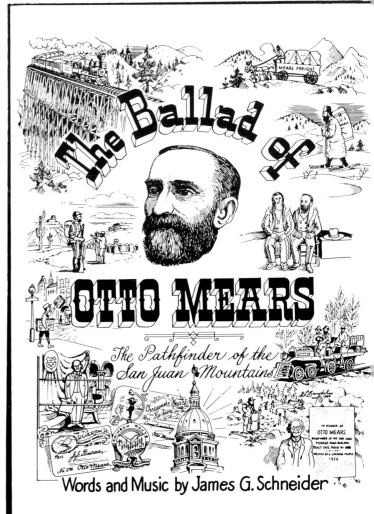

JOHN GIBBS ENGSTROM COLLECTION

The Ballad of Otto Mears, with words and music by James G. Schneider, was published in a limited edition of only 900 copies in 1970 to commemorate the fame of Otto Mears, *Pathfinder of the San Juan.*

His New York relative, in turn, passed him on to another uncle in California. Mears was reshipped, sailed to Panama, crossed the Isthmus by horse, and arrived in San Franciso by ship in 1851. In the meantime, his uncle had departed for Australia and Mears was left on his own at the age of 11.

A lady who had traveled with him from New York took him to her home, and after some discussion, Mears started selling newspapers to help pay for his keep. Subsequently, he moved to Walkerville, California, where he clerked in a store and learned tinsmithing. He continued to "bum" around California, doing odd jobs, and in 1859 he became a gold miner at Wabuska, Nevada. He claimed to have been naturalized as a U. S. citizen in San Francisco and voted for Abraham Lincoln in the 1860 presidential election. On the seventeenth of August, 1861, upon the outbreak of the Civil War, Mears enlisted in the Union Army—company H, First Regiment of California Volunteers—at $50.00 per month. The regiment sailed to Los Angeles and then marched across the desert to New Mexico, where the Texans had invaded. Mears' regiment arrived on the scene just in time for the battle to be over.

The march was made during the driest season in 30 years. The regimental surgeon, J. M. McNulty, reported to the surgeon general in Washington as follows:

The march of this column from the Pacific Ocean to the Rio Grande is somewhat remarkable, from the fact that almost the entire distance is a desert waste, with great scarcity of water and that of the worst quality.

Men marching day after day through the burning sands and nearly suffocated with alkali dust required to be made of stern stuff—of such were the men composing this column. Men inured to mountain life in Calif., pioneers and miners; men self-reliant and enduring; men equal to any emergency, if guided by a firm hand and clear head. That they were equal to a great emergency is evidenced by the fact that they conquered vast deserts, and accomplished a march not equaled in modern times, traversing a distance of nearly a thousand miles and almost the entire route over a sterile waste.

Mears' outfit then came under the command of Kit Carson, who was fighting the Navajo Indians. The Navajos eventually were defeated and forced to a reservation at Fort Sumner, New Mexico. During this campaign, the quartermaster gave Mears the job of furnishing bread to the troops. He camped about 150 miles from Albuquerque, New Mexico, and built adobe ovens for baking the bread. Since the Union Army gave him a pound of

ROBERTSON MEARS PITCHER COLLECTION

Otto and Mary Mears — about 1916 — near the time of their Golden Wedding Anniversary.

flour for each pound of bread—more flour than needed—with typical acumen, he sold the extra flour for a handsome profit of $1,500.

Otto Mears was discharged from the army at Las Cruces, New Mexico, near El Paso, Texas, in August of 1864. He and his friends, Isaac Gotthelf and Fred Walsen (the latter to be an on-and-off business partner for the next 38 years) went north to Santa Fe. When Mears arrived in Santa Fe, he collected the $200.00 bonus in gold that California owed him as a veteran. Shortly thereafter, he became a storekeeper and worked for Elsberg and Amberg for a short time, then he managed a store owned by the Staab brothers in his own name. Mears left Santa Fe in 1865, and—with Isaac Gotthelf—established a general store at Conejos, near present-day Antonito, Colorado.

At that time, lumber was selling for $80.00 per 1,000 feet and the Federal government was paying $20.00 per 100 pounds for flour at Fort Garland. Mears grasped at the opportunity and proceeded to build the first sawmill and the first gristmill in Conejos County. With the exception of the up-and-down type blade, the sawmill was constructed

EARLY DAYS ON THE WESTERN SLOPE OF COLORADO —
RICHARD A. RONZIO COLLECTION

Chief Ouray lived in this old homestead in the Uncompahgre Valley while he was staying at the Los Pinos reservation. Other Indians established farms in various places while they were under the jurisdiction of the second Los Pinos Indian Agency, but Ouray's were the only permanent improvements.

entirely of wood held together with rawhide. The stones for the gristmill were of lava found near Conejos.

It soon became apparent that there was not enough grain grown near Conejos to make the gristmill profitable—so in 1866, Mears homesteaded a 200-acre wheat ranch 40 miles to the north, near Saguache.

Soon after, Saguache County was organized and Otto Mears became the first county treasurer.

The same year, he started a general store in a building on his homestead. To facilitate bringing in goods, Mears began operating pack trains from Denver to Saguache via La Veta Pass. Packing rates were 10 cents a pound, and there were no roads to pack on.

Mears found that the Mexican custom of cutting grain by hand and threshing with sheep was uneconomical, so in 1867 he brought into the San Luis Valley the first powered mower, reaper and threshing machine. To add to his problems, the U.S. Army dropped its price on flour to $5.00 per hundred. Otto thereupon decided to take his wheat over Poncha Pass to California Gulch (near present-day Leadville), where he could get $12.00 per hundred pounds.

While going down the pass, his wagon turned over, spilling loose wheat down the hillside. Just then, Major William Gilpin—who had been the first U.S. Territorial Governor of Colorado—happened by. Major Gilpin suggested that Mears take out a charter for a toll road, as he could make a lot of money on it. Gilpin also told Mears that someday the road would be needed for a railway

grade. Otto thought Gilpin was "rather crazy" since at the time there was not even a railway to Denver; however, he took out a charter anyway. Using hand tools, Mears constructed a 50-mile road from Saguache over Poncha Pass to Nathrop, on the Denver-Leadville road—and promptly started collecting tolls.

On October 20, 1867, Fred Walsen transferred the title of his ranch to Mears in exchange for a $1,000 note. Twenty-five days later, on November 14, 1867, Mears mortgaged the combined Mears-Walsen ranches for $4,450, probably to pay for the construction expenses of the toll road. In February of 1868, Mears had the opportunity to sell part of the ranch. Fred Nagel advanced Mears the purchase price, and Otto paid off the $4,450 loan on February first, transferring the title to Nagel on the eighth. Otto later sold the remainder of the ranch to Isaac Gotthelf.

On March 2, 1868, the Utes finally signed the *Kit Carson Treaty*, relinquishing their claim to the San Luis Valley. They were to move west of the Continental Divide in Colorado. Territorial Governor Hunt made preparations for the move and chose a site 45 miles west of Saguache for the new Los Pinos (The Pines) Indian Agency. Before anything more was accomplished, however, Governor Hunt was discharged from his position and General Edward McCook took his place. This caused considerable delay in the removal of the Utes.

By the time temporary Indian Agent Speer arrived on the scene, the Utes had had time to reconsider the treaty and decided not to move.

EARLY DAYS ON THE WESTERN SLOPE OF COLORADO —
RICHARD A. RONZIO COLLECTION

The Los Pinos Indian Agency on the Uncompaghre River, 1868.

Otto Mears, while trading with the Utes for the past several years, had gained their respect and learned to speak their language. It was said that Mears spoke fluent Ute with a Russian accent. Speer asked Mears to help, so Otto went to Denver and brought back Governor McCook and a party of army officers. Upon their arrival in Saguache, Mears acted as interpreter and helped convince the Utes to leave. Soon afterward, Otto was getting contracts from the Federal government to supply the Utes with beef and other merchandise.

On July 8, 1869, Otto paid-off his $1,000 note to Fred Walsen.

On October 17, 1870, Otto Mears married Mary Kampfshulte, a German immigrant girl living near Granite, Colorado, one of the settlements north of Nathrop on the Denver-Leadville road. Mears had met and courted her during his journeys hauling goods to Leadville from Saguache.

Two daughters—Laura and Cora—were born to Otto and Mary Mears while they were living in Saguache. Laura, born on January 14, 1872, married Marshall David Smith in the spring of 1902; Cora, born on November 25, 1879, married James Robertson Pitcher, Jr., in the fall of 1904. Both these men subsequently served as officials of

This drawing portrays the final exodus of the Northern Utes from Colorado, in 1881. They are shown crossing the Grand (now Colorado) River near the Utah border.

EARLY DAYS ON THE WESTERN SLOPE OF COLORADO —
RICHARD A. RONZIO COLLECTION

STATE HISTORICAL SOCIETY OF COLORADO COLLECTION

STATE HISTORICAL SOCIETY OF COLORADO COLLECTION

SUNDANCE PHOTO BY DELL A. McCOY

This is the colorful little mining community of Ouray — named for the famous Ute Indian chief. It was in this town that Otto Mears' electric railway would have terminated, providing a direct connection with the Denver & Rio Grande. Ouray lies "pocketed" in one of the most beautiful U-shaped mountain valleys to be found anywhere in North America — with spectacular, soaring mountains on three sides.

Opposite page, above — following the approval of the second Brunot Treaty in 1873, savage Indian and ruthless white man posed side-by-side to record the solemn occasion on a glass-plate negative. In the back row (from left to right), Ute Indians Washington, Susan, Johnston Number 2, Jack and John; in the center row, representing the white men, U. M. Curtis, Major J. B. Thompson, General C. Adams and Otto Mears; in the foreground are Chief Ouray and Pi-ah.

Opposite page, below — an interior view showing how some of the more well-to-do individuals furnished their living quarters while "taming" the wild West. The notation penned on the back of the card, from which this view was reproduced, reads: "Corner of sitting room in the bachlor domicile of Wm. Jas E. Wood, Silverton, San Juan Co., Colo. — Roughing it in the Far West, Nov. 1886."

41

Mears' railroads. Much later, Cora became the last president of the Silverton Northern Railroad.

Laura died childless about 1913, while Cora had four sons and died in 1948.

In 1871, Otto Mears, Enos T. Hotchkiss, and other Saguache businessmen formed the Saguache and San Juan Toll Road Company to build a road to the booming mining camps in the cañon of the Rio de las Animas Perdidas (meaning "River of the Souls Lost" in Spanish, when translated literally). By 1872, construction had progressed as far as the Lake Fork of the Gunnison River, from which point Mears built the "Blue Mesa Road" on to Cimarron. That year he also financed a newspaper in Saguache, *The Saguache Chronicle*.

By 1873, his toll road was completed to the little camp of Lake City. He gave up his pack trains and began freighting with large wagons from the railhead in Colorado Springs to Lake City and points in-between.

In 1872 and 1873 a second treaty, the *Brunot Treaty*, was negotiated with the Utes to move them out of the mountains to allow for the development of mining. Since the negotiations were making no progress, on the advice of General Adams, Mr. Brunot asked Otto for his assistance. Mears was instrumental in getting the treaty signed by arranging for a salary of $1,000 per year for Chief Ouray for ten years. The government later paid the traveling expenses of Mears, General Adams, Ouray and nine other Ute chiefs to show them the East Coast and Washington, D. C.

In 1874, while Enos Hotchkiss was poking around on Henson Creek a few miles west of Lake City, supposedly looking over a route for continuation of the Saguache and San Juan Toll Road to the Rio de las Animas, he discovered a rich ore deposit. In August, 1874, this ore body became the Hotchkiss mine, later to become famed as the Golden Fleece. By October, the townsite of Lake City was entered at the U.S. Land Office at Del Norte, with E. T. Hotchkiss, I. Gotthelf and O. Mears among the members of the first board of trustees.

In June, 1875, Mears financed Lake City's first newspaper, *The Silver World;* and it is this newspaper which is generally credited with having started the Lake City boom. In the following month he began construction of a road between Silverton and Animas Forks. Later, in the winter of 1875-'76, he was awarded the U.S. Mail contract to Ouray, with a requirement for one trip a week for the payment of $30.00 per trip. In March of 1876, this mail contract was placed in jeopardy when the carriers quit due to the deep snow, forcing Mears to carry the mail himself. He made the trip on skis,

taking three days to break the trail.

Otto Mears was one of the three presidential electors for the new State of Colorado, following the election in 1876, and personally delivered the votes to Washington. Upon his return from the East, he moved his general store from the old homestead to a new building in Saguache, and also became a partner in a hardware store which he opened next door.

Mears was back at work building roads again in 1877. In August he finished a road from Lake City to Animas Forks, completing the through route to Silverton. His road from the Lake Fork of the Gunnison to Ouray also was completed in 1877. In 1878, he built 20 miles of road from Gunnison to a connection with the Lake City road at Cibola; then in 1878-'79, he built a 60-mile toll road over Marshall Pass between his Poncha Pass road and Gunnison. After operating it for a year and a half, he sold it for $40,000 to the Denver and Rio Grande Railway for use as the right-of-way for their narrow-gauge mainline to Utah. In 1879 he erected a telegraph line from Fort Garland to Montrose— the first such facility to see use in the San Juans.

After the Meeker massacre in 1879, a new treaty with the Utes was prepared in 1880, calling for removal of the Indians to areas away from the invading *gringos* (English-speaking whites). Mears was on the Indian Commission that negotiated and enforced this last Colorado treaty. In order to get the Indians' agreement, Mears toured the reservation and paid 1,400 Indians $2.00 apiece out of his own pocket to sign, with the result that he was ordered to Washington in 1881 to stand trial for bribery.

At the trial, Mears' defense was that the Indians told him $2.00 cash in hand was worth more than government promises of interest on $1,800,000. Mears was acquitted and his $2,800 refunded!

The treaty provided that the Uncompahgre band of Utes were to be removed and settled ". . . upon agricultural lands on [the] Grand River [now the Colorado River], near the mouth of [the] Gunnison River, in Colorado, if a sufficient quantity of agricultural land shall be found there; if not, then upon such other unoccupied agricultural lands as may be found in that vicinity and in the territory of Utah."

In June 1881, Mears and commissioners J. J. Russell and Judge T. A. McMorris together with Ute Chiefs Sapavanaro and Guero, who had replaced Chief Ouray after his death the previous fall, searched the area around the site of Grand Junction for suitable land. The Indians were not satisfied, so after the inspection, the party selected a new site in Utah at the junction of the White and Green Rivers. The chiefs and all the commissioners

COLORADO RAILROAD MUSEUM COLLECTION

Otto Mears posed with his first grandson, James Robertson Pitcher III, and his son-in-law, James R. Pitcher Jr. (right), in July of 1906.

agreed to this site but when the time came for the move, the Utes were reluctant to leave. Mears and Judge McMorris, as the commissioners closest at hand, had to sign the order for General R. S. Mackenzie to remove them with troops on two hours' notice. These Utes were unhappy about being dispossessed of their tribal land in Colorado and Chief Cojoe—blaming Mears for their situation—attempted to murder him. Mears, with more constructive things in mind, submitted his resignation as Indian Commissioner.

In 1880, Mears built a 14-mile road from Animas City to Fort Lewis, and a 27-mile road from Dallas Divide to Telluride; 10 years later—in 1890—major portions of this route were to be transformed into the right-of-way for his Rio Grande Southern Railroad.

The burgeoning network of Mears toll roads was beginning to be remunerative; during 1880 he collected $100,000 in tolls from U.S. Army movements alone. In 1881 he extended the Telluride road from Vance Junction to Ames, about six miles, and built five miles of road from Ouray to Sneffels, which he was later forced to sell to Ouray County for $7,000.

After the discovery of the Guston and Yankee Girl mines near the summit of Sheridan Pass in 1882, Mears and Fred Walsen built 12 miles of road, the first *Rainbow Route*, between Ouray and Red Mountain. They continued this road on to

Silverton in 1883, and then rebuilt the nine miles of road from Silverton to Eureka.

In 1884, after a very hot campaign, Mears was elected a representative to the Colorado General Assembly from Saguache County. Although there were but 400 votes in the county at the time, the campaign had cost money and Mears had to borrow $16,000 to cover his expenses.

The Mears system of toll roads now totaled about 200 miles, with 8 to 10 toll stations. Toll charges on his roads depended on distance, cost of the road, and "what the traffic would bear." Crossing over passes between nearby towns cost $2.00 for a single rig and $4.00 for four horses. The highest toll was for the 24 miles from Ouray to Silverton—$5.00 for a single-span team and $1.00 for each additional head of stock.

Truly, a miniature transportation empire had been developed!

And so it had come about that, after 19 years as a Colorado citizen, this orphaned, unschooled, indefatigable Russian immigrant—now age 44— was tasting the fruits of his unflagging efforts applied to a chance suggestion. Nearly anytime anyone moved anything in the San Juans, Otto Mears made money!

Within the next three years, however, it grew more obvious that roads and wagons were incapable of handling the growing volumes of mineral production. Nor could the mines increase

SUNDANCE PHOTO BY DELL A. McCOY

The ruins of the Hanson mill are located in Mastodon Basin — high above Animas Forks. This site provides ample evidence of the great mining boom of former days. Local "wags" once claimed that some veins of ore ran from 10 to 100 feet wide — from the top of the mountain, straight down to the center of the Earth! The fabulously rich Gold Prince mine is located just around the bend in this old wagon road (now a jeep trail).

44

production to achieve their full potential if they must continue suffering under the limitations imposed by wagon freighting. The need was for volume transportation—possible only by rail—and late in the summer of 1887, the Silverton Railroad, utilizing the roadway of Mears' and Walsen's *Rainbow Route* toll road north out of Silverton, started construction.

As the transportation magnate of the San Juans, Otto Mears was the natural nucleus around which this venturesome new enterprise was formed. Mears was elected president; the other officers of the new company were old friends—poker playing "buddies" and associates in building the business society of the San Juans.

George Crawford, vice-president of the new railroad, was a local mining entrepreneur who years later developed the audacious scheme of draining the Red Mountain mines by driving the Joker Tunnel.

John W. Wingate, secretary of the company, was born in Boston in 1845 and served as a Union captain in Company E of the 117th New York Infantry during the Civil War. He came to Colorado in 1871 to work as a carpenter on the bridge gang of General Palmer's new Denver and Rio Grande Railway, and he became a great friend of Oliver P. Posey, another Civil War veteran from Whitewater, Wisconsin. Together, in 1872, they raised potatoes on rented ranchland at the head of Cherry Creek in Douglas County, giving them a stake for future operations.

Wingate started contracting in Colorado Springs, and in 1873 joined Stevens and Tower in freighting the first sawmill into Silverton from the railhead at Colorado Springs, taking a route over Ute Pass into South Park, over Mears' toll road across Poncha Pass south to Del Norte, and finally west over the range to Howardsville and down along the Rio de las Animas to Silverton. Construction of the sawmill on Mineral Creek at the south end of town was started, but the party was obliged to quit and winter at Del Norte.

SAN JUAN COUNTY HISTORICAL SOCIETY

Otto Mears is shown here at the site of the dedication plaque honoring him — located at Bear Creek Falls on the Million Dollar Highway in 1927. The plaque later was removed during a road-widening project, and after years of neglect, was rededicated in 1970.

In 1874, Wingate turned to mining, first working placer claims at Parrott City, and then becoming manager of the Hotchkiss mine—soon to become famous as the Golden Fleece—near Lake City. Wingate and Posey pooled resources with Alva Adams, later to be elected as governor of Colorado, and opened a hardware store called

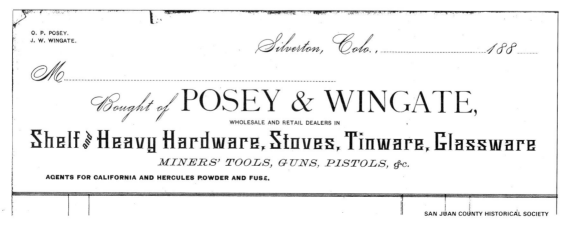

O. P. POSEY.
J. W. WINGATE.

Silverton, Colo., _____ 188 __

M

Bought of POSEY & WINGATE,

WHOLESALE AND RETAIL DEALERS IN

Shelf *and* Heavy Hardware, Stoves, Tinware, Glassware

MINERS' TOOLS, GUNS, PISTOLS, &c.

AGENTS FOR CALIFORNIA AND HERCULES POWDER AND FUSE.

SAN JUAN COUNTY HISTORICAL SOCIETY

Adams and Posey in Del Norte, the gateway to the San Juan, with branch stores in Alamosa and Silverton. The store was later Posey and Wingate. In 1888, the partnership was dissolved, the Silverton store continuing operation under the name, Adams and Wingate.

Wingate first married a girl from Posey's hometown, and after her death, married the widow of one of the Greene brothers who had built the smelter on the northeast edge of Silverton in 1874. His friend, Oliver P. Posey, who owned the North Star mine just outside Silverton, also invested in the new Silverton Railroad and subsequently became a director of that company.

Fred Walsen, treasurer of the railroad, was Otto Mears' old army comrade from the California Volunteers and his sometime partner in the stage and toll-road business. Oftentimes, Walsen's funds were called upon to bail out various Mears enterprises when other money was tight.

Chief engineer of the Silverton Railroad at the time it was formed was J. H. Ernest Waters. In 1881 a young, new civil engineer, he had been hired by John A. Porter to assist in the reconstruction at Durango of the old Greene smelter which was being dismantled and moved from Silverton. Waters later was associated with Porter in the prolific Smuggler Union and Sheridan Mendota mines above Telluride.

Adair Wilson, engaged as the company's attorney at the time the Silverton Railroad was organized, was prominent among the members of the legal profession in Denver. Subsequently, during the 10 years from 1896 to 1905, he served as a judge, and finally as chief justice with the Colorado Court of Appeals.

In the summer of 1888, at the first annual meeting of the Silverton Railroad, two additional men entered the official picture. J. A. Porter was elected vice-president in place of George Crawford, and C. W. Gibbs, who had been hired by Mears earlier that spring, was confirmed as chief engineer in place of J. H. Ernest Waters. Crawford and Waters both continued as directors of the railroad, however.

John A. Porter, born in Connecticut in 1850, and briefly a student at the Columbia School of Mines in New York, studied from 1869 to 1872 at the largest and most prestigious mining school in the world—the Royal Academy of Mines in Freiburg, Germany. On his return to the United States in 1873, he became an assayer with the Richmond Consolidated Mining and Smelting Company at Eureka, Nevada.

Judge George Greene, Silverton storekeeper and one of the pioneer inhabitants of the settlement,

JOHN GIBBS ENGSTROM COLLECTION

Charles Wingate Gibbs, innovative locating engineer of the San Juans.

asked Porter to come to Silverton to supervise construction of a new smelter. This was the Greene smelter, built in 1874 on the northeast edge of the town. The plant's machinery had to be hauled by team and wagon from Colorado Springs, at that time the nearest terminal of the Denver and Rio Grande Railway. Upon completion of this project, Porter returned to Nevada, where he served from 1878 to 1880 as metallurgist and superintendent of the K. K. mine in Eureka.

When Porter returned to Silverton in 1880 to become manager of the San Juan and New York Mining and Smelting Company, which had bought the Greene smelter and the Aspen mine, he recommended the smelter be moved to the projected townsite of Durango. The ready availability of ample fuel and water at the new location was the principal reason for Porter's proposal.

Most *aficionados* of Colorado narrow-gauge railroad history are aware that the Denver and Rio Grande picked the townsite of Durango, rather than the already-established settlement of Animas City, partly for the purpose of making profits on town lots, but a less well-known reason was *Smelter Hill.* General William J. Palmer and Dr.

JOHN GIBBS ENGSTROM COLLECTION

Charles W. Gibbs, in the canvas chair, was relaxing in the sunshine with his surveying
crew when this photograph was taken.

William A. Bell, both of the D&RG, together with John A. Porter, the mining engineer, were involved in the founding of Durango. Porter's strong preferences for the site involved closeness to the Rio de las Animas, easy access to nearby coal beds, and the steep slopes of Smelter Hill (as it came to be known), which provided the advantages of gravity feed for the metallurgical operations.

Upon arrival of the Denver and Rio Grande in Durango on July 27, 1881, and its completion to Silverton on July 8, 1882, Porter's unitized operation achieved success; lower-grade ores now could be processed economically. To further reduce cost, he helped Mears build his railroads, and then developed the Porter coal mine, the first revenue-producing industry on the Rio Grande Southern, five and one-half miles by rail west of Durango, when that fabled line started construction in 1890.

Charles Wingate Gibbs, the new chief engineer of the Silverton Railroad, was born in Maine on June 19, 1859, and attended Maine State College, graduating as a civil engineer in 1879. In 1886 he

went to work as an assistant to Thomas H. Wigglesworth on the Colorado Midland Railroad. Then, during the spring of 1888, Gibbs was hired by Otto Mears to construct the northern end of the Silverton Railroad, and went on to engineer the more complicated northern two-thirds of the Rio Grande Southern in 1890 and 1891.

In 1889 he married Adeline Hammon of Colorado Springs, raising three daughters, Helen, Eloise and Martha. With the receivership of the Rio Grande Southern in 1893, he set up practice as a mining and civil engineer in Durango where he remained until 1897. He then moved to Ophir and Telluride where he worked as a civil engineer for the mines until 1904. After working in Nebraska for a short time, he joined the Utah Construction Company and from 1906 to 1927 worked mostly on railroad location surveys in Utah, Nevada, California and Mexico.

He retired to a walnut farm in California in 1927 and died in 1948, at age 89, after a fall.

John L. McNeil, who served as treasurer of the

Silverton Railroad from 1889 to 1904, and also as general manager in 1895, was born in New York in 1849. He came to Denver in 1870, and moved to Del Norte in June of 1876. At the latter place he founded "The Bank of San Juan," the first bank in southwestern Colorado. He was joined by Alfred P. Camp in the fall of that year; both continued as bankers for the balance of their lives. Camp married McNeil's sister.

McNeil's Del Norte bank was the delivery point for bullion from the Greene smelter in Silverton and the town served as the wintering place for many of the Silverton miners. By 1880, after the Denver and Rio Grande had bypassed Del Norte and founded the town of Alamosa, McNeil and Camp moved their operation to the new town. Camp then was sent to Durango when that town was founded, to open a branch of the Alamosa Bank of San Juan.

Moses Liverman, who was appointed superintendent of the Silverton Railroad in 1889, is a man whose relationships with Otto Mears are not entirely clear. Born about 1849, Liverman enlisted in and fought with the 8th Wisconsin during the Civil War while still no more than a boy. Subsequently an early participant in the Black Hills gold rush, he also spent considerable time in Washington as clerk of a Congressional committee, and it is probable that he and Mears became acquainted during the latter's visits to the Capitol in connection with the Ute Indian problems.

Apparently a resident of Silverton in 1889 when Mears made him an official of the railroad, he continued that association for about seven years, until late 1896. Signing the passes of the Silverton Railroad in his capacity as general manager of the road in 1892-'93-'94, Liverman also was one of the directors of the Silverton Northern Railroad when that line was organized by Mears and his friends in the fall of 1895. It is said that a profound disagreement with his employer led to his discharge from Mears' service in 1896, when he was replaced by Alexander Anderson. Liverman afterwards moved to Denver, where he died December 31, 1902, following a short illness.

William "Billy" E. Booker, originally a fireman on the Denver and Rio Grande, was hired directly for two positions—master mechanic and locomotive engineer—on the Silverton Railroad in the fall of 1889. While it is rumored that he suggested to Mears the purchase of D&RG engine Number 42, which became the Silverton's Number 100, on the basis of his earlier experience as a fireman on the locomotive, the story is unlikely since the engine was purchased before Booker was hired. He remained with the Silverton Railroad and the Silverton Northern, serving as general superintendent on

both roads from 1919 to 1923, when he retired.

Alexander Anderson was hired by Mears in 1892 to fill the job of auditor of the Silverton Railroad, with offices in Denver. While it was not apparent at the time, of course, Anderson was to be the savior of both the Silverton and Silverton Northern roads in the years to come.

A native of Scotland, born in 1861, Anderson had emigrated to the United States when he was 20 and worked on various Eastern railroads for 10 years until accepting the position offered by Mears. Three years after moving to Denver, he married Adelaide Stimson, a resident of the capital city, and in 1896 he was promoted and transferred to Silverton where he replaced Moses Liverman as superintendent of both of Mears' mountain railroads.

When William Jennings Bryan, the *Silver Knight,* was defeated in his bid for the U.S. presidency in 1896, Mears left Colorado in disgust, and upon 35-year-old Alexander Anderson—known as "Alex" or "Sandy" by his friends—devolved the day-to-day management of the two narrow-gauge railroads. As a resident of Silverton, Anderson suffered severely from altitude sickness and the effects of an old case of sunstroke, from which relief could be obtained only by moving temporarily to lower altitudes.

In 1899 Anderson was appointed receiver of the Silverton Railroad, and in managing both that property and the Silverton Northern, he juggled the accounts to keep the companies more-or-less solvent, ran the office in the depot, bossed the track gang when sidings had to be built or moved, argued with the D&RG over rate problems, rental and repair costs for leased engines, and when necessary, even fired the locomotives himself. Regarded by his contemporaries and associates as a "quiet, silent man, with much force of character," Anderson was the archetype, all-'round railroad man, which no doubt was why Mears hired him in the first place.

During the winter of 1903-'04, Anderson went to Scotland for his health and to visit his mother—returning to Silverton in late March, 1904. He finished building the extension of the Silverton Northern to Animas Forks from Eureka; then, after Mears returned to Silverton seven months later to reorganize the Silverton Railroad into the Silverton Railway, Anderson—now secretary of the company—moved to Denver where he died of appendicitis in February of 1907, at age 46.

While handling the affairs of the Mears railroads in Silverton, Anderson reported weekly to Mears and once a month to C. H. Graham, vice-president of the Silverton Railroad, in Philadelphia. Anderson's letters are the principal source of the history related here for the nine years from 1896 to 1904.

W. Z. Kinney of Silverton, Cyrus W. Davis of Waterville, Maine, and Henry M. Soule of Boston, Massachusetts, were major investors in the Silverton mines—Kinney serving as the local manager of the properties. In succession, the two Easterners bought the Harrison mine in 1893; the Gold King mine in 1894; built the Silverton, Gladstone and Northerly Railroad in 1899; bought Rasmus Hanson's Sunnyside Extension mine in 1903, renaming it the Gold Prince; then bought the Old Hundred mine in 1905 and the Tom Moore mine in 1906. Each company was bigger than the one preceding.

Willis Z. Kinney was born in New York state in 1860, and after an early farm life, moved in 1880 to Pueblo, Colorado, where he went to work in one of the smelters. Having learned a bit about the smelting end of the mining business, he then prospected around Silver Cliff for two years. In the spring of 1883 he shifted his prospecting and mining efforts to the Silverton area; 10 years later, Davis and Soule hired him to manage the Harrison mine. When this mine proved a disappointment, Kinney persuaded the two financiers to buy the Gold King mine from Oscar Nelson's widow for $15,000.

Kinney was given full charge and an interest in the new company, and made the mine into one of the richest properties in the San Juans. He served as local manager for Davis and Soule until 1909, and was described by *The Silverton Standard* as a "genial, whole-souled man with a prodigious amount of persistence and rugged determination, that has been accentuated and brought out by the crude, but effective concentrating process of a long battle with Dame Nature among the mines and mountains of Colorado."

Kinney was a regular member of the late-night poker games with Mears and his "cronies" in the back room of what is now the *Parlor* on Greene Street in Silverton. He did not always win and gained a reputation for writing personal checks to cover his gambling losses; then, on his way home, scribbling a stop-payment note against the check and slipping the note under the front door of the bank.

One evening, during a game in Silverton, Kinney found himself in need of more cash and started to write a check for the necessary funds. His friends, wise to his stop-payment trick, insisted on cash. The money he had salted away at Gladstone would not do him any good where it was, so he hastily authorized a midnight special train composed of only an engine and caboose to run up to Gladstone for the needed cash. The minimum amount required to stay in the game was $1,000!

The 15-mile round-trip to Gladstone, needless to say, was made in record time, rumored to be 35 minutes. The locomotive, probably Number 32, on the return leg of the journey careened downgrade so fast the engineer later said, "We nearly fell into town, the trip was so quick!"

One of the employees longest in Mears' service on his Silverton railroads was an engineman named Edward "Pete" Meyer. Pete originally had learned his trade as a fireman on the Gunnison Branch of the Denver, South Park and Pacific, but in 1899, he signed-on as a fireman on Kinney's Silverton, Gladstone and Northerly. The job lasted only two years, however, until he was fired in 1901. Otto Mears—or rather Alex Anderson—immediately hired Meyer as a locomotive engineer on the Silverton Railroad. He later reported that the SRR trackage to Ironton was gone at the time he went to work for the road in 1901.

He was engineer of the construction train during the 1904 building of the Animas Forks extension of the Silverton Northern. In 1906 he took a train to Corkscrew Gulch on the SRR and removed the circular shed covering the unique old 50-foot gallows turntable. The materials were brought up to Animas Forks and apparently re-erected as a cover over the 50-foot iron turntable there. Normally, Meyer was the engineer on the Animas Forks run. He is quoted as saying:

> One car of coal and one empty was all my engine could pull up to Animas Forks, and I never handled more than three loads down. After making sure the brakes were okay, I'd start down; my brakeman rode the cars and clubbed each as soon as they got rolling. If the rails were wet or rusty, I'd let 'em down on sand, holding to a slow walk; it sure was some relief to get stopped safely at Eureka.

But apparently he did try longer trains on occasion. At one time he wrote Morris Abbott:

> Five or six was the maximum safe load, but I once took eight loads of ore down from Animas Forks. We had all the brakes tied down. I used the engine brake as much as I dared, but was afraid the tires (on the engine drivers) would heat up and come loose. I never tried that again, as the cars just made the curves at Eureka.

According to Pete, the normal speed limit was 10 miles per hour from Silverton to Eureka, and 4 miles per hour on the heavy grade between Eureka and Animas Forks.

During the rebuilding of the north end of the Denver and Rio Grande's flood-damaged Silverton

Branch in the late fall of 1911, Mears was riding in the cab of the locomotive on the construction train with Pete, who was running rather cautiously on the unfamiliar track. The 71-year-old Mears, becoming impatient, inquired, "What's the matter ——'fraid?"

"No, but the road is pretty rough, so I thought I'd be careful," Meyer replied as he let the engine pick up speed.

A bit of this and Mears had a change of heart, "Well, it's all right if you stay on the track, but if you go off, where are you?"

In 1929, Pete replaced Joe Dresback as superintendent of the Silverton Northern, while continuing to serve as locomotive engineer as well.

In February, 1929, when the D&RGW's Silverton Branch again was blocked—this time by a snowslide above Needleton—Pete and Tom Lonergan took a work train down to clear away the obstruction. Pete's son was fireman. Silverton Northern engine Number 4 overturned during the bucking operations and Pete was trapped in the cab, his legs pinned down by the framework. Only the big snowplow mounted on the pilot beam up front kept the engine from going on over and crushing the engineer to death; after his painful rescue, Pete spent some time in the hospital and the locomotive had to be sent to Alamosa for repairs.

Pete handled the work train that dismantled the Animas Forks Branch in 1936. The turntable from the end of the line finally was delivered to the county highway yard in Durango. In 1940, he started the dismantling work on the Gladstone Branch from the upper end.

In August of 1938, James D. Osborn visited Silverton, took some pictures reproduced elsewhere in this volume, and gossiped with Pete Meyer and Billy Logan, the original fireman on SG&N engine Number 32. Three years later, *Railroad Magazine* published Osborn's tale about Edward H. Hudson, who had been hired as a conductor by Anderson in 1903 and was named superintendent of the Silverton and Silverton Northern roads on October 20, 1905, after Arthur Ridgway departed to return to the D&RG. Osborn left the conductor nameless, but the only such employee later to become superintendent was Hudson.

Quite a large quantity of timothy was being shipped into Silverton, via the D&RG, and handled from there on the SN. Through some kind of high finance, each car of this hay carried a sizable cash freight refund. One day the skipper in question learned about the cash refund, and immediately got chummy with the D&RG freight agent in Silverton. Together, the pair hatched a

remunerative plot. None of the cars of hay would be shown on any SN wheel reports. By this device, the pair would get the SN refund and split it between them.

For several weeks the conspirators basked in luxury. One day Mr. Mears discovered the D&RG was being paid quite a refund on cars of hay which were being handled onward by the SN. He billed the D&RG for his share of the refund; but was notified his refund had been paid, and to whom.

The big boss could hardly wait for the erring conductor, so he could blast and then discharge him. At length, the culprit pranced into the depot with more of Mears' cash refund bulging in his pockets. The firing ceremony was brief and to the point. But after the conductor had gone away in disgrace, Mears got to thinking. He paced the floor. He had an idea in his head that he couldn't get out. Suddenly he saw the light. He hurried uptown and located the former employee.

"Mister," he said, "I want to hire you back—as my superintendent."

The ex-conductor tried to stammer something, but was interrupted.

"I made a mistake in firing you," the chief explained. "You're too clever to be running one of

ROBERTSON MEARS PITCHER COLLECTION

James Robertson Pitcher Jr., 1879-1933, and Cora Mears Pitcher, 1879-1948, third and fourth presidents of the Silverton Northern Railroad, taken about 1916.

COLORADO RAILROAD MUSEUM COLLECTION

Cora Mears Pitcher and her three boys (left to right), Otto, Robertson and James, were "camping out" in a business car in Alamosa during January of 1911, waiting for a slide to be cleared on the Silverton Branch of the Denver & Rio Grande.

my trains. I need a smart official. I have a better chance to watch my super than I have a conductor. Do you want the job?"

The answer was, "Yes!"

James Robertson Pitcher, Jr., one of Otto Mears' sons-in-law, and president of the Silverton Northern after the death of his wife's father in 1931, was born on November 10, 1879, in Short Hills, New Jersey. As one of five children of an underwriter, he was raised at the family estate and became acquainted with Cora Mears, the younger daughter of the Mears family, during the period when the San Juan pioneer and his dependents were living on the East Coast after Bryan's defeat for the presidency. Cora Mears was born on November 25, 1879, in Saguache.

Pitcher was successful in his courtship of the girl, for on October 26, 1904, he and Cora Mears were married. From February 3 to November 30, 1906, Pitcher served as treasurer of the Mack Brothers Manufacturing Company while Otto Mears was president of the firm. On the latter date, both Mears and Pitcher, who was a tall man towering over his short father-in-law, returned to Silverton to prepare for a projected boom in mining, particularly in the areas around Eureka and Animas Forks. In the next few years Pitcher served as Mears' right-hand man, managing the family properties when Mears was away.

James and Cora Pitcher gave the elder Mears couple their only grandchildren—four boys: James R. Pitcher, III, born July 8, 1906, in New York City; Otto Mears Pitcher, born August 3, 1908, in Silverton; Robertson Mears Pitcher, born January 12, 1910, in Denver; and William Kingsbury Pitcher, born July 19, 1919, in Los Angeles. The oldest grandson passed away in September of 1972; the three younger brothers still survive, as of this writing.

James R. Pitcher, Jr., succeeded Otto Mears as president of the Silverton Northern Railroad when his father-in-law passed away on June 24, 1931, but his term ended shortly thereafter when he himself died on December 26, 1933, in Pasadena, California.

Thomas Francis Walsh, whose activities in Colorado's San Juan region were quite independent from those of Otto Mears, none-the-less had a significant impact on the affairs of the latter man. Walsh was born in Ireland in 1851 and came to the United States at the age of 14. He participated in the Black Hills gold rush in Deadwood, South Dakota, in 1876; and, after marrying Caroline Reed of Wisconsin in 1879, moved to Colorado. There he operated the Grand Hotel in Leadville for awhile and then built bridges for W. A. H. Loveland's Colorado Central Railroad, which was under construction at the time.

Three children were born to Tom and Caroline Walsh, but only the middle girl, Evalyn Walsh (McLean), who much later bought the Hope Diamond with the family fortune, survived the parents. Walsh made a small fortune during the Leadville and Rico booms, only to lose his wealth in the Silver Panic of 1893.

In 1894, the Walshes moved to Silverton where he built a new smelter to treat the low-grade copper-silver ores brought up from the depths of the Guston mine on the north side of Sheridan Pass. This smelter operated until 1896. Meanwhile, Walsh—who now owned a fancy home with a bay window in Animas Forks (still standing as of the autumn of 1974 and a famous building among the remnants of that high-altitude ghost town)—had been nosing around for good claims. In 1895, he entered Imogene Basin, high on the side of Mount Sneffels, southwest of Ouray, while looking for more siliceous ores for his smelter. He bought the

SUNDANCE PHOTO BY DELL A. McCOY

Ghost of the past, the "Walsh" House which is still standing at Animas Forks.

Hidden Treasure mine and the Gertrude adit, paying $10,000 for the latter, and assembled a group of claims which he named the Camp Bird mine after the Canada Jays—or "camp robbers"—which stole his lunch.

His Camp Bird claims turned him into a millionaire. In 1902, he sold them to a British syndicate for $5,200,000 and moved to Washington, D.C., where he joined "high society." He died there of lung cancer in 1910.

Such were the characteristics of those independent, hardy, rugged individualists who were attracted to Colorado's San Juan Mountains during the pioneer days. Neither the hostility of their surroundings, the high altitude, the severe weather, the unfriendly Indians, nor the primitive, harsh conditions of their existence, deterred them. From the perspective of modern times, it seems remarkable that it was possible for the diversity of their interests and talents to be channelled into development of the common good. The resultant benefits to the area, and to themselves, were beyond imagination.

MORRIS W. ABBOTT COLLECTION

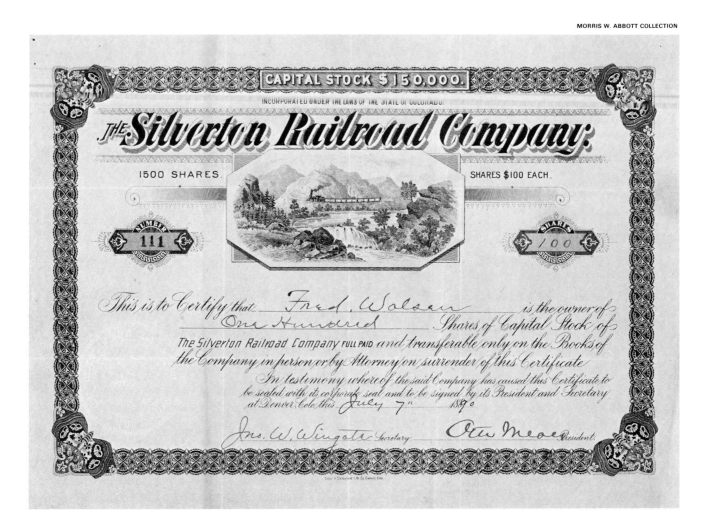

CHAPTER

III

In 1892, Otto Mears issued three unbelievable gold filigree passes, one of which is shown above.

Mears and Gibbs Build the Silverton Railroad
1887 - 1895

Up the steeps of the Great Divide,
Over the chasms deep and wide,
Yard by yard was the line surveyed,
Foot by foot were the timbers laid,

Drill and chisel, and pick and spade;
Each to the labor gave a share,
Till crag and peak and boulder bare
Were cleft, to make a roadway there.
— The Great Divide, 1890.

THE SILVERTON Railroad, first of Mears' four railroads, was begun in 1887, following the old survey extending up Mineral Creek, made in 1883 by Thomas Wigglesworth for the Denver and Rio Grande Railway. The new railroad was incorporated on July 5, chartered on July 8, and the first construction contracts were let by the end of the same month. The original officers were Otto Mears, president and general manager; George Crawford, vice-president; John W. Wingate, secretary; Fred Walsen, treasurer; J. H. Ernest Waters, chief engineer; and Adair Wilson, attorney. Local mines along the route helped in financing the railroad's construction by purchasing stock. The Yankee Girl, for example, bought at least $4,000-worth during the road's first few months. On the eleventh of August, 1887, Mr. Wingate advised the treasurer of the Yankee Girl mine that 150 men were working on the grade and that tie-placement was well underway. Mears went to Denver that week to order 30-pound rail.

With this concrete evidence of less expensive transportation for low-grade ores now at hand, the New Guston Company, Ltd., of London, was formed in September of 1887, and on June 30 the following year, the Guston mine reopened under new management.

Tracklaying progressed and by October 21, 1887, the rails reached as far as Burro Bridge, the eastern terminus of the horrid pack trail to Ophir that climbed along the Middle Fork of Mineral Creek, crossed over Ophir Pass, and dropped down the Howard Fork of the Rio San Miguel to the town and mines of Ophir.

The people of Red Mountain town were impatiently awaiting the arrival of the end-of-track. The settlement's *third* newspaper, *The Red Mountain Mining Journal,* had been launched on October 1 by Gid R. Propper, an itinerant editor with previous experience on other papers in the San Juans, and in his very first issue Propper included such stories as:

It has been casually suggested that when the graders begin moving dirt through Red Mountain, a day be set apart by a number of our citizens and leisure hour people and that they make 500 feet of grade for the railroad. At the same time we should arrange to have a silver spike in the most central part of the track. The people of Chattanooga are to have a ball; the people of Silverton, at the instigation of the Jockey Club, raised $500 to celebrate the first train down from Red Mountain. Now, we must certainly do something to show our appreciation of the coming event.

The graders are between Chattanooga and Old Congress Town.—

MRS. MARVIN GREGORY COLLECTION

In the summer of 1888, Red Mountain was a boom town, growing up rapidly near the National Belle mine. In this street scene, you are looking northeast along Main Street, where new construction and one of the scrapers used for grading the Silverton Railroad can be seen.

Red Mountain is prolific in weddings. It is a lonesome place to live in and the young people are not to be blamed for doubling up. A man who will sleep alone during a winter in Red Mountain either has no affection for the fair sex or they have none for him. Besides, Red Mountain needs an increased population.—

On November 27, 1887, he ran the following story, not only to fill space, but also to boost the morale of the townfolk faced with the fast-approaching winter:

As a class, all are united and nothing intervenes to mar the happiness of all who have cast their winter lot in the camp, and a silver lining and plumage of hope and prosperity are now assured.

The mines are on all sides. The men have but a short walk to work and the whistle for meals and shift time breaks the gloom of what may seem an isolated or desolate camp. It is a town of happiness unconfined the year 'round.—

* * * * *

On the Silverton Railroad there was happiness, too, for on November 2, 1887, the road bought its first locomotive—second-hand D&RG Class 60 2-8-0 Number 42, named the *Anglo Saxon* (Baldwin number 4938), manufactured in 1880. Before delivery to the Silverton, the engine was overhauled and rebuilt at the Burnham shops in Denver. In the process, an exchange of boilers took place with a second engine in the shop, the running gear of

Number 42 receiving the boiler from another Class 60 2-8-0—Number 283 (Baldwin number 6057), built for the D&RG in 1882. The original boiler from Number 42, in turn, was installed on the running gear of D&RG Number 283, and that engine remained in service on the Rio Grande system until sold to the Nevada County Narrow Gauge in 1933 as their engine Number 8.

The hybrid locomotive purchased by Mears for his new Silverton Railroad venture was given the number 100 and was named *Ouray*, the name duly inscribed in capital letters on the side panels of the cab, and Mears tendered his check for $6,500 to the Denver and Rio Grande to complete the transaction.

By January 28, 1888, the first six miles of the Silverton Railroad were in operation to Burro Bridge, and 15 additional miles were under construction. At this time, Mears also ordered his first passes for the new railroad from John Morris and Company of Chicago. Imprinted on white buckskin, the passes were 2½ x 4-inches in size, and today are among the real rarities of railroadiana.

The folk in Red Mountain town, to while away the winter and at the same time combat the loneliness of their isolated snowbound high-altitude site —pending railroad connection with the outside world—concocted various forms of entertainment. The Red Mountain Lyceum and Dramatic Association gave its first performance on February 8, 1888, the program consisting of community singing, a guitar solo, a soliloquy from Shakespeare, and a debate. Apparently less interested in such mental excercise than in physical exertion, the Knights of Pythias, the Free Coinage Dancing Club, and the Sky City Miners' Club all gave frequent balls. Editor Propper observed to the readers of his *Red Mountain Mining Journal*:

The town is five years old and as yet there is no graveyard. Two children have died from unnatural causes. We should be contented.

* * * * *

In the spring of 1888, Charles Wingate Gibbs, having left the Colorado Midland, was engaged in the construction of the Rock Island's western extension approaching Colorado Springs (from the east). He was glad to accept the opportunity to serve as chief engineer of the Silverton Railroad when approached by Otto Mears. Gibbs started construction at Burro Bridge in late May, 1888, when the snow melted. By June 1, seven miles were in operation, and on the tenth of the month, he was camped at Chattanooga.

There he installed the first of three major

bridges on the Silverton—across Mineral Creek—and more importantly, created the first of his many innovations in railroad location engineering, the *Chattanooga Loop.* Here he made the railroad rise 550 feet in a quarter of a mile as the crow flies, detouring up Mill Creek, then lining out 200 degrees of curve with a 30-degree (194-foot) radius —a total distance of one and three-quarter miles, all on five-percent gradient! Having proved workable, these were to be the standard grade and maximum curvature for the balance of the road. Few tighter curves were to be built on any of the Mears railroads; a 32-degree curve was located on the mainline of the Silverton Northern at the Sunnyside mill in Eureka, at the start of the extension to Animas Forks, and a 40-degree curve was required near the end of that branch. On the Silverton, Gladstone and Northerly—which did not become a part of the Mears system of railroads until 1915—there were a dozen curves ranging between 30 and 40 degrees.

Never afraid to challenge the hallowed precepts of location engineering, Gibbs used no transition spirals from tangents to curves, used no compensation for curvature on his grades, frequently put no tangents between reverse curves, and in his vertical curves went from dead level to a five-percent grade in 60 feet. The effects of the latter practice can be observed in the worn underside of the pilot on engine Number 100 in the photograph taken at the Yankee Girl mine in 1891 by S. G. White (see the frontispiece).

As of July 1, 1888, the Silverton Railroad reported ownership of one locomotive, Number 100, the *Ouray,* one passenger car, the *Red Mountain,* and one baggage-mail-express car, later given the number 5. By the twenty-second of that month, Chief Engineer Gibbs had crossed over the summit of Sheridan Pass and was camped at the Guston mine (which he called the "Gustine" in his correspondence) on the north side; regular trains were running to Chattanooga, where they served the Hoosier Boy, Silver Crown and Silver Ledge mines.

The first annual meeting of the company was held in Silverton on July 25, 1888, and two new officers were installed. While Otto Mears continued as president, John A. Porter was elected vice-president. John W. Wingate and Fred Walsen remained as secretary and treasurer, respectively, and attorney, Adair Wilson, was given the more estimable title of *solicitor.* Charles W. Gibbs was confirmed as chief engineer; George Crawford and J. H. Ernest Waters, while relinquishing their previous titles, remained as directors.

The second major bridge, a high trestle, was

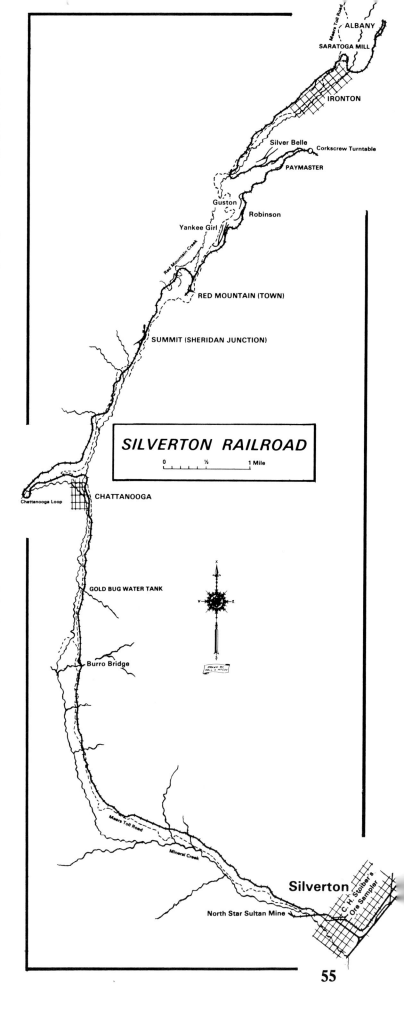

SILVERTON RAILROAD

SUNDANCE PHOTO BY DELL A. McCOY

A warm Indian summer day provided a beautiful time for a hike along the old Silverton Railway grade to Corkscrew Gulch turntable — near the the base of Red Mountain Number 1. Autumn normally is the most colorful time of the year in the San Juans, with bright, sunny days and crisp, cool nights. During its heyday, this railroad had the reputation of being the steepest (5-percent grades), the crookedest (30-degree curves) and the best-paying road in Colorado.

W. J. CARPENTER PHOTO —
CHARLES S. RYLAND COLLECTION

The **Mule Shoe Curve** — or Chattanooga Loop — on the Silverton Railroad, meant the beginning of a heavy grade to locomotive engineers. In June, 1891, engine 100 was seen pulling baggage car 5 and coach 3, the *Yankee Girl,* downgrade to Silverton. The famous Million Dollar Highway now uses this route.

installed across Porphyry Creek, about half-way between Chattanooga and the top, and by August 10, trains were running to within a mile of the summit of the pass. Then, on September 19, 1888, at the open-handed invitation of Otto Mears, the noted photographer, Thomas M. McKee of Mont-rose, journeyed to the site with his camera, tripod and glass plates to celebrate—in the form of some

superb views—the arrival of the first train at Red Mountain town. Here, Gibbs had devised the second of his engineering masterpieces, the *depot in a wye.*

The settlement known as Red Mountain had shifted back and forth over the saddle of Sheridan Pass—on the flanks of Red Mountain peak—several times during the 1880's. Finally, with the

MRS. MARVIN GREGORY COLLECTION

Looking north along Main Street of Red Mountain town, one was able to see this view in 1889. When this scene was recorded, a covered wagon, loaded down with "flatlanders," had just arrived in the settlement.

arrival of the Silverton Railroad, the townsite was established next to the National Belle mine; the neighboring village of Congress immediately became a ghost town when its inhabitants abandoned the place and moved to the final site of Red Mountain! The town then consisted of about 600 souls, with three newspapers, a postoffice, the National Belle mine (which produced silver ore worth up to $14,000 a ton), numerous saloons, the depot inside a wye, and a jail. Considerably worse for the years of harsh weather and vandalism, only a few moribund mine buildings and the jailhouse were still in existence as of 1974.

The ingenious track plan at Red Mountain town came about because of the location and size of the townsite. This place features a large, peculiar outcropping known as *the Knob*—composed of a very hard rock produced when the silver ore was deposited—and the rocks east of the Knob, which are not much softer. In consequence, the whole town was built along the approach to and in a very small glen between the steeply sloping sidehills. With no room for a balloon loop, and not enough overburden for excavation of a turntable pit, Gibbs resorted to constructing a wye. The legs of the wye were about 150-feet long—enough to accommodate

only a locomotive and two cars. The track arrangement made for some very interesting—and sometimes complex—switching moves.

Only one small, flat area next to the track was suitable for a depot. This was at the junction of the two creeks in town, coincidentally the only place to put a wye without the trouble and expense of blasting or major excavation. So the depot was built on piles, inside and along the main track, across the top of the wye. A privy was placed inside the east leg of the wye—to save space, and to keep patrons and employees from being delayed by train operations in moments of stress!

The jail was undoubtedly a howling success. It was located on the main street, only 80 feet from the depot, and just across the tracks and down the hill from the big mine. Built on solid bedrock, especially leveled for the occasion, it was never broken out of (as far as can be determined). The wood in the structure weighed about 40 tons, so it was virtually immovable. There was no heat, and no glass in the two north-facing windows; therefore at 10,920 feet above sea level, a night in the *carcel* must have exerted a very sobering influence, if the poor hombre did not freeze to death in the meantime.

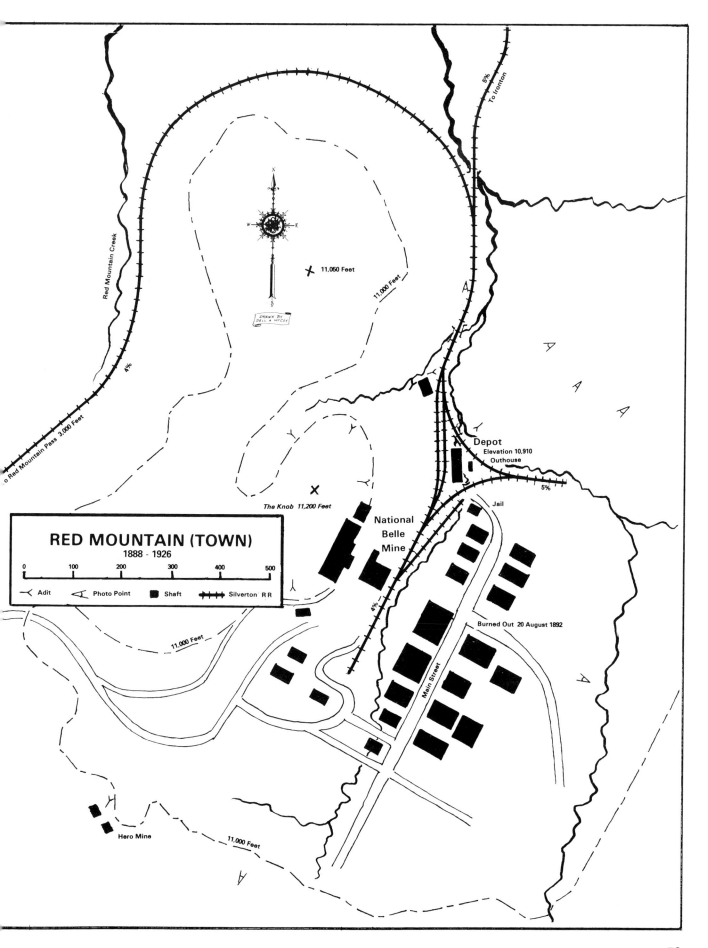

Red Mountain Creek

To Ironton

5%

N

$\times$ 11,050 Feet

11,000 Feet

DRAWN BY
DELL A. McCOY

To Red Mountain Pass 3,000 Feet

4%

Depot
Elevation 10,910
Outhouse

5%

$\times$ The Knob 11,200 Feet

Jail

National
Belle
Mine

Burned Out 20 August 1892

4%

Main Street

11,000 Feet

RED MOUNTAIN (TOWN)
1888 - 1926

| 0 | 100 | 200 | 300 | 400 | 500 |

$\prec$ Adit $\prec$ Photo Point   ■ Shaft   ┼┼┼┼ Silverton R R

Hero Mine

11,000 Feet

59

RAINBOW ROUTE, SILVERTON, R.R., COLO.

W. J. CARPENTER PHOTO —
CHARLES S. RYLAND COLLECTION

Photographic stop, above the Chattanooga Loop.

Gibbs finished construction for the year by October 29, 1888, having built 11.2 miles of narrow-gauge railway in five and one-half months, under the worst possible circumstances, through cramped and restrictive areas, and amid avalanche runs. Although the railway was more-or-less complete to Ironton, through traffic could not go the whole distance until the third major bridge could be erected—a long curved trestle across Red Mountain Creek at a place later known as Joker. On November 1, the contractors turned the new line over to the operating company.

Opposite page — the Chattanooga Loop was the setting of this 1888 photograph, with Silverton Railroad Number 100, D&RG boxcar 431X and Silverton Railroad baggage car Number 5 on the upper leg. Sister engine, D&RG Number 22, the *Alamosa,* was resting with a handcar in tow on the lower leg of the loop.

W. J. CARPENTER PHOTO —
COLORADO RAILROAD MUSEUM COLLECTION

The stockholders of the Silverton Railroad, at a meeting late in September, voted to raise $350,000 to add five extensions to the line, as follows:
1. From Ironton to Ouray by way of Uncompahgre Cañon;
2. From a point near Ouray to the Virginius mine;
3. From Silverton to Howardsville, Eureka, Animas Forks and Mineral Point, and from there to a junction with the mainline;
4. From Animas Forks to Lake City; and
5. From Silverton along Cement Creek Valley.

Gibbs already was at work surveying the route from Ironton to Ouray. Some of these branches so optimistically projected in those booming times actually were built, but at much later dates and after Gibbs had vanished from the scene.

Mears ordered his passes for the coming year—1889—to be stamped from solid silver produced by the Red Mountain mines. Manufactured by the Diamond Palace in Denver, they were 3.65 x 2.2

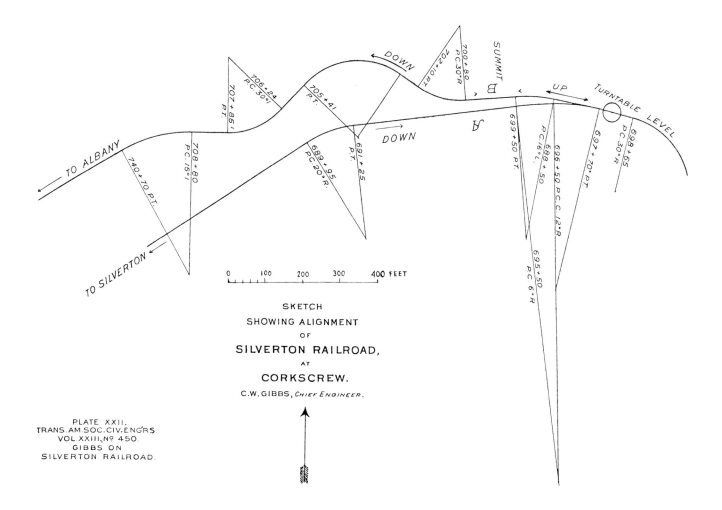

SKETCH
SHOWING ALIGNMENT
OF
SILVERTON RAILROAD,
AT
CORKSCREW.

C.W. GIBBS, CHIEF ENGINEER.

PLATE XXII.
TRANS.AM.SOC.CIV.ENG'RS.
VOL.XXIII, N° 450.
GIBBS ON
SILVERTON RAILROAD.

inches in size, and were of two types. The first had the year, *1889*, engraved in the die, which was produced in relief on the silver; in the other, only the *18* portion of the year was embossed on the silver, while the *89* portion was engraved by the jeweler, along with the names of the recipients, as the passes were issued.

During the winter, the switchback at Corkscrew Gulch had posed some severe operational problems; so, after the spring thaw in 1889, Gibbs added the third of his more audacious contrivances, a *turntable on the main track*. In use by June 14, this unique and ingenious solution to a vexing problem allowed full operation to Ironton.

There were several reasons behind the installation: the poor tracking qualities of the 2-8-0's working in reverse, especially in snow, presented a continuing problem. Of even greater import, safety and efficiency of operation demanded that the locomotive be on the downgrade end of the cars to work the mine spurs. Neither the approach to, nor the steep, crooked, narrow Corkscrew Gulch itself, affording any space for a passing siding, a loop or a wye, and without a means for running the locomotive around the cars, the train had to drop down all the way to the far end at Ironton in order

to return and work the mine spur at the Silver Belle. That Gibbs was extremely careful in thinking through problems before starting construction, there can be no dispute; since the 50-foot turntable was long enough only to turn the locomotive while the coupled cars were fed through the table by gravity both ways.

So pleased was Gibbs with the practicality of his arrangement, when subjected to actual operation, that he thought the matter worth bringing to the attention of his professional colleagues, and in Volume XXIII, No. 450, of the *Transactions of the American Society of Civil Engineers*, issued in September, 1890, he publicized his achievement in the following words:

SAN JUAN COUNTY HISTORICAL SOCIETY

62

AMERICAN SOCIETY OF CIVIL ENGINEERS,

INSTITUTED 1852.

TRANSACTIONS.

Note.—This Society is not responsible, as a body, for the facts and opinions advanced in any of its publications.

450

Vol. XXIII.—September, 1890.

THE TURN-TABLE ON THE MAIN TRACK OF THE SILVERTON RAILROAD IN COLORADO.

By C. W. Gibbs, M. Am. Soc. C. E.

WITH DISCUSSION.

The Silverton Railroad is a short line but 17.5 miles long, and has the reputation of being the steepest (5 per cent. grade), the crookedest (30 degree curves) and the best paying road in Colorado; and is owned by one man, Otto Mears. It also has a turn-table on its main track, and it is the purpose of this paper to describe it and explain why it was so placed.

This road leaves the Denver and Rio Grande at Silverton, and runs over a divide 11,113 feet above sea level, then down into the rich mining country beyond. The country is very rough and rugged, and in order to reach the town of Red Mountain it was necessary to run up on a switchback, as no room for a loop could be found. A wye was, therefore, built, and the engine could be turned while the train stood on the main track. The engine was thus placed ahead of the train, only the train is pulled out of the station rear end ahead. It runs thus till the turn-table is reached. The train is stopped at a point marked *A*, Plate XXII; the engine uncoupled, run onto the table, is turned and pulled up to a point near *B*, where it is stopped. The train is then allowed to drop down to the turn-table and the engine backed onto it. In coming up from Albany the train is stopped on the down grade between the summit at *B* and the table; the engine is taken off, turned on the table and run up to about *A*; the train is then allowed to drop to the table as before and the engine backed up and coupled on, taking not over five minutes in going either way.

The reason of putting the table in was that there were no mines to the east of Ironton as shown on Plate XXI, but between the turn-table and the loop there were several that it was very desirable to reach, and the side hill is so steep that it is impossible to make a loop on it.

This table is the source of a great deal of comment from tourists, of whom there are many during the summer months, as it is on the line known as the "circle," so extensively advertised by the Denver and Rio Grande Railroad.

The road is used both for a freight and passenger road, and as before mentioned, is the best paying road in Colorado, two engines being kept busy hauling ore to Silverton from the Red Mountain district.

The object of writing this paper was to describe what the author thinks is quite a novelty, being the only turn-table that he has ever heard of which is used upon a switchback in this manner, and where the grades are adjusted as they are to let the train run by gravity on the table from both ways.

Plate XXI is a print from a photograph of the map filed in Washington and is about 9,000 feet to the inch.

Plate XXII is an enlarged sketch of the line near the turn-table.

DISCUSSION.

J. FOSTER CROWELL, M. Am. Soc. C. E.—It occurs to me that the use of the turn-table being simply to turn the engine during transit, while the train waits, and moreover, as the service is a special one on a spur line, it would have been better to obtain an engine capable of running in either direction and not requiring to be turned, rather than resort to a turn-table in the main track which contains an element of danger as well as of delay to the traffic. The device, however, is an ingenious one to meet the peculiar conditions of the line; and if experience with it proves satisfactory, there are other problems on a larger scale relating to change of direction in mountain location that it may help to solve.

C. W. GIBBS, M. Am. Soc. C. E.—If a special engine had been procured, as Mr. Crowell suggests, it would have been at an extra expense, owing to the limited number wanted; and even with a special design, it might have been difficult for any engine to have backed its load over so steep a grade and such sharp curves without more danger than was suggested there might be at the turn-table. The delay to traffic amounts to nothing, for there are no competing lines, nor do I expect there ever will be. The turn-table has now been in actual operation every day since June, 1889, and no accident has ever occurred.

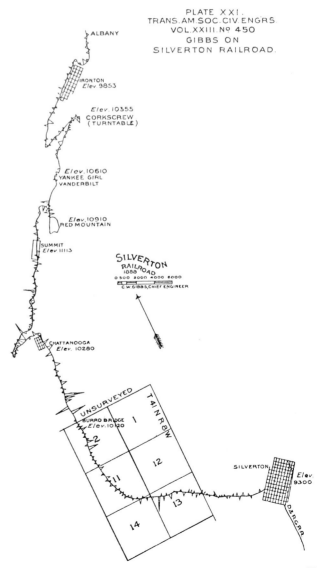

PLATE XXI.
TRANS. AM. SOC. CIV. ENGRS.
VOL. XXIII. Nº 450
GIBBS ON
SILVERTON RAILROAD.

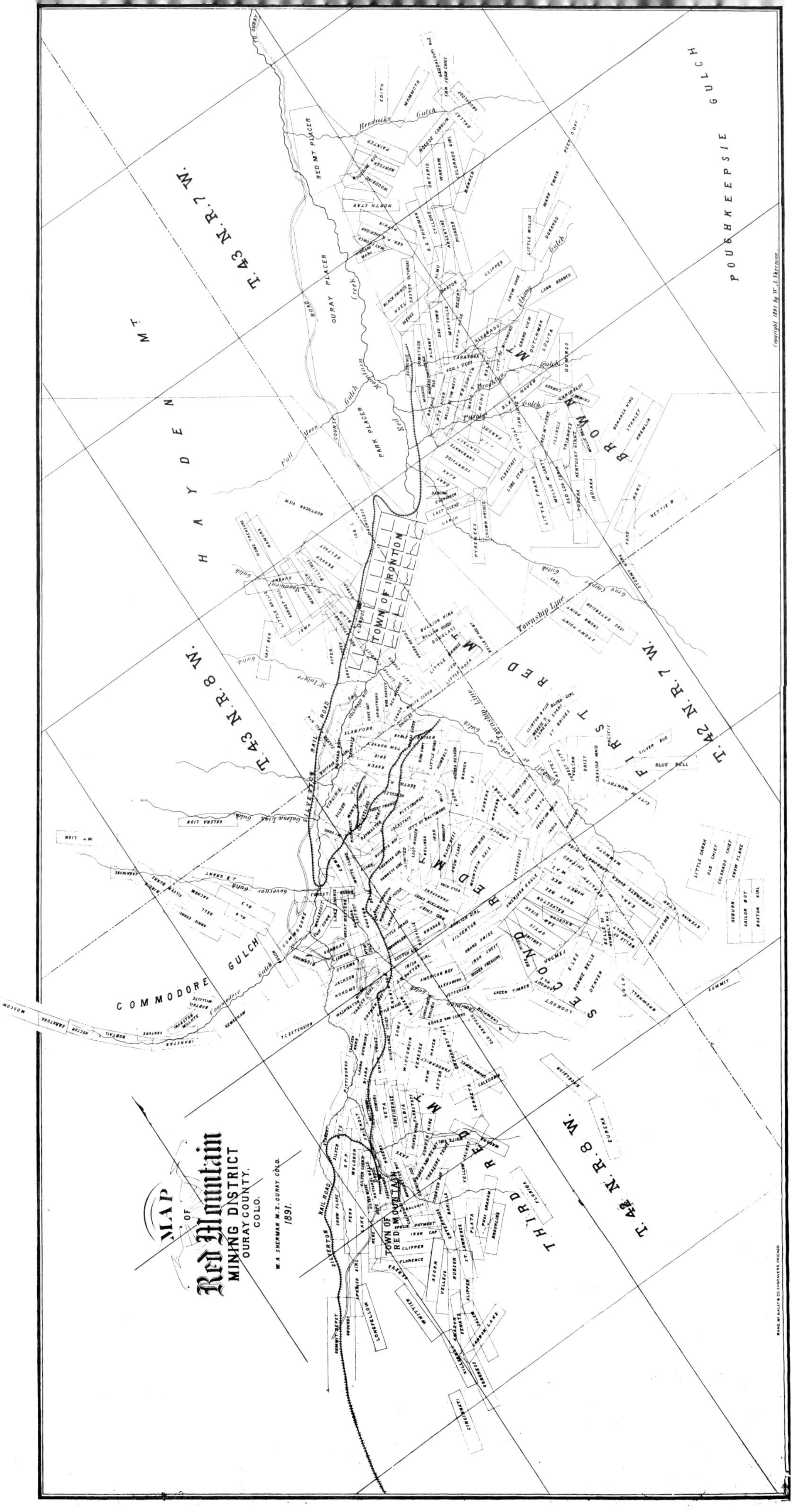

SAN JUAN COUNTY HISTORICAL SOCIETY

THIS MAP OF THE
RED MOUNTAIN
MINING DISTRICT
WAS ORIGINALLY
PRINTED IN 1891

Opposite page — Corkscrew Gulch turntable was brand new when portrayed in this magnificent view during June of 1889. The track leading to the turntable (at the left) came down from Red Mountain town, while the other track (to the right of the train) continued downgrade to Ironton. Spirit Gulch and Commodore Gulch can be seen on the far side of Red Mountain Creek.

COLORADO RAILROAD MUSEUM COLLECTION

MAP
OF
Red Mountain
MINING DISTRICT
OURAY COUNTY,
COLO.
W. A. SHERMAN M. E. OURAY COLO.
1891.

Nº 560
THE TURNTABLE

THOMAS M. McKEE PHOTO — RICHARD A. RONZIO COLLECTION

The first Silverton Railroad passenger train into Red Mountain town arrived on September 19, 1888. In this historic photograph, passengers were transferring to the stage line to continue their trip along the original "Rainbow Route" to Ouray. When this view was produced, Otto Mears was standing next to the steps of the combination baggage-chaircar, *Red Mountain*.

The view printed below is another picture of the first passenger train into Red Mountain town. The equipment was carefully positioned at the north end of *the Knob* for this group shot. Otto Mears proudly stood next to the pilot of his only engine, Number 100, the *Ouray*. C. W. Gibbs stood in front of the drivers, while Ernest E. Ingersoll, noted author, impressed upon a beautiful lady the wonder of all the riches lying in the ground just waiting to be mined. Notice that the pilot of Number 100 scraped the rails at this point — where the grade changed.

THOMAS M. McKEE PHOTO — RICHARD A. RONZIO COLLECTION

WILLIAM H. JACKSON PHOTO — WILLIAM PLUNKETT COLLECTION

Due to a forest fire, which occurred several years earlier, the approaches to Corkscrew Gulch turntable were nearly treeless when W. H. Jackson photographed this view in 1889. Silverton Railroad Number 100 was drifting downgrade on the lower leg of the mainline to Ironton — in the valley below. Beyond Ironton, the line can barely be discerned heading toward the end-of-track at Albany.

In a closeup view of the scene printed on page 65, the picture below shows that carpenters were completing the covered shed of the tail-end track of the Corkscrew Gulch turntable. Notice the sawhorse on the roof ridge leading to the turntable. A smoke vent was being built at the peak of the roof. Meanwhile, Silverton Railroad Number 100 was heading upgrade toward Red Mountain town with the *Yankee Girl* and baggage car 5.

W. I. CARPENTER PHOTO

WILLIAM H. JACKSON PHOTO —
FRITZ KLINKE COLLECTION

The William H. Jackson view above reveals both levels of the Chattanooga Loop (Mule Shoe Curve). You are looking south — down Mineral Creek — toward Bear Mountain. People who thought they could see the image of a bear eating something held in its paws, led to the naming of this mountain. The town of Chattanooga, nestled in the park below, was protected by the high peaks on all sides.

WILLIAM H. JACKSON PHOTO —
JACKSON C. THODE COLLECTION

It was a foggy day in Red Mountain mining district when the noted photographer, William H. Jackson, shot a series of three glass-plate negatives — about 1890. The first picture was taken looking north from the Silverton Railroad mainline, about halfway between the Genessee-Vanderbilt and Yankee Girl mines, and shows the latter mine quite well. The train consisted of SRR Number 100; the combine, *Red Mountain;* and a D&RG boxcar. The engine was about to pick up boxcar 4008 from the lead track to the Yankee Girl spur, and would then continue backing upgrade into Red Mountain town.

5647. YANKEE GIRL MINE.

SWITCHBACK AT RED MOUNTAIN.

WILLIAM H. JACKSON PHOTO —
JACKSON C. THODE COLLECTION

The second Jackson photo of that day was taken 3000 feet to the south, as the train — now towing boxcar 4008 — went through the switch leading to the Red Mountain wye.

SILVER MEDALLION PASS

SILVER FILIGREE PASS

Opposite page — the third of the ''foggy day in Red Mountain town'' series of Jackson photographs was taken looking south into town from very nearly the same spot as the second view. It gives us the only print known of the north end of the depot. Car 4008 was dropped on the mainline to shorten the train for switching on the National Belle spurs, as well as the 100-foot legs of the Red Mountain wye; it was picked up again on the trip out of Red Mountain to Silverton.

WILLIAM H. JACKSON PHOTO —
JACKSON C. THODE COLLECTION

RED MOUNTAIN.

3346. YANKEE GIRL MINE, RED MOUNTAIN, W. HO. CO.

WILLIAM H. JACKSON PHOTO —
JACKSON C. THODE COLLECTION

William H. Jackson was sufficiently unhappy over the foggy background he had obtained in his 1890 shot of the Yankee Girl mine to come back later that year (or the next) to duplicate his earlier view. Nothing much had changed but the size of the tailings dump (at the left), and a new log cabin had been constructed. However, no train can be seen in this view, only a boxcar and gondola waiting to be picked up.

W. J. CARPENTER PHOTO —
CHARLES S. RYLAND COLLECTION

In this closeup view of the D&RG's engine 22 — leased by the Silverton Railroad — Otto Mears was standing next to the tender. This Class 60 engine was the only wagon-top boilered locomotive of its class, and was named *Alamosa*.

MOORE PHOTO — RON MORSE COLLECTION

This photograph was taken from the tail of the wye at Red Mountain town, and shows a train already turned and ready to head toward either Silverton or Ironton. Silverton Railroad Number 100 was on the point of this train, with baggage car Number 5 in tow, followed by a D&RG stockcar, the *Yankee Girl* coach and a D&RG flatcar.

75

#84
NATIONAL BELLE MINE, ON RAINBOW ROUTE, SILVE

CHARLES GOODMAN PHOTO — RICHARD A. RONZIO COLLECTION

In 1890, the inhabitants of Red Mountain town went about their business at the National Belle mine, as a freighter unloaded goods from a boxcar on a siding beside the depot. The train crew probably was up the hill in town, having lunch at the local "beanery," while the *Ouray* simmered by herself on the wye. *The Knob* was a famous landmark of this locale, honeycombed with gold and silver. Once the train crew returned, they

would pick up their train and head on down to Ironton, dropping off cars along the way at various mines. Then, in the late afternoon, their work would find them picking up carloads of ore, as the *Ouray* worked its way over Red Mountain Pass, and on down the mountain, back home to Silverton. Originally called Sheridan Pass, this pass reaches an elevation of 11,018 feet, one of the highest trans-mountain routes in Colorado.

NKEE GIRL MINE.
RED MOUNTAIN COLORADO.
U.S.A.

78

S. G. WHITE PHOTO —
STATE HISTORICAL SOCIETY OF COLORADO

S. G. White of Ouray posed locomotive Number 100, the *Ouray,* and its crew on the lead track of the Yankee Girl mine in 1891. This outstanding view — as reproduced at left — is an excellent portrayal of the Red Mountain mining district.

On the following page is a panoramic scene, photographed on September 11, 1900, by Whitman Cross. It shows almost the entire business end of the Silverton Railroad in one picture. It was taken from high on the divide between Full Moon and McIntyre gulches — looking southeast — and displays the entire railroad from Corkscrew Gulch turntable (on the left) to Red Mountain town (on the right). Paymaster and Silver Belle trackage can be seen in the left half of the view, while Red Mountain Number 2 is in the center of the right half of the scene — with the Guston - Yankee Girl complex on its face. All of these mines had been shut down when this view was produced, and the railroad was slumbering.

WHITMAN CROSS PHOTO — U.S. GEOLOGICAL SURVEY

Photo Area

Fold

Page Edge

Corkscrew Turntable

Paymaster Coal Spur

Cora Be

Passing Siding 150 Fe

Paymaster Ore Spur

Coal Spur

Silver Belle Mine

Ore Spur

Emma Mine

White Cloud Mine

Joker Tunnel

Main Street

Ironton Depot IRONTON

Red Mountain Creek

OURAY & RED MOUNTAIN TOLL ROAD

Page Edge

Robinson Powerhouse

Fill

Fill

Fill

Robinson Mine

Irish Girl Mine

J. R. Dutton Mine

Genessee-Vanderbilt Mine

RED MOUNTAIN (TOWN)

uston Mine

Wilde Mine

Yankee Girl Mine

Union Trust Mine

Treasury Tunnel Mine

Red Mountain Creek

OURAY & RED MOUNTAIN TOLL ROAD

SHERIDAN JUNCTION (SUMMIT)

RED MOUNTAIN MINING DISTRICT MAP

0   ½ Mile

S. G. WHITE PHOTO —
STATE HISTORICAL SOCIETY OF COLORADO

During late summer of 1892, Mr. S. G. White, a photographer from Ouray, produced this view — looking east upon a scene of mining prosperity at the Yankee Girl mine. All the trees on the mining claims had been logged-off to be used for mine props and timbering. The Silverton's Shay, Number 269, was starting down the "roller coaster" switchbacks to reach the Yankee Girl mine, with five 10-ton boxcars in charge — in what is regarded as one of only three photographs known of this geared engine. Silverton Railroad's 2-8-0, Number 100, with coach Number 3 and baggage car Number 5, were waiting on the mainline for the switch to be cleared before resuming their trip to Ironton. This scene has been enlarged on the two preceding pages.

WILLIAM H. JACKSON PHOTO —
WILLIAM PLUNKETT COLLECTION

This closeup reveals the Silverton's Number 100, as it rolled downgrade from Corkscrew Gulch turntable — with baggage car Number 5 and the chaircar, *Yankee Girl.* The wagon-top roof — with which the baggage car was equipped — was the earliest design used on railroad coaches in Colorado, due to the relatively low cost involved in building it.

The two styles of 1889 silver passes are shown below, left, and on the preceding page. The one to the left is the earlier "A" style, while the one to the right is the later "B" style. The pass reproduced directly below is an example of the famous buckskin pass.

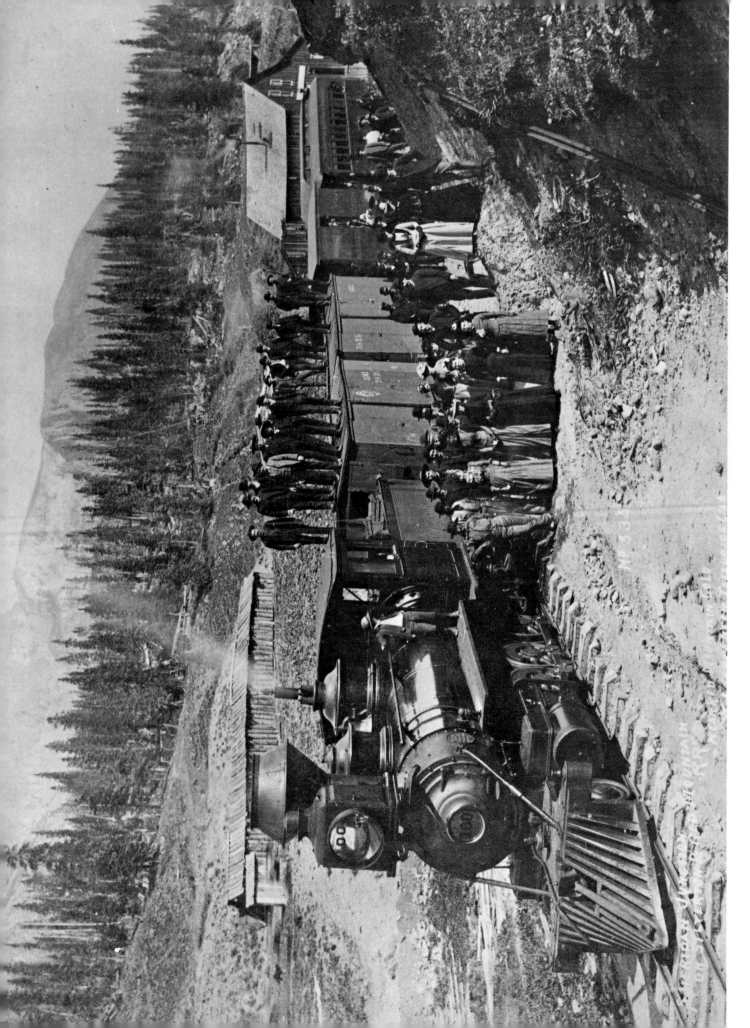

W. J. CARPENTER PHOTO

In the scene above, it would appear that Sheridan Junction was a good spot for picture-taking. In addition to Silverton Number 100, D&RG boxcars 3103 and 4512, the Silverton baggage car and the coach, *Yankee Girl*, were captured on glass in this 1891 view.

The Silverton's Number 100, a D&RG boxcar, and the combine, *Red Mountain*, are portrayed in the 1890 scene below, as they emerged from the covered turntable at Corkscrew Gulch — heading toward Ironton. Waiting on the upper leg of the switchback is a leased D&RG engine.

WILLIAM H. JACKSON PHOTO —
STATE HISTORICAL SOCIETY OF COLORADO

62900. RED MOUNTAIN

WILLIAM H. JACKSON PHOTO —
STATE HISTORICAL SOCIETY OF COLORADO

WILLIAM H. JACKSON PHOTO —
STATE HISTORICAL SOCIETY OF COLORADO

The closeup scene above reveals the depot grounds of Red Mountain town, with a mixed train sitting on the mainline. The end-of-track was just out of sight, below the National Belle's mine dump. Beyond the depot, the original Ouray & Red Mountain Toll Road wandered down to Ironton, after circling around through Red Mountain town.

When photographed during the winter of 1893 — after the big fire — Red Mountain town looked like this, covered with a blanket of snow, an altogether normal occurance. This view was photographed from nearly the same spot as the one above, but the town is noticeably emptier. Sadly enough, it never recovered its former bustling glory.

Opposite page — when photographed in 1890, Red Mountain town was at its peak population. The National Belle mine on *the Knob* (to the left) was producing carloads of silver, and the town's merchants were busy making merry sounds in their cash registers. The fire of August 10, 1892, destroyed most of the buildings and the majority of the town's people moved elsewhere after their belongings had gone up in smoke.

MRS. MARVIN GREGORY COLLECTION

91

BRUMFIELD AND GILBERT PHOTO —
RICHARD A. RONZIO COLLECTION

The subject of the view above was the Guston mine on Red Mountain. The Silverton Railroad's mainline was occupied with a train coming past the Robinson powerhouse, heading toward Red Mountain town. The Robinson mine had a spur at this building for delivering carloads of coal. Two boxcars were spotted on another spur — to the left, below — and further downhill yet another spur swung in to serve the Guston mine complex.

WILLIAM H. JACKSON PHOTO —
RICHARD A. RONZIO COLLECTION

Kendall Mountain rises above Silverton in the 1890 photograph printed below. You are looking east, along the Silverton Railroad grade. Parts of the original toll road had been covered by the new railroad grade — making new roadwork necessary, including a new bridge over Mineral Creek. The North Star Sultan mine can be seen at the right.

MOUNTAIN MINES

DETROIT PHOTOGRAPHIC

WILLIAM H. JACKSON PHOTO —
JACKSON C. THODE COLLECTION

Above — in this 1888 Jackson view of miners' homes, you can see the Guston mine buildings (left) and the Robinson mine's combination shafthouse and powerhouse, located on the newly completed Silverton Railroad grade (right).

BRUMFIELD AND GILBERT PHOTO —
RICHARD A. RONZIO COLLECTION

At left — this 1890 closeup shows SRR Number 100 smoking up the sky as she climbed the grade to Red Mountain town — past the Robinson powerhouse.

Opposite page, above — snow-shovelers found a good excuse to take a breather at the Red Mountain depot in 1891, the only year the Silverton Railroad ran all winter.

Opposite page, below — Number 5 was a leased Class 60 2-8-0 from the Rio Grande Southern. It is shown here at Red Mountain Pass (Sheridan Junction). The crew was picking up boxcars full of concentrate while making up a train to head into Silverton. This scene was photographed during mid-summer of 1892.

No. 50
SNOW SHOVELLERS, SILVERTON R.R.
COLO.

BRUMFIELD & GILBERT OURAY

BRUMFIELD AND GILBERT PHOTO —
JACKSON C. THODE COLLECTION

E. ADAMS PHOTO — MORRIS W. ABBOTT COLLECTION

HIGHEST POINT ON THE RAINBOW ROUTE
11,000 FT. ALTITUDE

WILLIAM H. JACKSON PHOTO — STATE HISTORICAL SOCIETY OF COLORADO

Mining folk needed strong faith while living in the San Juan mining district — as evidenced by the little white church in Ironton. This view was shot in 1889, from near the lower leg of the Corkscrew Gulch turntable track, looking north. The SRR depot is to the left and slightly above the church. The mainline passed by Ironton on the grade in the background — on its way to the end-of-track at Albany. A boxcar can be seen sitting on the depot house track.

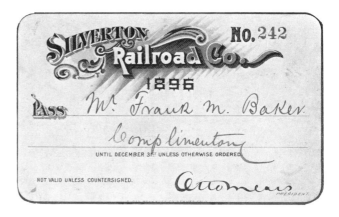

96

WILLIAM PLUNKETT WATERCOLOR

Red Mountain town was a scene of busy activity once the mixed train arrived. The depot agent was busy selling tickets, while outside, freighters unloaded goods that had arrived from Silverton and beyond. The train crew clanked equipment about the wye and spotted cars on the sidings — while picking up other cars to makeup the train for the outward-bound trip.

STATE HISTORICAL SOCIETY OF COLORADO COLLECTION

Cora Mears' gold filigree pass — shown full size. (Cora was the daughter of Otto Mears.)

RICHARD A. RONZIO COLLECTION

The main street of Red Mountain town looked like this before the fire of 1892. Several hotels lined the street, along with a postoffice, restaurants and saloons. The large building at left was the Red Mountain Hotel.

To supplement the Silverton Railroad's engine Number 100, Mears leased from the Denver and Rio Grande their Class 56 2-8-0, Number 65, the *San Cristoval*, from January to July of 1889. The same locomotive again was leased from January 1 to 23 in 1890; it was often asked for specifically when the Silverton needed a spare locomotive.

The employees working for the Silverton Railroad in 1889, along with their titles and monthly salaries, were: John E. Fitzgibbon, and after September, William E. Booker, locomotive engineers, at $165.00; William Hyndman, fireman, at $100.00; Charles Spear, conductor, at $125.00; J. V. Kilbourn, agent, at $125.00; J. A. Atkinson, agent, at $50.00; C. W. Gibbs, chief engineer, at $175.00; and Moses Liverman, superintendent, at $150.00.

The rail laid in 1889 cost $1,250.00 for five carloads of used 30-pound material; 48,000 track spikes cost $1,200.00; rail braces, splice bars, track bolts, washers and nuts added another $1,500.00; and 15,000 hand-hewn ties cost $7,500 delivered in

Silverton. The foundation, turntable house and sheds at Corkscrew Gulch cost $6,000.00 and the enginehouse at Summit (at the top of Sheridan Pass) cost $500.00, while the other buildings there cost $4,500.00. The depots at Ironton and Red Mountain cost $2,500.00 and $1,500.00, respectively.

Chief Engineer Gibbs finished the long trestle across Red Mountain Creek at Joker in the spring of 1889. The last major bridge on the railroad—on the Treasury Tunnel Branch across the same stream much higher up the valley—was not built until the early 1900's, years after Gibbs had left the property.

By July 12, 1889, Mears had assigned Gibbs to start the survey and grading of the Eureka Branch, which later became the Silverton Northern Railway. The maximum planned grade and curvature, respectively, were 2½ percent and 20 degrees (288-foot radius).

Over on the Silverton Railroad, the extension from Ironton to Albany, one and one-half miles, was completed by September 20, 1889, while work continued on the Eureka Branch. During this period of activity, Moses Liverman, another of Mears' Silverton friends, was given the appointment as superintendent of the company.

Since the smelting processes in use at the time recovered none of the high copper content of the ores from the Red Mountain district—where Mears was part owner of several properties—he very typically was instrumental in organizing a consortium which built a new refinery in 1889. This was known as the Standard Smelter and was located on the bank of the Rio de las Animas just outside the south edge of Durango.

As of the autumn of 1889, Mears and his associates came to realize that not even Gibbs—with all his unorthodoxy—could devise a way to get the Silverton Railroad from Albany on down the precipitous cañon of the Uncompahgre River to Ouray. The difference in elevation over the five-mile distance was a staggering 2,100 feet, requiring an average grade of eight percent, and no space was available for switchbacks. Gibbs therefore was sent to make a preliminary survey of the northern end of what was to become the Rio Grande Southern Railroad; the southern end of the same line having been partially surveyed by Thomas Wigglesworth in 1881 for the Denver and Rio Grande. Mears and some of his friends incorporated the Rio Grande Southern Railroad on October 2, 1889, and Gibbs was instructed to make a more detailed survey of the northern half.

For 1890, complimentary passes for the Silverton Railroad again were delightfully imaginative. They were beautiful little watchfob medallions, stamped from solid silver, 1-1/2 inches high by 1-1/8 inches across, with a crescent of blue enamel lettered, "RAINBOW ROUTE," at the top and two blue enamel scrolls at the bottom, one lettered, "SILVERTON," the other lettered, "RAILROAD." But perhaps because he was so involved with his activities on the Rio Grande Southern in 1891, Mears issued no fancy passes for that year.

Early in 1890, Mears traveled to the East to raise money for the Rio Grande Southern. While on this trip he stopped at Lima, Ohio, and bought a 37-ton, two-truck, three-foot gauge, Shay geared locomotive—Lima Machine Works shop number 269. Although never considered entirely successful, the Shay saw a variety of uses on both the Silverton and Rio Grande Southern lines during the following few years.

Activity in the Red Mountain mining district by 1890 had burgeoned to the point where the new town of Guston—centered around the Guston mine—had a year-'round population of 332; by the

MRS. MARVIN GREGORY COLLECTION

This was all that was left of Red Mountain town after the fire of 1892. This view looks west, showing a portion of the main street and the church on the hillside.

Silverton Railroad

Otto Mears, President
Denver, Colo.

Moses Liverman, Gen. Manager and Ticket Agent, Silverton, Colo.

S. K. Hooper, Gen. Passenger and Ticket Agent, Denver, Colo.

October 23, 1889	Mls.	Psgr.	Mixed	
[LEAVE				
Silverton 1	.0	†7.00 A.M.	†1.10 P.M.	....
Burro Bridge	5.0	7.34	1.44	....
Chattanooga	7.5	7.49	1.59	....
Summit	12.5	8.11	2.21	....
Red Mountain	15.0	8.25	2.25	....
Vanderbilt	15.5	8.26	2.36	....
Yankee Girl	16.0	8.27	2.37	....
Paymaster	17.0	8.45	2.55	....
Ironton	20.0	9.00 A.M.	3.10 P.M.	....
[ARRIVE				

STATIONS	Mls.	Psgr.	Mixed	
[LEAVE				
Ironton	.0	†9.00 A.M.	†3.20 P.M.	....
Paymaster	3.0	9.25	3.35	....
Yankee Girl	4.0	9.43	3.53	....
Vanderbilt	4.5	9.44	3.54	....
Red Mountain	5.0	9.50	4.00	....
Summit	7.5	9.58	4.09	....
Chattanooga	12.5	10.21	4.31	....
Burro Bridge	15.0	10.36	4.46	....
Silverton 1	20.0	11.10 A.M.	5.20 P.M.	....
[ARRIVE				

CONNECTION—1With Denver & Rio Grande Railway

† Daily, except Sunday

DELL A. McCOY WATERCOLOR

Red Mountain town, the National Belle mine, the Red Mountain depot and the Silverton Railroad's mixed train form this twilight scene of early winter, 1889 — just before the railroad closed for the season.

RICHARD A. RONZIO COLLECTION

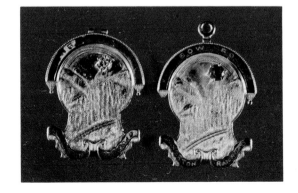

Made of gold from the Sunnyside Extension mine (later known as the Gold Prince mine), this 1890 locket pass was the only one of its kind. The name of the owner, Rasmus Hanson, is engraved on the inside lid, with a photograph of Otto Mears inside.

100

summer of 1891, 1,000 hardy souls were living there. The Reverend William Davis stumped all about the district seeking a place where he would be welcome and could build a church. Guston was the only place which opened its arms to him, and the Congregational church which resulted was built on a knoll just west of the Guston mine. A feature of this frame building was a stone belfry housing both the customary bell and another quite unusual means of calling the flock to worship—a standard mine whistle! Since the miners were so accustomed to having their whole existence governed by such noisy devices, the whistle at the church was intended to make them feel at home—and no doubt it did.

During these years, the Red Mountain district was shipping 20,000 to 25,000 tons of ore (2,000 to 2,500 boxcar loads) to the smelters, and importing 15,000 tons (1,500 gondola-car loads) of coal per year. This coal, after 1891, came from the mines at Porter, Hesperus, and later, from Perins Peak, a few miles west of Durango on the south end of the Rio Grande Southern. To handle all this business, the Silverton Railroad was working overtime, and in January of 1890, it leased from the Denver and Rio Grande two of the Class 56 2-8-0's—Number 38, the *Mancos*, and Number 65, the *San Cristoval*, the latter locomotive mentioned previously.

In its issue of February 8, 1890, the *Silverton Weekly Miner* reported that a special mercy train, with borrowed D&RG engine Number 32 handling a coach, took Dr. J. W. Brown from Silverton to the scene of an accident at Red Mountain in 23 minutes, surely a record. Three weeks later, the Silverton's engine Number 100, suffering the effects of more than two rugged years of hard, strenuous work in the San Juans, was sent to Denver for overhaul at the Burnham shops. It was to be reserved for passenger service after the Shay came out from Ohio and was put in service.

Upon his return from the East Coast, Otto Mears incorporated the Rio Grande Southern Construction Company on March 4, 1890. A separate construction company (with directorate interlocked with that of the railroad) to build the line, and upon completion, turn it over to the operating company, was standard practice in those days. This method of doing things at least insured that there would be a profit in building the railroad, even if the operating company should happen to go broke.

The Shay geared locomotive was delivered in Durango by the D&RG on April 19, 1890, lettered "SILVERTON RR. CO.," with the builder's number, "269," on the sand box. It had been given the name, *Guston,* in recognition of the impor-

THE SILVERTON MINER, 1907 —
MORRIS W. ABBOTT COLLECTION

The view above is of Rasmus Hanson, developer of the Sunnyside Extension mine in Mastodon Gulch, above Animas Forks. The mine was later named the Gold Prince mine. Rasmus Hanson died in 1909.

tance of the big mine and small town that were helping to keep the line so busy. Rather than being assigned immediately to the Silverton, however, it was used on the initial construction of the south end of the Rio Grande Southern. Under the direction of Thomas Wigglesworth, grading was started on March 30, 1890, and construction of the line was completed as far west as the coal mines at Porter by the first of December. The coal bed at that location, three miles away in a direct line, but five and one-half miles by rail from the Durango depot, was the same seam later worked at the Calumet mine on Perins Peak, four miles to the north. At Porter, though, the adit was down at the level of the arroyo, where the production from the mines could be handled on the mainline with a minimum of additional railroad construction. The mines, being underground, could be worked without interuption from the weather throughout the winter season.

The Porter mine was the first revenue-producing industry on the Rio Grande Southern, supplying all the fuel for that road, the Silverton Branch of the D&RG, and of course, Mears' Silverton Railroad. The mine was owned by John A. Porter, vice-president and director of the Silverton, and owner

DENVER PUBLIC LIBRARY WESTERN COLLECTION

The Silverton's Shay, Number 269, is shown here as it rested at the Silverton depot in November, 1892. The engine was waiting to be traded to the Rio Grande Southern In exchange for RGS Number 34, a Class 56 engine (which had come to the RGS from the Rio Grande Western). The initials, "RGS," had been scribbled on the negative, and the Shay's gear covers had been raised for inspection. *Guston* was her name.

of several precious-metal mines around Telluride, as well as the former Greene smelter, which he had moved from Silverton to Durango some years earlier.

The Shay—still designated by its shop number, 269—worked the coal mine traffic through the winter, until April 19, 1891, when construction of the RGS was resumed. Then—joined by RGS engine Number 11 (ex-D&RG Number 29, the last of eight Class 40 2-6-0's purchased from Baldwin in 1876-1878 and sold to the RGS in January of 1891) — the Shay returned to construction work, continuing until December 19, 1891, when the southern and northern portions of the road were joined at milepost 84, midway between Dolores and Rico. At last, the geared engine was available for the assignment originally intended.

A new office building, one of the costliest in town, was erected by the Silverton Railroad during the late summer of 1890, according to the columns of the *Silverton Weekly Miner* of September 25. The front portion was used as the office, the remainder of the building being utilized as a private apartment for the superintendent, at that

time, Moses Liverman. This building, later known as the Silverton Northern office, evidently is the one which survives to the present day in Silverton.

In October and November of 1890, two additional Class 56 locomotives—Number 61, the *La Jara,* and Number 67, the *Weminuche*—were leased by the Denver and Rio Grande to the Silverton Railroad; and, in December, the weekly newspaper reported that three engines were hardly enough to handle all the business on the road. It was stated that the company could not get along the next year with less than four locomotives.

Normal operations on the Silverton, from the very beginning of its history, occupied the months from mid-May to the following mid-January. The mines, continuing to work all winter, stockpiled their ores for shipment in the spring. But the winter of 1890-'91 was mean and difficult, with the snowy and frigid weather coming early to the San Juans, and Superintendent Liverman was pushed to the very limit to keep the railroad open until Christmas. On the worst day, engine Number 100, with the usual train of two cars, derailed six different times during the return run from Ironton

PRICE FAMILY COLLECTION

The miners of the National Belle mine posed for this "distinguished" group portrait during the late 1880's.

over the pass to Silverton.

Because of problems encountered in keeping the road open that winter, Mears acquired a snow-flanger, constructed of reinforced timber, during the spring of 1891. Very probably purchased from the D&RG, it was assigned number 3 when added to the roster of equipment owned by the Silverton Railroad.

At the annual meeting of the Silverton Railroad on July 22, 1891, Otto Mears was re-elected president; John A. Porter, vice-president; Moses Liverman, secretary and superintendent; John L. McNeil, treasurer; and Adair Wilson, general counsel —with George Crawford and J. H. Ernest Waters continuing as directors.

That same month, the first serious accident on the railroad occurred near Burro Bridge. Engine Number 100 derailed and turned on its side—and as engineer William Spear was being thrown from the cab, his leg was caught under the injector, causing him to be badly scalded. The coaches were coasted on down to Silverton, using the hand brakes to control their speed.

Earlier that spring, at about the time the flanger

was purchased, the Silverton also acquired another second-hand coach: Number 3, with the name, *Yankee Girl,* 34 feet, 8 inches long over end-sills, with duckbill roof-ends and 13 windows on each side. While the origin of this car is uncertain, it is most likely that it came from the D&RG or very possibly from the Rio Grande Western in Utah. By 1896, it had been converted to a combination coach-baggage, some of the seats having been removed and baggage doors cut in the sides. It ultimately became listed as Silverton Railway Number 11; and, as of 1974, the tattered, bedraggled remnants still could be found alongside the Silverton Branch of the Denver and Rio Grande Western at Tefft Spur.

Anticipating another long, hard winter like the one preceding, the railroad from September to November of 1891, again rented a Class 56 engine, Number 55, the *Tomichi,* from the Denver and Rio Grande, hoping to clean up all the business before the snow fell. But the winter of 1891-'92, in contrast to that of the year before, was extremely mild, and for the one and only time in its history, the Silverton Railroad was able to operate through-

103

OO RAINBOW ROUTE, SILVERTON. R.R. COL.

#18

RICHARD A. RONZIO COLLECTION

This hitherto unpublished 1892 photograph doubles the amount of known information about the elusive Silverton Railroad Shay, Number 269. Since few Shays were delivered with pilots instead of steps, this view is a distinct surprise. The Shay was on the upper leg of the Corkscrew Gulch turntable trackage; eight

boxcars were spotted on the lower leg of the line — near the Silver Belle mine — while in the distance, the town of Ironton can be seen. The Shay may have been slow, but it clearly could pull more cars than either of the other SRR engines, numbers 100 or 101. The man sitting on the pilot beam certainly had a good view!

out the winter, producing a good profit in the process.

The year, 1891, also witnessed out-of-the-ordinary developments in the mines of the Red Mountain district. The Silver Ledge at Chattanooga caught fire and burned, with considerable loss; the Genessee-Vanderbilt started what was to become the standard way of saving a mine that had become too deep for the pumps to stay ahead of the water. It opened a horizontal tunnel, or adit, starting near the tracks of the Silverton, and pushing a drain and tramway tunnel 820-feet long into the old shafts. This not only immediately dewatered the mine by draining the water to the level of the tunnel, but also permitted the use of smaller pumps to keep the lower workings from flooding.

The coming of 1892 was welcomed by Otto Mears with the wonderful new idea for his complimentary passes, once again made of pure silver produced by the mines in the Red Mountain district. Very ornate and delicate in design, and about 1½ x 2½ inches in size, they were manufactured for Mears by S. Spitz Jewelers of Santa Fe, New Mexico. Today, renowned as the *Mears Silver Filigrees,* these rare and bizarre passes are the most sought after of all such things.

Spitz billed Mears for a total of 544 silver filigree passes at a cost of $4.00 each, and also charged him $15.33 apiece for three additional passes of the same style, but made of gold! Lettered for the Rio Grande Southern R.R. and Silverton R.R., each pass when issued to the fortunate recipient was enclosed in a fine leather pass case, accompanied by a small, printed card stating, "This pass is made of Colorado Silver by Native Workmen." Poole Brothers of Chicago, foremost printers of railroad tickets, timetables and maps at the time, received the order for 500 of the leather cases, charging Mears $75.00 for the lot.

On March 28, 1892, the annual report of the Silverton Railroad for the year, 1891, was released. Over the personal signature of either Otto Mears or John L. McNeil, pioneer banker of the San Juans, and at that time, treasurer of the railroad, the company sent a formal transmittal letter with each copy of the report to provide additional information. It read as follows:

March 28, 1892

My dear Sir,
I beg to hand you, herewith a report from the Auditor of the earnings of the Silverton Railroad for the years 1889, 1890 and 1891, showing also the mileage bonded debt, floating debt; also a list of

DON STOTT COLLECTION

In 1891, Red Mountain town was at its peak. On August 20, 1892, a disastrous fire burned most of the town. Upon losing their belongings, homes and shops, most of the residents moved elsewhere in the district — or left the area for good.

the equipment. I also enclose a map showing the line of the railroad from the town of Silverton to the Saratoga Mine, with the side-tracks, spurs and stations on the line.

I may add for your information that this road is built through the famous Red Mountain district of the San Juan country in which are located the well-known Yankee Girl and Guston mines, besides many other producing properties.

This is the only road that can be built up through this district because of lack of room. The mines mentioned are large producers, and there are many more which are being developed rapidly. This is one of the best known mining districts in the State of Colorado. From Ironton to the town of Ouray, which is reached by another branch of the Denver and Rio Grande, the distance is seven miles over a very precipitous country.

The reason the road has not been extended to Ouray is because of the excessive cost, but capitalists are now engaged in making estimates and plans for an electric road to cover this distance to follow the line of the Mears Toll Road, as indicated on the map. A line of this kind can be built to operate much more cheaply than a [standard steam-powered] railway line, and we have good reason to expect that this gap may be so filled during this year. At the present time, stages make daily trips each way over the toll road, and the trip from Silverton to Ouray is a favorite one with tourists, on account of the beauty and grandeur of the scenery on the toll road.

Our relations with the Denver and Rio Grande Railroad Company are friendly and cordial; each road charges its own local tariff on all shipments in and out. The freights originating on our road bring in a large revenue to the Denver and Rio Grande, in fact they make two-hundred and fifty miles of that Company's track remunerative.

There is every reason to expect that the earnings for the year 1892 will be increased in the same proportion as in the past, and will continue for a great many years. The Silverton Railroad is also authorized to build up the Animas River, which you will see indicated for a short distance on the map. We would like very much this year to extend the road in that direction some twelve to fifteen miles, in order to reach a very rich and valuable mining district. There are a great many very extensive mines of low grade material lying between Silverton and the summit of the range toward the northeast, and our project in offering to you the bonds of the present line of the Railroad is to obtain funds to extend the line up the Animas River.

We can offer you at present time $400,000, out of a total issue of $425,000. These bonds are issued in denominations of $1,000 each. The interest is payable semi-annually on the first day of April and the first day of October at the rate of six per cent. per annum in United States gold coin.

As a matter of convenience to English purchasers we will pay the interest without charge for transferring the funds, at the banking house of Montague & Co., 60 Old Broad Street, London.

I hand you, herewith, a map giving you an idea of the portion of the State of Colorado in which the San Juan country is located and also showing route of proposed new line.

Yours very truly,

Otto Mears
President
P.S. The floating debt was created by the purchase of additional equipment.

February 15, 1892

REPORT OF EARNINGS AND EXPENSES
OF THE
SILVERTON RAILROAD
For the Years 1889, 1890 and 1891

1889

Gross Earnings from Frt. Pass. Exp. etc.	$ 80,881.66
Less Operating and all other Expenses	34,285.04
	46,596.62
Less Interest on First Mort. Bonds, 1 year	25,500.00
Net Profit ------------------------	$ 21,096.62

1890

Gross Earnings from Frt. Pass. Exp. etc.	$105,673.39
	51,127.22
	54,546.17
Less Interest on First Mort. Bonds, 1 year	25,500.00
Net Profit ----------------------	$ 29,046.17

1891

Gross Earnings from Frt. Pass. Exp. etc.	$121,611.38
	57,548.37
	64,063.01
Less Interest on First Mort. Bonds, 1 year	25,500.00
Net Profit ------------------------	$ 38,563.01

Length of line	17 miles
Length of side-tracks	8 miles
Total ------------------------	25 miles

JOHN GIBBS ENGSTROM COLLECTION

The four passes issued to C. W. Gibbs from 1888 through 1892 are shown above. The 1888 pass is one of the very rare buckskins, the 1889 pass is one of the first type, while the 1890 pass is a silver watchfob, with blue enamel ribbons at the top and bottom, and the 1892 pass is one of the silver filigrees.

Capital Stock $350,000.00
Bonded Debt 425,000.00
Floating Debt 32,502.76
——————————

Alex. Anderson
Auditor

****

March 26, 1892

—— E Q U I P M E N T ——

3 Locomotives;
2 Passenger Coaches;
1 Baggage and Express Car;
50 Freight Cars

Alex. Anderson
Auditor

——————————

NOTE: The listing of three (3) locomotives in the letter above is interesting when it is known that only engine Number 100 and Shay Number 269 were included in the ownership records of the Silverton Railroad at the time. Denver and Rio Grande Class 60 2-8-0 Number 203, the Navajo, *[Grant serial number 1365], built in 1881, was on*

lease to the Silverton, however—from before June 1, 1891, to at least April 1, 1892—and this engine apparently was included as the third locomotive listed in the annual report.

****

About the time the annual report was issued in early 1892, the Silverton Railroad at last obtained relief from its dependency upon the Denver and Rio Grande for extra motive power. This came about because Otto Mears, in equipping his Rio Grande Southern — then abuilding — had purchased second-hand from the D&RG a total of 21 locomotives, including 19 of the "big" Baldwin Class 60 2-8-0's. In addition, there were 13 smaller locomotives, including passenger power acquired from the Rio Grande Western, in Utah.

Since the profits from the Silverton were being used to finance construction of the RGS, one or more engines from the latter road were on loan to the Silverton during almost the entire year. There were only 86 days in those 12 months when an RGS engine was not on the Silverton; two served on the road all that summer. RGS engine Number 8 (ex-D&RG Number 248) was there from Janu-

DENVER PUBLIC LIBRARY WESTERN COLLECTION

Despite the piles of snow, Red Mountain town looked spruce in this photograph, taken during the winter of 1891-1892. All of these buildings were destroyed in the fire of 1892.

ary 1 to April 12; Number 5 (ex-D&RG Number 245) from July 7 to November 19; Number 7 (ex-D&RG Number 247) from August 14 to September 2; and Number 6 (ex-D&RG Number 246) from September 2 to October 10. In addition, RGS Number 34, one of the Class 56 2-8-0's acquired from the RGW, was transferred to the Silverton's ownership on November 27 and renumbered Silverton Number 101, the railroad giving up the much-bartered Shay in exchange.

Used rolling stock for his two roads also was purchased by Mears during the first three months of 1892. Of 117 boxcars, all of 10-ton capacity, available from the Rio Grande Western, 67 were ordered for the Rio Grande Southern and 50 for the Silverton Railroad. These cars were from a group of standard 24-foot boxcars originally built in 1882 and 1883 by the Denver and Rio Grande, with iron work by Billmeyer and Small of York, Pennsylvania, financed under the Series "E" issue of the Colorado Rolling Stock Trust certificates. The 1882 cars had cost $544.95 to build, while the 1883 cars had originally gone on the books at $545.76 each.

Back in July of 1886, in partial settlement of the controversy over the corporate separation of the Denver and Rio Grande Western Railway in Utah from the Denver and Rio Grande Railway in Colorado, 121 D&RG narrow-gauge boxcars, with numbers ranging from 4237 to 4366, had been transferred to ownership of the Utah line, the 1882 cars being valued at $297.83 and the 1883 cars at $317.31 each for purposes of the settlement. (D&RG cars not transferred were numbers 4238, 4246, 4250, 4258, 4264, 4266, 4268, 4283 and 4332.) Upon reorganization of the Utah line as the Rio Grande Western in May of 1889, these cars were renumbered RGW 4000 to 4120; and within another year they were rendered surplus when the RGW rebuilt their line to standard-gauge in 1890.

The Rio Grande Southern bought the lower-numbered RGW cars, eventually receiving 57 boxcars surviving from the original batch carrying numbers 4000 to 4067. The Silverton Railroad ordered 50 of the RGW cars, numbered from 4068 to 4120, presumably all built in 1883. The new owner assigned numbers from 500 to 549 to the cars, in the same sequence that they had been numbered on the RGW. Thirty-seven of the box-

MOORE PHOTO — CHARLES S. RYLAND COLLECTION

Number 100 of the Silverton Railroad had just arrived at Red Mountain station — with the combine, *Red Mountain,* and chaircar Number 3, the *Yankee Girl.* The wye for turning locomotives is plainly visible in this view. At this time, Number 100 was sporting a new cab, probably required because of a derailment.

cars were actually delivered between December 4, 1891, and February 19, 1892; cars assigned Silverton numbers 504, 510, 513, 521, 525, 529, 531, 535, and 545 through 549 were never received.

Costing from $75.00 to $180.00 each, with an average price of $141.62, the boxcars for the Silverton represented an investment of $5,240.00. Freight charges from Utah (or more likely Grand Junction, the eastern terminus of the RGW) to Ridgway came to $5.00 per car; repairs at the Rio Grande Southern's Ridgway shops, to put the cars in condition suitable for service, totalled $1,137.17, varying from zero to $85.89, and averaging $30.75 per car. By April of 1894, the number of boxcars had been reduced by one to a total of 36; all of them continued to be carried on the Silverton or Silverton Northern rosters up to June, 1906. But there the story of the boxcars appears to end, for no later mention of any of them has been uncovered. One such car—perhaps one of these—survived as a shed in north Silverton as of the summer of 1974.

The Shay apparently had seen hard usage in construction and coal-hauling service on the south end of the Rio Grande Southern. Since it was a geared engine, it was quite slow, of course, and thus not particularly well suited to line-haul work on the Silverton. Late in 1892, Otto Mears, as president of the Silverton Railroad, made a deal with Otto Mears, the president of the Rio Grande Southern, to return it to the latter road in exchange for engine Number 34, as previously related.

In the long run, the trade was a good deal for both railroads. The Silverton obtained an engine that endured until 1923 on the Silverton Northern, and the RGS, when it finally sold the Shay in 1899, received $2,000.00 more than it originally had paid

On the two following pages — from left to right are Red Mountain Number 1, Red Mountain Number 2 and Red Mountain Number 3, looking down on the mining district which was served by the Silverton Railroad. The old railroad grade is visible all the way from the Paymaster mine (left) to Red Mountain Pass (right). Notice the National Belle mine, just to the right of *the Knob.* This view was photographed from the Black Bear jeep road, looking toward the northeast.

RONALD F. RUHOFF PHOTO

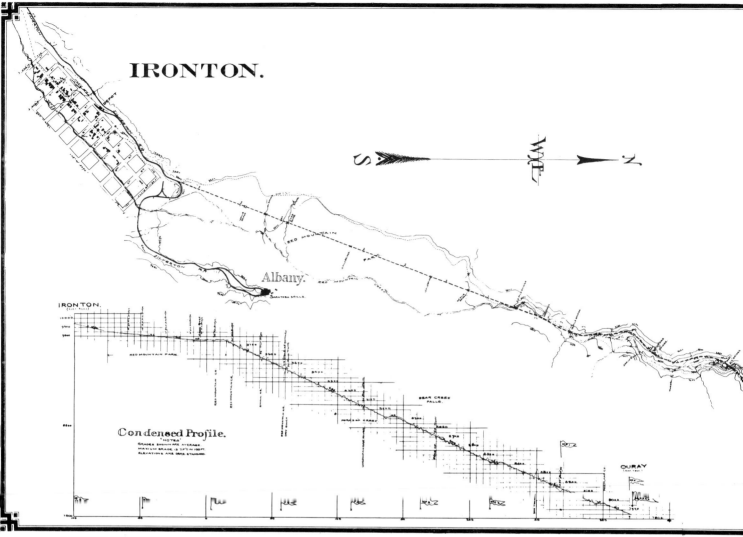

IRONTON.

Condensed Profile.

IRONTON.

Albany.

OURAY

JACKSON C. THODE COLLECTION

In 1892, R. L. Kelly produced this survey for the prospectus of the Ouray & Ironton Electric Railway,

Light & Power Company — which was never built. This reproduction is from the original survey, showing that

for the engine traded to the Silverton. Supposedly, the Shay never again was used by the Rio Grande Southern after the engine made the long journey from Durango north to Ridgway, although it was renumbered 34—the second locomotive to carry that identification on the road.

The outcast finally was sold to the Siskiwitt and Iron River Railroad at Ashland, Wisconsin, in July of 1899. From there it went to the Thompson Brothers Lumber Company, and then to the Fidelity Lumber Company, both at Doucette, Texas—subsequently moving on to Waynesboro, Mississippi, first with the Turkey Creek Lumber Company, and then the Stark and Oldham Brothers Lumber Company, who ended its pioneering and adventurous career in 1928 by dismantling it for scrap.

As hinted in the letter accompanying the Silverton Railroad's annual report, President Mears and

Chief Engineer Gibbs continued to scheme regarding the closing of the gap between Ironton and Ouray. Mears, along with Fred Walsen, Charles Munn, James H. Casanova and William H. Wallace, even went so far as to incorporate the *Ouray and Ironton Electric Railway, Light and Power Company* on November 20, 1891. Capitalized at $800,000, the company arranged for a new survey in 1892 by the eminent locating engineer, R. L. Kelly, who lined out a route for an electric railway with 7-percent grades, 35-degree curves, a tunnel and a complete spiral loop!

The idea of electrical propulsion no doubt was encouraged by the success of L. L. Nunn in generating hydroelectric power on the Rio San Miguel at Ames; and, for the first time ever, developing the means for long-distance transmission of electricity at high voltage. Not only did Nunn make the Gold King mine near Ames successful, but he also sent

114

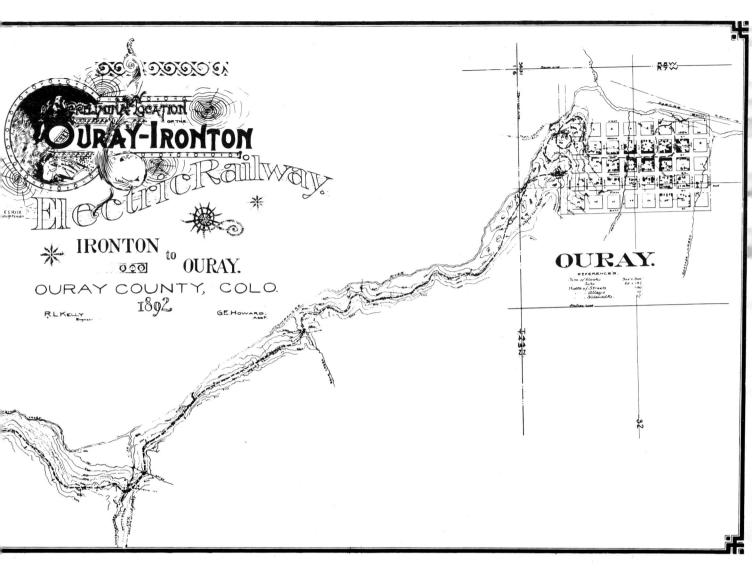

the grade would have been a fairly uniform seven percent, and would have included several loops and a complete spiral to negotiate the steep cliff face encountered at the south edge of Ouray.

surplus power over 13,366-foot-high Imogene Pass above Pandora to serve the Camp Bird mine area near Ouray. This, or a development of similar nature, probably was in mind as the source of power for the proposed Ouray and Ironton Electric Railway. But the whole project was permanently shelved, in company with many other plans, when the Silver Panic struck in 1893.

In mid-August of 1892, engine Number 100 came due for an overhaul. Since Mears was president of both the Rio Grande Southern and the Silverton Railroad, this time the locomotive was sent off to the RGS shops at Ridgway for the work, rather than to the D&RG Burnham shops in Denver as had been the practice in all the preceding years.

On August 20, 1892, a fire started in the Red Mountain Hotel in the little town at the foot of the Knob. Despite the strenuous efforts of one of the best volunteer hosecart and pumper companies in southwestern Colorado, the fire spread quickly, destroying all the buildings along the main street near the depot. At least 15 structures burned to the ground; only the jailhouse and the Silverton Railroad's depot were saved from the conflagration in the north end of town. Faced with the continuing decline in the price of silver, the inhabitants never rebuilt that section of Red Mountain town, and the little settlement entered upon its long, slow course of decay to the status of a ghost town.

In the fore part of 1893, as in 1892, Otto Mears continued his use of silver filigree passes for special friends and valued customers. At this time, an unusually large pass of the filigree design was issued, while at least one solid stamped silver pass dated 1893 has survived. Someone attached a souvenir spoon bearing the likeness of Mears on the handle at a later date. (Originally, the spoons

DELL A. McCOY WATERCOLOR

A RAINBOW ON THE RAINBOW ROUTE — The front-cover view (reproduced above) represents a Silverton Railroad mixed train of 1889, which was climbing the five-percent grade above Chattanooga. You are looking down the valley of Mineral Creek toward Bear Mountain. (Can you see the image of a bear on the mountainside?) To view this same scene today — minus the train, of course — you must travel up the south side of Red Mountain Pass on the Million Dollar Highway. Incidentally, this highway supposedly got its name from ore-bearing gravel used on the original road surface — back when the route between Durango and Ouray was improved for automobile and truck traffic.

Opposite page — this closeup photograph reveals the Red Mountain depot trackage on the upgrade portion, not far from the end-of-track. The backside of the depot grounds shows where their "comfort stop" was located — near the tail of the wye. The depot was supported by piles driven into the rocky ground. This was necessary because the structure was built over a creek bed.

CHARLES GOODMAN PHOTO — RICHARD A. RONZIO COLLECTION

116

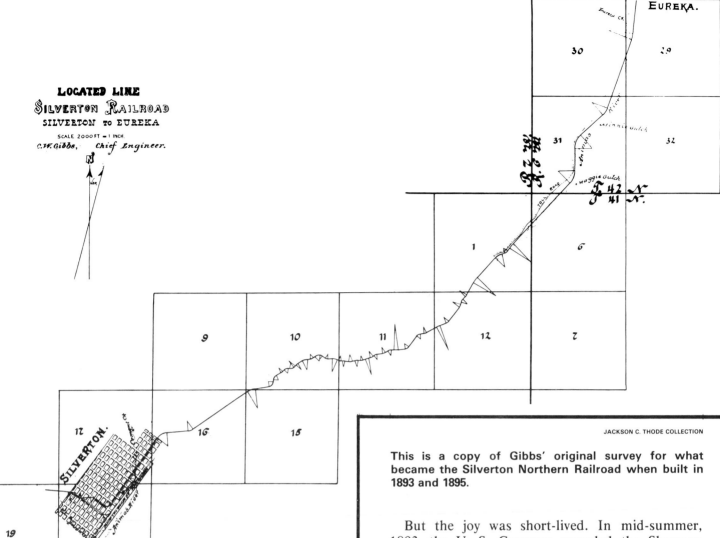

JACKSON C. THODE COLLECTION

This is a copy of Gibbs' original survey for what became the Silverton Northern Railroad when built in 1893 and 1895.

But the joy was short-lived. In mid-summer, 1893, the U. S. Congress repealed the Sherman Silver Purchase Act of 1890. This legislation had supported the silver mining industry by insuring that 16 silver dollars were minted for every gold dollar produced, thus serving to keep a floor under the price of silver. Twenty-five years before, in 1868, the precious metal had brought $1.326 per ounce; by 1892 the price had dropped to $.874 per ounce. With the repeal of the Silver Purchase Act in 1893 the price continued to plummet until it reached a low of $.588 an ounce in 1898—virtually destroying the silver mining industry, and forcing most of Colorado's mines to close, bringing about a general depression in the mining districts. This, in turn, seriously affected all the railroads of Colorado.

Opposite page — the highest spot on the Silverton Railroad was at Sheridan Junction, 11,018 feet above sea level. Here, you see SRR combine, *Red Mountain*, and a D&RG boxcar parked in front of the Sheridan Junction Hotel, which provided passengers with a few moments to view the alpine scenery. The old prospectors' trail now called the Black Bear jeep road, led to Telluride from here — on the other side of the mountain range.

JACKSON C. THODE COLLECTION

were passed out as favors at a dinner given by Mears.) These were the last of the elaborate passes; as the supply of silver filigrees began to ebb in 1892, and in 1893 attractive card passes imprinted with the Silverton herald came into use for the first time.

It was at this time that rail finally was put down on 2.2 miles of the grade which Gibbs had originally surveyed and started in 1887 as the lower part of the Eureka Branch. Although the Stoibers had opened their new Silver Lake mill at the mouth of Arrastra Gulch in 1890, their operation was carried on without railway service until the summer of 1893, when the extension from the end of the D&RG on Cement Street in Silverton was completed along the Rio de las Animas. Ed and Lena Stoiber, now luxuriously ensconced in their palatial new office and mansion known as *Waldheim*, close-by the power house serving the Silver Lake mine and mill, were at last relieved of reliance on horsedrawn transportation for their needs!

VAUGHAN JONES PHOTO — RICHARD A. RONZIO COLLECTION

This wintery scene reveals the Red Mountain depot and National Belle mine as they looked in 1891. The jail can be seen above the combination car, *Red Mountain.* Back of the depot, passengers had to walk over wooden planks to reach the privy.

Not yet two years old, the Rio Grande Southern was thrown into receivership on August 1, 1893, and Otto Mears was forced out of the company. As the infamous Silver Panic took its deadly toll—and Congress failed miserably to help areas dependent on silver mining—the profitability of the mines in the San Juan mining districts quickly deteriorated. Furthermore, water problems were worsening as the mines went deeper; not only were these mine waters loaded with sulfuric acid (derived from the reaction of air and water with the sulfide ores) which corroded everything in the mines, but the cost of pumping increased continually. That same year, pending the erection in Silverton of a new smelter with an improved process, the English companies which owned the Red Mountain mines restricted the output of their properties, with a resultant adverse impact on the business of the Silverton Railroad.

In 1894, the Silver Belle mine, on the line between Corkscrew Gulch and Ironton, closed—

after reaching a depth of 706 feet—the first of the Red Mountain mines to shut down. By the summer of that year, the local economy had come upon such evil times that Mears was now in danger of losing the Silverton Railroad, also. In a letter dated June 8 to Charles H. Graham, a Philadelphia investor and vice-president of the Silverton, Mears wrote:

There is no way for me to raise any money here on any other property I have. I am very sorry the circumstances are such that it is impossible for me to do anything at present. It is very hard for me today to raise even sufficient money for my household expenses.

The unthinkable had come about! Charles W. Gibbs, chief engineer par excellent, was out of a job—and Otto Mears, the redoubtable *Pathfinder of the San Juan,* was on the verge of going bankrupt!

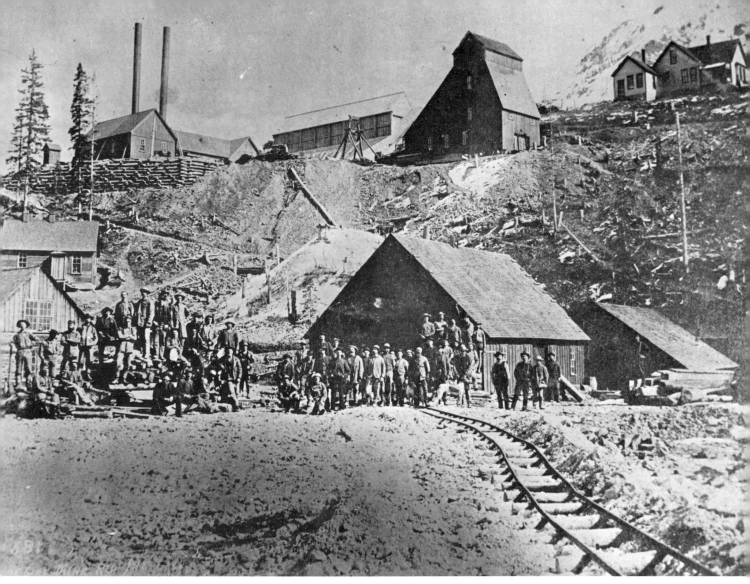

RICHARD A. RONZIO COLLECTION

In 1889, the Yankee Girl mine employed a large group of men. The track in the fore-ground was the mine's waste track coming from the tunnel at the first level, 75 feet below the shaft opening in the shafthouse. The two smokestacks are from the powerhouse.

Perhaps recalling the hardships of 30 years before—when he had come to Colorado with so little in the way of possessions—Mears was not one to give up. Watching the pennies, exercising every bit of his ingenuity, scrimping, manipulating and maneuvering, he managed to keep his Silverton Railroad functioning as a going concern.

Within another few months, the new smelter anticipated by the Red Mountain mine owners became a reality. Built and operated by Thomas F. Walsh, this new matte smelter was located on the site of the old Martha Rose smelter on Mineral Creek in Silverton and was designed to treat the low-grade ores from the Guston mine. Walsh treated about 100,000 tons of Red Mountain ore before closing the plant in 1896. From then until the Kendrick smelter on Cement Creek opened in 1900, no smelting operations were active in Silverton.

Some of the mines located along the line of the Silverton Railroad as of June, 1895, bore intriguing names. Among these were the Aspen, Gray Copper, Colorado Boy, Armstrong, Buffalo Girl, Virginia, Silver Belle, Monte Cristo, Paymaster, Guston, Cora Belle, Scotch Girl, Robinson, Yankee Girl, Highland Chief, Drunkard's Dream, Union Trust, Vanderbilt, National Belle, Caledonian, Bobtail, Andalusia, and Magnet. The total mileage of the Silverton Railroad at this time was 23 miles, which included the spurs to the different mines.

Struggling constantly to keep his enterprises afloat, Mears wrote a letter to General Manager Moses Liverman from Denver on July 22, 1895,

121

Santa Fe, N.M. 6/18. 1892

Mr. Otto Mears. Prest
Rio G.S. R.R. Co

TOURISTS SPECIALLY INVITED TO
VISIT OUR WORK SHOPS.

BOUGHT OF

S. SPITZ, MANUFACTURER OF MEXICAN FILIGREE JEWELRY.

South Side of Plaza.

ALL WORK PROMPTLY AND NEATLY EXECUTED

DIAMOND SETTING & REPAIRING.

C. & O. LITHO. CO. DENVER.

TERMS

COLORADO RAILROAD MUSEUM COLLECTION

stating that the railroad's June payroll of $2,391.50 was much too high—and unless he cut down on expenses, the road would be forced into receivership. In another letter, two months later, Mears wrote Liverman on September 25 that the 30-cents-per-day rental being charged by the Denver and Rio Grande for the caboose was too much. They wanted $350.00, if the Silverton was interested in buying it, and Mears thought that too high, too.

Three days later, however, Alexander Anderson, auditor of the company in Denver, advised the superintendent that D&RG caboose number 0516 was now the property of the Silverton Railroad (the original cost to the D&RG in 1880 had been $720.00). The caboose was renumbered 17 on the Silverton, and later became Silverton Northern number 1005.

In February, 1896, as had been the case in all but one of the previous years, the Silverton Rail-

road was completely closed for the winter, this time by several snowslides. Later in the year, the Yankee Girl—that venerable and rich property just beyond Red Mountain town—found it necessary to shut down because of water problems.

All through its existence, up to this time, the Silverton Railroad had depended upon passenger business as an important asset to its welfare. Until the Silver Panic of 1893, the road charged 20 cents per mile for passengers, and no reduced fares were in effect for round trips. Mears must have measured the miles with a rubber ruler; the early timetables show distances about two miles farther between Silverton and Sheridan Pass than tabulated by later surveys, and about three and one-half miles greater than actual distances for all stations beyond Sheridan Pass—or Summit, as it was often called. In fairness to Mears, though, part of the extra mileage may have been the result of

D. & R. G. Form 477—S-92-2M.

BILL FOR VOUCHER.   604

Department No. _____   Auditor's Voucher No. _____

To *S Spitz*

Chargeable to   Address *Santa Fé N.M.* Dr.

33

79 ~~State Other~~ $100.00   Stop for Pay *J W Gillerly Treas* $1000.00
Sud & Cos, Sil R.R. 7,549.50   canceled in Address
                        500.00   *June 9 2 Jo. Entry.*
1892   Total, $2,149.50

May 31 *For 527 Sil Fil Passes @ 4.00* $2108.00 $210
        3 Gold " " @ 15.33⅓   4600
        7 Sil to replace Centre @ 1.00   700 $2161.00
                                                      1150
        Credit 16 Dwt 18 Karet Gold @ 7²⁴

Bill against Sil RR 4/21/92

Bill attached $2149⁵⁰

Correct: _____   Certified: _____   Approved: _____

Otto Mears

Place of delivery of all materials and supplies must be stated in Bill for Voucher.

COLORADO RAILROAD MUSEUM COLLECTION

As can be plainly seen by this pair of statements, there was considerable discussion as to who should pay how much for the fancy 1892 silver and gold filigree passes. This order was the main one for filigree passes, but several considerably smaller orders are known to exist.

two-way travel over the *roller coaster,* the switch-backs at the Yankee Girl mine.

In the following table of mileages, changes from one timetable to another are shown, and a comparison of these timetable figures with the actual mileages surveyed by R. L. Kelly.

The first schedule in effect on the Silverton Railroad was dated October 23, 1889. Continuing

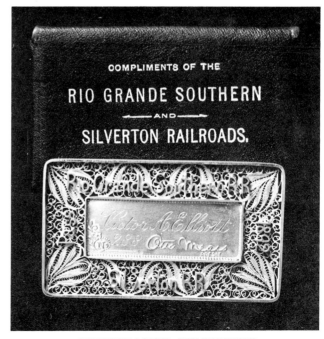

COLLECTION OF A. D. RAMSEY — PHOTO BY RALPH HAWES

	Oct. 23, 1889 to July, 1891	Aug. 3, 1891 to Sept., 1893	October 1893	Mainline Distance 1892 Survey By R. L. Kelly
Silverton	0.0	0.0	0.0	0.0
Burro Bridge	5.0	6.4	6.0	5.0
Chattanooga	7.5	8.9	9.0	7.3
Summit	12.5	12.9	13.0	10.7
Red Mountain	15.0	14.5	14.0	11.9
Vanderbilt	15.5	14.9	15.0	12.5
Yankee Girl	16.0	15.1	15.0	12.7
Paymaster Coal track	-	-	16.0	13.7
Corkscrew Gulch	-	17.0	17.0	14.1
Paymaster Ore track	17.0	17.5	18.0	14.5
Joker	-	-	-	15.0
Ironton depot	20.0	20.0	20.0	16.5
Albany	-	-	-	18.0

MORRIS W. ABBOTT COLLECTION

A unique 1893 solid silver pass — never issued — was at some later date attached to one of the Mears' souvenir spoons.

Trip Around the Circle

Through Realms of Gold and Silver,

VIA

Between Silverton and all points in the famous

Red Mountain Country

Connects with the Denver and Rio Grande
R. R. at Silverton and Ouray, and
completes the famous trip

"AROUND ◊ THE ◊ CIRCLE"

Over Denver and Rio Grande Railroad, acknowledged to be the most magnificent mountain trip in the known world, including daylight ride of six miles in CONCORD COACHES through the Uncompahgre Canon which is unequalled in its grandeur and adds greatly to the pleasure of this delightful journey.

OTTO MEARS,
President, DENVER.

MOSES LIVERMAN,
Gen. Superintendent,
SILVERTON.

S. K. HOOPER,
Gen. Pass. Agt.,
DENVER.

until late July, 1891, it showed a mixed train leaving Silverton at 7:00 a.m., arriving in Ironton at 9:00 a.m., leaving Ironton as a passenger train at 9:10 a.m. and arriving in Silverton at 11:10 a.m. In the afternoon, another passenger train left Silverton at 1:10 p.m. and arrived in Ironton at 3:10 p.m., then returned as a mixed train, leaving Ironton at 3:20 p.m., and arriving in Silverton at 5:20 p.m. Trains ran daily except Sunday.

From August 3, 1891, until September of 1893, schedules were rearranged from 30 minutes to 10 minutes later, with trains being offered daily. In October, 1893, however, as a result of the Silver Panic, the passenger trains were dropped in favor of one mixed train daily, leaving Silverton at 7:30 a.m., arriving in Ironton at 9:20 a.m., departing Ironton 10:00 a.m. and returning to Silverton by 11:50 a.m.

Circle tours, sponsored by the D&RG, provided a popular tourist attraction at the turn of the century. They ran from Salida to Alamosa, to Durango, to Silverton, where the passengers changed to the Silverton Railroad for the ride to Ironton. There they transferred to horse-drawn coaches of the Pioneer Stage Company for the eight miles between Ironton and Ouray. From Ouray the tours continued on the D&RG — back to Salida, by way of Montrose, the Black Canyon and Gunnison. Major S. K. Hooper, a D&RG passenger agent, was the one who dreamed up these tours, and this 1890 "flyer" exuberantly advertised about them.

124

ROBERT E. SLOAN PHOTO

The residents of Red Mountain town could have enjoyed this view from the cafe on Main Street back in the days when the hills were crawling with prospectors. This view reveals *the Knob* on Red Mountain and the remains of the National Belle mine. The stub track of the Silverton Railroad ended near the left side of this photograph.

In the view below, the Albany mill can be seen at the end of the main street in Ironton — as of 1889. The Albany mill was the end-of-track for the Silverton Railroad. In Ironton, trail riders could fortify their thirst for strong drink before heading up among the rocky crags.

RICHARD A. RONZIO COLLECTION

125

RICHARD A. RONZIO COLLECTION

G. W. Moore of Ouray took this 1892 view (above) of the snowsheds at the Corkscrew Gulch turntable on the switchback of the Silverton Railroad.

A leased D&RG engine blew off steam for this portrait of the town of Chattanooga and the famous loop. In this view we are looking south, down Mineral Creek.

RICHARD A. RONZIO COLLECTION

126

CHAPTER IV

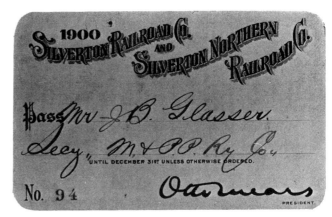

COLLECTION OF A. D. RAMSEY — PHOTO BY RALPH HAWES

The Anderson Years
1895 - 1904

IN 1895, the dreadful effects of the Silver Panic of two years earlier began to show signs of easing in the San Juan region. The mines at Eureka—some miles up the Rio de las Animas from the end of the Silverton Railroad's branch to Ed and Lena Stoiber's Silver Lake mill—were in operation, and plans were even afoot to construct a new ore-processing plant at the edge of town, to be known as the Sunnyside mill.

Alert to this opportunity for additional business, Otto Mears made the decision to extend his railroad to Eureka. Having been badly burned in the Rio Grande Southern fiasco, and with the Silverton Railroad on the ragged edge of going under, Mears determined to detach the two miles of line previously built out of Silverton and incorporate it with the new branch as a separate railroad so it could not be dragged down if the Silverton were to fail.

Thus, the Silverton Northern Railroad was incorporated on September 20, 1895, with the charter being granted on November 4 and organization completed on December 20 of that year. Fred Walsen, Otto Mears, Alexander Anderson, Jerome B. Frank, Thomas L. Wiswall and Moses Liverman were variously involved as incorporators, stockholders and/or directors; Walsen was elected president; Mears, vice-president; and Anderson, secretary and treasurer. At the meeting on December 20, the stockholders decided to issue $300,000 in five-percent, 50-year bonds to be dated January 1, 1896, with the International Trust Company of Denver as trustee. They also agreed to purchase the Silverton and Animas Forks Toll Road Company from Mears for use as right-of-way. The

directors optimistically projected the road on past Eureka to Animas Forks, then to Mineral Point and thence to Lake City by way of Henson Creek. The plans even called for a three-quarter-mile tunnel through the mountains!

Over and above the money represented by the bond issue, much of the estimated cost of the road—$600,000—was borne by the mining companies along the proposed route, following the precedent set originally in financing the Silverton Railroad. Edward G. Stoiber advanced $3,000 to be used for construction, against which freight could be charged at a favored rate for a five-year period.

Construction of the line started in the fall of 1895, beginning at milepost 2.2 where the North Star bridge to the Silver Lake mill at Arrastra Gulch was located. The rail used was 30-pound steel, presumably second-hand material from the Denver and Rio Grande; ties were green, untreated cottonwood and fir. Since construction was incomplete when winter set in, the usual delay was incurred until work could be resumed in the spring of 1896. In May of the new year, Anderson ordered the necessary parts for a dozen number nine switches to fit the 30-pound rail.

By mid-June of 1896, Anderson had moved from Denver to Silverton, taking over as superintendent of the Silverton Northern from Moses Liverman, and finished building the new road as far as Eureka. Late that month, Lena Stoiber drove the railroad's golden spike at the outer terminal. Built at a cost of $272,400, the completed portion of the road was turned over to the Silverton Northern Railroad Company on July 1. Legal title to the lower two miles of track between Silverton and

SUNDANCE PHOTO BY DELL A. McCOY

In this view from the grade of the Silverton Railway, Chattanooga Park basked in the late afternoon sunshine. Mineral Creek winds its way down the valley toward Bear Mountain, in the distance. Today, very little remains of the mining town that once stood here, although many tons of ore continue to be shipped out of the nearby district.

Arrastra Gulch—built and owned by the Silverton Railroad—was obtained by turning over $40,000 in first mortgage bonds to the original owner of the track, and on August 5, the board of directors voted to give Mears an additional $140,000 in bonds in payment for the new construction to Eureka.

While construction of the Silverton Northern was being completed, Mears took time to rebuild the old four-mile-long toll road on up the steep cañon from Eureka to Animas Forks. Several years later, this stretch was to be rebuilt yet again as the Animas Forks Branch of the Silverton Northern.

Mears also found time that year to campaign vigorously for the presidential candidacy of William Jennings Bryan, the *Silver Knight,* whose attraction for Coloradans was the advocacy of renewed mining subsidies in the form of coinage of silver at a rate fixed at one-sixteenth the value of gold. But when Bryan failed to win the 1896 election, Mears gave up in disgust and left Colorado as a lost cause.

He moved to Washington, D.C., where, energetic as ever, he built the Chesapeake Beach Railroad during the years from 1897 to 1899. He served as president of this shortline railroad until 1902 and then moved to New York City, where he helped the Macks found the Mack Brothers Motor Car Company, and served as its first president.

Not until 10 years after moving to the East—during the last month of 1906—did Otto Mears finally decide to return to Colorado to live. During the long absence from his old haunts, he made brief visits periodically to Denver and the San Juans, but a local manager, resident at the scene, was a necessity in the situation. Thus, to Alexander Anderson fell the countless duties of overseeing all the facets of operating both the Silverton and the Silverton Northern railroads during that time.

When Anderson arrived in Silverton in the summer of 1896, he found that the two roads were physically separated by about a mile of D&RG trackage, including the Silverton yard. This partitioning meant that for three hours in the middle of the day—while the daily D&RG train was switching—nothing could move between the Silverton and Silverton Northern. Anderson immediately started making plans to alleviate the problem by building the necessary connecting trackage. But the plans all came to naught, for one thing or another always seemed to come up to delay the construction—until the connection was finally made in October of 1903.

He also found that several bents supporting bridges on the Silverton Northern had fallen down during the winter, and that all the bridges on the Silverton Railroad—in particular the high trestle at Porphyry Gulch—were in need of careful in-

THE SILVERTON RAILROAD CO.

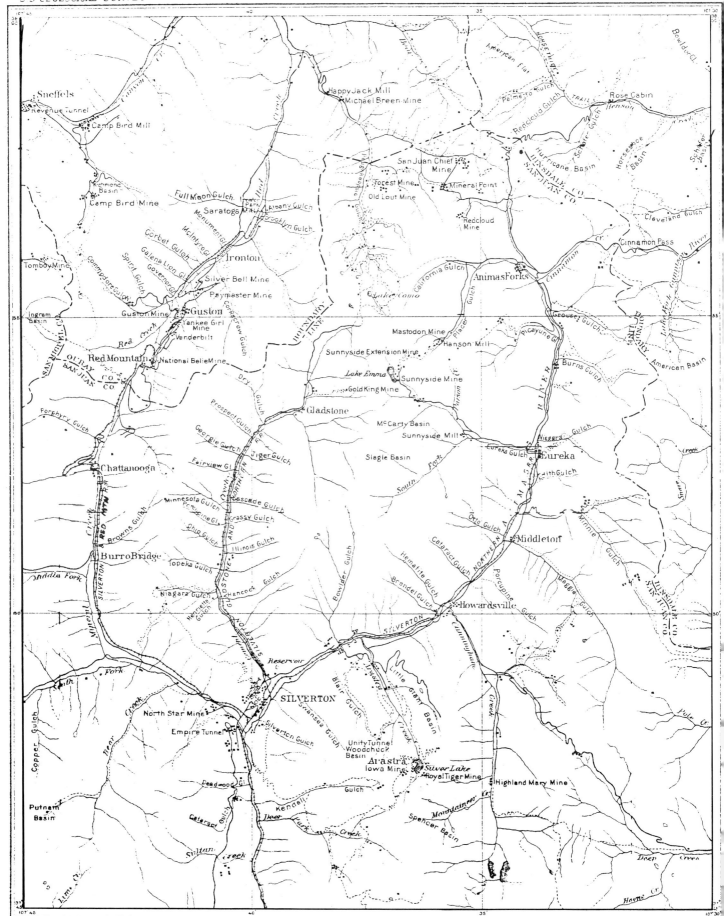

OUTLINE MAP OF THE SILVERTON QUADRANGLE, COLORADO

Scale

spection by a competent bridge and building (B&B) man. In addition, 3,000 new ties were needed. On the traffic side he established a through rate of $2.00 a ton for ore to be carried from Chattanooga (at SRR milepost 7.3) to Rickett's mill at Howardsville (at SN milepost 4.7). Of the sum, $1.33 went to the Silverton while 67 cents was allocated to the Silverton Northern.

Another project facing Anderson was equipping the Silverton Northern Railroad with locomotives and rolling stock. Mears, with neither the desire nor the capital to invest in new equipment, wrote to Moses Liverman, general manager of the Silverton Railroad Company, on December 8, 1896, directing him to turn over 1 locomotive and 10 boxcars to the Silverton Northern. The ex-Silverton boxcars were renumbered 100 through 109 on the SN, while the engine, Silverton Number 101 (previously Rio Grande Southern Number 34), was designated Silverton Northern Number 1.

Through Anderson's first winter at Silverton, both the Silverton Railroad and the Silverton Northern were closed; the latter line, subjected to numerous snowslides, remained shut down until April 27, 1897. Then, shortly after the Silverton was re-opened for the summer, the National Belle mine at Red Mountain town closed down. The Guston mine, working on level 14 at a depth of 1,300 feet, also suspended operation and the New Guston Company, Ltd., was liquidated.

These discouraging developments, together with no apparent prospect of any business from mines on down the valley from the Guston, led Anderson to close the northern 7½ miles of the Silverton Railroad. No longer would there be any maintenance of the railroad beyond Red Mountain town; the track left lying on the deserted roadbed would provide a handy and inexpensive source of supply for any material needed to keep the active portion of the railroad in service.

By August of that year, the Silverton Railroad's mixed train was running with little traffic; only one engine was in use—and a Sunday school excursion was big business. John L. McNeil, who was serving as general manager of the road from Denver, inquired about two used Baldwin combination motors as a means of transporting passengers and less-than-carload (LCL) shipments at lower expense than the cost of an entire train. The Baldwin machines turned out to be standard-gauge, so McNeil wrote the Schenectady Locomotive Works asking for a quote on a combination motorcar and coach, 36 feet in length and with enough power to handle an extra coach, if necessary, on a six-percent grade. Nothing came of this inquiry, either —probably due to impracticability, as well as excessive cost.

As a measure of the penny-pinching being practiced, the following letter from Anderson to McNeil on September 16, 1897, is illuminating:

> One of our engines struck a milk cow yesterday on Northern about a quarter of a mile above station. Butcher will not buy the cow. I have had her appraised and seen the owner. I can settle claim for $30.00 which is less than appraised valuation. If you approve of it I will make payment and get release.

Anderson complained to Mears that 25 cents was too much to pay for a red spruce tie cut to the standard length of 6½ feet, with a cross section of 6½ x 7 inches. He was to order some 32,000 ties, paying that price and much more, in the next seven years.

In the middle of December, 1897, George Crawford finally ordered coal for the Yankee Girl mine, pleading, "Don't close down the road till we get it."

By February of 1898, the pumps had been pulled out of the Yankee Girl and that mine, like the Guston and National Belle, was full of water. Anderson took advantage of the reduced traffic on the Silverton to send engine Number 100 into Alamosa for repairs by the D&RG shops there;

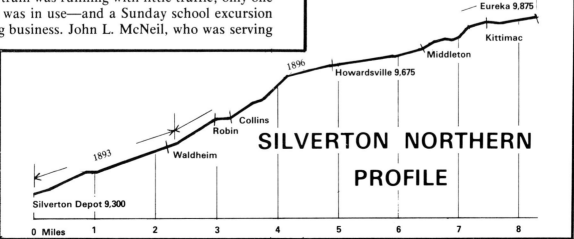

SILVERTON NORTHERN PROFILE

Eureka 9,875
Kittimac
Middleton
Howardsville 9,675
1896
Collins
Robin
1893
Waldheim
Silverton Depot 9,300

0 Miles 1 2 3 4 5 6 7 8

with the Rio Grande Southern no longer under the control of Otto Mears, that road's shop facilities at Ridgway now held no attraction for such work.

On May 29, 1898, Anderson re-opened the Silverton Railroad, but only as far as Summit, since the mines beyond that point had stockpiled but 600 tons of ore and the snow was 6 to 20-feet deep—more snow than in the previous 15 years. He discovered, too, that the Guston and Yankee Girl mines had dug out a frozen water pipe, throwing the dirt on the tracks to a depth of four feet—another factor which no doubt influenced his decision not to go beyond Summit until later in the year.

The D&RG was applying pressure on the road to pay for use of trackage, the depot and the two-stall roundhouse in Silverton. (Built in 1882, across the main track from the depot, this original building burned down in 1902 and was replaced by a new, smaller structure which lasted until 1938.) Consequently, Anderson was giving much serious thought to moving the Silverton's "roundhouse" (a rectangular shed 30 x 60 feet in size, 20 feet in height) from Summit down to Silverton.

An outsider entered the picture later in the year. With the intention of connecting the Silverton Railroad and the Rio Grande Southern, despite a decided lack of interest on the part of both roads, Andrew S. Meldrum, a mining engineer who was employed as trainmaster on the RGS, and was later to serve as superintendent of that company, started to drill a four and one-fifth mile tunnel between the Red Mountain and Telluride districts. Starting his tunnel at an elevation of 9,971 feet, from a point about 3,500 feet southeast of the Smuggler Union mill at Pandora, Meldrum managed to tunnel east about 2,600 feet before the year 1900, when he abandoned attempts to finish the bore. Simultaneously, he started tunneling west at an elevation of 10,000 feet, beginning at a spot on the Silverton Railroad's right-of-way, 1,750 feet north of the future site of the Joker tunnel. On this end of the tunnel, 1,200 feet were completed before the funds ran out. In a sense, Meldrum's dream was fulfilled during World War II when the Idarado mine (the old Treasury tunnel, or Hammond's tunnel, on the Silverton Railroad—across the valley from the Guston) finally connected into the Smuggler Union mine. The result, though, was a tunnel too small and crooked to handle railroad-sized equipment.

An employees' timetable, dated June 11, 1898, for the combined Silverton and Silverton Northern railroads indicates that a water tank existed at the Gold Bug mine between Burro Bridge and Chattanooga. Maps of the time, however, indicate that the Gold Bug was on Cement Creek, with a *Gold Finch* mine close to milepost 7 on the Silverton. Operating rules in the timetable include such statements as, "Trains must not exceed schedule under any circumstances," and, "The general rules and regulations of the operating department of the D&RG Railroad Company will govern employees of this company."

In mid-June of 1898, W. Z. Kinney, superintendent of the Gold King mine at Gladstone, approached Anderson about building a railroad up Cement Creek. Mears, still sour on Colorado mining, was not going to sink any more money in the San Juans; in any event, he was in Delaware building the Chesapeake Beach shortline. Thinking that in his disenchantment with the area, Mears might entertain a proposal to dispose of his investment in the Silverton Railroad, Anderson wrote to McNeil to see if he could raise enough money so that the two of them could take control of the company and build the new branch. McNeil was not interested to quite that extent, so Anderson was unable to swing the deal.

The gap between his two railroads in Silverton continued to bother Anderson. He found it would take 5,218 feet of track, at a cost of about $3,500, to build a direct connection between the two lines. Costs for moving the roundhouse from Summit would approximate $600.00, while another $270.00 would be required to supply it with water from a connection with the city water mains near Gus Stoiber's sampling works in the southwest corner of town.

The Silverton Railroad was opened to Guston in June of 1898. But with that mine full of water, only the Silver Ledge and the Congress were working. Furthermore, 1,000 old ties were in need of replacement. On the Silverton Northern, only the Silver Lake, Iowa and Royal Tiger mines were working, although others were in production above Eureka and also over at Gladstone. The following month, Anderson moaned to C. H. Graham, the vice-president in Philadelphia, that the Congress had closed and the only business on the Silverton all month had been five cars from the Silver Ledge at Chattanooga. The railroad could not pay the interest on its bonds, even at three percent; passenger revenues were only just enough to cover operating expenses.

In August, Anderson's problems with the Denver and Rio Grande were compounded. Mr. Shoemaker, the agent at Silverton, asked him to remove the Red Mountain and Eureka telephones from the depot, complaining of unnecessary trouble over the phones. In addition to that, Anderson was worried about the D&RG roundhouse collapsing under a

SUNDANCE PHOTO BY DELL A. McCOY

After a steep climb up a rocky, narrow trail, Silver Lake finally is reached at 12,200 feet above sea level. Beyond the lake, Kendall Peak soars up to 13,451 feet — featuring a blanket of snow nearly all year 'round. The mountain ridge reflects in the mirror-like surface of the lake. The Silver Lake mine buildings are plain to see; however, the Iowa-Tiger mines are too far away to be discerned. The Iowa was on the left bank, while the Tiger was on the right bank. A cableway ran across the middle of the lake to connect the two.

heavy load of snow and continued to pester Mears about moving the Summit roundhouse to town. Rickett's mill at Howardsville required a spur, and he managed to complete that construction in-between other tasks. Finally, by October, C. S. Thompson, in charge of the B&B department on the D&RG, agreed to repair the roundhouse, and Anderson was able to postpone moving the enginehouse down from Summit.

The Silver Ledge mine at Chattanooga closed down in November; now only the Congress and Silver Belle mines were shipping over the Silverton Railroad—at a rate of one-half car a day, the latter evidently freighting its ore by wagon to Red Mountain for loading on the cars. Responding to an inquiry from the ICC in December, 1898, Anderson reported that neither the caboose nor the flanger were equipped with air brakes or automatic couplers; when tried a few years earlier the automatic couplers had separated on the sharp curves.

Just before the Silverton Northern shut down for the winter, the machinery for Judge John Terry's new Sunnyside mill at Eureka arrived in Silverton and was taken to the construction site at the end of the line.

Following the failure of Anderson's and Kinney's abortive attempt of the previous year to finance a line up Cement Creek, the stockholders and management of the Gold King mine at Gladstone incorporated and chartered the Silverton, Gladstone and Northerly Railroad on April 6, 1899. This new railroad was to be built for the purpose of bringing their ores and concentrates down to Silverton, thereby reducing shipping costs under wagon haulage and increasing the tonnage which could be mined economically.

The original directors were Henry M. Soule, Charles E. Bibber and J. Walter Davis of Boston; Cyrus W. Davis of Waterville, Maine; E. J. Lawrence of Fairfield, Maine; John Blackman of St. Stephens, New Brunswick; Fred A. Jones and G. Whetmore of Saint Johns, New Brunswick; and W. Z. Kinney and George A. Barnes of Silverton, Colorado. John W. Chipman was the first president, C. W. Davis the vice-president, H. M. Soule the treasurer, and Kinney was appointed general manager. The proposed route was from Silverton to Gladstone; and, here again, on north to Lake City.

It might be reasonably asked why all three of the Silverton railroads were so dead set on pushing northeast to Lake City. Before the turn of the century, this place was a real boom town. In 1876, with 500 buildings and a population of 2,500, it was larger than either Silverton or Ouray. In addition, the D&RG had built a branch into

Lake City in 1889 from Sapinero on the old narrow-gauge mainline.

If any of the three Silverton roads could build the 17 miles from Animas Forks to Lake City by way of Denver Pass and Henson Creek, or the 25 miles from Eureka by way of the Lake Fork of the Gunnison River, distances and times between the San Juan region and Denver would be greatly reduced. Using mileages in the D&RG's 1890 timetable, for instance, it appears that distances would be trimmed by 153 miles, with corresponding reductions in time of about 14 hours. Further, if goods were interchanged at Gunnison with the narrow-gauge Denver, South Park and Pacific or its successors: the Denver, Leadville and Gunnison, and later, the Colorado and Southern, the distance to Denver would be 241 miles less than by way of the southern route, and the time about 16 hours less—based on 1899 timetables.

Similarly, if the Silverton Railroad could have built to Ouray, a project really stopped only by the 1893 silver devaluation, 106 miles of travel and about four hours in time could have been saved on the all-important connection with the Colorado capital.

The Silverton, Gladstone and Northerly Railroad was built by the Rocky Mountain Construction Company, a Maine corporation, with James Dyson as engineer in charge. When construction started in April, the Silverton and Silverton Northern roads provided the necessary work trains.

As construction progressed during the next month, some dickering—looking to regular operation of the new line after completion—went on between the opposing managements. Anderson wanted $400.00 to $500.00 per month above costs to run the trains in regular operation; he figured $95.00 a month for coal and oil alone. Kinney, on the other hand, would offer the Mears manager no more than $400.00 per month; Mears thought even Anderson's estimate was low and wanted a higher figure. Having reached an impasse, Kinney decided to lease an engine from the D&RG and hire a crew at monthly rates of $125.00 for the engineer, $90.00 for the fireman, $115.00 for the conductor and $75.00 for the brakeman, when the time came to inaugurate service.

When Judge Terry's Sunnyside mill was finally opened at Eureka in mid-May of 1899, the smelters in Durango were shut down due to a strike by employees. There being no other place to haul the ores and concentrates, the SN and the SRR continued to provide the construction train on the new SG&N, charging $10.00 a day for the locomotive. Then in June, C. W. Davis, SG&N vice-president, offered new proposals for regular operations: the Mears roads could either run a train each way daily on the new line at mutually agreed hours, or they could operate and maintain the new road with costs of opening the line after each snowstorm to be borne by the SG&N, and with no deduction from the SN charge when trains could not run, through no fault of the Silverton Northern company.

Mears, when presented with Davis' proposal, replied to his manager, saying:

> I wouldn't attempt to maintain their road at any price. After we built the SRR, it cost $2,500.00 per month to maintain it for the first two years; it will cost them $1,000.00 per month for equipment and the men to run the road.

The seven miles of 45-pound rail used in building the Silverton, Gladstone and Northerly from Silverton to Gladstone were all spiked down by July 2, 1899, and the road was turned over to the operating company on July 21. Original cost of the line is not known, but by July 1, 1904, at the time of the road's first mention in *Poor's Manual of Railroads*, total investment recorded for road and equipment (including three engines, combination car Number 1, and 20 freight cars) was $230,000. A reasonable estimate for cost of the road alone would seem to be in the neighborhood of $177,000.

When the Silverton, Gladstone and Northerly went to work hauling loads of ore down along Cement Creek from Gladstone, Kinney—as a sharp businessman—tried to continue the same low rental of $10.00 per day that he had paid for the use of the engine during construction. Anderson violently disagreed. Kinney then fixed a maximum allowance of $450.00 per month to be paid for the use of SN-SRR locomotives and crews; at that price, Anderson informed him, the Mears roads would do without the business. Despite the brusque refusal, though, Kinney evidently saw nothing wrong in asking Anderson to break in the new station agent and officeman for the SG&N.

In the nearly four months since its incorporation in April, the new railroad had accomplished a great deal, completing all the legalities, obtaining right-of-way, locating and grading its line, and building its track. The ready availability and low cost of rented motive power and equipment had been a godsend; even when Anderson finally could tolerate no more of Kinney's bargaining, the latter encountered no difficulty in leasing a locomotive from the Denver and Rio Grande. Whether indicative of poor construction of the railroad, or of poor condition of the engine, is not clear, but it was rather frequently in the ditch.

Following the customary practice of acquiring second-hand equipment, the Silverton, Gladstone and Northerly, on August 1, 1899, bought its first engine. C. M. Hobbs, purchasing agent for the Denver and Rio Grande and subsidiary Rio Grande Southern, sold the latter company's engine Number 32 to the new railroad, where the same number was retained. A Class 56 2-8-0, built in 1880 (Baldwin number 5185) as D&RG Number 77, the *Rinconida,* it had been included in the Denver and Rio Grande equipment transferred to the D&RGW Railway in Utah in settling the 1886 controversy previously mentioned. Worked on the Utah line as Number 77, without change in number, it had been valued at $4,744.72 in the transfer transaction, but cost $1,200.00 when it returned to Colorado in 1891 as one of the 13 Rio Grande Western engines purchased by Otto Mears for the RGS. While in service on the latter road, its condition apparently showed considerable improvement, for the sale price to the SG&N was $3,252.00! That extra $2.00 covered the cost of a rerailing frog added to the engine's equipment at the last moment.

W. D. Lee, the Rio Grande Southern's superintendent at Ridgway, was instructed to put the engine in first-class condition and to letter it properly for the new owner. The engine moved from Ridgway on August 31, 1899; when it reached Silverton under its own steam on September 7, in the charge of locomotive engineer Holland, it was accepted by W. Z. Kinney as the Silverton, Gladstone and Northerly representative.

Contrasting with its second-hand motive power, the SG&N bought a brand new combination car, Number 1, to accommodate its passengers; 10 new 32-foot boxcars, numbered 1000 to 1009, built by American Car and Foundry; and a "service car" of unknown type.

The new road was a success—surplus earnings the first year, after dividends to the stockholders, were $35,366.21.

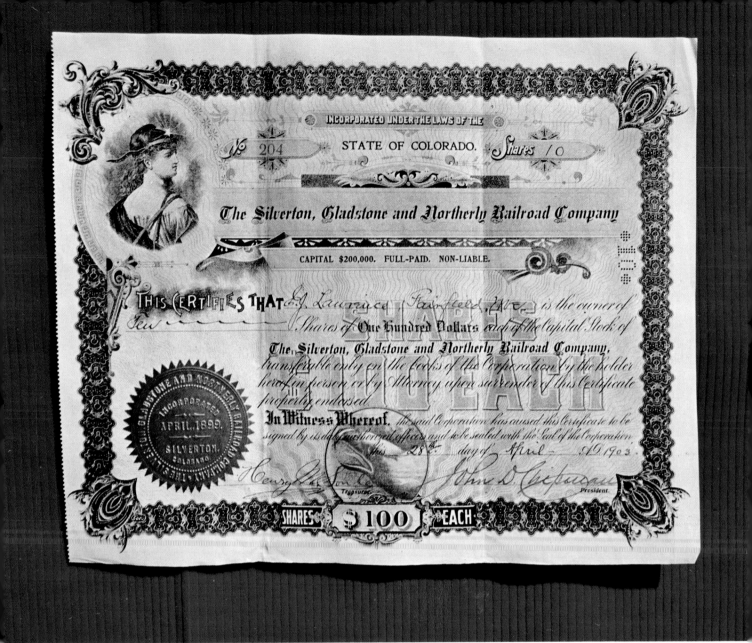

ROBERT E. SLOAN COLLECTION

Stock certificates were impressive examples of the engraver's art back around the turn of the century. This certificate was issued by the Silverton, Gladstone & Northerly Railroad Company during April of 1899.

At the left are examples of Silverton Northern, and Silverton Railway tickets, and a Silverton Railroad bond coupon of 1899.

SAN JUAN COUNTY HISTORICAL SOCIETY

Opposite page — this formal portrait of Silverton, Gladstone & Northerly locomotive Number 32, the *Gold King,* and combination car Number 1 was produced early in September, 1899. The photographer was looking east when he shot this view — at the base of the large Gold King mill, still under construction. The train was sitting on the north leg of the wye. Notice the unusual switchstand, which featured an arrow.

JACKSON C. THODE COLLECTION

137

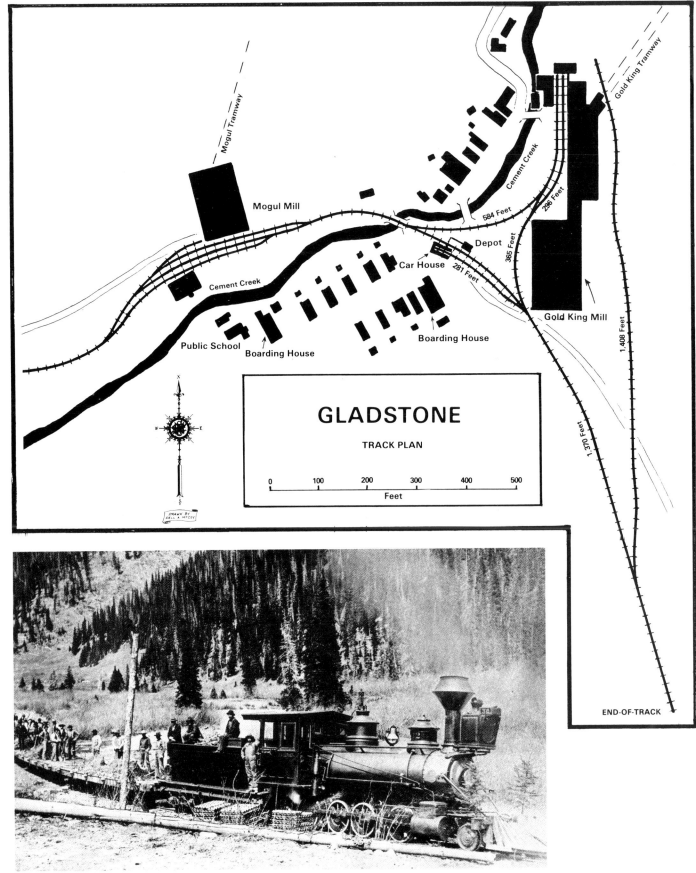

GLADSTONE

TRACK PLAN

Mogul Tramway

Gold King Tramway

Mogul Mill

Cement Creek

Cement Creek

584 Feet

296 Feet

365 Feet

Depot

Car House

281 Feet

Public School

Boarding House

Boarding House

Gold King Mill

1,408 Feet

1,370 Feet

END-OF-TRACK

DRAWN BY
DELL A. McCOY

0   100   200   300   400   500

Feet

THOMAS T. TABER COLLECTION

Silverton, Gladstone & Northerly engine 32, the *Gold King,* was pulling a work train when this view was made during the fall of 1899. The engine was hauling a work train, helping to ballast new track. Notice the rail joiners stacked beside the locomotive.

The first locomotive fireman on the SG&N was "Billy" Logan, a boomer from the Denver, South Park and Pacific. Another fireman was Edward "Pete" Meyer, who joined the road in 1899 at the tender age of 18, and whose earlier experience had been gained on the Gunnison Division of the South Park line. In 1901, when discharged by the SG&N, Meyer was immediately hired by Alexander Anderson as locomotive engineer for the Silverton and Silverton Northern railroads, where he remained to run engines until the final abandonment of the SN in 1942.

Pete Meyer probably was the source for the following tale, extracted from James D. Osborn's article in *Railroad Magazine* of February, 1941:

One winter morning in 1895, Charles Speer, a new conductor, started to Eureka with an engine and a four-wheeled caboose. In the crummy were two hardrock miners. A few miles above Silverton he cut the engine loose from the little red chariot to buck a few snowslides. Leaving the crummy motionless on the main line, Charley went ahead with his engine. The crew were busily bucking slides when a miner dashed up the track.

"Mr. Conductor," he shouted, out of breath, "there's a snowball in your caboose!"

Charley gave him a funny look. "What do you mean, a snowball?"

"That's what I mean. It's in your caboose, a great big one!" the miner tried to explain.

Supposing that a slide had come down and buried his chariot, Charley climbed on the engine and motioned the hogger back. When they reached the scene he scowled. There was no snow piled around or over the way-car, which was sitting comfortably on the rails where he had left it. Madder than a hornet, Charley leaped from the engine and hurried into the caboose. It was filled from floor to ceiling with solidly packed snow!

The miner hadn't lied. Up the mountain-side a small chunk of snow had started rolling. As it rolled, the mass had built up in the soft, wet snow until it was a 12-foot wheel about two-feet thick when it hit the caboose. Fortunately, the miners had seen it coming in time to duck to safety.

That was too much for Charley Speer. He didn't mind slides, but when snowballs began wearing his name on their noses he decided to quit. He went to the Denver and Rio Grande. There he hired out and spent the rest of his railroad life.

* * * * *

By late 1898, business conditions on the Mears roads had reached the point where plans were being made to place the Silverton Railroad in receivership to stop outside debts. A strike at the smelters in Durango, both now owned by the Omaha and Grant Smelting Company, had totally paralyzed the mines at Red Mountain and Ironton, no ore having been shipped since May. In spite of

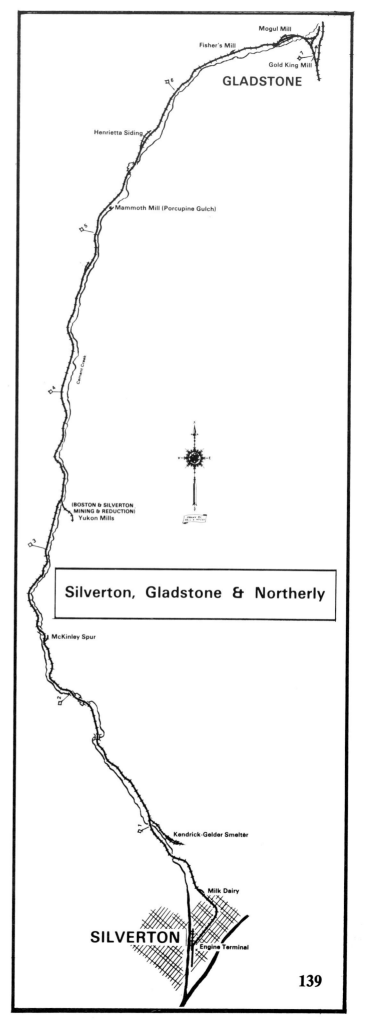

Silverton, Gladstone & Northerly

A. M. FAYNE COLLECTION

this, in July the new Treasury tunnel mine graded a 2,000-foot spur from the Yankee Girl trackage to their tunnel across the valley. Anderson bought 1,100 new ties and used some rail from Hammond's spur to build the new track to the mine.

The Treasury tunnel was an extremely difficult property to work. Hydraulic pressures of the underground water were so strong in places that blasting powder literally was blown out of its holes. To counteract this problem, the powder charges had to be put into gas pipes, which were then force-fitted into the holes. Using such means, the Treasury tunnel was worked successfully for many years.

Anderson continued to worry about the lack of a connection between his two railroads in Silverton, since the Denver and Rio Grande was steadily raising its freight rates and was forcing the SRR and SN out of the depot. Adding insult to injury, the Silverton, Gladstone and Northerly was using the Denver and Rio Grande's roundhouse to store its locomotive. Consequently, Anderson bought a warehouse building for $350.00 from Moses Liverman and George C. Logan to store all the goods and fixtures of both the Silverton and Silverton Northern companies.

By 1899, the Paymaster and Genessee-Vanderbilt mines were closed, having joined the Yankee Girl, Guston and National Belle in being flooded with water. This was the time—as might be expected—that was chosen by the U.S. Geological Survey to dispatch the noted geologists, Whitman Cross and F. L. Ransome, to undertake a geologic survey of the area and the mines. Many of the photographs taken by these two men during their explorations are spread throughout this book.

Because of the smelter strike, Ed and Lena Stoiber had been dickering to sell their Silver Lake properties, and finally succeeded in doing so early in August. The buyers were Simon and Daniel Guggenheim, owners of the local Guggenheim Exploration Company, and the American Smelting and Refining Company. The price paid the Stoibers totaled $1,300,000.

Anderson was finally appointed receiver of the Silverton Railroad on August 18, 1899. In November he got wind of a chilling rumor: the Gold King people had bought the Sunnyside Extension mine from Rasmus Hanson's widow and subsequently had made a major strike on the other side of the mountain. Since the closest access to the new discovery was by way of Animas Forks, the rumor indicated that the Silverton, Gladstone and Northerly was planning to cross the Silverton Northern and build up the Rio de las Animas to Animas Forks, and then across the passes to Lake City.

The threat was enough to change the senior Fred Walsen's mind about not extending the road until

Opposite page — Silverton, Gladstone & Northerly engine Number 32 was posed at Gladstone in 1899 for this impressive photograph. Dump rock and junk from the mill was being used here as fill material.

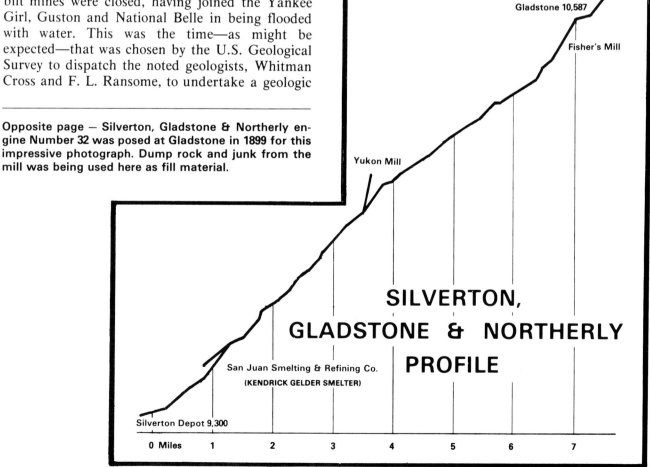

SILVERTON, GLADSTONE & NORTHERLY PROFILE

Gladstone 10,587

Fisher's Mill

Yukon Mill

San Juan Smelting & Refining Co.
(KENDRICK GELDER SMELTER)

Silverton Depot 9,300

0 Miles   1   2   3   4   5   6   7

F. L. RANSOME PHOTO — U.S. GEOLOGICAL SURVEY

Looking southeast from the road to the Barstow mine in Commodore Gulch, the Red Mountain mining district obviously covered a large portion of the mountain. Mines, gulches and mountain peaks visible, from left to right, are: White Cloud; Guston, directly below the peak of Red Mountain Number 2; Robinson; Champion Gulch; Yankee Girl; and, at the extreme right, the Genessee-Vanderbilt and Red Mountain Number 3.

revenues would pay the cost. In addition, the change in management of the Silver Lake mine and mill now made it necessary to firm up title to the Silverton Northern right-of-way, which had been very loosely handled back in the Stoiber days. Fred Walsen, Jr., secretary of the railroad, had managed to misplace the first right-of-way plats; and since they could not be found anywhere, a second set had to be drawn.

Over the winter, Silverton Northern engine Number 1 was sent to the shops in Alamosa for a $900.00 overhaul; after it was returned, the old pioneer, Silverton Railroad Number 100, was sent over for a similar overhaul, this one costing $1,400.00.

In May of 1900, after the winter's layoff, Anderson reported that Kendrick was building a new smelter on Cement Creek at the north edge of town; it was to become known as the San Juan Smelting and Refining Company. He put 500 new pine ties into the Silverton Northern and ordered 10,000 new pine ties for the Animas Forks extension and to take care of replacements needed on the Silverton Railroad. Mr. Burroughs, owner of

the Astor mine at Grouse Gulch, and Colonel Channing F. Meek (who a few years later was to become deeply involved in the Yule Marble Company and its associated Crystal River and San Juan Railway) in September were trying to persuade Anderson to extend the Silverton Northern to their mines up the Rio de las Animas above Eureka, promising enough money to pay for the job.

Anderson was having trouble with L. B. Jackson and Company at Eureka at this time; four D&RG boxcars full of coal, delivered to the customer in the preceding 30 days, were still on hand unloaded. Since the cars were not being handled promptly, Anderson warned Jackson that for such delays in the future, the D&RG would charge demurrage. Free for the first 48 hours, each car would then accumulate a penalty of 50 cents a day for the first five days, $1.00 a day for the next five days, and $2.00 a day thereafter. Anderson disbursed $919.00 to lay a total of 2,000 additional feet of trackage in the Sunnyside yard at Eureka, at the Iowa tramhouse, and to serve the power house at Waldheim.

WHITMAN CROSS PHOTO — U.S. GEOLOGICAL SURVEY

The Guston - Robinson mining complex is shown here (far left), with the settlement of miners' houses (near the center) on typical landslide topography. The Congregational Church (also near the center) used a mine whistle to call in the flock. *The Knob* can be seen just above the church, while Sheridan Junction was just around the hillside, atop Red Mountain Pass (to the right).

Early that fall the Silver Ledge mine at Chattanooga was the only mine working on the Silverton Railroad. On the far side of Red Mountain Pass, Charles Newman was opening claims near Ironton and wanted the rails relaid beyond Guston through the Corkscrew Gulch turntable to Ironton. He offered only 75 cents a ton to ship out his ore, however, and would not pay for rebuilding the right-of-way that had been abandoned since 1897. Anderson told Vice-President C. H. Graham in November of 1900 that the Silverton road was in only fair condition—the 30-pound rails were badly worn; heavier rail and at least 15,000 ties were needed to put the railroad in first-class condition.

In October of 1900, the Silverton, Gladstone and Northerly asked the Rio Grande Southern for another Class 56 engine. A year previous, in September of 1899, the RGS had disposed of engine Number 33, another of the locomotives transferred to Utah in the D&RG-D&RGW fracas of 1886, and purchased from the RGW by Otto Mears for the RGS in 1891. Built in 1880 (Baldwin number 5225) as D&RG Number 78, the *Sandia,* she went to the Utah company, where she worked as Number 78 without a number change, with a valuation of $4,383.53 in 1886. Five years later,

when bought for the RGS, the locomotive cost Mears $3,000.00.

The D&RG-RGS, in disposing of small, outdated surplus power around the turn of the century, included this engine among several sold to a dealer in used locomotives—George M. Dilley and Sons of Palestine, Texas. The Dilley firm laid out $3,200.00 for RGS Number 33, but found the condition of the engine so bad that their complaints finally resulted in cancellation of the deal and the engine was returned to the Burnham shops in Denver. As the reader has no doubt guessed, this ill-kept little machine, after some additional work at Burnham, ended up as the property of the Silverton, Gladstone and Northerly, being purchased at a price of $3,200.00 during 1900, and given Number 33 in the roster. Notwithstanding the work done at Burnham, W. D. Lee of the RGS at Ridgway had to undertake more repairs, even going so far as to cannibalize minor parts from the Rio Grande Southern's first ten-wheeler, Number 22, in April of 1902, to keep the engine serviceable on the SG&N.

In early 1900, the Silverton, Gladstone and Northerly also purchased 10 new 32-foot gondolas, numbered 2000 to 2009, from American Car and

WHITMAN CROSS PHOTO — U.S. GEOLOGICAL SURVEY

Looking southeast, with Ironton in the foreground and the Corkscrew Gulch turntable just behind — on Red Mountain Number 2 — W. Cross of the U.S.G.S. made this view on September 14, 1900. The White Cloud mine is at the left of the mouth of Corkscrew Gulch. Ironton started her decline to ghost town status at this time.

COLORADO RAILROAD MUSEUM COLLECTION

Foundry, and bought four miles of rail—enough for a proposed two-mile-long extension to the Natalie Occidental mine south of Gladstone. This was part of the basis for the rumor about the SG&N building to Animas Forks and Lake City that had so frightened Anderson a few months earlier.

The Yankee Girl mine produced a total of $3-million in values by 1900, with an aggregate of $8-million up through the next half-century to 1954. Total production of the Guston mine from discovery to 1901 was $2.5-million. The Silver Belle mine, up the hill above Ironton, produced about $178,000 in values from 1887 to 1890; the Congress mine on Red Mountain turned out $220,000 in 1883 alone. During the three decades from 1871 to 1900, total mineral production of the mines in the region encompassed by the U.S.G.S. Silverton Quadrangle was about $35-million. The Genessee-Vanderbilt and the former Treasury tunnel, known in recent years as the Idarado, were still in operation as of this writing — in 1975.

During the first 10 years of the Twentieth Century, the town of Silverton and its citizens embarked on a massive building program. The miners' union, with a membership of more than 1,300 men, built its hall at the corner of Eleventh and Greene streets in 1901, expending more than $35,000 on the structure. A telephone system to serve the town—with a line to the Sunnyside mine near Eureka—was installed in August of the same year, while a line was also put into service to Durango. In 1902, Silverton purchased the private water company for $40,000 and in the year following, built a new brick jail at Fifteenth and Reese streets; this building presently is devoted to the more-constructive activities and collections of the San Juan County Historical Society. A fine new library, financed from funds donated by Andrew Carnegie as part of his nationwide philanthropic program of library aid, was built at Tenth and

The cover (above, right) of this $500.00 gold bond was artistically lettered, making it look quite attractive. Despite the fancy artwork and flowing language found in the bond, investors never got a chance to clip all the pretty little coupons — one of which is printed here (below, right).

Opposite page — a $500.00 gold bond of the Silverton, Gladstone & Northerly — decorated with flowery legal language about defaulting, which did not help at all when the line folded in January of 1915; the investors lost their shirts. The bond bears an engraving of a high-wheeled 4-4-0 American-type locomotive of the sort that never got within 100 miles of this narrow-gauge shortline.

COLORADO RAILROAD MUSEUM COLLECTION

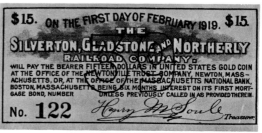

MORRIS W. ABBOTT COLLECTION

The brand new Gold King mill at Gladstone, as shown here, reveals the tail-end track of the wye. A portion of Storm Peak is to the right. The upper spur track was under construction at the time, where felled logs rest above the mill. SG&N locomotive Number 32 and combine Number 1 were waiting for the photographer, along with Gladstone folk.

The view below, photographed in 1897, shows that the Silverton Railroad's Number 100 steamed well — as the plume of steam makes obvious. The engine was ready to tackle the steep five-percent grade above the Chattanooga Loop with a four-car train. In her consist she had two SRR boxcars, an SN boxcar and the SRR's combine, *Red Mountain.*

RICHARD A. RONZIO COLLECTION

A. M. PAYNE COLLECTION

A train consisting of Silverton Northern engine Number 1, Silverton Railroad boxcar 500 and the Silverton Railroad's combine, *Red Mountain,* is shown here as it rounded the 24-degree curve at Eureka. The steep canyon leading to Animas Forks is in the background. When this view was photographed — in 1896 — track braces were used instead of tie plates to anchor the rails.

Reese streets at the same time.

In 1907, the new City Hall—constructed of dark stone quarried along South Mineral Creek—was built at a cost of $40,000, and the next year a new San Juan County Courthouse was completed at a cost of $100,000. Both of these buildings are located at Fourteenth and Greene streets. The Grand Hotel was acquired through a tax sale and operated during this period by Henry Frecker, a recluse who had come to Silverton from Victor, Colorado. The impressive old hostelry, today considered an outstanding example of Victorian architecture, was known as the *Imperial* during most of the first half of this century, has main-

tained its attraction to visitors through all the years, and continues in business to the present time as the renowned *Grand Imperial.*

In the last month of 1900, a new right-of-way plat for the Silverton Northern was drawn up and filed with the government. When this was rejected, Otto Mears hired Ben L. Allen, a civil engineer from Pence, Kansas, to re-survey the railroad. Allen performed the necessary work between May 22 and June 6, 1901, and he and Mears then filed the revised plat on the final day. In July, Anderson sent the legal forms for perfecting title to the railroad's right-of-way to Mears on the East Coast for further handling.

149

RICHARD A. RONZIO COLLECTION

In this scene, Silverton Northern locomotive Number 1 was chuffing about the Sunny-side yard, delivering empty freight cars to the mill (out of view at right). This photograph of Eureka was taken in 1899, and the lens was pointed down the valley toward Silverton.

The Big Five Tunnel, Ore Reduction and Transportation Company built a new mill at Howardsville in 1901, at the same time excavating the grade for a siding to serve the new facility. Anderson, checking up on what was being done, discovered that the mill building encroached on the Silverton Northern's right-of-way and that the grade on the siding varied from 0.4 to 2.7 percent. He wrote to William P. Daniels, in charge of the Big Five operation, asking that the grade be made more uniform, and advising that the SN would lease the necessary part of its right-of-way covering the encroachment. In the same letter he told Daniels that although he could not authorize him to ride his rail velocipede or bicycle on the tracks, because of the liability, others along the line managed to engage in such practices without permission.

Anderson ordered 1,000 red spruce ties with cut ends and two opposite sides hewn parallel, no bark, for 32 cents a tie, loaded at Durango or at Bell's Spur on the D&RG's Silverton Branch, and started a rate discussion with that road over cost of moving the ties. He offered 3½ cents per hundred pounds, the big road countered with seven cents per hundred; then agreement finally was reached at three cents per hundredweight for ties to be used on the Silverton Railroad, and four cents per hundredweight for those bound for the Silverton Northern.

The Stoibers, it will be recalled, had made a sizeable contribution toward construction costs of the Silverton Northern; in return, as agreed, they had received an unpublicized, under-the-table 50-percent rebate on freight charges over the road. Just before they finally departed from the Silverton area for good in late May, 1901, they informed the new owners of the Silver Lake mill of the confidential rate of 20 cents per ton on coal delivered to the power plant, and Anderson's hopes for increased revenue thus were neatly undercut.

In October of 1901, Mrs. M. B. Murrell asked the Silverton Northern to build an extension up Cunningham Gulch to her Highland Mary mine. When interviewed by Anderson, she guaranteed two cars per day, either inbound or outbound, but he was unable to promise any immediate construction. This trackage, in fact, was delayed for another four years before it could be put down.

150

Anderson's problems with the Denver and Rio Grande now were compounding, for he found his roads caught in a rate squeeze by the big railroad; the tariff on coal was doubled to $2.00 per ton, while the Silverton, Gladstone and Northerly was being charged $1.00 a ton for general freight. It was only after a series of protesting letters, forcibly arguing for a change, that the D&RG finally reinstated the old rate.

Another problem arose over ties needed for the Mears roads. None were available from any source closer than Lumberton, New Mexico, some 82 miles east of Durango on the D&RG narrow-gauge mainline, and again the big road turned the situation to its own advantage. At first, Anderson was charged freight on the ties at one cent per ton-mile, then the D&RG raised the rate to 15 cents per hundred pounds, and finally settled on 10 cents a hundred. Anderson was properly outraged at having to pay 12 cents a tie for freight!

Still other difficulties confronted him when the D&RG applied pressure on the Silverton and Silverton Northern roads to repair some of their bad-order boxcars. Anderson placed an order for nearly enough spare parts to build three 10-ton boxcars from scratch in November, 1901, and enough for two more the following January.

In November an unfortunate accident in the Silver Lake yard cost Michael Corliss, an employee of the Silver Lake mine, a leg. He sued the railroad for damages, but lost his suit.

In December of 1901, mine operator and former Silverton Railroad director, George Crawford, ordered 225 tons of coal to start working the Hudson and National Belle mines near Red Mountain town. He also aired plans to reopen the Guston mine.

In mid-December, recognizing Anderson's excellent management and hard work on behalf of his two roads, Otto Mears allowed his manager a bonus of $1,000. The response was typical of the Scotsman:

My dear Mr. Mears, I received your recent letter on which you allowed me $1,000 for my past services. I thank you very much for your kindness and trust that I shall always prove worthy of your confidence and respect.

* * * * *

Encouraged by this tangible evidence of Mears' confidence, Anderson attempted to initiate action on a matter which had occupied his mind for several months. He wrote C. W. Davis, an officer of the Silverton, Gladstone and Northerly, as follows:

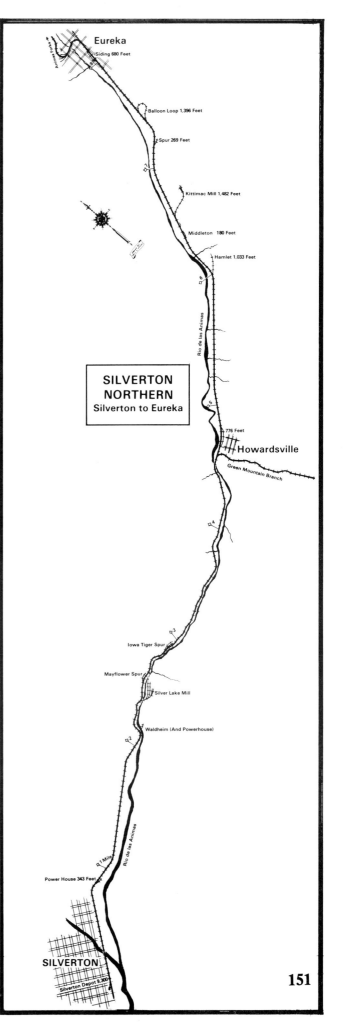

SILVERTON NORTHERN
Silverton to Eureka

151

SUNDANCE PHOTO BY DELL A. McCOY

Above — autumn colors add golden warmth to this view of Silverton — sitting in the middle of Bakers Park. The bell-and-clock tower of the county courthouse stands out above the trees, next to the jail building (to the left of the courthouse). Looking south, the canyon carved by the Rio de las Animas will be virtually silent until next summer, as the last trainload of tourists has departed for the the season. Shortly, the town will return to its long, peaceful — and often snow-filled — winter season.

Opposite page — this view of Silverton — looking north — was taken from the old Durango-Silverton toll road, on the side of Sultan Mountain, August 23, 1900. Mineral Creek and the Silverton Railroad entered town from the left. The Walsh smelter is barely in the picture (at the base of Anvil Mountain), almost hidden by the pine trees in the left foreground. Cement Creek and the SG&N entered town in the center of the view, between Anvil Mountain and Storm Peak, the highest mountain in the photograph. The Rio de las Animas and the Silverton Northern came into town from right, center. The yard of the D&RG can be seen to the right of the main part of town. In the foreground, the floodplain of the Animas stands out quite distinctly. The Silverton Branch of the D&RG is on the near side of the river, and the spur to the Little Dora mill is barely discernable — leaving the main track where it curves to cross the bridge over Mineral Creek. To the right of the river is Kendall Mountain.

WHITMAN CROSS PHOTO — U.S. GEOLOGICAL SURVEY

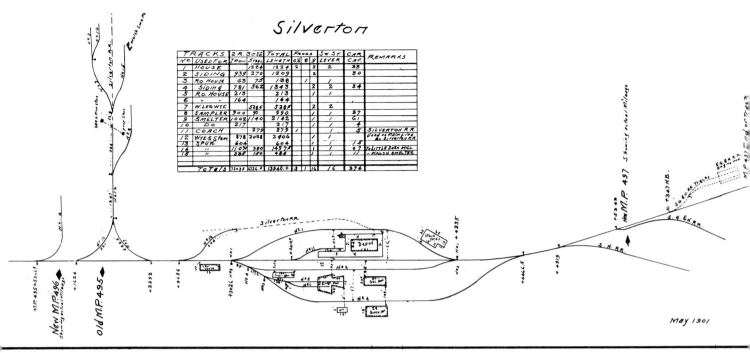

JACKSON C. THODE COLLECTION

December 21st 1901

Cyrus W. Davis, Esq.
Waterville, Maine
My dear Sir:

It has occurred to me lately that the three little roads here—the Silverton; Silverton Northern; and Silverton, Gladstone and Northerly—might be consolidated and a saving in management and operation thereby effected to the benefit of all. Would your people be willing to accept, any four or five per-cent bonds (with a proportion of the stock) of a company organized to acquire the three roads in payment for the transfer of the SG&N? If your people would not care to accept the securities of another company for their property, at what price in cash could your road be bought?

I will appreciate the favor of a reply at your early convenience and I will probably leave here soon and want to work on this when in the east. I have little doubt of my ability to push the matter to a successful close, if your people agree to it.

Wishing you the compliments of the season, I am, with best regards for you,

Yours very truly,

Alex Anderson

* * * * *

In February of 1902, Anderson reported to Vice-President Charles H. Graham in Philadelphia that the Silverton Railroad had been closed down as usual on the first of January and that Davis of the Silverton, Gladstone and Northerly had declined to entertain any negotiations regarding a merger. A letter to Mears at the same time reported that earnings on the Silverton Northern were poor. A teamster named George Boss had succeeded in taking the mail contract away from the railroad, and if Mr. Mears would allow an extra $250.00 per month for the crew, Anderson would operate two straight passenger trains to Eureka every day, in addition to the daily mixed train, and drive Boss out of business.

At this time, the Silverton Railroad was deriving most of its income from hiring its train crews to the Silverton Northern, which had none! The standard monthly fee was $500.00—transferred out of one pocket into the other.

In March, still vexed over the physical separation of the two roads in Silverton, Anderson re-estimated the cost of building a connection between the Silverton and the Silverton Northern. He arrived at a total close to $4,500, including rails and ties, figuring on 6,000 feet of track, with the necessary sidings, and estimating $350.00 for a bridge over Cement Creek, 60 tons of 30-pound rail at $2,100.00; 3,000 ties at $1,000; spikes, track bolts and splice bars at $265.00; parts for six switches and the frogs for crossing the Denver and Rio Grande at $425.00; and labor at $300.00. He also pointed out to Mears that if they did not build a track to the town's new power plant, the work would be done by the D&RG or the SG&N. Switching revenues from the power plant would approximate $300.00 a year, and perhaps other industries would build on the line.

During the Christmas seasons of both 1900 and 1901, the privately-owned electric plant serving the town had failed due to overload. This alone would have peeved the city fathers, but they also thought the rates too high and deliberately set out to put the Silverton Electric Light Company out of business. For a while, both the town and the private company had electric lines strung around town. In the long run, this was not too significant. The Animas Electric Light and Power Company plant at Tacoma was soon built. By 1907, Silverton was buying its electricity from them, and by 1914, the town power plant was in a state of disrepair, not having been in operation for several years. Anderson explained the situation more fully in another letter to Mears the following month, telling him that Mayor Ballou had told Anderson that if the Silverton Northern would extend its track, the town would locate the municipal plant on the line. Anderson again pointed out to Mears that the switching charges would amount to something, and that with a connection between the two Mears roads around the D&RG yard, they could operate trains without regard to the D&RG time card. As things presently stood, they were shut out of the yard for three hours a day.

He also asked Mears again for the extra money for passenger service, emphasizing that the mixed train was unavoidably irregular and that people would be able to depend on the passenger trains. He had 3,000 new ties on hand at Florida, over east of Durango, and needed them within a week, due to the early thaw in the weather; if Mr. Mears would take up the matter of freight rates on ties with the D&RG, it would be helpful.

Rumors were flying thick and fast in the spring of 1902! Colonel Meek, according to the gossip, would be building from Lake City to Burroughs Park; the Silverton, Gladstone and Northerly, it was rumored, was to be extended to Lake City. When Anderson used these as excuses to press for building the branch to Animas Forks that summer, Mears responded only by approving the extra money for the passenger train operation.

Gratified at having won at least part of his argument, Anderson planned a commuter train for the workers in the mines and mill at Eureka, leaving Silverton at 6:45 in the morning and arriving at Eureka by 7:00 a.m. The second train would leave for Eureka at 9:30 and depart on the return to Silverton at 10:00, then leave at 11:15 a.m. for Red Mountain after arrival of the Denver and Rio Grande train from Durango. In other words, a passenger could leave Durango at 7:00 a.m., or Eureka at 10:00 a.m., and reach Ouray by 3 o'clock the same afternoon.

Another train would leave for Eureka at 2:45 p.m. and return to Silverton at 6:00 p.m. He calculated that 50 workmen, at $1.00 per man, alone would net $200.00 per month.

By July, the Silverton Railroad was in even

THE SILVERTON MINER, 1907 —
MORRIS W. ABBOTT COLLECTION

The livery stable of teamster, George Boss, on Blair Street in Silverton, earned quite a reputation early in 1902 when Boss succeeded in taking the Animas River mail route — between Silverton and Animas Forks — away from the Silverton Northern Railroad.

deeper trouble. Anderson needed $3,000 to work the road through the fall and the court authorized him, as receiver of the railroad, to borrow the money at 10-percent interest from the Silverton Northern. But the SN did not have the money either, so Anderson, as manager of the latter road, turned once again to Fred Walsen and borrowed the funds at eight-percent interest on the strength of the probable fall earnings from the Silver Ledge mine at Chattanooga. To handle that business, he installed a two-track siding and a *kite* track for the Silver Ledge, taking the rails from the spur to the Bobtail mine. The Treasury tunnel, or Hammond's tunnel, was being actively pushed by September, and George Crawford, now in New York, had a few men working at Red Mountain.

In his frequent letters to Silverton Railroad Vice-President C. H. Graham, Anderson repeatedly pointed out that the railroad would not do much toward providing a return on Graham's investment until the mines were reopened and the railroad rebuilt. Graham, as a result, teamed up with George Crawford, and assembling a group of unsuspecting investors, incorporated a unitized company, the "Red Mountain Railroad, Mining and Smelting Company," on October 6, 1902, in Arizona. The plan was to drain the Guston, Robinson, Yankee Girl and Genessee-Vanderbilt mines by drilling a drainage tunnel from a point between Corkscrew Gulch and Ironton where the railroad's bridge crossed over Red Mountain Creek.

SUNDANCE PHOTO BY DELL A. McCOY

The snow-capped beauty of Trico Peak — rising to an elevation of 13,321 feet — aligns with the old Silverton Railway grade. The photographer was near the Paymaster mine when this view was shot about two years ago. A glimpse of the Million Dollar Highway, which crosses Red Mountain Pass, shows to the right.

WHITMAN CROSS PHOTO — U.S. GEOLOGICAL SURVEY

Looking north from the mouth of Gray Copper Gulch, this striking view of Ironton Park shows the Saratoga, or Albany, mill. The abandoned roadbed of the Silverton Railway is just barely visible in the foreground of this photograph, taken on September 12, 1900.

The drainage tunnel at Joker (the name seemingly quite appropriate in the view of those "unsuspecting investors"), finally was started in 1904, eventually extending for 4,800 feet in a straight line from the level of Red Mountain Creek to the shaft of the Genessee-Vanderbilt, with side branches drilled into the Guston, Robinson and Yankee Girl mines. This was the most convenient route because it drained as much of the mines as possible for the least amount of tunneling.

When the tunnel was completed in 1907, the Red Mountain mining district revived almost immediately. Water levels in the mines were lowered by 410 feet in the Guston, by 435 feet in the Yankee Girl, and at the Genessee-Vanderbilt by 625 feet below the railroad, or 925 feet below the original mine opening. Operation of the mines was eased now, too, since the ore no longer had to be lifted to the surface, but was trammed out to

the mouth of Joker tunnel where it could be loaded into cars. Since the Saratoga mill at Albany, below Ironton, had ceased operation during the Silver Panic, the Silverton Railroad now normally ended at Joker.

In either 1902 or 1903 the only fatal accident to take place on any of the three little Silverton roads occurred. Engineer Bally Thompson backed an engine off a short rail on the Silverton Railroad wye at Sheridan Junction (Summit) and was crushed when the locomotive turned over.

The snows came early in the fall of 1902. Anderson bought an engine-pilot snowplow from the Denver and Rio Grande in November, but had to shut down the Silverton for the season by December 5. He ordered 10,000 yellow pine ties from John F. Bell of Rockwood to be used during the next year's construction and maintenance.

In January, 1903, the *Silverton Standard* re-

157

WHITMAN CROSS PHOTO — U.S. GEOLOGICAL SURVEY

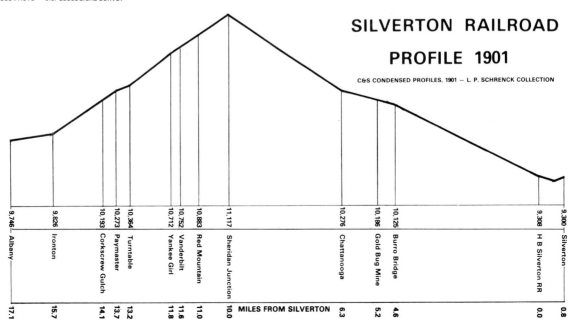

SILVERTON RAILROAD

PROFILE 1901

C&S CONDENSED PROFILES, 1901 — L. P. SCHRENCK COLLECTION

Elevation	Station	Miles from Silverton
9,746	Albany	17.1
9,826	Ironton	15.7
10,193	Corkscrew Gulch	14.1
10,273	Paymaster	13.7
10,364	Turntable	13.2
10,712	Yankee Girl	11.8
10,752	Vanderbilt	11.6
10,883	Red Mountain	11.0
11,117	Sheridan Junction	10.0
10,276	Chattanooga	6.3
10,186	Gold Bug Mine	5.2
10,125	Burro Bridge	4.6
9,308	H B Silverton RR	0.0
9,300	Silverton	0.8

MILES FROM SILVERTON

Taken from a knoll near a cabin at the mouth of Galena Lion Gulch — looking east across Red Mountain Creek — this view shows the extensive damage caused by a forest fire, which had burned nearly all the trees several years before the photographer recorded this scene. The rejuvenation of the area, under George Crawford's Red Mountain Railroad, Mining & Smelting Company, was still a number of years away. The mountain in the center is Red Mountain Number 2, while on the right is Red Mountain Number 3, with Champion Gulch between them. The steep bedrock slopes on the near side of Red Mountain Number 2 are the source of the many landslides that make up the ripple-surfaced hillside below; each ripple is a separate landslide that slipped down the hill. The mines in the left photograph are the Paymaster, with coal track above the mine and ore track below; the White Cloud; and the American Girl. In the right photograph (from left to right) can be seen the Cora Belle (above the tracks); the Guston, with the pyramidal-roofed office; and the Robinson, just at the mouth of Champion Gulch.

Silverton had its own brewery — shown here as it looked in 1903 — which was built of stone. Ruins of this facility lasted until 1959, when some of the stone was used to build a shrine on Anvil Mountain overlooking the town. The brewery was located southwest of Silverton at the base of Sultan Mountain.

THE SILVERTON STANDARD, 1903 —
MORRIS W. ABBOTT COLLECTION

VAUGHAN JONES PHOTO —
RICHARD A. RONZIO COLLECTION

This crowd of oldtimers probably was attending a convention which ended up at the Gold King in Gladstone in 1900. Notice the Sunday-go-to-meeting dress of the group, and each one has pinned on a name tag. A part of the fanfare was the beautiful ride up Cement Creek behind locomotive 32, with accomodation in the comfortable combine, Number 1.

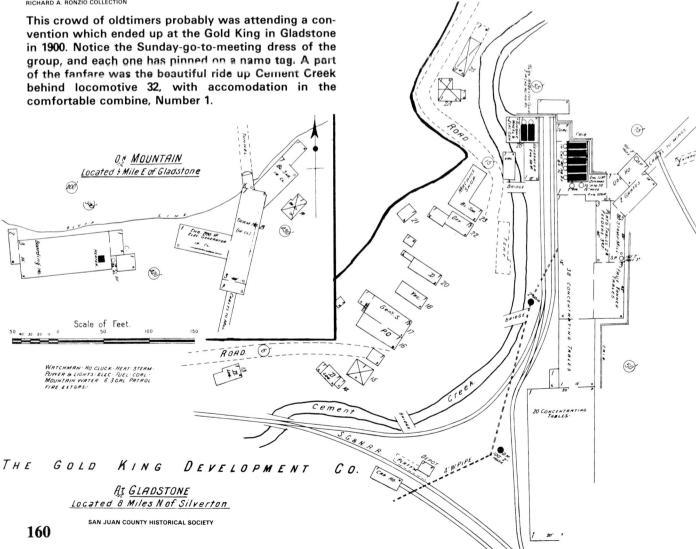

ON MOUNTAIN
Located ¼ Mile E of Gladstone

Scale of Feet.

WATCHMAN - NO CLUCK · HEAT STEAM ·
POWER & LIGHTS · ELEC · FUEL · COAL ·
MOUNTAIN WATER · 6 3 GAL PATROL
FIRE EXT.GRS.

THE GOLD KING DEVELOPMENT CO.

At GLADSTONE
Located 8 Miles N of Silverton

SAN JUAN COUNTY HISTORICAL SOCIETY

160

JACKSON C. THODE COLLECTION

As evidenced by this 1902 scene, the Gold King mill at Gladstone was served by two cableways — seen climbing the hill to Ross Basin. Both ended at the shafthouse as shown in the plan on the facing page. The enlarged mill had two 24-foot 10-ton boxcars spotted for loading — RGS 1603 and SN 103.

L. P. SCHRENCK COLLECTION

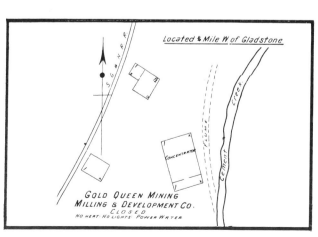

SAN JUAN COUNTY HISTORICAL SOCIETY

SAN JUAN COUNTY HISTORICAL SOCIETY

SG&N locomotive 32 or 33 was photographed spotting two empty 24-foot boxcars for loading at the Gold King mill during 1901. The clearing between the trees was for a cable tramway going to the pithead in Ross Basin.

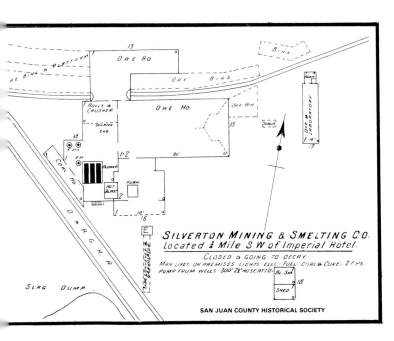

SAN JUAN COUNTY HISTORICAL SOCIETY

THE SILVERTON MINER, 1907 —
MORRIS W. ABBOTT COLLECTION

This was the Martha Rose — later the Walsh — smelter at the southwest corner of Silverton in 1903. By, or shortly after, this date the smelter was under lease to the Red Mountain Railroad, Mining & Smelting Company.

162

"SAN JUAN COUNTY" BOOKLET — THE SILVERTON STANDARD
MORRIS W. ABBOTT COLLECTION

Dusty streets were a major summertime problem for merchants and housewives, so the Silverton town fathers saw to it that the community went first-class, operating a water-sprinkler wagon to cut down on "air pollution." The impressive Grand Hotel and Hub Saloon are on the left side of the view. You are looking northeast, up Greene Street, at the corner of Twelfth Street, and the year was 1903.

ported that in 1902 (before the Joker tunnel was started) the Silverton Railroad had operated only as far as Red Mountain, bringing out 482 tons of ores and concentrates, and carrying in 3,448 tons of freight. The biggest shippers, in order, had been the Brooklyn Bonner at Burro Bridge, the Yankee Girl and Genessee-Vanderbilt at Red Mountain, and the Silver Ledge at Chattanooga.

Gus Stoiber was one of the principals in the

Bonner—in August 1905, he suffered a stroke on board the down passenger train from Red Mountain after visiting the Bonner and died at his house at 767 Reese Street.

The Silverton Northern had moved 23,442 tons (1,828 carloads) of ores and concentrates outbound, and inbound had carried 21,210 tons of freight. The Silverton, Gladstone and Northerly had handled 14,428 tons from the Gold King mine,

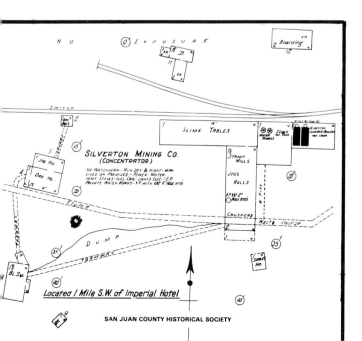

SAN JUAN COUNTY HISTORICAL SOCIETY

"SAN JUAN COUNTY" BOOKLET — THE SILVERTON STANDARD
MORRIS W. ABBOTT COLLECTION

The North Star mill was served by a spur from the Silverton Railroad at the southwest corner of Silverton.

ON THE LINE OF THE S & N R R

MORRIS W. ABBOTT COLLECTION

The lead track to the Silver Lake mill yard left the Silverton Northern mainline in this scenic canyon area, two miles out of Silverton. In this view, you are looking west as a freight train drifted toward Silverton along the Rio de las Animas.

while ingoing freight had totalled 10,411 tons. New shippers along this line were the Grand Mogul, Henrietta, Natalie, Big Colorado, and the Boston and Silverton Mining and Reduction Company, also known as the Yukon mill.

At the beginning of 1903, passenger fares on the Silverton Railroad from its home terminal were 65 cents to Burro Bridge, 80 cents to Chattanooga, $1.30 to Summit and $1.50 to Red Mountain—or 10 cents per mile. Fares on the Silverton Northern were 25 cents to Waldheim or Howardsville, and 50 cents to Middleton or Eureka.

During the first month of 1903, Silverton Northern engine Number 1 was away from its home road for a short while, hauling coal on the branch between the Rio Grande Southern mainline and the coal mine at Perins Peak; Anderson had rented the locomotive to the Boston Coal and Fuel Company for $8.00 a day while the coal company's engine was being repaired. The next month, in preparation for the start of the extension to Animas Forks, Anderson ordered all the ties that

T. B. Northrop of Rockwood could make.

In May, Anderson wrote P. B. McAttee, the new D&RG general agent at Durango, asking that at least some of the boxcars owned by the two Mears roads be returned to Silverton. He also requested that whenever the Durango coal mines were to load coal ordered by the two roads, empty Silverton Northern or Silverton Railroad cars should be supplied for the purpose. It had been at the urgent request of the superintendent of the big road's Fourth Division that the SN and SRR had spent considerable money rebuilding boxcars, he told McAttee, and it was unfair for the D&RG now to keep them tied up in the Durango yards.

Anderson's campaign during the past three years for extending the Silverton Northern on into the high country at Animas Forks—a project fostered by the renewed mining activity in that area and encouraged by rumors concerning the SG&N building a branch to the Sunnyside Extension via the little settlement—at last brought solid results. Thomas H. Wigglesworth was re-employed

164

as locating and construction engineer, and on May 28, 1903, he assembled a surveying crew of young men who had worked for him previously in Durango. Roy Goodman was level-man, George Vest Day (son of David F. Day of *Solid Muldoon* newspaper fame) was rodman, and Harold Sievers and Charles Kiel were other crew members. Day was commissioned to set up camp at Animas Forks and rode the train that day from Durango to Silverton, then took the Silverton Northern on to Eureka and packed the crew's gear on up to the town. Wigglesworth and the rest of the crew arrived in camp on June 1.

During the first week of June, Wig (as Wigglesworth was often called) started with a preliminary survey at Cinnamon Pass, the most likely route to Lake City, and worked west down the mountainside to Animas Forks, then south toward Eureka. By using switchbacks the engineer succeeded in working out a five-percent grade down the steep east side of the Rio de las Animas, but since the rockwork would be prohibitively expensive, all the while he was looking longingly at Mears' toll road, mostly on the west side of the cañon.

Finally, in July—when Mears was back in Silverton at last—Wigglesworth remarked to the boss, "If it wasn't for the road, we could put this railroad over on the better side."

"Well, why not?" Mears replied. "It's mine; I built it. Go ahead and take it if you want it!"

So the survey was immediately shifted to the toll-road location, and construction was begun.

In June, Anderson ordered 15,000 tie plates for use in constructing the extension. He also ordered 1,000 each of 12 types of tickets for the Silverton Northern—one-way, round-trip (return) and commutation—between Silverton, and Waldheim, Howardsville, Middleton and Eureka.

Effective July 3, 1903, Anderson posted a new timetable of train schedules and fare charges for both the Mears railroads:

SILVERTON NORTHERN RAILROAD

Passenger Trains Will Hereafter Be Run Daily As Follows:

A.M.	A.M.	P.M.				A.M.	A.M.	P.M.
6.50	9.30	4.00	Lv.	Silverton	Arr.	7.52	10.42	5.37
6.56	9.36	4.06		Waldheim		7.46	10.36	5.31
6.59	9.30	4.09		Collins		7.43	10.33	5.28
7.04	9.44	4.14		Howardsville		7.38	10.28	5.23
7.09	9.49	4.19		Middleton		7.33	10.23	5.18
7.20	10.00	4.30	Arr.	Eureka	Lv.	7.25	10.15	5.10

Fares:

Between Silverton and	Waldheim	10 cents
	Howardsville	25 cents
	Eureka	50 cents

On Sundays round-trip tickets will be sold at above rates.
Commutation Tickets at reduced rates can be purchased at the office.

SAN JUAN COUNTY HISTORICAL SOCIETY

The mainline of the Silverton Northern is to the left, beside the Rio de las Animas, in this view — with a spur and siding leading to the lower terminal of the Iowa tramway. This was about one-half mile upstream from the Silver Lake mill. The rock pinnacles here and at the Silver Lake mill are due to vertical faulting and cementation of the crushed rock by hot mineral-bearing solutions.

SILVERTON RAILROAD

P.M.				A.M.
12.35	Leaves	Silverton	Arrives	3.00
1.02		Burro Bridge		2.33
1.14		Chattanooga		2.21
1.29		Summit		2.06
1.35	Arrives	Red Mountain	Leaves	2.00

Silverton, Colo., July 3rd, 1903. A.

RICHARD A. RONZIO COLLECTION

A panoramic camera recorded this view of Eureka in 1899. To the left, two boxcars have been spotted for loading at a small mill. Near the center, the passenger platform and the

Mid-summer of 1903 saw the start of grading and track-laying on the extension of the Silverton Northern from Eureka to Animas Forks. The 400 men employed to do the grading were billeted in four boardinghouses—at Eureka, Animas Forks and at two locations between the towns. Mears had already requisitioned four miles of 40-pound rail at $25.00 a ton delivered in Silverton; and, during one week in the middle of July, when he visited the construction site, additional orders for men and materials went out thick and fast. Before he departed, Mears wired D&RG purchasing agent Hobbs in Denver asking where the rail was and when it would be shipped, and ordered 10 stub switches of number nine frog angle.

Anderson ordered several harp switchstands, as well as four horse-drawn graders and dump carts with harness, for immediate delivery. He also ordered 3,000 yellow pine ties from Ed Roberts of Rockwood for delivery by August 25 at the latest, at a price of 25 cents for first-class ties and 13 cents for any second-class ties accepted.

Wigglesworth's survey crew had the use of the railroad velocipede built by the Silverton Northern's shopmen for Lena Stoiber when she and her husband were running the Silver Lake mine and mill. This rig consisted of a light framework upon which two bicycle frames were mounted side-by-side, all supported on four flanged, pressed-steel wheels on a pair of axles. The bicycle drive-chains were connected directly to the rear axle, and the contrivance was light enough in weight to be lifted and handled easily by one person.

Marion A. Speer, a youngster who worked on the construction that summer, recorded his memories in a letter to Morris W. Abbott some years ago. Recalling that in 1903, at the age of 18, he had run away from the family farm in the hill country of Texas, he continued:

It was my ambition to have some schooling that would help me in life or to [do] something better than farming the rough hillsides of a farm in Montague County. I entered the Colorado School of Mines at Golden, Colorado, in the fall of 1903. I finished there in 1909. I did not have a cent when I left Texas. I worked on a farm near Golden for my board and room, mornings, evenings, Saturdays and sometimes Sundays. After the second year, the American Smelting and Refining Company took me over and seen me through school. I followed

166

unusual water tank (improved with wooden insulation) can be seen next to most of the town's buildings. The new Sunnyside mill is back of the branch track to Animas Forks.

mining, gold, and silver, until 1916.

The Silver Lake mine was developed by the Stoibers and by them sold to the American Smelting and Refining Company. I worked there until 1914 when the mine failed to pay expenses.

I had an uncle living at Silverton, Colorado, and to him I went when I left Texas. I was just a kid, small for my age. I could not get any kind of work to do. Otto Mears was getting ready to build the narrow gauge extension from Eureka to Animas Forks. I went to his construction engineer, Mr. Wigglesworth, who gave me a job as a "Nipper". My job was to carry dull tools from the road builders to the blacksmith shop and sharp tools back to the men. It was hard work and when night came I was ready for the bunk. I was not used to the high altitude and this hurt some until I got used to it. I lay my good health and strong body today to my work in the high mountains of Colorado.

One day Mr. Wigglesworth came to me and said that he would have to let me go as the work was too hard for me. This was hard news and I sat down and bawled like a baby. I told him that I was saving my money to go to school that fall. As proof I took him to my bunk and showed him the paper and letters I had from the Colorado School of Mines. He told me to stay on, as anyone who worked like I did needed a break. The next morning he gave me a Mexican or an Indian, I do not know which, to help me out. I had it easy from then until the road was finished to Animas Forks.

On the sixth of August, 1903, Anderson wrote to Mears in Denver advising him that Wigglesworth estimated grading on the extension would be completed by the fifteenth. To speed the work, the road hired about 125 Navajo Indians as construction laborers and paid their fares to Silverton via the Denver and Rio Grande. This gang, supplementing the large force of local men, was put to work on the big fill extending north half-a-mile from the Sunnyside mill at the edge of Eureka.

The Indians were not very diligent laborers, much preferring to drop everything to enjoy the fun and excitement of chasing the numerous marmots (Western woodchucks) playing along the grade. Mears, who had returned to the scene upon receiving Anderson's letter, reacted explosively to such carefree joy and wasted effort; hiring some local lads he gave them each a .22 caliber rifle and instructed them to get rid of the pesky little varmints.

MORRIS W. ABBOTT COLLECTION

Waldheim, the combination mansion-office of Ed and Lena Stoiber, may have been the finest residence of the area. They ran the huge Silver Lake mining complex from this building. Behind Waldheim one can see the powerhouse, together with the bridge over the Rio de las Animas, from which trackage ran into a covered coal shed. The mansion survived until 1945, when it was torn down. The photographer was looking southwest when he shot this picture, with the Silverton Northern mainline in view beside the Animas.

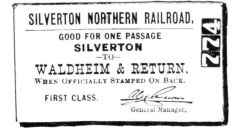

SAN JUAN COUNTY HISTORICAL SOCIETY

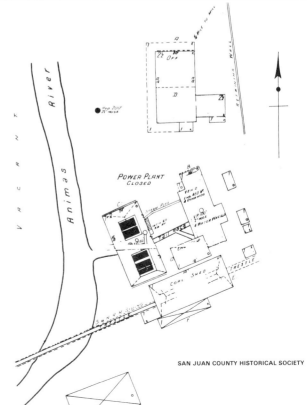

SAN JUAN COUNTY HISTORICAL SOCIETY

SUNDANCE PHOTO BY DELL A. McCOY

The photographer was looking down on the old Silverton Northern grade in this autumn scene. The late fall colors of 1974 brought beauty to the Mayflower mill site (right hand corner). The Mayflower bucket tramway was suspended all the way across the canyon, with only the cables to support it. Silverton is in the far distance, at the base of Sultan Mountain. The Mayflower mill now is operated by the Standard Metals Corporation.

169

THE SILVERTON MINER, 1907 —
MORRIS W. ABBOTT COLLECTION

Howardsville was located near the Rio de las Animas, as shown in this 1903 view — looking toward Sultan Mountain (on the horizon). This was milepost 4.6 on the Silverton Northern. The school house at the far right was the lone survivor among all these buildings in 1975.

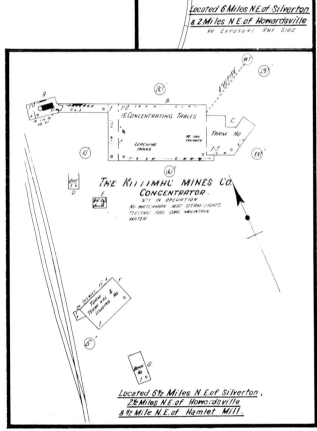

SAN JUAN COUNTY HISTORICAL SOCIETY

No doubt recalling his friendly and successful association with the Utes during his younger days, the old gentleman now tried his hand at bossing a crew of Navajos. This time, however, things were different; neither side could understand the other. When Mears tried to use hand signs to communicate, the Indians only mimicked him. The old man lost his temper at such impertinence, quit trying to be a straw boss, and went back home to Denver in a huff!

On August 14, Anderson advised in yet another letter to Mears that the Indians had been discharged at noon that day; it cost $778.50 to pay them for the 3½ days they had been on the job (including the time spent chasing marmots). Wigglesworth still had a dozen men working on the grade, while two of his engineer corps, also on hand, could not yet be dispensed with—to Anderson's regret. The rails, splice bars and fastenings had left Salt Lake City on the eleventh, being routed by way of the Rio Grande Southern, but had not yet arrived. Nor had the old rails at the end of the Silverton Railroad been brought up from Ironton. Wigglesworth reported that 4,000 feet of grading remained to be done, half of which was in solid rock, an indication that his estimated completion date established earlier in the month was considerably wide of the mark. (In fact, the date was premature by about 15 months!) Cost of construction from the beginning now totalled $9,737.21.

And—oh, yes!—Otto's older daughter, Laura, and her husband, Marshall Smith, had just moved to Silverton. The couple were living in the hotel, and Smith was working on repairs at a mill for $3.00 a day.

On August 21, Anderson ordered the timber for the bridge across Cement Creek on the connecting track through town between his two railroads.

One uncertainty over which Anderson was agonizing was a strike called for the entire San Juan region by "Big Bill" Haywood's Western Federation of Miners. The Silverton miners did not want to go out, it was true, but the prospect of revenues lost from a shutdown of the mines was a worry when the Silverton Northern was spending money hand over fist.

THE SILVERTON MINER, 1907 —
MORRIS W. ABBOTT COLLECTION

The view above shows the Hamlet mill on the Silverton Northern, located near milepost 6. A short spur track served the mill when it was photographed about 1903.

The SN had a short spur to the Kittimac mill at milepost 7 — at Minnie Gulch. In the scene below, SN Number 1 was switching boxcars at this mill.

THE SILVERTON MINER, 1907 —
MORRIS W. ABBOTT COLLECTION

171

SUNDANCE PHOTO BY DELL A. McCOY

Wreckage of the Silver Lake mine litters the foreground in this 1974 view of Silver Lake. Looking southeast, across the lake, you can see the ruins of the Iowa mine, part way up the hillside. On the opposite bank, the Tiger mine stands out at the water's edge. Raw ore from these two mines was partially reduced here before being trammed down to the Iowa-Tiger mill in Arrastra Gulch.

SUNDANCE PHOTO BY DELL A. McCOY

The winter snows of early 1975 made travel into Arrastra Gulch almost impossible, and one cannot help but wonder how hundreds of miners carried on their work at the top of this gulch. The rich Silver Lake mine was high up in the crags — between the two peaks in this view. The abandoned SN railroad grade is just visible at the bottom of this scene, while the Rio de las Animas can be seen on the opposite side of the canyon. Some of the ore from this mine was so rich, it was said that a single carload could make a man rich.

173

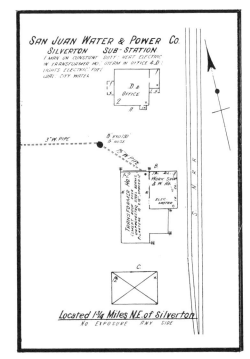

"SAN JUAN COUNTY" BOOKLET — THE SILVERTON STANDARD
MORRIS W. ABBOTT COLLECTION

SAN JUAN COUNTY HISTORICAL SOCIETY

The ore from the Iowa-Tiger mill was trammed down to the lower cableway terminal on the Silverton Northern, about half-a-mile east (or upgrade) from the Silver Lake mill. This 1903 photograph shows a mixture of D&RG and SN 10-ton boxcars, including SN 100, at the near end of the line.

The Silverton, Gladstone & Northerly Railroad had a spur track serving Charles Thompson's dairy at the north end of Silverton in 1907. His dairy cows were pastured south of Silverton during the summer months, and his dairy was known for its very wholesome milk.

THE SILVERTON MINER, 1307 —
MORRIS W. ABBOTT COLLECTION

Candlelight was the light source used by miners stoping-out a vein in the Gold King mine in 1899, as recorded in this view.

"SAN JUAN COUNTY" BOOKLET — THE SILVERTON STANDARD
MORRIS W. ABBOTT COLLECTION

On the second of September, Anderson sent his men to Ironton to get the rail to be used in building the connection between the Silverton and the Silverton Northern. The 21,123 feet of 40-pound rail ordered from the D&RG for the Animas Forks extension, on the other hand, had apparently gotten misplaced somewhere in the transfer from standard to narrow-gauge cars in the Grand Junction yard, and the work to Eureka had to be stopped for lack of rail.

Several days before the month ended, Anderson

174

Here we see an early view of the Highland Mary mine, which was located up near timberline, in a cirque near the head of Cunningham Gulch.

RICHARD A. RONZIO COLLECTION

hired Edward H. Hudson away from the D&RG at Durango. Entered on the payroll as a conductor at $125.00 per month, Hudson much later was to become superintendent of the Silverton Northern.

That period in late September of 1903 was a time both favorable and unfavorable for the two little railroads under Anderson's management. Wigglesworth's original survey for the extension to Animas Forks now was not worth much because the line was being built across the valley on Mears' old toll road. In consequence, a new survey of the branch would be necessary after construction finally was done. With no rail on hand for work on the extension, Wigglesworth brought his crew back into Silverton to prepare for the connecting track and bridge in town.

Business on both roads was bad, and the two engines—Silverton Number 100 and Silverton Northern Number 1—were in poor shape. Anderson ordered a full set of flues for the first locomotive and asked the D&RG's people at Alamosa for the loan of another engine until the "One-Spot" could be fixed.

At last—late in the month—the 40-pound rail arrived from Salt Lake City, having been on the way for more than six weeks. The Denver and Rio Grande immediately presented their statement for $3,224.69 to cover the cost; the amount was for the original full weight, even though the rails were undersize from much previous wear. But Anderson had good news to report to Vice-President C. H. Graham: Mr. Geisel, of the Barstow Mining and Milling Company, operators of the Bobtail mine, was building a $15,000 boarding house for his workmen and would require 100 cars of coal and lumber. While nothing was being shipped currently from the Silver Ledge at Chattanooga, Crawford's plans at Red Mountain were working out and Hammond's tunnel had uncovered a good ore body, five feet in width, in their mine across the valley from the Yankee Girl.

By the first of October, 1903, Anderson had taken charge of the construction work himself, for Wigglesworth had departed; reading between the lines in Anderson's correspondence, it appears that

The Highland Mary mill was located three and one-half miles up Cunningham Gulch — about 1,000 feet higher than Howardsville. Mrs. M. B. Murrell wanted Alex Anderson and Otto Mears to build a spur to her mine in 1901, but the line only made it part way in 1905. This mill was in active production until 1949.

CARL SKOWRONSKI COLLECTION

he and the engineer had quarreled. But now, with the track materials on hand and nowhere else to use the men at the moment, Anderson's pet project ever since his arrival in Silverton seven years before —the connection through town between his two railroads—was underway at last. Cement Street, the first street toward town from the D&RG depot, did not have much traffic and Anderson persuaded the town fathers to let him use a portion of the thoroughfare as the route for the connection.

Although the timbers needed for the two small trestles over Cement Creek — ordered from the D&RG in mid-August — had not yet arrived, Anderson put his trackmen to work installing the switch for the connection in the Silverton Northern mainline on the east bank of Cement Creek, and a diamond crossing frog in the adjacent D&RG spur leading to the Silverton, Gladstone and Northerly. When the bridges over the creek were built, the new track would lead south down Cement Street some seven blocks. There it would turn to the right on a 20-degree curve, run up Sixth Street for three blocks to another 20-degree curve to the left just beyond Greene Street, and finally join the Silverton Railroad out on the tail of the D&RG wye over on the west edge of town, near Fifth and Snowden streets, where the two roads connected just below Gus Stoiber's sampling works.

Someone must have been spying for the D&RG, for in the midst of the work, Anderson received a letter from H. E. Whittenberger, superintendent of the D&RG's Fourth Division at Alamosa, scolding him for installing the crossing frog so near the bridge over Cement Creek; and, even worse, for connecting into the D&RG track at Fifth Street without permission. However, Anderson—presuming that all arrangements had been made—had merely followed the orders given him by Otto Mears.

The trestles were in and the main track of the connection was finished by October 15, 1903. Anderson wanted to install two extra sidings along the connection in the area of the D&RG yard, but some of the big road's trackage was in the way and there is no evidence that the D&RG ever moved its line to accommodate the SN. A spur was put down, however, to the Doyle Machine Shop on Cement

A whisper of a chill breeze skittered across beautiful Silver Lake as this photograph was recorded on Ektachrome film. In this late summer scene you are facing directly toward Kendall Peak. One of the pit-heads of the Iowa-Tiger mines is visible on the far shore (to the left), while the second, and larger one can be seen along the near shore. The tailings are from the Silver Lake mine (at far right) and have nearly cut the lake in half.

SUNDANCE PHOTO BY DELL A. McCOY

176

MORRIS W. ABBOTT COLLECTION

Fisher's mill — on the SG&N — was located beside the wandering shortline's main track. In this view, taken in 1902, you are looking upstream, toward Gladstone.

Street, in the block between Tenth and Eleventh streets, and it is entirely possible that Doyle's facilities saw some use as a backshop for both of the Mears roads.

The connection through town between the Silverton Northern and the line over Red Mountain Pass, sad to relate, lasted hardly a year longer than Anderson had agonized over the problem before it was built. In 1911 or 1912, when the Silverton Northern enginehouse was erected in the block between Eighth and Ninth streets, beside Cement Street—and the SG&N was being operated as part of the Mears empire—all the rail in the connection from the enginehouse over to the Silverton Railroad was pulled up.

During the brief period that construction of the connection was being handled, the D&RG master mechanic at Alamosa, P. Gratz, tried to furnish an engine to substitute for the two ailing Mears loco-

motives at Silverton. In the process, four different Class 60 2-8-0's, built for the D&RG by both Grant and Baldwin in the heyday of the narrow-gauge more than 20 years previously, were offered. The first locomotive, Grant-built Number 216, arrived on October 6; it had flanges on the center drivers and thus could not negotiate the curves on the Silverton Railroad. Anderson sent it back and asked for a Class 56 engine, Number 65. Without regard to that request, though, engine Number 201, another Grant, arrived on October 19. It turned out to be useless, with four blisters on the firebox, a crack in the side sheet, 30 flues and 6 staybolts leaking, and it was so lame it could not haul anything up the Red Mountain road. On the twenty-first, Baldwin locomotive Number 285 arrived; and, like the others, it was of no use, for it continually derailed on curves owing to excessive endplay in the axles of the blind drivers, caused by

The Boston & Silverton Mining & Reduction Company's "Yukon mill" was located at milepost 3.4, on the east side of the Silverton, Gladstone & Northerly. This was at the mouth of Illinois Gulch. The Yukon mill was a major producer of concentrate when this scene was recorded in 1903.

"SAN JUAN COUNTY" BOOKLET — THE SILVERTON STANDARD
MORRIS W. ABBOTT COLLECTION

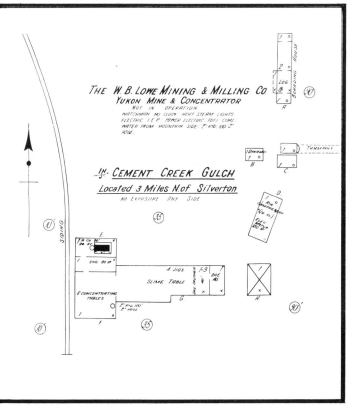

SAN JUAN COUNTY HISTORICAL SOCIETY

FREIGHT BILL.

Silverton Station,_____190____

To THE SILVERTON, GLADSTONE & NORTHERLY RAILROAD CO., Dr.

For Transportation and Advanced Charges, from_____Via_____

BILLING REFERENCE	DESCRIPTION OF ARTICLES	SEPARATE WEIGHT	WEIGHT	RATE	AMOUNT
Pro. No.					
W. B. No.					
Date of W. B.					
Car Initials,					
Car No.					
Consignor,					
(Give complete reference.)	Total,				

This form is the only authorized receipt to be given for payment of Freight Bills.

Received payment,_____190____

_____Agent.

SUNDANCE PHOTO BY DELL A. McCOY

The ore buckets were swaying in the breeze as they awaited the resumption of operations at the Mayflower mine — high above the valley in Arrastra Gulch. Outlined in the snow, you can perceive the trail to Silver Lake, cutting its way up the mountainside.

This Silverton Northern switch lock (see at right) was found near the SN enginehouse by Tom Pollock. The patent date was September of 1912, with "SN Ry" stamped in the hasp.

WILLIAM PLUNKETT PHOTO

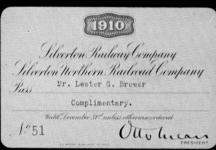

These examples of the Silverton shortline paper passes were issued over a period of years by Otto Mears. One of the original buckskin passes is shown in the upper lefthand corner.

Insulators which were once used along the Rainbow Route are (from left to right): from the power line found at *the Knob* on Red Mountain (Hemingway patented, 1893); from a telegraph line along the Silverton Northern (purpled with age, but originally was clear); and from the telegraph line at Red Mountain (patented May 2, 1893).

WILLIAM PLUNKETT PHOTO

181

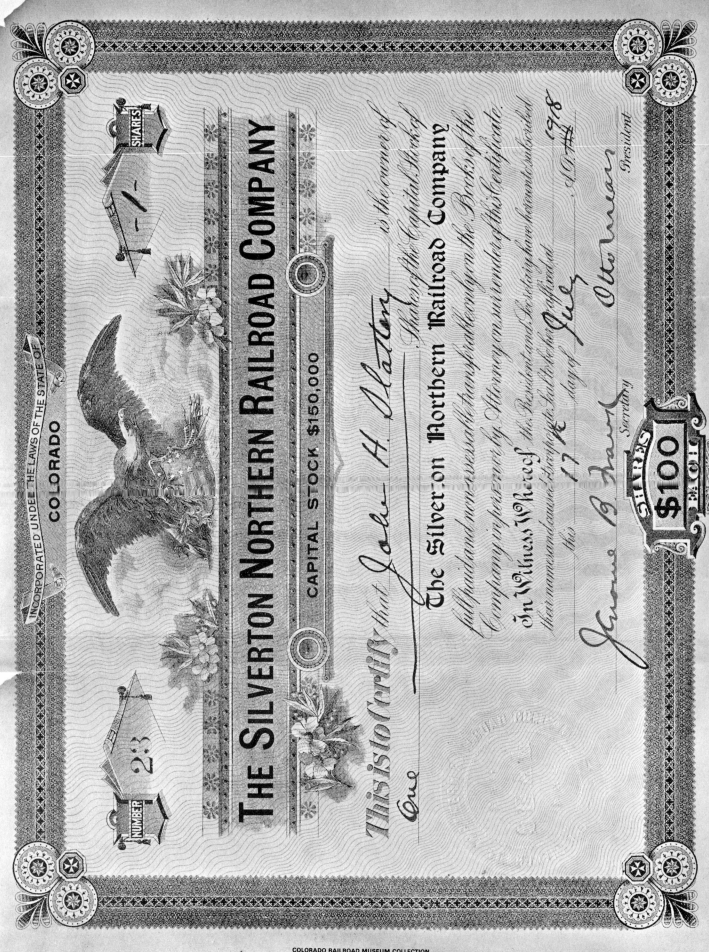

THE SILVERTON NORTHERN RAILROAD COMPANY

INCORPORATED UNDER THE LAWS OF THE STATE OF
COLORADO

CAPITAL STOCK $150,000

SHARES
$100 EACH

NUMBER 23

SHARES —1—

This is to certify that John H. Slattery is the owner of One Share of the Capital Stock of The Silverton Northern Railroad Company

full paid and non-assessable transferable only on the Books of the Company in person or by Attorney on surrender of this Certificate.

In Witness Whereof the President and Secretary have hereunto subscribed their names and caused our Corporate Seal to be hereaffixed this 17th day of July 19 # 1918

James B. Davis
Secretary

Otto man
President

COLORADO RAILROAD MUSEUM COLLECTION

wornout hub plates. Finally, on the twenty-fifth, engine Number 281, another Baldwin product, arrived, and—to the relief of all—proved to be satisfactory.

Anderson had directed an inquiry to the Chicago Car and Locomotive Works about used engines which might be available. The number, "2," apparently was reserved in the roster for such an engine, but in the end, the available locomotives were not suitable—one was too small, the other had too long a rigid wheelbase for those tight 30-degree curves.

When Anderson wrote to Mears late in October, he suggested that the Silverton Northern needed a new locomotive—not a cast-off from the Denver and Rio Grande—the next year. It looked as though the roads would need 10,000 ties in 1904; prices had risen to 36 cents a tie and the Denver and Rio Grande was taking all it could get from around Rockwood. And now that the big road was using its new 30-foot, 25-ton cars with a gross loaded weight of 75,000 pounds in interchange service, the bridges on the Silverton Railroad, especially the high trestle over Porphyry Creek near the top of the pass, probably were too weak to withstand the added weight. As a final vexation, the D&RG was taking all the coal that could be mined around Durango, and could not be talked into giving any to the two little roads headquartered in Silverton.

On November 10, Anderson advised Mears of the reductions he had made in train schedules for the winter on the Silverton Northern. Three trains now were operating daily—a passenger train at 6:00 a.m., a mixed train at 10:00 a.m., and another passenger train at 4:00 p.m. Traffic was averaging 70 passengers a day at 25 cents per passenger. He planned to send the Company's engine Number 1 to Alamosa for repairs about March 15; cost of the work probably would run about $2,000.

When the Big Five Tunnel, Ore Reduction and Transportation Company appropriated water from Hematite Creek for their milling operations at Howardsville, Anderson succeeded in having the company also put in a standpipe for the railroad as a settlement to avoid litigation. Then the Denver and Rio Grande loosened up on the coal supply at Durango and Anderson just managed to lay-in 200 tons, enough to last for three months during the winter.

The altitude at Silverton, combined with the effects of the constant encounters with the Siberian-type climate found at Red Mountain Pass and Animas Forks, finally took its toll of Anderson's health, and about the first of 1904 he was forced to

seek a lower elevation and more moderate climate to recover from his high-altitude sickness. Hence he decided to return to Scotland for a visit with his mother. T. J. McKelvey, who had started as agent for the Silverton Railroad at Red Mountain town in 1892, and then moved to Silverton as agent for both of the Mears roads in 1899, temporarily assumed the job of running the roads during Anderson's absence.

McKelvey continued Anderson's practice of submitting periodic reports, and informed Mears that Master Mechanic W. E. Booker had recommended installation of an automatic sander on engine Number 1 while it was in the shop. This would feed sand automatically, both ahead of the drivers in forward motion, and behind the third pair when backing up. He also wanted to put a new Ohio injector on the right-hand side, replace the old obsolete six-inch air pump with a larger eight or nine-and-a-half-inch pump, and thought consideration should be given to replacing the link-and-pin drawheads on the engine with automatic couplers. McKelvey also told Mears that his new son-in-law, Marshall Smith, apparently did not care to learn railroading, seeming to prefer the mining game to any other business.

On his return from Scotland on March 23, 1904, Anderson stopped off to visit Mears and the two men signed a contract to purchase from the Baldwin works a new Class 76, inside-frame Consolidation (2-8-0) for the Silverton Northern. Assembled by early May under construction number 24107, the engine and tender reached Pueblo on a pair of flatcars on May 17, and after being moved over to Alamosa sometime during the following four days, the locomotive and tender were unloaded May 21 onto the narrow-gauge rails in the Denver and Rio Grande yard. There they were switched to an out-of-the-way spot where they could await the arrival of Silverton Northern Master Mechanic Booker and the man from the Baldwin Locomotive Works to "set up" the engine by installing the side and main rods, coupling the engine and tender together, connecting up water and air hoses, and making all the numerous other final adjustments required before the engine could be fired up for the first time. Assigned road number "3," this welcome engine was the first brand-new motive power for the Mears roads since the Shay—finally going into service on the Silverton Northern on June 9, 1904.

The Silverton, Gladstone and Northerly also had ordered a new locomotive from Baldwin at about the same time; this engine, too, was assembled in May of 1904. A Class 88 outside-frame Consolidation, built under construction number 24130, it

SILVERTON NORTHERN R. R.
COMPANY

60 Ride Commutation Ticket.

Form L 60   No. 414

BETWEEN

SILVERTON

AND

HOWARDSVILLE

FOR
OR ANY MEMBER OF HIS FAMILY
If used within sixty days from date of sale
to be stamped hereon.

NOT GOOD ON TRAINS NOT SCHED-
ULED TO STOP AT STATIONS NAMED

POOLE BROS. CHICAGO

SILVERTON NORTHERN R. R.
COMPANY

60 Ride Commutation Ticket

Form L 60   No. 390

BETWEEN

SILVERTON

AND

WALDHEIM

FOR
OR ANY MEMBER OF HIS FAMILY
If used within sixty days from date of sale
to be stamped hereon.

NOT GOOD ON TRAINS NOT SCHED-
ULED TO STOP AT STATIONS NAMED

POOLE BROS. CHICAGO

THE S. G. & N. R. R. CO.
UNLIMITED TICKET
GOOD FOR ONE FIRST CLASS PASSAGE
WHEN STAMPED ON BACK

GLADSTONE to SILVERTON

No. 4464

The S. G. & N. R. R. Co.
UNLIMITED TICKET
Good for One First Class Passage
when Stamped on Back.

Silverton to Fisher's Mill

No. 590

THE SILVERTON NORTHERN RAILROAD CO.
Gladstone Branch.
UNLIMITED TICKET
GOOD FOR ONE FIRST CLASS PASSAGE
WHEN STAMPED ON BACK.
SILVERTON TO GLADSTONE
NO. 11858

THE SILVERTON NORTHERN RAILROAD CO
Gladstone Branch
UNLIMITED TICKET
GOOD FOR ONE FIRST CLASS PASSAGE
WHEN STAMPED ON BACK.
Gladstone to Silverton
NO. 11858

The S. G. & N. R. R. Co.
UNLIMITED TICKET
Silverton to Mammoth
No. 1521

The S. G. & N. R. R. Co.
UNLIMITED TICKET
Mammoth to Silverton
No. 1521

SILVERTON NORTHERN R. R.
COMPANY

60 Ride Commutation Ticket.

Form L 60   No. 157

BETWEEN

SILVERTON

AND

ASTOR

FOR
OR ANY MEMBER OF HIS FAMILY
If used within sixty days from date of sale
to be stamped hereon.

NOT GOOD ON TRAINS NOT SCHED-
ULED TO STOP AT STATIONS NAMED

POOLE BROS. CHICAGO

SILVERTON NORTHERN R. R.
COMPANY

60 Ride Commutation Ticket.

Form L 60   No. 79

BETWEEN

SILVERTON

AND

EUREKA

FOR
OR ANY MEMBER OF HIS FAMILY
If used within sixty days from date of sale
to be stamped hereon.

NOT GOOD ON TRAINS NOT SCHED-
ULED TO STOP AT STATIONS NAMED

POOLE BROS. CHICAGO

6-15-15-1-500
THE SILVERTON NORTHERN R. R. CO.
J. B. PITCHER, JR., General Manager.

100 MILE TICKET.
Form 7.
No. A 242

Agent will detach this stub and
return with weekly report to Auditor.

ISSUED TO

Of

GOOD BETWEEN ALL STATIONS ON
THE SILVERTON NORTHERN RAILROAD,
THE SILVERTON RAILWAY,
THE SILVERTON, GLADSTONE & NORTHERLY
RAILROAD.

STAMP DATE OF
SALE HERE

AUDITOR'S STUB.
To be taken up by Conductor upon pre-
sentation of first mileage and returned with
report.

STAMP DATE OF
SALE HERE

No. A 242
Form 7.

6-15-15-1-500
THE SILVERTON NORTHERN R. R. CO.
J. B. PITCHER, JR., General Manager.

300 MILE TICKET.
Form 6.
No. B 393

Agent will detach this stub and
return with weekly report to Auditor.

ISSUED TO

Of

GOOD BETWEEN ALL STATIONS ON
THE SILVERTON NORTHERN RAILROAD,
THE SILVERTON RAILWAY,
THE SILVERTON, GLADSTONE & NORTHERLY
RAILROAD.

Form 7   No. A 242
THE SILVERTON NORTHERN R. R. CO.
J. B. PITCHER, JR., General Manager.

100 MILE TICKET.

ISSUED FOR THE USE OF

When officially stamped and countersigned
by the ticket agent and upon the conditions
named in the contract attached to and made
part hereof.

THIS TICKET IS GOOD BETWEEN ALL
STATIONS ON
THE SILVERTON NORTHERN RAILROAD,
THE SILVERTON RAILWAY,
THE SILVERTON, GLADSTONE & NORTHERLY
RAILROAD.

Not good unless officially stamped and
countersigned by ticket agent.

Agent.

Date Sold

No. B 393
THE SILVERTON NORTHERN R. R. CO.
J. B. PITCHER, JR., General Manager.

300 MILE TICKET.

ISSUED FOR THE USE OF

When officially stamped and countersigned
by the ticket agent and upon the conditions
named in the contract attached to and made
part hereof.

THIS TICKET IS GOOD BETWEEN ALL
STATIONS ON
THE SILVERTON NORTHERN RAILROAD,
THE SILVERTON RAILWAY,
THE SILVERTON, GLADSTONE & NORTHERLY
RAILROAD.

Not good unless officially stamped and
countersigned by ticket agent.

Agent.

Date Sold

MORRIS W. ABBOTT COLLECTION

Opposite page — as you can see, printing at the turn of the century could be as colorful and ornate as anything produced today. With these interesting tickets, a commuter could travel on the SG&N and the SN for a very long time.

MORRIS W. ABBOTT COLLECTION

Silverton Northern locomotive Number 1 was rolling downgrade toward Silverton with three D&RG freight cars and the Silverton Railroad's caboose. Notice the brakeman decorating the top of one of the boxcars, ready to apply the handbrakes in case of emergency. The lamp on top of the caboose aided the engineer in backing at night. One question arises about this scene: Where is the harp switchstand for the Silver Lake spur?

185

SILVER LAKE MILL

RICHARD A. RONZIO COLLECTION

The photograph on this page presents a different view of the Silver Lake mill. Taken sometime after 1907, the mill yard had had two more spur tracks added, while the main mill structure was a new building altogether. A disastrous fire probably brought this about. Notice that there were far fewer skylights in the new structure. The accompanying drawing clarifies the complexity of the mill trackage and buildings.

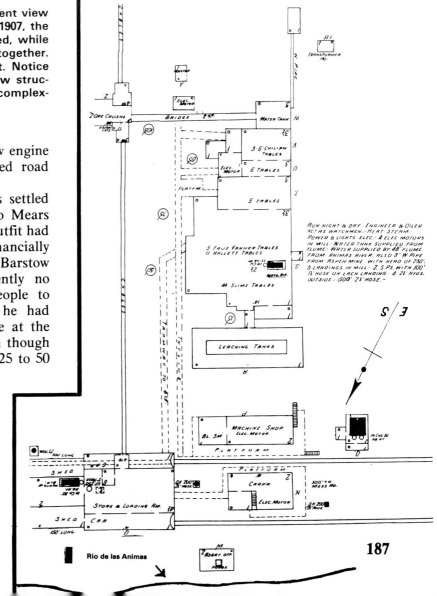

was slightly larger and heavier than the new engine on the Silverton Northern. It was assigned road number 34.

By April 21, Anderson once again was settled down in Silverton and sent off a letter to Mears reporting that Geisel of the Bobtail mine outfit had offered to assist the Silverton Railroad, financially or otherwise, in building the spur for the Barstow Mining and Milling Company. (Apparently no pressure was applied by the Bobtail people to make Anderson replace the rail which he had borrowed to build the additional trackage at the Silver Ledge during the fall of 1902.) Even though Geisel held forth the enticing promise of 25 to 50

Opposite page — during the fall of 1903, the Silver Lake mill was concentrating ore by the trainload. The pithead was near the top of Kendall Mountain, and ore traveled to the mill via cable tramway. The Silver Lake mill was the biggest producer on the Silverton Northern, turning out over $7-million-worth of ore.

DENVER PUBLIC LIBRARY WESTERN COLLECTION

187

DENVER PUBLIC LIBRARY WESTERN COLLECTION

This closeup view of D&RG engine Number 281 shows her switching cars on the SN during the late fall of 1903. This 2-8-0 was leased to the SN during the period when the railroad was converting to automatic couplers. A brakeman was uncoupling the engine in preparation for the cars to be shoved to the far track in the Silver Lake mill yard. The harp switch stand had already been positioned for the switching move. The mill was still in the midst of a construction program, as later photographs reveal more buildings and additional trackage.

188

THOMAS T. TABER COLLECTION

Silverton Northern Number 3, shown above, was fresh from the Baldwin works in the summer of 1904, and was double-heading a train with SN Number 1. Master Mechanic William E. Booker was performing an inspection job on the locomotive at Silverton.

tons of ore daily for the railroad, Anderson had to reply that the work could not be done until after the snow disappeared. Engine Number 100 was hardly fit to run in the yard and Anderson planned to send it to the shop at Alamosa as soon as he could line up the loan of a spare from the Denver and Rio Grande.

Despite agent McKelvey's reservations about Marshall Smith's interest in railroading, Mears told Anderson to put the son-in-law on the payroll, and Smith was given charge of the gang handling the grading on the extension to Animas Forks. In early May of 1904, Smith began work at the rock cut above Picayune Gulch, while Anderson followed along with the track gang. However, progress was extremely slow; Wigglesworth, it now appeared, had grossly underestimated the difficulty and cost of clearing rock from the grade, and additional delay was incurred during the second

week of the month when tons of rock and dirt— loosened in the spring thaw—slid down onto the grade already built. By May 23, with leased Denver and Rio Grande engine Number 208 serving on the construction train, the track was laid only as far as the Tom Moore mine, about a mile and a half above Eureka.

* * * * * * *

It is not inappropriate here to diverge for a moment to concern ourselves with the performance of Thomas Wigglesworth. This experienced civil engineer was no novice in mountain railroad construction, having served well and capably on much of the expansion of the Denver and Rio Grande in the early 1880's, as well as during the later construction of the Colorado Midland and Rio Grande Southern lines—in expansionist times —with seemingly limitless money supplies. It is not

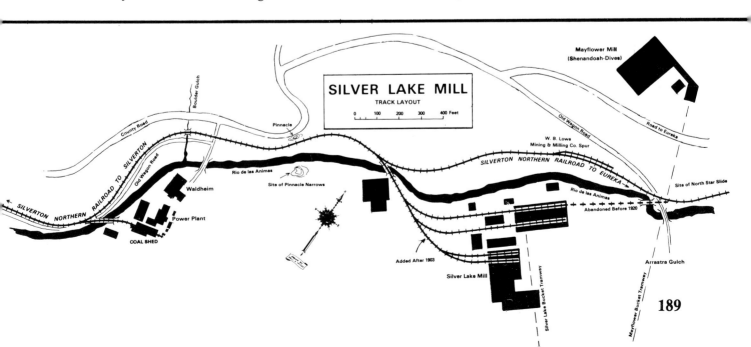

Opposite page — looking northwest across Silver Lake, the Iowa-Tiger mine buildings can be seen to the far left, while the Silver Lake mine and original mill are in view in the center. Arrastra Gulch is just beyond the lake, over a sheer cliff. Storm Peak and Tower Mountain are in the distance. The Iowa-Tiger used a cableway to move their ore from the other pithead (on the right, out of sight). The ore from both pitheads was partially processed in the complex in view. It then was transported by the second cableway over the ridge of Kendall Mountain (left center) and down to the mill in Arrastra Gulch. The Silver Lake mine moved their ore down through Arrastra Gulch by another cable line to their mill on the Silverton Northern. Snowfences to guard against avalanches are discernable on the hillside above the Silver Lake mine buildings.

SAN JUAN COUNTY HISTORICAL SOCIETY

THE SILVERTON MINER, 1907 —
MORRIS W. ABBOTT COLLECTION

This Silverton "streetcar" had a full load, as reported in one of the *Silverton Standard's* promotional books.

believable that he now would be incapable of estimating accurately the grading requirements on the extension of the Silverton Northern between Eureka and Animas Forks. Having gained considerable insight during the RGS days into the attitudes, outlook and methods of handling men characteristic of Otto Mears, it is much more probable that he hesitated to give the old man—all in one jolt—the true picture and the costs involved. To do so would have meant, quite probably, the loss of his job—on the spot—and such work was not in abundant supply in the early 1900's.

* * * * * * *

Four-thousand tons of ore had been stockpiled during the winter months at Red Mountain, primarily by George Crawford, awaiting movement on the Silverton Railroad during the spring of 1904, but before this tonnage could be handled, considerable work was required to reopen the road. Anderson did not have enough engines to provide power for the necessary work train, and got off a telegram to Gratz, the D&RG's master mechanic at Alamosa, asking that the repairs to Silverton Northern Number 1 be hurried and the engine returned as soon as possible.

Anderson also requested W. A. Morey, engineer in charge of the Bridge and Building Department of the D&RG in Denver, to arrange for McNamara's bridge gang to erect two new timber trestles

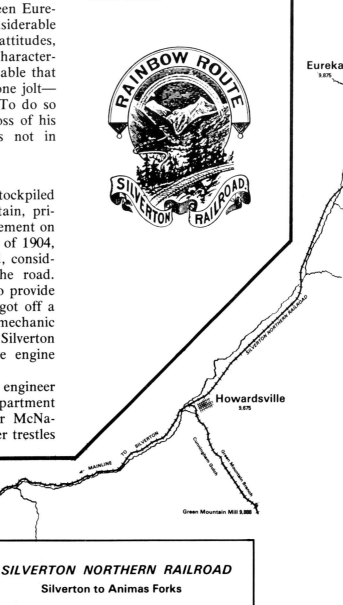

SILVERTON NORTHERN RAILROAD

Silverton to Animas Forks

0   ½   1 Mile

SUNDANCE PHOTO BY DELL A. McCOY

Opposite page — Silver Lake, a *tarn,* or bedrock lake, was carved out by one of the glaciers that sharpened all the peaks of the San Juan Range. This body of water was the spectacular setting for both the Silver Lake mine and original mill, and the Iowa-Tiger mining complex. The Silver Lake mine buildings are the only ones plainly visible in this scene. The large four-story structure was a boarding house for workers, and had the distinction of "featuring" an attached four-story privy. The peak of Kendall Mountain is in the background. Since the entire area is above timberline, no trees can grow here, only tundra vegetation.

SAN JUAN COUNTY HISTORICAL SOCIETY

In the scene above, you are looking down from nearly the same elevation as Silver Lake — along the narrow trail leading down into Arrastra Gulch. Beyond is the canyon of the Rio de las Animas. The trail zig-zags down through the rockslides, past the Mayflower mine buildings (at the base of the cliff at right). Past the Mayflower mine, an old wagon road winds down through the gulch into the Animas Canyon — where the Mayflower mill and dump stand out prominently.

on the Animas Forks extension — one of five panels, the other a larger, eight-panel structure. Anticipating the requirements for the several sidings and spurs at Animas Forks, he also ordered the parts for four number six and four number nine stub switches.

Crawford was applying increased pressure to get the Silverton Railroad opened to Red Mountain so his ore could be moved. From the opposite side, Mears was applying pressure to get the Animas Forks Branch finished as soon as possible. Anderson's right-hand man in the office was about to quit; Wigglesworth, although his work had been left undone the previous fall, did not return after having departed in a huff over his dispute with the manager. The track and rock gangs on the extension were too far apart for Anderson to supervise properly all by himself.

A bit of welcome relief appeared on May 28 when Silverton Northern engine Number 1 finally showed up after being overhauled. Anderson's pleasure, however, was very brief, for everything else now seemed to fall apart. Alamosa refused to accept Silverton Number 100 for overhaul ahead of 12 other engines needing work and already standing in line. T. J. McKelvey, the thoroughly competent agent at Silverton—who also handled much of the office work for Anderson—resigned on June 1 to start a general store at Animas Forks. Not only had the balance of the rail for the extension, on order from the Denver and Rio Grande, failed to show up, but the supply of ties had run out, and Anderson could find no empty cars to send after more. Marshall Smith's 16-man rock gang was costing $54.00 a day, and although composed of the most qualified men from the track crew, the men were encountering extremely slow going.

Desperate to placate the increasingly irritated Crawford and keep his track men busy, while the rock gang hacked away at the unyielding granite, Anderson sent some of the crew over to the Red Mountain line and put them to work repairing track. This lasted for less than two days; Mears, thinking his men on the ground had progressed with their work on the extension much farther than was really the case, was far less concerned with reopening the "Silverton and Red Mountain line" than in getting the new branch open. In unmistakable terms, Anderson was ordered to cease work on Red Mountain Pass and get the men back at work on the new line. Then, when Anderson went to the "front," he found that some of the grading done by Marshall Smith—particularly in the area just north of Cinnamon Creek—could not be used at all!

Tactfully and carefully—avoiding any mention of this latter problem in his next report to Mears—Anderson pointed out that the son-in-law was a very reliable employee, took much interest in the work in his charge, and was of great assistance. Mears also was advised that Geisel's company was going to advance the money necessary for the spur to the Barstow Mining and Milling Company mill; just as soon as C. W. Gibbs (the very same civil engineer, of course, who had laid out the Silverton Railroad some 17 years before) returned from the East, Anderson planned to have him stake out the line for the spur. In the meantime, Geisel was loading his ore at the Yankee Girl.

Finally—to top all the other problems—frame bridge 470-A on the Denver and Rio Grande's

Walsh House

McKelvey's Store & Post Office

Gold Prince Bucket Tramway

Kinney Street

Hanson Street

Gold Prince Mill

Proposed Frisco Mine Extension

ANIMAS FORKS

TRACK LAYOUT

0   100   200   300   400   500

Feet

Siding 510 Feet

50-Foot Turntable

MAINLINE TO SILVERTON

End-of-Track

Silverton Branch just above Rockwood had burned out, and Anderson was having to run a crew 26 miles down there and back each day with a train to meet the daily passenger run from Durango.

On June 2 the injector on rented D&RG engine Number 208, whose none-too-good condition now was reflecting the further rigors of hard daily work, quit outright. Anderson returned the locomotive to the owner in disgust, anticipating the arrival of the Silverton Northern's brand-new Baldwin engine, Number 3, out there somewhere along the narrow-gauge enroute to Silverton. He also ordered timbers for reinforcing the bridges between Silverton and Eureka so that the road could handle the new 25-ton D&RG cars which were showing up ever more frequently.

His relief at receiving—at last—the first brand-new locomotive to be owned by the road was tempered somewhat on June 9 by the unsettling discovery that when filled with water, coal and supplies, ready for work, she was heavier than ordered. Only the insertion of more ties in the track, to support the additional weight, would make it possible to use her regularly without danger.

Track-laying on the extension, due to the chronic shortage of rail, was averaging only 66 feet (or little more than two rail lengths) per day. When the additional rail on order for so long finally did arrive a week later, it was found to include a lot of 35-pound material, as well as some badly worn stuff, and time had to be taken to sort out the best rail for use.

While Marshall Smith continued grading work through late June and July, track construction continued, also; at some places along the new extension, the track just could not be laid over the surveyor's stakes since Wigglesworth had put in several "streetcar curves" to avoid the masses of solid granite along the way. Anderson's plea for help was answered by the loan of a young Denver and Rio Grande civil engineer to rework the survey, Arthur Ridgway.

Confronted not only with the problems of operation and construction, Anderson also was faced with money difficulties; he had been able to meet the May payroll from funds on hand, but now had to arrange a loan of $10,000 to cover the June payroll, the payment for the rail, and an expenditure for half the cost of the new engine ($8,648.75), Number 3. He was able to borrow $2,000 from good old dependable Fred Walsen, and also succeeded in arranging a $9,000 line of credit from Alfred P. Camp of the First National Bank of Durango—with an interest rate of eight percent for both loans.

Through July 21, construction costs of the Silverton Northern's extension from Eureka toward Animas Forks totalled $31,050, and Anderson

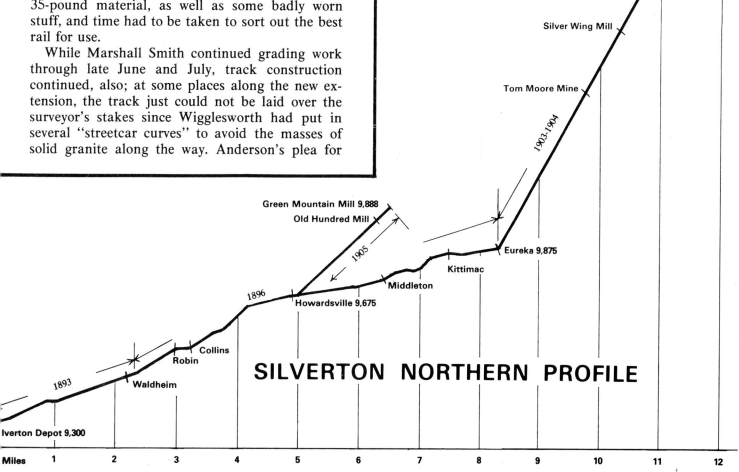

SILVERTON NORTHERN PROFILE

Animas Forks 11,080

Lion Tunnel

Sioux Mine

Silver Wing Mill

Tom Moore Mine

1903-1904

Green Mountain Mill 9,888

Old Hundred Mill

1905

Kittimac

Eureka 9,875

Middleton

1896

Howardsville 9,675

Collins

Robin

Waldheim

1893

Iverton Depot 9,300

Miles 1   2   3   4   5   6   7   8   9   10   11   12

DELL A. McCOY WATERCOLOR

The turntable at Animas Forks is the subject of this water color reproduction — with Silverton Northern locomotive Number 3 being turned before heading back down the branch to Eureka and Silverton. This 50-foot steam-driven turntable was at 11,100 feet elevation, near the end-of-track on the SN's Animas Forks Branch. The year represented is 1905. Originally this turntable was at Marshall Pass on the D&RG. Niagara Peak is directly above the turntable and locomotive.

196

could not again avoid raising his estimate for the whole job—this time to $40,000 (still a long way from the actual final cost, as will be seen). James McNamara's bridge gang arrived on August 2 to put in the new bridges; faced with the cost of this "foreign" labor, Mears contributed $5,000 to help meet the payroll. And now the weather entered the picture as an important factor, for the usually lovely fall days in the high country turned to almost continuous rain. Under such conditions, every move of the work train was risky, for the rails insisted in spreading on the green ties under the weight of the engine and cars.

Fifty-seven-hundred feet of track remained to be built; in the miserable weather less than 500 feet were being spiked down daily, and there was still the grading to be finished at Animas Forks, where the flat in the floor of the valley had to be built-up to accommodate all the necessary switches, spurs, sidings and a turntable.

By August 15, 1904, Master Mechanic Gratz of Alamosa—having finally been able to squeeze in Silverton engine Number 100 for work a bit earlier in the summer—finished the overhaul at a cost of $2,000 and the pioneer locomotive was sent home with a D&RG engineer at the throttle. The track on the extension, at last, was across the Rio de las Animas bridge at Grouse Gulch and in a week was expected to reach Cinnamon Creek where the second and smaller of the two bridges was being built by McNamara's gang. Mears, obviously disappointed with the performance of Marshall Smith, on the sixteenth abruptly sent his son-in-law off to Salt Lake City. Anderson discharged the least-productive men on the track crew and hoped to work more economically with the remainder; Mears, very clearly, was upset by all the delays which had occurred.

Unpaid bills for the most recent construction work amounted to $4,000 and the $2,000 obligation for the overhaul of engine Number 100 was still owed to the D&RG. The regular August payroll was $1,400, the construction payroll for the month totaled $3,000, and a $1,000 payment was due the Mack Brothers Motor Car Company of Allentown, Pennsylvania, for a railbus being built by the firm at the order of President Mears. But attention was required for other necessities as well, and on August 28, Anderson ordered two more cars of yellow pine ties from A. T. Sullenberger of Pagosa Springs for the Silverton Railroad.

Anderson managed to accumulate $2,000 before the payrolls had to be met on September 10, and in a letter more stiff and formal than usual (apparently he felt he was in the doghouse), he expressed his regrets to Mears about some of the

blunders that had been made (evidently by Marshall Smith), including some grading that was wide enough for double track.

At the meeting of the Silverton Northern's board of directors on September 7, 1904, Mears prematurely reported completion of the branch (in fact, more than two additional months would pass before construction was finished), and the board authorized payment to Mears' construction company of $27,000 in cash and $80,000 in first mortgage bonds in order to gain possession of the title to the extension.

The second-hand 50-foot iron turntable for turning engines at the end of the extension at Animas Forks arrived on October 1, 1904. Built by the Keystone Bridge Company of Pittsburgh, Pennsylvania, from plans drawn by Joseph A. Beaumont and dated February 26, 1881, it had been installed originally at the summit of Marshall Pass on the Denver and Rio Grande's narrow-gauge mainline between Denver and Salt Lake City.

On October 7—about the time the turntable was being hauled up to Animas Forks—Alexander Anderson sent a telegram to Arthur Ridgway, who had returned to his temporary job on location with the Rio Grande and South Western Railroad near Lumberton, New Mexico, after rectifying the streetcar curves in Wigglesworth's survey. Ridgway, if he wanted the work, would be hired as superintendent of the two Mears railroads, with the additional responsibility of engineering, locating and supervising construction of another branch off the Silverton Northern up Cunningham Gulch. A contractor from Pueblo would be hired to handle the construction itself. Plainly, Mears and Anderson had learned an expensive lesson—the hard way!

Mr. Madding's gang finished putting in the turntable at Animas Forks about November 6, 1904, and the last of the rail, 2,400 feet of 30-pound material, arrived shortly thereafter. Now, nine weeks after Otto Mears had officially notified the board of directors of its completion, the extension to Animas Forks finally was finished.

The investment totaled $107,169—or about $27,000 per mile, very expensive for a branch-line—and especially for one to be used only for about 12 years, from 1904 to 1916.

No doubt there was a great sigh of relief, and great joy as well, in the Mears camp at the completion of this four-mile addition to the Silverton Northern Railroad. Certainly there appeared every justification for having built the extension; a veritable flood of traffic descended upon the railroad immediately after the construction was done.

SAN JUAN COUNTY HISTORICAL SOCIETY

Opposite page — this view was taken looking down Eureka Gulch at Lake Emma and the Sunnyside mine at an elevation of 12,250 feet. Lake Emma is a *tarn,* or glacially-scoured-bedrock lake and is surrounded on all but one side by the highest mountains in the region, Hanson Peak (to the left), Hurricane Peak (directly behind the camera) and Bonita Peak (to the right). Begun in 1873, the Sunnyside mine eventually was connected by tunnels from the Gold King and Gold Prince mines. Today it is once again a producing mine, currently being worked by the Standard Metals Corporation.

SAN JUAN COUNTY HISTORICAL SOCIETY

Here, we see the Sunnyside mill and halfway house on the east side of Bonita Peak, between the mine at Lake Emma and Eureka. The cable tramway ran through this first mill, which partially processed the ore. Notice the wooden box inside the trestlework. This was filled with rock and was used to pull up slack in the cableway. The Sunnyside mine is 1,500 feet higher in elevation and two miles farther up Eureka Gulch. Eureka and the main Sunnyside mill (now abandoned) was 750 feet below and two miles down the gulch. The halfway house allowed buckets to transfer between two separate cables, permitting the cableway to run in two sections, each two miles in length.

At the head of Mastodon Gulch, the Gold Prince Mines Company, owned by Cyrus Davis and Henry Soule, also vice-president and treasurer, respectively, of the Silverton, Gladstone and Northerly, was expanding its mine at a furious pace. On one side of the small basin at the lower edge of Animas Forks, construction was underway on the associated Gold Prince mill. The latter, a huge structure housing 100 stamps with a capacity of 500 tons of ore a day, was the largest concentrating mill in the state of Colorado—and with a price tag of $500,000, was probably the costliest as well.

Outside dimensions of the mill building proper were 336 feet by 184 feet. The walls of the upper and lower terminals were constructed of inch-thick boards covered with tar paper, and this assembly was covered overall with number 22 corrugated sheet-steel siding. The mill was made as fireproof as possible.

The Gold Prince mine, up on the mountain, and the Gold Prince mill, down in the valley, were separated by more than two miles of rough mountain country, all at timberline or above in elevation. The mine received its supplies and conveyed all its ores to the mill over a Bleichard cable tramway, 12,600 feet long, the construction of which required in excess of 50,000 feet of steel cable. Operating at a speed of 350 feet per minute, the tramway could carry 50 tons per hour.

At the mine a first-rate boarding house was built to accommodate up to 150 men. All construction materials for that and other buildings, as well as the supplies, and much of the machinery and equipment for the mine, were hoisted up from Animas Forks over the cable tramway.

Illustrative of the volume of traffic generated for the Silverton Northern by construction of just the Gold Prince mill alone, the foundations and floors of the building required over 400 carloads of structural steel—all brought into Eureka on the Silverton Northern and then shoved up the steep four miles of the extension to Animas Forks two and three cars at a time!

The benefits and rewards of the strenuous, back-breaking effort devoted to construction of the railroad's extension were offset in some respects, for Alexander Anderson's health—never the best in the high altitudes as we have seen—was broken. During October of 1904, even before completion of the additional trackage, he moved to a lower elevation in Denver, where he continued in Mears' employ as secretary of the Silverton Northern Railroad until his death by appendicitis in February, 1907.

Truly, Alexander Anderson was no less a sturdy pioneer than those who had gone before him.

THE MARY M.

Through all the years when the activities just related were transpiring, the guiding spirit of Otto Mears toward his small, shortline railroad empire in Colorado was, of necessity, essentially that of an absentee owner. Notwithstanding his frequent and recurring visits to the San Juans, and his occasional attempts at on-the-ground supervision, he and his family—including a son-in-law (after his daughter, Cora, was married in October of 1904) and his first grandson (born in July, 1906)—were residing in New York City, where Mears was a director active in the affairs of the Mack Brothers Company of Brooklyn.

It will be recalled that John L. McNeil, while serving as general manager of the Silverton Railroad in 1897, had looked into the possibilities of a steam-powered motorcoach—either new or used—in an attempt to develop an inexpensive commuter operation. The inquiries, of course, had had the full backing of Otto Mears as president of the railroad; and now, in his association with the Macks, it was not unnatural that Mears should revive the idea by suggesting to the Mack brothers some type of railbus. It was clear to Mears that an arrangement of this type might be feasible, in the light of the progressive developments which were taking place in the evolution of the internal combustion engine.

The Mack organization started construction of their first railbus in 1903 at their Brooklyn shop. The machine took the form of a modified large "touring car"—essentially an automobile with a close-coupled four-wheel pilot truck, two pairs of larger shaft-driven rear driving wheels, and three open-bench seats accommodating six people. The car was finished in 1905 in the new Allentown, Pennsylvania, plant of the Mack Brothers Motor Car Company, and ultimately was purchased by the Uintah Railway. On that steep and crooked western Colorado narrow-gauge road, it became rather well known during its many years of useful service.

The second Mack railbus originally was destined for the Silverton Northern Railroad. Mears had plans drawn up and these, together with a proposed contract for purchase, were sent out to Alexander Anderson in Silverton for his inspection and approval. Certainly no "yes man," Anderson returned the papers to Mears with a less than wholly enthusiastic response on May 3, 1904:

I have not signed the agreements, as Secretary of the Company, and leave that to you, as President, after calling your attention to the following matters: the agreement calls for a payment of $1,000 on each of the following dates: 1904—May 1st, July 1st, Sept. 1st, Nov. 1st, Dec. 1st; 1905—Jan. 1st, March 1st and April 1st. According to these dates $1,000 is now past due and the Company will pay for the machine before having a chance to try it. My recollection was that we were not to make payment until Sept. or Oct. which months would be far more convenient for us than making payments at once, as they seem to wish.

In the specifications they guarantee a speed of 10 miles per hour up a 5% grade. Can they not guarantee that speed on a 6% grade? Most of the grade between Eureka and Animas Forks is in the neighborhood of 6% and the speed should be guaranteed on a 6% instead of a 5% grade.

The automobile should also have a sandbox, but I do not see it on the blue prints or in the specifications, and I think their attention should be called to this.

Some other points may occur to you, but the above are the only suggestions I have to make.

Never having lost his verve for innovation, Mears quite apparently was intrigued with the gasoline-engined contrivance; and despite the financial straits of his Silverton Northern, he had the Macks continue construction work on the bus.

Near the end of 1904, the Mack company's business had expanded to the point where larger quarters were needed, and early in 1905 they purchased a new and larger plant in Allentown, Pennsylvania, after incorporating the Mack Brothers Motor Car Company on January 2 for that purpose. The as-yet-unfinished railbuses, numbers 1 and 25, were shipped from Brooklyn to the new Allentown factory for completion.

By April 28, 1905, the day before Otto Mears was elected president of the Mack Brothers Motor Car Company, word of the new railway motorbus got back to Silverton and the *Silverton Weekly Miner* printed the following story:

Sometime next month, probably by the 15th, the Silverton Northern Railroad will inaugurate a novelty in passenger traffic which, if successful, will revolutionize railroad traffic in the mountains, especially as to sight-seeing. The experiment consists of a railroad automobile, constructed to run on the rails and capable of carrying twenty-eight people, and with power also to haul a passenger coach. The motive power is gasoline as in other automobiles, but of course the wheels are of iron and flanged like car wheels.

The machine is the first of the kind ever built and was designed and constructed under the supervision of Otto Mears. It was ordered last fall and is now about ready for delivery. It is claimed that the machine will take a six per cent grade with

ease. Its advent will be awaited with great interest and the Silverton Northern will certainly have a boom in passenger travel this summer.

* * * * * * *

The bus was completed with the passenger compartment remodeled from an old streetcar body, and after the machine was painted, it was given the name, *Mary M.*, after Mrs. Mears. The finished bus left Allentown on August 22, as related in an article in the Allentown *Morning Call* of August 23, 1905:

The Mack Motor Car Company yesterday shipped to Denver, Colorado, a large motor car to be run on a narrow gauge (36 inch) railroad track. The car was consigned to the Silverton & [sic] Northern Railroad Co. It is rated at 90 h.p. and seats 28 people. The car is named the "Mary M."

* * * * * * *

The bus arrived in Denver and was unloaded on D&RG tracks, but it never reached Silverton, nor the Silverton Northern Railroad. It is entirely probable that the financially strapped SN just could not afford the machine, which cost as much as a new Baldwin Consolidation steam locomotive.

The *Mary M.* was tried out by the D&RG, but that company decided against purchasing the bus. It has been suggested, also, that the *Mary M.* went to the narrow-gauge Uintah Railway as their motorbus Number 50. However, Henry Bender, author of the authoritative book, *Uintah Railway,* covering the history of that company, declares that the *Mary M.* never was Uintah Railway property.

In all likelihood, just as Alexander Anderson had feared, the unique railway motorbus could not handle the steep grades and so was of little use in Colorado's three-foot-gauge territory. Where the *Mary M.* went is anyone's guess at present. Quite possibly it was returned to the Allentown plant, rebuilt to standard-gauge, and sold to some Eastern road.

MORRIS W. ABBOTT COLLECTION

SAN JUAN COUNTY HISTORICAL SOCIETY

This imposing structure was Judge Terry's new Sunnyside mill, built at the mouth of Eureka Gulch in 1899 — on the west side of the Animas Canyon. An extension had just been completed on the right side of the building when this picture was taken. The cable tramway ran from the long horizontal tower-like structure straight up the hillside. This and several other photographs adorned an album printed to entice prospective buyers to purchase stock as an investment in the Sunnyside project.

202

CHAPTER

V

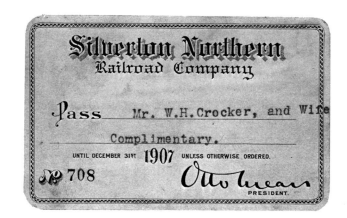

Silverton Northern
Railroad Company

Pass   Mr. W.H.Crocker, and Wife

Complimentary.

UNTIL DECEMBER 31ST 1907 UNLESS OTHERWISE ORDERED.

№ 708   Otto Mears
                                                PRESIDENT.

Otto Mears Returns to Silverton
1904 - 1911

THE LAST HALF of the opening decade of the Twentieth Century would see Otto Mears once again taking an active role on the local level in the management of his Colorado railroads. The apparent return of prosperity to the mines in the area where he had pioneered in so many ways was irresistible in drawing the old *Pathfinder of the San Juan* back to his early stamping grounds.

Nonetheless, until the transition could be accomplished, a local representative would continue to be necessary. Before the faithful Alexander Anderson was forced by ill health to leave Silverton —in October of 1904—one of his last duties was to arrange for a replacement, a man who would be a day-to-day manager for Otto Mears. Anderson contacted Arthur O. Ridgway, the young D&RG civil engineer who had come to the rescue earlier that summer in reconciling track location with Wigglesworth's survey stakes on the extension to Animas Forks. Ridgway—at work during the preceding year and a half as engineer in charge of locating and building the Rio Grande and South Western, a 33-mile logging railway out of Lumberton, New Mexico — was notified that he had been hired as superintendent of the Silverton and the Silverton Northern railroads.

Ridgway's tenure in this capacity, it developed, was to be for only a year. One of his first chores after entering Mears' employ was to supervise the installation at Animas Forks of the 50-foot iron turntable, which had been brought over from the D&RG after being removed from the top of Marshall Pass.

During the same month that Anderson and Ridgway were changing locations, Otto Mears returned to Denver briefly from the East Coast to organize a new company. Together with Anderson, George Crawford and J. A. Ewing of Leadville, Mears officially formed the Silverton Railway Company on November 3, 1904. Four days later, the assets of the old Silverton Railroad—in receivership since August 18, 1899—were transferred to the new Silverton Railway.

Almost immediately following this reorganization, the Red Mountain Railroad, Mining and Smelting Company—which had been formed in 1902 by George Crawford and C. H. Graham (the vice-president of the now-liquidated Silverton Railroad)—began in earnest to drive the Joker Drain Tunnel. Starting at the level of Red Mountain Creek, down the valley from Guston, where the railroad's bridge between Corkscrew Gulch and Ironton crossed the stream, the tunnel extended 4,800 feet in a straight line to the Genessee-Vanderbilt shaft, with side tunnels into the Guston, Robinson and Yankee Girl mines. As originally conceived, the tunnel was to project on beyond the Vanderbilt to the National Belle, Congress and Hudson mines, but this extension never became a reality.

Crawford began the Joker tunnel on July 9, 1904, and by December 11 had driven the first 300 feet. At that time, he installed an electric generator, an air compressor and two pneumatic air drills, and the progress in tunneling jumped to 10 feet per day. The tunnel varied in diameter—where the rock was solid, the clear dimensions were 7 feet wide by 8 feet high; where timber supports were

ROBERT E. SLOAN PHOTO

The Joker tunnel, and the boarding house of the Red Mountain Railroad & Smelting Company were in the foreground of this 1974 photograph — along with the American Girl dump. In this view, one is looking southeast from the Million Dollar Highway at Red Mountain Number 2.

JERRY B. HOFFER PHOTO

The Joker tunnel boarding house was in a rather tattered condition in the summer of 1973. The tunnel opening was just above the railroad grade, to the left of the photograph.

needed, the cross section was expanded to 10 by 11 feet. Grade of the bore rose at 3 inches per 100 feet, and a track for the little mine cars used in hauling out the muck was laid to a gauge of two feet, utilizing the old, worn 30-pound rail recovered from the nearby abandoned line of the Silverton Railroad below Corkscrew Gulch. In the tunnel floor a water drain two feet deep by four feet wide was excavated under the ties of the mine track. Electric lights were added as tunneling progressed.

While Mears quite evidently was paying a great deal more attention to his Colorado railroad properties now that Alexander Anderson no longer was active on the ground as his local manager, his interests with the Mack brothers in their work with gasoline-engined conveyances also continued at a high level. The new, enlarged Mack plant at Allentown, Pennsylvania, was activated early in 1905 and on April 29, Otto Mears was elected president of the Mack Brothers Motor Car Company.

As a reminder of the frailty of man's hopes and dreams, an inverted Joker tunnel tramcar sat in the old tailings pond, in front of the abandoned tunnel.

JERRY B. HOFFER PHOTO

The old gentleman must have been in a quandary—two widely divergent and geographically far-apart activities, each of prime importance, commanded more of his attention than could be given to either. However, a solution to the problem was devised by mid-summer of 1905. At this time, Otto Mears and George Crawford—officers of the new Silverton Railway Company—leased the railway to the Red Mountain Railroad, Mining and Smelting Company, with George Crawford as general manager. One condition of the lease provided that the old 30-pound rail of the Silverton Railway—by this time badly worn (and actually missing in some spots)—was to be replaced with heavier 45-pound rail.

As the new superintendent during this time, Arthur Ridgway was busy on the Silverton Northern, supervising the survey and construction work on the one-and-one-half-mile Green Mountain Branch from Howardsville up Cunningham Creek, originally proposed to Alexander Anderson by the owner of the Highland Mary property in 1901. Mears, involved on the East Coast, and having learned an expensive lesson on the Animas Forks extension the previous year, did not serve as contractor for construction of the new line this time, but sub-contracted the entire job. The three-and-one-half-percent grade was simple and straight, progress was rapid, and the branch was soon completed.

To the right is a detail shot of the coupler and underframe arrangement of the Joker tunnel tramcar.

JERRY B. HOFFER PHOTO

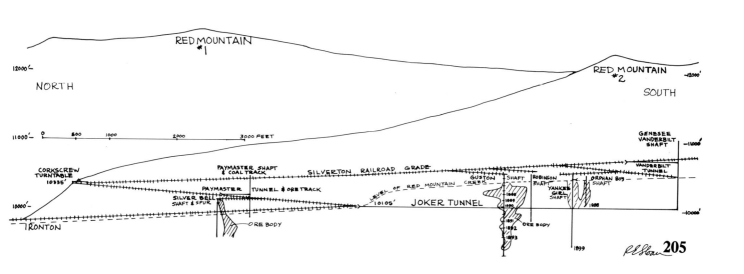

SUNDANCE PHOTO BY DELL A. McCOY

Fading light from the setting sun painted the autumn leaves and Telluride Peak from Nature's pallet. Telluride Peak — 13,509 feet above sea level — looks down on the old ties which once carried the weight of ore trains. The photographer was standing beside the abandoned Silverton Railway grade, not far from Corkscrew Gulch. Ironton Park is below and to the right.

Opposite page — Chattanooga Loop on the Silverton Railway provided a challenge for the survey crew who staked out the grade for Otto Mears. The challenge was met head-on with a sharp curve and extra-steep grade (five percent). Portions of the old railroad grade are visible in this modern-day photograph — in the loop area and above the highway (to the right).

ROBERT A. LeMASSENA PHOTO

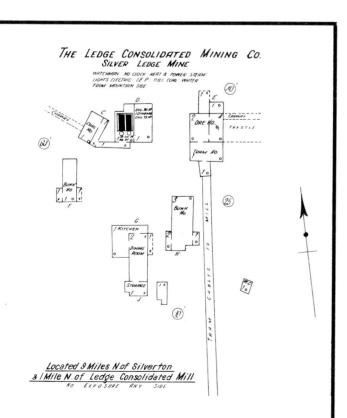

THE LEDGE CONSOLIDATED MINING CO.
SILVER LEDGE MINE

WATCHMAN - NO CLOCK HEAT & POWER STEAM:
LIGHTS ELECTRIC 1 E.P: PIEL COAL WATER
FROM MOUNTAIN SIDE

Located 9 Miles N.of Silverton
& 1 Mile N.of Ledge Consolidated Mill

NO EXPOSURE ANY SIDE

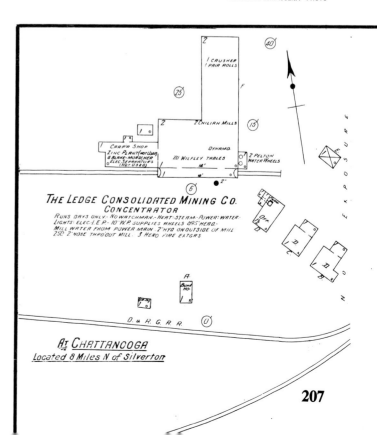

THE LEDGE CONSOLIDATED MINING CO.
CONCENTRATOR

RUNS DAYS ONLY - NO WATCHMAN - HEAT - STEAM - POWER: WATER:
LIGHTS: ELEC: 1 E.P: 10 W.P. SUPPLIES WHEELS 89.5'HEAD:
MILL WATER FROM POWER MAIN 2"HYD ON OUTSIDE OF MILL
250 2" HOSE THRO'OUT MILL 3 HAND FIRE EXTGRS

AT CHATTANOOGA
Located 8 Miles N of Silverton

207

THE SILVERTON MINER, 1907 —
MORRIS W. ABBOTT COLLECTION

Red Mountain Number 3 and the Yankee Girl - Genessee-Vanderbilt area is shown here as it looked in 1907. The operations of the Red Mountain Railroad, Mining & Smelting Company finally drained these mines with the Joker tunnel. This allowed the mine owners to resume production.

ROBERT E. SLOAN COLLECTION

RICHARD KINDIG COLLECTION

Silverton Northern Number 1 had been outfitted with a wedge plow for snow-bucking — as of 1905 when this picture was taken. The rest of the snow-removal train consisted of SRR flanger Number 1, SN engine Number 3, and SRy combine Number 11 (ex-Number 3, the *Yankee Girl*). The train was working its way north, along the Rio de las Animas, plowing through snowdrifts a short distance out of the Silverton yard.

RICHARD A. RONZIO COLLECTION

As shown in this 1907 view, Silverton Railway Number 100 had been re-equipped with automatic couplers and a new round oil headlight. This engine was on lease to the Red Mountain Railroad, Mining & Smelting Company and was helping to replace old 35-pound rail with new 45-pound rail. Red Mountain town and depot are to the right, while the stub switch for the Ironton line is near the locomotive tender. The line to Ironton dropped away on a five-percent grade to the left of Number 100, while the engine itself was on the four-percent grade that circled around *the Knob* to reach Red Mountain Pass. Otto Mears' toll road also passed this spot, heading down to Ironton.

SUNDANCE PHOTO BY DELL A. McCOY

In your imagination, you can almost see a little narrow-gauge train working its way over the small trestles in this valley — as the passengers were thrilled with the beautiful scenery along the way. Since the abandonment of the SG&N, Cement Creek has taken its toll of the bridge-builders' art. Kendall Mountain looms up in the background of this 1972 view.

210

RAYMOND F. SPENCER WATERCOLOR

SG&N locomotive Number 32 was switching cars at the yard of the Gold King mill in Gladstone.

SAN JUAN COUNTY HISTORICAL SOCIETY

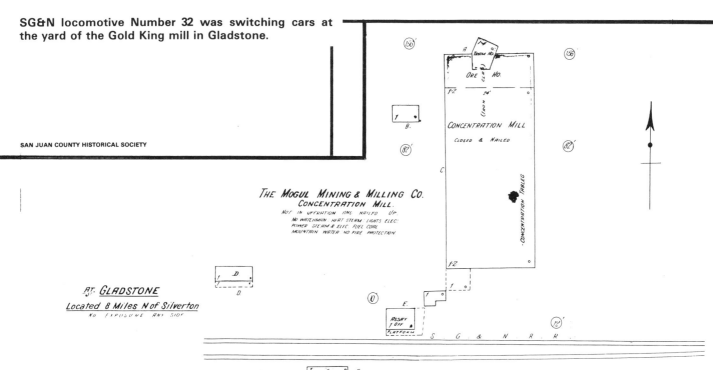

THE MOGUL MINING & MILLING CO.
CONCENTRATION MILL.

NOT IN OPERATION TIME NAILED UP.
NO WATCHMAN HEAT STEAM. LIGHTS ELEC.
POWER STEAM & ELEC. FUEL COAL
MOUNTAIN WATER NO FIRE PROTECTION

AT GLADSTONE
Located 8 Miles N of Silverton
NO EXPOSURE ANY SIDE

CONCENTRATION MILL
CLOSED & NAILED

ORE HO.

S G & N R R

Three locomotives now were required to handle all the business on the Silverton, and Silverton Northern lines, including the Animas Forks and new Green Mountain branches, and Superintendent Ridgway needed another engineer to supplement the two regular men, Pete Meyer and Billy Booker. He hired a 35-year-old boomer, Otto Herbert "Oh Hell" Albertson, who previously had worked on the Colorado Midland, the Santa Fe, and the Chicago and Alton roads.

Ridgway picked up Albertson by appointment in Ouray the morning after the new man was hired. After making the stage trip up Mears' toll road to Red Mountain with Ridgway, "Oh Hell" rode the engine down to Silverton, and that afternoon Billy Booker took him back over the Silverton Railway once more. The following day, Oh Hell had the train to himself, with only the fireman as a guide. His pay as engineer was $5.00 a day, with nothing for overtime.

Albertson's normal run was on the Silverton Railway; but, on occasion, he took freight trains over the Silverton Northern to Animas Forks, and ran the construction train up to the mile-long extension of the Animas Forks Branch to the Bagley tunnel. While working on this branch one day, a section of the frame of his locomotive broke.

Under Mears' inherently frugal policies, it was never the practice on his roads to have a spare engine on hand. Since the D&RG had none to lend at the moment, and a trip to the shop at Durango would require too much time, Ridgway suggested having the trouble fixed at the shop of one of the larger mines. The locomotive was jacked up and the broken parts removed and welded, but the welder failed to line up the pieces properly and the bolt holes did not fit. As a result, the SN had to send to Denver for jigs to relocate the holes, and new bolts had to be machined in Silverton. Since the engineer was expected to do all the work on his engine, Oh Hell had to work through one night, all the next day and the following night to get his locomotive back together, with not one penny in overtime pay.

The first snow of the winter of 1905-'06 came in November and rapidly built up drifts so deep that the Silverton Railway had to be closed for the season. Thereupon Oh Hell was out of a job. For a short time he worked as a carpenter's helper rebuilding one of the mills at Gladstone, but with word that his father-in-law at Montrose was ill, he quit work, hired a horse and rode the animal in mid-winter along his regular route over Red Mountain Pass to reach the D&RG train for Montrose at Ouray.

Arthur Ridgway, after completing the Green Mountain Branch, left Mears' service in October of 1905 to return to the D&RG. Mears, in addition to his apparently routine duties as president of Mack Brothers Motor Car Company in Pennsylvania, temporarily had to actively manage both his roads by himself—hiring his former black sheep conductor, Edward H. Hudson, to replace Ridgway as superintendent on October 20, 1905. When Oh Hell Albertson returned to work at the beginning of the summer of 1906, he did not get along with Hudson, and in September left for a job with the Utah Copper Company as the engineer of a stripping train in the new open-pit copper mine just starting development at Bingham, Utah.

The Denver Post on October 24, 1905, reported that Otto Mears—now handling the affairs of the Silverton Northern after Ridgway's departure—planned to spend most of his time managing his Colorado properties; he now owned or controlled all but a few shares of the SN stock, having bought out his long-time associate, Fred Walsen. The branchline built that summer from Howardsville up to the new Green Mountain mill was in commission and freight traffic was very heavy due to the probability of closure by snow. He proposed to put the road in shape the following year for full-time operation and was, in fact, signing a contract that very day for lumber and timber to build snowsheds between Eureka and Animas Forks. Construction was planned for next spring, after the winter layoff.

Mears still retained a controlling interest in the Silverton Railway, also—which *The Denver Post* referred to as the "Silverton and Red Mountain railroad" (as the line was frequently called in the popular press of the day)—and he was personally managing both roads. He told the newspaper that roadbed and ties were in place between Red Mountain and Ironton, ready to receive rail, and that the rail was on hand in Silverton.

The story in *The Denver Post* revealed, too, that as had been rumored the preceding April, Mears still was considering a cog railway down the cañon from Ironton as a means of reaching Ouray. Mears was quoted as saying that, "The road from Ironton to Ouray depends on what Ouray does." He had asked them to take $8,000 to $10,000 of stock in the road and said he would raise the necessary $400,000 to build the road the following year.

As indicated by the newspaper article, Mears had started making elaborate plans that summer for all-weather, year-'round operation during the coming season, including construction of a large and substantial engine facility for the Silverton Northern in the line's headquarters town. There was to be a six-stall roundhouse, 70 feet long, at

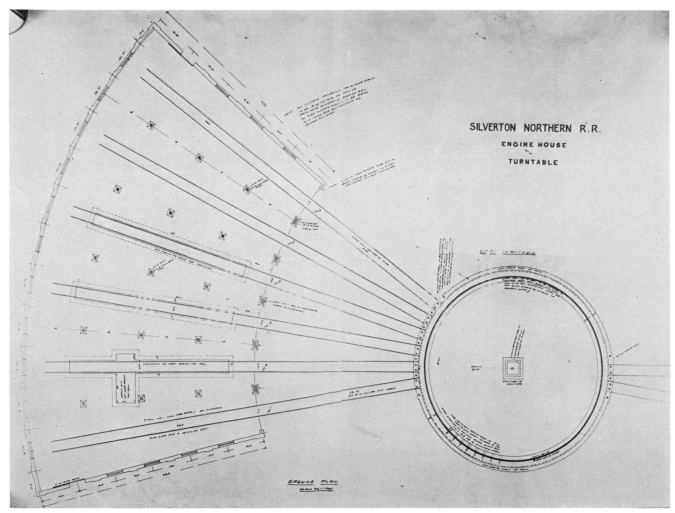

GROUND PLAN

STATE HISTORICAL SOCIETY OF COLORADO COLLECTION

the corner of Sixth and Cement streets; a 60-foot steel turntable; and coaling, sanding and other servicing facilities which were to be located between the two leads to the turntable. The roundhouse was to be patterned after the Denver and Rio Grande's structure at Salida, and Mears purchased reams of blueprints from the big road, covering every aspect of construction of the upstate enginehouse, then had plans drawn up for the proposed new Silverton Northern facilities.

One might wonder if the old pioneer's thoughts about returning to Silverton's high altitude were making him lightheaded, or if he were suffering from delusions of grandeur. Why should a small road such as the Silverton Northern need so elaborate an engine facility? Further consideration suggests some of the probable logic behind Mears' thinking: First, it should be recognized that six locomotives normally were in operation out of Silverton at that period (Silverton Northern numbers 1 and 3; Silverton, Gladstone and Northerly numbers 32, 33 and 34; and Silverton Railway Number 100). The second new Silverton Northern locomotive, Number 4, probably was on order from

the Baldwin Locomotive Works as well. In addition, from time to time, the D&RG had an engine in town for more than a day, working in the yard.

All four railroads in Silverton had taken turns during the years in using the rickety old D&RG two-stall enginehouse; when it finally burned down in 1902 it was replaced with a smaller structure which provided absolutely nothing in the way of space or machinery necessary for continuous maintenance of locomotives. Mears undoubtedly intended that some of the facilities and space in his new Silverton Northern roundhouse would be made available for lease to the other lines.

Furthermore, Cyrus Davis and Henry Soule, owners of the productive Gold King mine at Gladstone and the Gold Prince in Mastodon Gulch above Animas Forks, had organized another Maine corporation, The Old Hundred Mining Company. The Old Hundred owned 30 claims on the southwestern slope of Galena Mountain, northeast of Silverton on Cunningham Creek, above the Green Mountain Branch. The claims were worked in levels, starting 1,000 feet above the mill and continuing almost to the top of the moun-

RICHARD A. RONZIO COLLECTION

SAN JUAN COUNTY HISTORICAL SOCIETY

Not all the miners rode ore buckets to and from work in the Gold King mine. Many lived in the boarding house shown above, as it appeared in 1906 — located on the southwest side of Bonita Peak. The cableway ran downhill from beside the mine dump (to the left).

Opposite page — the Gold King mill had its capacity increased by 50 percent in 1901, four years before this picture was taken. The new barn-like addition to the mill forced the SG&N to rebuild the east leg of their wye, while they had to extend the tail of the wye for a quarter of a mile to the south. A switchback was laid in this new trackage, enabling the line to double-back behind the mill. Coal was delivered to the wooden chutes at the extreme left edge of the picture — to be fed by gravity to bins located near the boilers. Men were hired to shovel gondola carloads of coal, being paid per car worked. In this scene, Number 32 was on the switchback, as carloads of wood were being delivered to be used as mine props. The bucket tramway line entered the mill near the smokestacks (to the left and above the upper track level). Ore concentrate was loaded into boxcars spotted on the lower track level. Storm Peak occupies the horizon, sheltering the Natalie-Occidental mining complex — where an extension of the SG&N was planned, but never built.

RICHARD A. RONZIO COLLECTION

A panoramic camera captured this fascinating "wide-angle" view of Gladstone. To the left is the Mogul mill, while to the right is the Gold King mill. This scene has been reproduced (across the top of these two pages) from a halftone originally printed in 1905.

tain, the various levels being connected to the mill via an aerial tramway system. The mill was located on the Silverton Northern's right-of-way.

The mill and adjacent powerhouse were of the most modern design in the area, the powerplant containing steam boilers capable of developing 700 horsepower. Certainly, any investment and activity of this magnitude could be justified only by continuous operation, a factor assuredly not overlooked in the thinking of astute Otto Mears.

A parallel viewpoint, just as encouraging, arose from the construction underway at Davis' and Soule's Gold Prince complex in and above Animas Forks. So monstrous and expensive an affair as the Gold Prince mill, with its capacity of 500 tons of ore per day, surely could not but favorably influence Mears' outlook toward continuous utilization of his own properties.

Hence, the need for full-time operation of the Silverton Northern was everywhere apparent and Mears formulated his plans accordingly. In support of the scheme, an all-weather engine facility was a must. There would be need, also, for a depot of some sort at Eureka and Mears had plans for a new station building, 39 x 22 feet in size, with a hipped roof, for the town. Actual construction of

this utilitarian structure, unfortunately, never came about. News of the full-time train service projected by his railroad, as well as of the improvements contemplated by Mears was, of course, welcomed gladly by the local mine operators.

The principal obstacles to year-'round operation of the Silverton Northern between Silverton and Animas Forks were the many snowslides that ran down the steep slopes of the Rio de las Animas cañon every winter, blocking the tracks. Mears reasoned that since the snowshed built by Gibbs at Corkscrew Gulch on the Red Mountain line so many years before had proved to be the solution to operating problems caused by deep snow at that point, the same idea should work elsewhere. He envisioned a series of sturdy snowsheds covering the Silverton Northern's tracks at all the bad slide areas. Some of the sheds were even to have bunkhouses built into them so that snowshoveling crews could be stationed there as necessary during the winter to help keep the line open between the snowsheds.

As if confirming Mears' optimism regarding the desirability and need for continuous operation of his railroad, in December of 1905, the *Silverton Standard* reported that the Old Hundred, Mogul

Miners often rode ore buckets to and from the pitheads, as shown in this **1906** view (below). The line illustrated is the Gold King bucket tramway, which transported ore down to the mill, out of sight in the valley below.

SAN JUAN COUNTY HISTORICAL SOCIETY

MORRIS W. ABBOTT COLLECTION

The Mogul mill at Gladstone was brand new when this photograph was recorded in 1907. The cable tramway carried ore buckets up the hillside — to the left, in the clearing — to the pithead, located on Hurricane Peak. The Gold King mill can be seen (to the far right) just above the houses, which had been provided for Mogul and Gold King mill workers.

and Green Mountain mills were expected to be working steadily all winter long, although the Gold Prince mill at Animas Forks perhaps would not be able to do so. The roof of the new Mogul mill at Gladstone was being installed and that mill was expected to be in operation the following February. Two-hundred to three-hundred more men were at work than in the previous year.

Alas! The best-laid plans of mice and men often go awry! In February, 1906, the same newspaper reported that Silverton was closed to the world! All trains were stalled by snowstorms and the region was completely isolated. Five men were lost in a snowslide at the Sunnyside mine above Eureka and the Iowa mill in Arrastra Gulch was crushed down to the table by a slide from Little Giant Mountain. Several towers of the Green Mountain tramway were swept away, involving $1,500 in damage. At the Natalie Occidental mine on the Silverton, Gladstone and Northerly, $5,000 in damages were incurred when the boardinghouse, office and compressor room were smashed by an avalanche of snow sweeping down off the mountainside above.

The Gold King, Sunnyside and several other mines suspended operation until railroad service could be resumed, and considerable fear developed in the communities over possible shortages of coal and other goods. On March 24, concussion associated with another slide caused a great deal of damage to the six-month-old Green Mountain mill in Cunningham Gulch, killing the foreman in the process and destroying several Silverton Northern freight cars. Another slide that same day destroyed the boarding house at the Shenandoah and 12 men died in the disaster.

While the whims of old Mother Nature were bringing such adverse and discouraging problems to the San Juans in the first months of 1906, the picture was quite the opposite on the East Coast. There the activities and promotions of the Mack brothers in the automotive field were meeting with growing success. Maintenance work handled in the Brooklyn plant of the Mack Brothers Company was expanding at such a rate that the partners decided to establish a separate entity for the manufacturing side of the business in New York City, and in January of 1906, the Macks and Otto Mears incorporated the Mack Brothers Manufacturing Company. Mears gave up his position as head of the Mack Brothers Motor Car Company on January 9 and some three weeks later, on February 2, was elected president of the new firm. James Robertson Pitcher, Jr., husband of Mears' daughter, Cora, was made treasurer of the company soon thereafter.

SAN JUAN COUNTY HISTORICAL SOCIETY

The townsite of Gladstone occupied the valley in this scene — looking down the bucket tram line of the Gold King mill in 1906. The Mogul mill is just visible behind the trees (to the right), across the track and company houses. Anvil Mountain (in the distance) forced the trackage of the SG&N to curve to the left to reach Silverton.

Opposite page — the abandoned grade of the Silverton, Gladstone & Northerly winds its way through the narrow, deep canyon of Cement Creek, near Silverton. Beyond Bakers Park, Kendall Mountain rises to an elevation of 13,451 feet. In this 1969 view, notice that some of the old SG&N trestlework still remains. The photographer was facing toward the southeast.

SUNDANCE PHOTO BY DELL A. McCOY

THE SILVERTON MINER, 1907 —
MORRIS W. ABBOTT COLLECTION

The pithead of the Mogul mine was on Hurricane Peak, a mile and one-half west of the Sunnyside mine.

Mears' renewed belief and confidence in the mines of the San Juans was given further impetus when the Animas Power and Water Company completed its hydroelectric generating plant on the Rio de las Animas at Tacoma, 24 miles south of Silverton, in April of 1906. The cost of power for the mines throughout the district was cut by 50 percent as a network of three main power lines spread out from the Silverton substation on the Silverton Northern above town. One line extended to the Guggenheim's Silver Lake mine and the Iowa mine, another went to the Animas Forks district, and the third one went to Gladstone and Red Mountain, and stretched all the way across the rocky crags to Tom Walsh's Camp Bird mine above Ouray.

Further broadening the base of mining prosperity that year, one branch of the Joker tunnel being bored by George Crawford's Red Mountain Railroad, Mining and Smelting Company finally reached the Yankee Girl shaft during the summer, with the main Joker tunnel reaching the Genessee-Vanderbilt in the following year. The mines, which had not worked in the 12 long years since 1894,

were drained of their water at a rate of 1,200 gallons per minute, allowing the owners to resume mining almost immediately, with little additional effort or investment.

About the first of May in 1906, the Silverton Northern received its second brand-new locomotive—another Class 76 Consolidation—from the manufacturer. SN engine Number 4 (Baldwin construction number 27977) was shipped from Philadelphia on April 23 and cost Mears $8,375. The principal feature distinguishing the new engine from two-year-old SN Number 3 was the tender capacity for both coal and water.

The new addition to the motive power roster had arrived just in time, for the Animas Forks Branch opened for the season on May 17, 1906, and the Silverton Railway was opened about June 10. The latter line was in good shape only to the summit, but before the end of the year, was rebuilt on through Red Mountain town, down to the Vanderbilt spur.

Mears, for some reason presently unknown, hired P. D. Rice to resurvey the entire Silverton Northern once again. Rice spent almost four months on the job, working from June 10 to October 3. While the survey was finished and a map drawn up, no record exists of it being filed.

On July 27, 1906, Mears was interviewed by the Silverton newspapers just before he left town on his way to Denver, and was said to be well pleased with the prospects for Silverton, Red Mountain, Animas Forks and the entire region. He stated that he was getting ready for a mammoth business due to the imminent reopening of the Red Mountain mines; the light rails on the "Silverton and Red Mountain" (i.e., the Silverton Railway) were being replaced with heavy rails, the roadbed was being put in good shape, and the rolling stock increased. (The old rail subsequently was used by George Crawford for mine tracks in the revived Guston, Yankee Girl and Genessee-Vanderbilt mines.)

Railroad business between Silverton and Animas Forks was exceeding expectations, according to Mears, with two trains daily each way. Men working in the mines at Eureka and Animas Forks lived in Silverton and were commuting to and from their work by train. So far as the extension from Animas Forks to Lake City was concerned, Mears said there would be no building that year, although he did have a corps of surveyors at work.

Mears' grandiose plans for elaborate improvements to his Silverton railway empire during this period did not overlook a thing—not only were a new roundhouse at Silverton and a depot at Eureka to be built, and a new engine purchased for service on the Silverton Northern, but passenger accommodations were to receive attention, also. Sometime in 1905 or early 1906, he purchased from the Pullman Company a narrow-gauge passenger car which had started life as one of the six buffet-sleepers (*Salida, Cimarron, Castle Gate, Provo, Salt Lake* and *Ogden*) built in 1883 for through service on the original mainline of the Denver and Rio Grande. With a wheelbase and carbody 10 feet longer than the usual narrow-gauge coach, the new car was a big one. Mears had it fixed up, painted it a rich Pullman green, emblazoned the name, *Animas Forks,* on the sides and started offering meals on the train!

The fancy coach had not been in service very long when it was involved in an accident on the regular trip north to Animas Forks on August 6, 1906. With engineer William Booker at the throttle and Arthur Hudson (not to be confused with Manager Edward H. Hudson) as the conductor, things went well until the train started around the curve about a half-mile north of the Contention mill, near milepost 6. The forward truck of the *Animas Forks* jumped the rails and the car tipped over on

its right side, dragging another coach with it, both cars falling clear of the track. By the time the two coaches hit the ground, of course, alert Billy Booker had his train stopped. Silverton Northern's manager, E. H. Hudson, and his wife were on the train, as luck would have it. However, few of the passengers were injured seriously, although there were a few broken ribs, and no doubt much of the crockery in the galley was in smithereens.

Only three or four days before this incident, another derailment of a different sort took place on the Silverton, Gladstone and Northerly. The *Silverton Standard and Weekly Miner* reported in its issue of August 4, 1906, that:

A carload of Gold King concentrate became detached from its moorings on the switch at the mill at Gladstone and ran wild down the track for half a mile with no obstacle to impede its flight until it struck the curve just below Fisher's mill, where it dumped the concentrates on the Big Five Company's patented millsite. Half a dozen prospectors

RICHARD A. RONZIO COLLECTION

The cable tramway towers at the top of the Gold King tramway are shown above.

SUNDANCE PHOTO BY DELL A. McCOY

The Silverton, Gladstone & Northerly grade curved past the McKinley mine, where a short spur existed. This mine probably was a fairly good producer, considering the size of the tailings pile and all the derelict equipment strewn about. Kendall Mountain is in the distance.

RICHARD A. RONZIO COLLECTION

In this view is the Silverton smelter, which was located at the north end of town. Built by Kendrick-Gelder in 1900, and operated as the San Juan Smelting & Refining Company, it was run by the Ross Company by 1907. However, it was permanently closed in 1908. Silverton Northern Number 3 was switching gondolas when this view was made — at least three years before the SN began operating the Silverton, Gladstone & Northerly.

This illustrates that the two railroads cooperated at least to some degree.

The builder's photograph (below) of American Car & Foundry's elegant combine, built for the Silverton, Gladstone & Northerly, was shot in 1905. The car was SG&N Number 2.

ARTHUR DUBIN COLLECTION

oiler Room
ine Room
King 1906

SAN JUAN COUNTY HISTORICAL SOCIETY

This probably was the cleanest room in the Gold King mill, as cleanliness was important around oiled machinery. In this view of the engine room — shot in 1906 — everyone was tensed up, as the switchboard operator was about to throw on the breaker to start the steam stationary engine and generator for the first time.

		S. G. and N. R. R.		
7		STATIONS (Mon. and Thurs. only)		8
4 00	Lv	..........Silverton..... .....Ar		5 40
4 40	Ar	..........Gladstone...... Lv		5 00

Opposite page, above — a new electric generator was being installed inside the new addition to the Gold King mill at Gladstone in 1906.

Opposite page, below — the boiler room of the Gold King mill must have been warm even in the bitter cold of winter. This 1906 view shows coal being fed into the furnace below the huge boilers which ran the machinery of the mill.

SAN JUAN COUNTY HISTORICAL SOCIETY

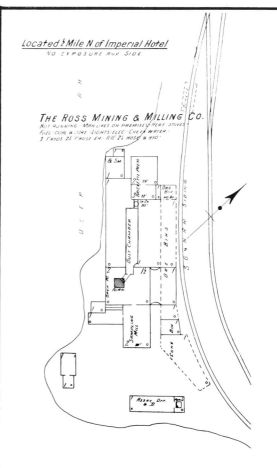

Located ½ Mile N of Imperial Hotel
NO EXPOSURE ANY SIDE

THE ROSS MINING & MILLING CO.

THE SILVERTON MINER, 1907 —
MORRIS W. ABBOTT COLLECTION

The extremely rich ore vein of the Gold Prince was being mined at this level in Mastodon Basin in 1907. The pithead is in the foreground, while the small mill and boarding house are farther away. The bucket tramway ran across the gulch — up to the notch on the side of Treasure Mountain (where a pack trail can be seen, also). At the notch, a mile and a half away, the angle station of the tramway was installed. In this view you are looking northeast, down Mastodon Gulch, with Seigal Mountain forming part of the Great Divide.

THE SILVERTON MINER, 1907 —
MORRIS W. ABBOTT COLLECTION

THE SILVERTON MINER, 1907 —
MORRIS W. ABBOTT COLLECTION

Opposite page, below — the angle station of the Gold Prince cableway was three-fourths of a mile west of Animas Forks, in Mastodon Gulch – later called Placer Gulch. This structure was made of steel and concrete to withstand the elements. Ore buckets on this line climbed the side of Treasure Mountain, then changed their direction — or angle of approach — in this building, permitting them to drop on down to the mill at Animas Forks.

This was the upper terminal of the bucket tramway serving the Gold Prince mine on Hanson Peak in 1907.

The Gold Prince mill was in full production when recorded in the view below, taken in June of 1905. A pair of unclaimed 1880, 10-ton freight trucks had been cast aside, beside the three-track yard. The combine, *Red Mountain*, can be seen on the near track, back by the mill. The boxcars were a mixture of D&RG 25-ton 3,000-series and smaller D&RG 20-ton 4,000-series cars.

RICHARD A. RONZIO COLLECTION

GEORGE L. BEAM PHOTO — JACKSON C. THODE COLLECTION

During September of 1906, a photographer produced this view, which has been printed two sizes (above and below). It was shot from the Cinnamon Pass road, looking west, up California Gulch. There you can see the new grade for the extension of the SN branch to the Frisco, or Bagley, tunnel. However, it is doubtful if rail was ever laid on this grade. Left to right, Treasure Mountain rises above the camp, with Tuttle Mountain in the distance and Houghton Mountain appearing to the right.

This closeup view of the scene on the opposite page shows the damage that was done to the structural steel of the Gold Prince mill when a snow-slide "let loose" from the slope of Cinnamon Peak. To the left of the mill (near the lefthand corner of the scene), you can see the 50-foot-steel-girder turntable and storage track (with a D&RG boxcar sitting on it). If you look closely, you can see a cable tramway tower in the center, while the little jail building is halfway between the tower and the turntable.

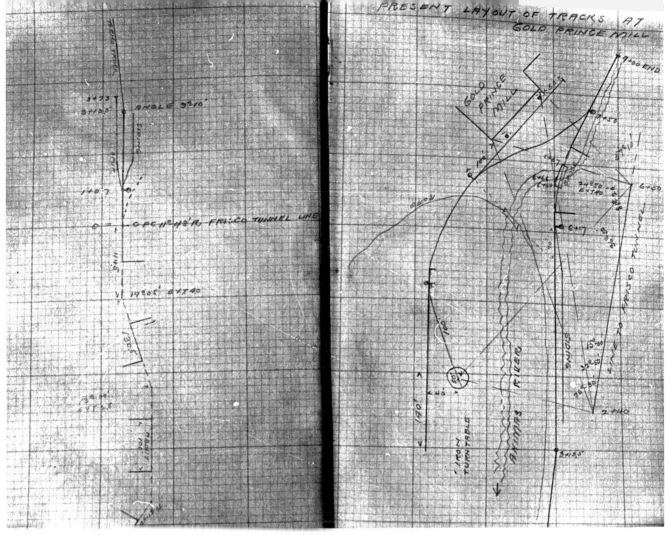

PRESENT LAYOUT OF TRACKS AT GOLD PRINCE MILL

SAN JUAN COUNTY HISTORICAL SOCIETY

This reproduction was photographed from the original "cross section book" of surveyor W. A. Beerbower, dated July, 1907. The sketch at left shows the proposed railroad route ending at the Frisco tunnel, while the sketch at right shows the Gold Prince mill with fewer railroad sidings than are in evidence from actual photographs of the mill.

THE SILVERTON MINER, 1907 —
MORRIS W. ABBOTT COLLECTION

This was the first and uppermost process utilized in the reduction of ore inside the Gold Prince mill at Animas Forks. The lump ore brought to the mill in tramway buckets was dumped into these Challenge feeders, which in turn, fed the ore to the stamps, the tops of which can be seen here.

THE SILVERTON MINER, 1907 —
MORRIS W. ABBOTT COLLECTION

The stamps — the lower parts of which can be seen in this view — proceeded to crush the lump ore into sand-size particles, the size of the original mineral grains in the rock. After a preliminary sorting in these jig tables, the sand flowed to the level below.

MORRIS W. ABBOTT COLLECTION

This was the Astor mine spur, about three-fourths of a mile above Eureka. A second spur is visible on the upper level, taking off from the mainline toward Animas Forks. The beginnings of cribbing for a snowshed can be seen to the left of the mainline, in this scene which was photographed in 1906.

SILVERTON NORTHERN R. R. CO.

GOOD FOR ONE PASSAGE
SILVERTON
—TO—
ASTOR & RETURN
WHEN OFFICIALLY STAMPED ON BACK.

FIRST CLASS.

239

General Manager.

The sand-size pulverized ore from the stamps (shown on the opposite page) was mixed with water and fed across these concentrating tables, which vibrated the ore under water. Since the gold and silver, as well as other metal sulfides, are heavier than quartz and other waste minerals, the ore and waste dripped off the tables at different places, allowing it to be collected and dumped or sacked, or recycled through the mill for additional processing.

THE SILVERTON MINER, 1907 —
MORRIS W. ABBOTT COLLECTION

233

GEORGE L. BEAM PHOTO —
JACKSON C. THODE COLLECTION

Opposite page — this view was taken looking south-east, down the main street of Animas Forks and the canyon of the Rio de las Animas. The slope of Cinnamon Mountain can be seen to the left, while Jones Mountain and Niagara Peak — on the Great Divide — can be seen on the skyline. Treasure Mountain is the hillside to the right. The Thomas Walsh house is the nearest house on the right side of the street. The back side of the Gold Prince mill is discernable to the left, with its cableway entering the open shed on the right side of the top level.

RICHARD A. RONZIO COLLECTION

When this snowshed was completed in 1906 — about a mile above Eureka — it was one of Otto Mears' proudest achievements. Mears hoped that this structure would thwart one of Mother Nature's most devastating snowslides, thereby permitting trains to operate on the Animas Forks Branch the year 'round. However, such was not to be the case. With the first big slide of the 1907 season, the snowshed was destroyed. Mother Nature had won the battle, and the branch went back to summer and fall operation only.

THE SILVERTON MINER, 1907 —
MORRIS W. ABBOTT COLLECTION

The Tom Moore boarding house, on the west bank of the Animas — near Picayune Gulch — had just been completed when this photograph was taken in 1907.

immediately struck up placer claim stakes, which they removed very soon, as the quick train crew on the Gladstone road fooled the prospectors and soon had the car on the track and contents reloaded and again enroute to the Durango smelter.

* * * * *

The Silverton, Gladstone and Northerly—as hinted by the newspaper story—also was happily participating in the revived prosperity of the mines. Evidently having foreseen such an encouraging turn of events in the San Juans some two or three years previously, in early 1905 the road decided to augment its equipment and ordered another new passenger coach from American Car and Foundry. The resulting product was an exquisite combination baggage-chaircar—38 feet, 6 inches long over end sills—with seating arrangements for 40 passengers. It was assigned number 2 and was the last piece of new rolling stock ever to be added to the

road's roster of equipment.

Probably because the little railroads were so busy, their small stock of freight cars seemed to suffer unusual attrition. Over on the Rio Grande Southern, to the west, for instance, a train crew reported to the head office at Ridgway that one of the new SG&N gondolas, number 2004—loaded with ties for Palisades—was wrecked at Glencoe and needed a new pair of trucks and a new body bolster immediately.

By the fall of 1906 — following up on Mears' plans of a year earlier for year-'round operation of the Silverton Northern—Mears and W. Z. Kinney (manager of Davis' and Soule's Gold King and Gold Prince mines, as well as of the SG&N) had developed a plan, and worked out and signed an agreement to keep the Animas Forks Branch open for shipping throughout the winter. Part of the plan called for a 500-foot-long snowshed at a bad slide area near the Silver Wing boarding house, not far above Eureka. With this additional protec-

236

SUNDANCE PHOTO BY DELL A. McCOY

The Frisco, or Bagley, tunnel was located part way up California Gulch — shown here bathed in sunshine on a September day in 1974. No evidence exists that rails ever reached this mine, although the roadbed was graded in 1906 and 1907. Hurricane Peak is in the distance, at an elevation of 13,447 feet above sea level.

THE SILVERTON MINER, 1907 —
MORRIS W. ABBOTT COLLECTION

Under Guggenheim-ASARCO management, the Silver Lake mill looked like this by 1907 (above). The ore buckets from the mine entered the top of the sloping building, and the ore then worked down through the stamps and concentrators by gravity.

238

SILVERTON NORTHERN R.R.

PROPOSED EXTENSION
VIA
ANIMAS FORKS TO FRISCO TUNNEL
July 1907
SCALE 200 FT

STATE HISTORICAL SOCIETY OF COLORADO COLLECTION

tion, it was thought that the railroad—with the help of the Gold Prince people—would be able to keep this portion of the Silverton Northern open all winter.

When completed by Mears in October of 1906, the new snowshed was built like a fortress—looking somewhat like an ancient wooden kremlin wall of old Russia. Massive timbers supported the roof,

which sloped up against the mountainside, the roof being so designed that downrushing snow would neatly slide on over and fall into the narrow cañon of the Rio de las Animas below.

The increasing intensity of his activities in the San Juans, combined with the extreme difficulty of effectively managing the operations of his little roads from New York City, finally brought Mears to sever his active association with the Mack brothers organizations on the East Coast. On November 30, 1906, he and James R. Pitcher, Jr., president and treasurer, respectively, of the Mack Brothers Manufacturing Company of New York City, resigned from their positions, as well as from the boards of directors, and surrendered their stockholdings to the Mack company. Leasing to the Macks the land on which the Brooklyn factory was located, Mears accepted in payment a small sum of cash and a four-cylinder tonneau automobile then being constructed.

Otto Mears—for the first time since 1896—was once again in a position to devote all his attention to his Colorado business interests; in January of 1907, after spending Christmas in New York City for the last time, the Mears and Pitcher families moved to Silverton. Pitcher immediately was made vice-president and treasurer of the Silverton Northern Railroad, replacing Fred Walsen, Sr., in the former position, and assuming the treasurer's

In 1904, Howardsville was provided with a depot, as shown near the bottom of this scene (to the left) — along the Silverton Northern track. The branch to the Green Mountain mill and the Old Hundred mill curved to the right, past the depot, and climbed into Cunningham Gulch, near the center of this view.

RICHARD A. RONZIO COLLECTION

239

SUNDANCE PHOTO BY DELL A. McCOY

In this scene of rugged mountain glory, the Silverton Northern laid its track up the steep grade out of Eureka. By now the Rio de las Animas is little more than a tumbling mountain brook. The photographer was looking south toward Galena Mountain, which rises to an elevation of 13,278 feet. Eureka Mountain is to the right. Otto Mears' short-lived snowshed was built about a mile downgrade from here.

SUNDANCE PHOTO BY DELL A. McCOY

The awesome beauty of an overwhelming avalanche was captured on color film during the winter of 1975 — as it roared down the face of King Solomon Mountain and slowly came to rest, after being thrown up against the side of Green Mountain. The bucket-tramway house of the Buffalo Boy mill was just barely out of the path of this slide run. The old Stony Pass road winds its way up through the gulch to the left, between Galena and Green mountains. Snowslides were greatly feared by the miners and railroaders because of the very real danger of being caught in one and being buried alive — which has happened more than once.

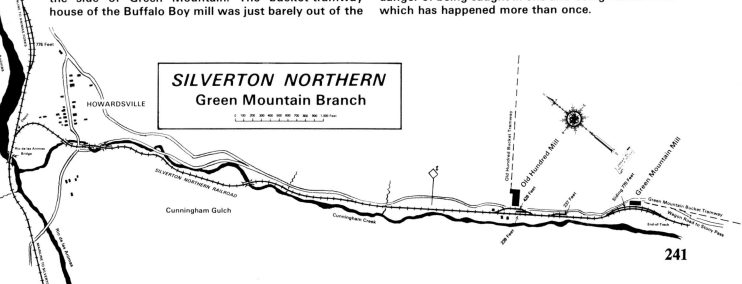

SILVERTON NORTHERN
Green Mountain Branch

0 100 200 300 400 500 600 700 800 900 1,000 Feet

MAINLINE TO ANIMAS FORKS

776 Feet

HOWARDSVILLE

Rio de las Animas Bridge

Depot

Rio de las Animas

MAINLINE TO SILVERTON

SILVERTON NORTHERN RAILROAD

Cunningham Gulch

Cunningham Creek

Old Hundred Bucket Tramway

Old Hundred Mill

628 Feet

229 Feet

227 Feet

Siding 770 Feet

Green Mountain Mill

Green Mountain Bucket Tramway

Wagon Road to Stony Pass

End-of-Track

241

VAUGHAN JONES PHOTO —
RICHARD A. RONZIO COLLECTION

Silverton Northern's locomotives 4 and 3 had their throttles open as they headed for the Silver Lake mill when this view was recorded at the power substation in 1907. Sultan Mountain is in the distance.

portion of the secretary-treasurer's duties of Alexander Anderson, whose health had continued to deteriorate after his move to Denver's lower altitude. Mears himself bought a substantial brick home in Silverton and had it remodeled — among other things, installing electric heating at a cost of $5,000. Pitcher built a large two-story house on Reese Street which remained in the family until the early 1960's. In only two more short weeks Alexander Anderson died in Denver, and Jerome B. Frank of the capital city was appointed to fill the vacancy as secretary of the company.

Harry C. Brown was a new employee brought in during 1906 to replace Anderson's former right-hand man, T. J. McKelvey, as bookkeeper and station agent for the Silverton Northern at Silverton; Brown stayed with the job until struck down by a heart attack some five or six years later. He apparently recovered and there is evidence that he returned to work for the SN. During the same period, E. S. Warner was employed as the station agent at Gladstone, over on the Silverton, Gladstone and Northerly.

After the move from the refinements of civilization in New York City to the rather primitive way of life found in Silverton, James Pitcher spent the first few months in his new surroundings familiarizing himself with the country, and the strange and manifold tasks of running a narrow gauge railway in the high and rugged mountains of his newly-adopted home—and then assumed the duties of general manager of the Silverton Northern, in addition to his two corporate assignments. He was to retain the position of general manager for more than the next quarter-century. The former "black sheep" conductor, Edward H. Hudson—who had met with much more success as the manager of the property in utilizing his talents—was made general superintendent.

The pride and joy of Otto Mears at the moment was the massive new snowshed just erected over the track above Eureka, for here was the means by which his promises for year-'round operation of the railroad could be carried out. After a thorough inspection of the new structure, he was confident that this "impregnable fortress" would be able to withstand the worst that Mother Nature could throw at it.

The ultimate test came early in 1907, when the first major snowslide of the winter came roaring down off the mountainside. As the cloud of powder

"Coming through on the Silverton Northern," SN's Number 4 — with wedge plow attached — meant business, as shown here outside of Silverton.

MORRIS W. ABBOTT COLLECTION

THE SILVERTON MINER, 1907 —
MORRIS W. ABBOTT COLLECTION

Looking west in 1907, SN Number 3 or 4 was blasting up the Animas Canyon. The train was just below the Tom Moore mine, at the mouth of Picayune Gulch — about 2.4 miles above Eureka. The main tunnel of this mine was called the Toltec and is marked by the dump pile and building in the center of this photograph.

SUNDANCE PHOTO BY DELL A. McCOY

A lonely ore bucket was swinging gently in the breeze as it waited for the Buffalo Boy
mine to open again. This aerial tramway ended at the Buffalo Boy's pithead, high on
Canby Mountain. This view was obtained from the old Stony Pass road during the fall of
1969. You are looking upstream in Cunningham Gulch.

snow which accompanies such avalanches settled slowly to earth, the rubble of what was left of Otto Mears' smashed pride and joy lay revealed at the bottom of the Animas cañon. The snowshed and Otto's hopes were gone, the Silverton Northern grade lay buried under tons of snow and debris, and Mears was never able to fulfill his contract with Kinney and the Gold Prince outfit.

Destruction of the snowshed, of course, demolished Otto Mears' dreams of turning the Silverton Northern into a fulltime railroad. Reluctantly, he pigeon-holed the entire scheme and went back to business as usual later in the spring of 1907. Today, only a handful of old drawings and blueprints and the battered remains of the snowshed survive as mute testimony to Otto Mears' ambitious plans for his little railroad empire.

In July of 1907, the Silverton Northern put a corps of surveyors to work locating the line for the remainder of the three-quarter-mile-long extension of the Animas Forks Branch up California Gulch to the N. R. Bagley tunnel (the Frisco tunnel) and the Mountain Queen mine. Rumors of the extension to Ouray flourished as usual; after repairs were made to washouts on the Silverton Northern, the Ross smelter was able to resume production.

OSCAR NELSON PHOTO — CARL SKOWRONSKI COLLECTION

The effects of the February, 1906, avalanche are evident in this view of the Iowa-Tiger mill — in the upper part of Arrastra Gulch. The slide came down Little Giant Mountain. Cable-tramway buckets transported ore down from Silver Lake; at the mill it was either transferred to a second cableway, or it was processed into concentrate. If either the lower tramway or the railroad was not running, raw ore (as well as concentrate) could be hauled by wagon down to Silverton for shipment on the D&RG or for local processing.

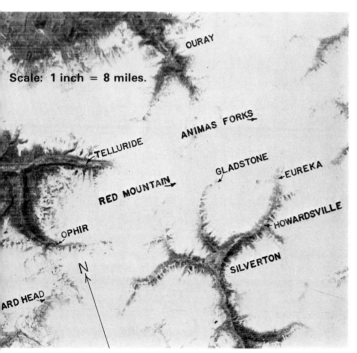

Scale: 1 inch = 8 miles.

OURAY

ANIMAS FORKS

TELLURIDE

GLADSTONE

EUREKA

RED MOUNTAIN

HOWARDSVILLE

OPHIR

SILVERTON

N

ARD HEAD

NASA - ERTS PHOTO

NASA-ERTS provided this satellite photograph of the central San Juan Mountains — taken on June 5, 1973, to show the snowpack in late spring and early summer, graphically illustrating why Otto Mears did not operate the Silverton Railroad or the Animas Forks Branch of the Silverton Northern until late May of each year.

The Silverton Railway, still under lease to George Crawford's Red Mountain Railroad, Mining and Smelting Company, finally was pushed on through Corkscrew Gulch turntable to Joker and Ironton once again.

Mears' inspired creation, the converted narrow-gauge Pullman, *Animas Forks,* suffered its second indignity in the summer of 1908, when it was derailed once more. Edward "Pete" Meyer was the engineer while Arthur Hudson was the conductor on this run, which unfortunately ran over some loose rail. New 45-pound rail was being laid near the Silver Lake mill and yard, two miles above Silverton, and it happened that one of the new rails had been carelessly left unspiked. Meyer's engine and the first coach rode over the spot with no trouble, but the second coach caught on the loose rail, and that car and the *Animas Forks* on the end of the train, tipped over—with a minimum of harm to the passengers. In consequence of the damage this time, the Pullman was extensively rebuilt once more during the winter of 1908-1909—coming out of the shop with a large open observation platform.

Superintendent E. H. Hudson left Mears' employ shortly thereafter, being replaced by William E. Booker.

The smallest of the three little lines headquartered in Silverton—the Silverton, Gladstone and Northerly—during the years from its beginning in

MORRIS W. ABBOTT COLLECTION

Wine List

SILVERTON NORTHERN RAILROAD CO
Car: Animas Forks

		Dolls.	Cts.

LIQUORS

Private Stock Whiskey	per drink	$	.20
Greenbrier Bourbon Whiskey	per drink		.20
Scotch Whiskey	per drink		.20
Holland Gin	per drink		.20
Burke's Ale	per pint		.40
Burke's Stout	per pint		.40
Benedictine	per drink		.25
Green Chartreuse	per drink		.25

WATERS

Manitou Water	per quart	$	.35
Ginger Ale	per quart		.50
Red Raven Splits	per half-pint		.20

WINES

Mumm's Extra Dry	per pint	$2.50	
White Seal Champagne	per pint	2.50	
Chateau Blanc Wine	per pint	.75	
LaRose Wine	per pint	1.25	
Grave's Wine	per pint	.75	
Imported Sherry	per quart	2.50	
Imported Port	per quart	2.50	
Saarbuch Steinwein Wine	per pint	1.25	
Liebfraumilch Wine	per pint	1.50	
Sparkling Burgundy	per pint	1.50	
California Port	per pint	1.25	

Cigars and Cigarettes			
	Total		

This wine list and order blank was used by the buffet-Pullman car, *Animas Forks*.

1900 through 1907 was a profitable enterprise, regularly earning the six-percent interest required on its bonds, with enough left over for management to pay out three to six-percent annually in cash dividends to the stockholders. In 1908, however, operating expenses increased while revenues dropped off drastically, reflecting in part, the closing of the Kendrick-Gelder smelter alongside the SG&N mainline in north Silverton. The peak of the recent mining boom had passed; now a decline was setting in among the mines, mills and smelters that was to last until the early days of World War I in 1915.

Looking southwest, down the Rio de las Animas, this 1908 view was taken just west of the Iowa mill spur. The Silver Lake mill was between the two bridges in the foreground and the low railroad trestle, which crossed the river half-a-mile downstream. The top of the mill can be seen through the trees in the fore-

GEORGE L. BEAM PHOTO —
JACKSON C. THODE COLLECTION

ground. The bridge on the left (of the two visible near the center) led to the wagon road up Arrastra Gulch, and the trail to the Iowa-Tiger and Silver Lake mines. The other bridge at this spot originally was a railroad bridge, which permitted trains to be switched from both ends of the Silver Lake mill yard (built in 1893).

New 45-pound rail can be seen along both sides of the grade, ready to replace the old 30-pound rail. This was the scene of the second wreck of the Pullman car, *Animas Forks*. When the coach ahead of it caught on the end of one of the newly-laid rails, it derailed and caused the *Animas Forks* to jump the track, also.

247

OLD 100 MILL

THE SILVERTON MINER, 1907 —
MORRIS W. ABBOTT COLLECTION

The lowest of the mills on the branch up Cunningham Gulch was the Old Hundred. This mill was one mile away from, and 200 feet above, Howardsville, while the mine itself was another three-quarters of a mile away, directly up the hill from the mill. This photograph was taken with the camera pointing toward the southeast. Galena Mountain is to the left and Canby Mountain is part of the Continental Divide in the center of the view. Stony Pass — the route traversed by the first prospecting parties coming into the area — is reached by way of this gulch. The Green Mountain mill is in the background (at right).

Silverton Northern R. R.				
*1	*3	STATIONS	*2	*4
7 00	3 00	Lv....Silverton....Ar	9 55	5 45
7 10	3 10	.....Silver Lake......	9 45	5 35
7 20	3 20	.....Howardsville.....	9 35	5 25
7 40	3 40	........Eureka........	9 15	5 05
8 15	......	Ar .Animas Forks. Lv	8 45	......

The photographer was looking down on the number 2 level of the Old Hundred mine — perched high on the side of Galena Mountain — when this view was taken.

STATE HISTORICAL SOCIETY OF COLORADO COLLECTION

THE SILVERTON MINER, 1907 —
MORRIS W. ABBOTT COLLECTION

The Old Hundred's aerial tramway terminal, boarding house and machine shop were high above the mill, on the second level of operations. This is called "Old Hundred Number 2."

THE SILVERTON MINER, 1907 —
MORRIS W. ABBOTT COLLECTION

The Old Hundred had a 40-stamp mill for crushing the ore to sand size. This 1907 photograph shows one row of eight stamps, one of the five rows of stamps which filled the mill building.

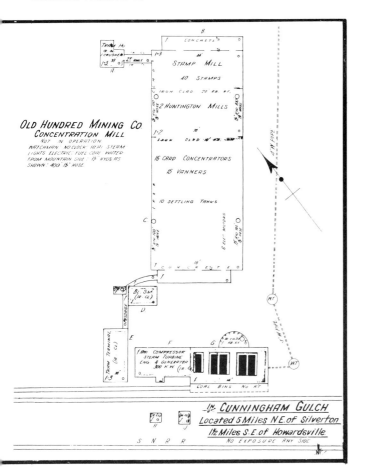

In the view at right, you are looking northeast, across Cunningham Gulch, where the Old Hundred occupied the mountainside — with mine openings at several levels above the big mill.

CHARLES S. RYLAND COLLECTION

MORRIS W. ABBOTT COLLECTION

Company houses and a boarding house are shown in this photograph of Gladstone, C. 1908. Notice the rather large privies behind the houses and the white clothing hanging on the lines. Hopefully, the wind did not blow coal soot from the smokestacks of the Gold King mill all over the laundry!

Silverton, Gladstone & Northerly gondola 2007 — of 1904 vintage — was wrecked on the Silverton Branch of the Denver & Rio Grande. The scene below presents the underbody detail of the car in a way not intended by the SG&N! Strangely enough, the trucks remained on the car.

M. G. BALLOUGH PHOTO — MARGARET B. PALMER COLLECTION
COURTESY OF JACKSON C. THODE

RICHARD A. RONZIO COLLECTION

One-fourth of a mile above the Old Hundred mill was the Green Mountain mill. The photographer who shot this view was attempting to record the tremendous havoc that snowslides can cause — the Nemesis of the San Juans. Besides the boxcars that the avalanche had shuffled around in the yard, notice the switchstand which had been bent over. The dark building, with white window frames, is the Green Mountain boarding house. The dump belonging to the Pride of the West mine is visible to the right.

This closeup features the Silverton, Gladstone & Northerly's enginehouse as it appeared from the back side.

L. C. McCLURE PHOTO —
DENVER PUBLIC LIBRARY WESTERN COLLECTION

THE SILVERTON MINER, 1907 —
MORRIS W. ABBOTT COLLECTION

HERB SCHWARTZ PHOTO —
SAN JUAN COUNTY HISTORICAL SOCIETY

The Green Mountain boarding house is in the foreground of this 1907 view, looking down Cunningham
Gulch. The bucket tramway ran to the Green Mountain
mill, below. From left to right, on the skyline, are
Macomber Peak, Hematite Basin, Gulch and Tower
mountains, Cataract Gulch, and Dome Mountain.

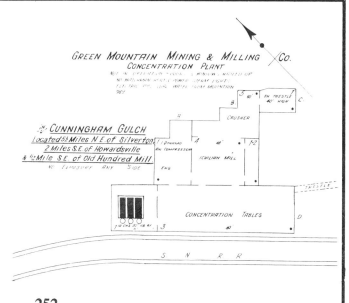

252

SAN JUAN COUNTY HISTORICAL SOCIETY

The old Posey & Wingate store — formerly owned by the incorporators of the Silverton Railroad — was being operated by the Crooke-Fuller Hardware Company when this picture was taken in 1908. The subject of the photograph was the elaborate Labor Day parade of that year. Musicians led the parade, followed by representatives of the carpenters' union, carrying tools of their trade.

Silverton Northern's Stover motorcar was given the number "1," prior to its delivery in Silverton. The view below was taken on the day the car arrived, August 3, 1908. Otto Mears (on the left) was standing beside Mr. Stover and J. R. Pitcher, Jr. The SN's master mechanic and driver, William E. Booker, was inspecting the vehicle's motor. The ladies inside the car probably were Cora Pitcher and Mary Mears, ready to enjoy a ride.

COLORADO RAILROAD MUSEUM COLLECTION

253

𝕭ill of 𝕱are

SILVERTON NORTHERN R. R. CO

Car: Animas Forks

			Dolls.	Cts.
SOUPS				
○ Chicken 25c	○ Vegetable 25c	○ Oxtail 25c		
○ Clam Chowder 25c	○ Clam Juice 25c	○ Tomato 25c		
○ Mock Turtle 25c	○ Mulligatawny 25c	○ Chicken Gumbo 25c		
○ Julienne 25c	○ Consomme 25c			
FISH				
○ Norway Mackerel 50c	○ Russian Caviar 50c	○ Smoked Sardines 35c		
○ Kippered Herring 50c	○ Bismark Herring 50c	○ Boneless Sardines 50c		
BEEF				
○ Chili Concarne 50c	○ Roast Beef 50c	○ Vienna Sausage 50c		
○ Lunch Tongue 50c	○ Beechnut Bacon 25c	○ Yacht Club Beef 50c		
○ Boned Chicken 50c	○ Chicken Tamales 50c	○ Liebig Beef 50c		
○ 2 Boiled Eggs 25c				
BREAKFAST FOOD				
○ Quaker Oats 25c	○ Egg O' See 25c	○ Shredded Wheat 25c		
VEGETABLES				
○ Baked Beans 35c	○ Corn on Cob 25c	○ Peas 25c		
○ Asparagus Tips 25c	○ Hominy 25c	○ Banquet Corn 25c		
○ Macaroni and Cheese 25c				
PUDDINGS *and* FRUITS				
○ Plum Pudding 25c	○ Stuffed Olives 25c	○ Plain Olives 25c		
○ Apricots 25c	○ Peaches 25c	○ Apricot Preserves 25c		
○ Marasch. Cherries 25c	○ Currant Jelly 25c	○ Marmalade 25c		
○ Pear Preserves 25c	○ Raspberry Preserves 25c			
RELISHES				
○ Tomatoes 25c		○ Mushrooms 25c		
CHEESE *and* BENT WATER CRACKERS				
○ McClaren Cheese 25c	○ Roquefort Cheese 25c	○ Chow Chow 15c		
○ Shelled Pecans 25c				
SANDWICHES				
○ Caviar 25c	○ Sardines 25c	○ Tongue 25c		
○ Tea 15c	○ Coffee 15c	○ Milk 15c		
○ Cream 25c	○ Biscuits and Butter 10c extra			
○ Bread and Butter supplied with all meats				
○ Wines and Cigars				

A separate check must be issued to each passenger.
No check issued for less than twenty-five cents to each person.

No. *Total*

NOTE: Parties are requested when ordering to make a cross at each individual item ordered, thus ⌧ ¶ Please report any complaints to the office

MORRIS W. ABBOTT COLLECTION

The menu and order blank for the combination cafe-sleeping car, *Animas Forks,* looked like this.

George Beam of the D&RG captured the mood of the mighty San Juans in this impressive picture, showing how tiny man's efforts were (and are) in the Animas

GEORGE L. BEAM PHOTO —
COLORADO STATE HISTORICAL SOCIETY

valley. It has been written that most of the real estate in the San Juan Region tilts at 45 degrees or more, and that Bakers Park is virtually the only flat area of any size to be found. This view was photographed while looking down on the town of Eureka from the SN railroad grade.

GEORGE L. BEAM PHOTO —
COLORADO STATE HISTORICAL SOCIETY

This closeup shows SN locomotive Number 1 and combine Number 2 of the SG&N at Eureka in 1911. The main street is just behind the train, along with the insulated, square-boxed water tank. No depot was ever built in Eureka.

Lack of their accustomed dividend in 1908, and the declining profits of the road, caused the stockholders to vote out John D. Chipman as president and W. Z. Kinney as superintendent, the two officers being replaced by Mark Gallert and D. M. Haynes, respectively. These changes in the active management of the road had little impact, however, for the next year saw matters continue to worsen rather than improve — even though the SG&N was still running two trains daily and reported carrying 3,916 passengers and 16,667 tons of freight in its revenue statistics for 1909. The stockholders, attempting vainly to reverse the trend, replaced three directors, voted in J. M. Johnson as vice-president and general manager, and elected John D. Chipman to replace Henry Soule as treasurer. But such meddling in the ranks of management would not be enough to save the railroad.

On August 3, 1908, the first passenger-carrying railway motorcar ever seen on the narrow-gauge lines in southwestern Colorado arrived in Silverton. Designed and built by Mr. Stover of Freeport, Illinois, this small, 12-passenger, 30-horsepower Stover motorcar carried construction number 114, with motor number R-2890. It had been shipped to Salida, unloaded onto the D&RG tracks there, and

then driven to Silverton, apparently by Stover, who encountered no difficulties in climbing over both Poncha and Cumbres passes. The *Silverton Miner* was delighted to refer its readers to Mr. Stover (the mechanic) or to Billy Booker (the chauffeur—and also master mechanic of the Silverton Northern) for more complete details. The Stover railcar made a number of short daily trial runs to Eureka and Gladstone, to the great pleasure of guests of Superintendent E. H. Hudson on the SN. Popularity of the new little car was assured.

Early in 1909, Otto Mears regained possession of the Silverton Railway from George Crawford's Red Mountain Railroad, Mining and Smelting Company when the lease was cancelled. This necessitated an addition to the passenger equipment, and Mears bought another used coach from the Denver and Rio Grande. New Silverton Northern coach, Number 4, was a sturdy, all-wood product built in Wilmington, Delaware, by Jackson and Sharp in 1882 for the D&RG as their coach Number 90, renumbered 314 in July of 1885. This newest addition to the passenger rolling stock became SN coach Number 4 in January of 1909 and lasted until the final end of the road.

As it had at the time of construction of the extension to Animas Forks five years previously, the weather in the San Juans again turned vicious in late 1909. On August 10 a monumental rainstorm —the heaviest ever recorded to that time—brought down a mud and rock slide near Needleton tank, 11 miles south of Silverton, totally blocking the D&RG branch along the Rio de las Animas. Silverton was isolated to all intents and purposes— with only wagons from Ouray and pack mules from Rockwood able to get through with supplies of any kind. The Silverton Branch was reopened by September 4, but that night another storm swept over the cañon—even worse than the one of August 10—and the D&RG branch was blocked again, and Silverton was once more isolated from the outside world for another three weeks, until September 26.

The Silverton Northern and the Silverton Railway, not so badly afflicted by the cloudbursts as the D&RG branch, were repaired and returned to operation by Mears with little trouble. Repairs to the D&RG, however, required a considerable amount of new grade, many ties and much replacement rail, and Mears was commissioned by the big road to go to work on the slides from the Silverton end of the cañon.

The early September storm also had overwhelmed two dams of the Telluride Power Company at Trout Lake, on the north side of Lizard Head pass. The resulting walls of water carried away much of the track and grade of the Rio Grande Southern at the mouth of Trout Lake and on down the cañon of the Rio San Miguel. Having accomplished the cleanup of three lines, Mears now went on to repair the RGS, rebuilding the Butterfly bridge and producing the twisting, crooked alignment just below Trout Lake—famed forever after as "Otto's Puzzle." By October 15, Mears had reopened the RGS as far north as Telluride—the balance of the road north of that town finally being reopened on December 17. Mears came home to Silverton on October 29, hailed as the Hero of the San Juans.

Having experienced at first hand the problems of using manual labor for railroad reconstruction due to rock and snow slides, Mears ordered the latest item of power-driven railroad work equipment. The American Hoist and Derrick Company of St. Paul, Minnesota, had developed a compact, rail-mounted, 30-horsepower self-propelled steam shovel in 1905 and Mears purchased one of these highly useful machines, receiving American Railroad Ditcher, serial number 578, during 1910.

At the time of the reconstruction problems of the various railroads in the San Juans, the Gold Prince mine near the head of Mastodon Gulch was steadily producing high-grade ore, and 40 stamps were pounding away continuously in the huge mill at Animas Forks. The concentrate, scheduled to go to the Durango smelter, had to be stockpiled when transportation was temporarily interrupted, and plans were made to keep the mill running after winter finally set in, with all the concentrate going into storage until spring. On the Guggenheim's Silver Lake property, on the other hand, a fire had

destroyed the midway terminal of the tramway; three transformers, all the machinery and 40 buckets were a total loss, the damage aggregating to $15,000 in amount. Late in 1909, the Gold King mine at Gladstone was closed by litigation and strikes, further darkening the financial picture of the SG&N railroad serving the property.

Quite typically, the unfavorable situation for the Gold King people was the knock of opportunity to Otto Mears. Subsequently, on January 1, 1910, he, Jack Slattery and son-and-law, James R. Pitcher, Jr., leased the Gold King mine, holding the lease until 1916. On the same day, Mears also obtained a lease on the Silverton, Gladstone and Northerly Railroad. Under the terms of the latter agreement, the lease could be cancelled by either party if the total came to less than $30,000 per year.

Now, the overall picture was completely altered. Mears now was able to operate all three of the little Silverton lines as a single integrated system—suddenly creating a surplus of locomotives and rolling stock. The two engines in poorest condition—old pioneer Silverton Railway Number 100, and venerable Number 32 of the SG&N—were deadlined. Among the passenger coaches, the two combination baggage-chaircars, built new for the SG&N in 1899 and 1905, were in much better condition than the antique relics on hand from the early days of the Silverton Railroad. Not wasting a thing, Mears sent the boiler of Number 32 and the carbodies of the 1888 arch-roof combination car, *Red Mountain,* and combine Number 11 (originally Number 3), the ex-*Yankee Girl*—both off the

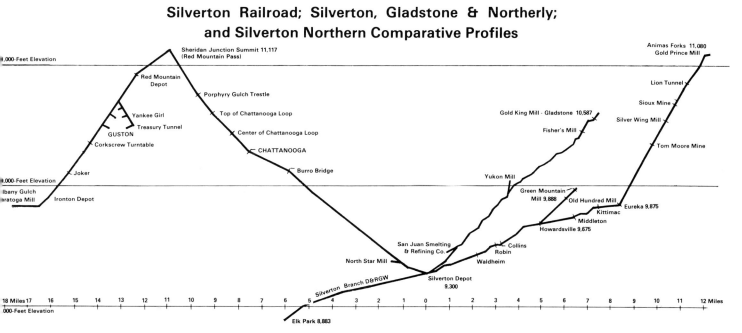

Silverton Railroad; Silverton, Gladstone & Northerly; and Silverton Northern Comparative Profiles

257

CHARLES S. RYLAND COLLECTION

The Red Mountain depot was the setting of this picture in 1909. Silverton Northern Number 1 still had the original peaked cab and Laird crossheads, but had been outfitted with a straight stack, larger air pump, extended smokebox and a round headlight — all as the result of its 1904 rebuilding. Also notice that the tender had been rebuilt, with the air reservoir moved to the top of the water tank. The *Yankee Girl* coach had been converted to a combine, painted green and relettered for the Silverton Railway as Number 11.

THE SILVERTON RAILWAY CO.

*5	M	STATIONS	*6
.....	0	Lv..........Silverton..........Ar	.....
.....	20	Ar...........Ironton...........Lv	.....

Connection with Stages for Ouray and intermediate stations.

The *Official Railway Guide* of 1910 showed nothing operating on the Silverton Railway.

SG&N combine Number 2 was shorter than this hand-shoveled snowslide, near Gladstone.

MORRIS W. ABBOTT COLLECTION

GEORGE L. BEAM PHOTO —
JACKSON C. THODE COLLECTION

The Ouray & Red Mountain Toll Road looked like this in 1909 — as the photographer looked southeast, toward Champion Gulch and Red Mountain Number 3. The sign over the buggy points to the Treasury tunnel now known as the Idarado mine.

Snow-shovelers were hired from among mine workers during March of 1909 to clear the Silverton, Gladstone & Northerly of 25 feet of snow.

MORRIS W. ABBOTT COLLECTION

CHARLES S. RYLAND COLLECTION

The Silverton, Gladstone & Northerly enginehouse appears in this picture, with the ditcher and derelict equipment lined up on the rip track.

Silverton Railway—down to Tefft (frequently misspelled "Teft") Spur at milepost 477.9 on the Silverton Branch of the D&RG. Here, where tumbling Cascade Creek meets the Rio de las Animas, Mears established a sawmill, cutting railroad ties, and bridge and mine timbers from the spruce, Douglas fir and ponderosa pine that grew along the valleys of Cascade and Lime creeks. The boiler from the engine powered the mill, while the combine carbodies were used as auxiliary buildings. The last remnants of these two cars and the engine boiler were still at the site as of June 1974.

While it is possible that this sawmill operation was established by Otto Mears at the time he was hired by the D&RG to rebuild yet again major portions of the Silverton Branch after the destructive flood of October 5, 1911, it is known that the two old combination coaches still were on hand in Silverton in 1912. And they certainly were at Tefft Spur by 1915.

The trackage of the three roads now comprising Otto Mears' railroad empire in the San Juans was all steep and crooked, even by the standards of the Denver and Rio Grande; some portions of Mears' little lines were absolutely outlandish in these regards. The five-percent grades, 30-degree curves and other unusual physical features innovated by Charles W. Gibbs on the Silverton Railway over Sheridan Pass (later called Red Mountain Pass) already have been noted.

The lower 9.3 miles of the Silverton Northern, between Silverton and Eureka, in contrast, were quite gentle—certainly by Mears' standards, and even by those of the D&RG. On this segment there were 45 curves, all but one of 20 degrees or less in curvature, excepting the final curve into the yard of the Sunnyside mill at Eureka, where the radius

tightened to 24 degrees, and the balloon loop at milepost 8.26 between Kittimac and Eureka, where the curvature reached 30 degrees. Steepest grade on this section was 2.5 percent, with an average of 1.35 percent over the whole distance.

The 3.92 miles comprising the Animas Forks Branch, on the other hand, was the most extreme of all the Mears roads, with an average grade of 5.77 percent and the maximum very close to 7 percent. In this relatively short distance, there were 85 curves, starting with a tight one of 32 degrees (182-foot radius) in the Sunnyside yard at Eureka. While most of the curves were approximately 20 degrees, there were six of 30 degrees (194-foot radius) and one extremely sharp curve 100 feet long of 40 degrees (147-foot radius) at milepost 11.97, where the track skirted the gorge of the Rio de las Animas just north of Grouse Gulch as the cañon closes in upon itself.

The Green Mountain Branch of the Silverton Northern, proceeded up Cunningham Gulch for 1.6 miles, left the mainline at milepost 5.45. On this branch the average grade was 3.59 percent, with a maximum of 3.8 percent. The branch began with a 24 degree (241-foot radius) curve 491 feet long; three other short 24 degree curves and one of 30 degrees were among the total of 15 curves.

THE SILVERTON MINER, 1907 —
MORRIS W. ABBOTT COLLECTION

Fred Goble's lumberyard in Silverton was fondly referred to as "Goble's Canon" in an issue of the *Silverton Miner* in 1907.

SUNDANCE PHOTO BY DELL A. McCOY

The Natalie Occidental mine prospered for a time — to the extent that the SG&N surveyed a route up the South Fork of Cement Creek. This would have entailed extremely steep grades for a railroad. Storm Peak encircles an alpine lake, just over the tree-crowned ridge above the mine site.

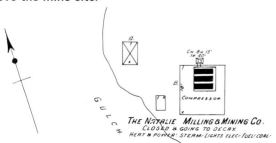

FRITZ KLINKE COLLECTION

SAN JUAN COUNTY HISTORICAL SOCIETY

The Silverton, Gladstone & Northerly depot and office building, on the east corner of Fourteenth and Mineral streets, was nearly brand new when this "portrait" was made in 1910. Silverton Railway locomotive

Number 100 sported an all-weather cab (added in 1888) as she waited on the mainline of the SG&N. The track in the foreground led to the SG&N enginehouse.

SAN JUAN COUNTY HISTORICAL SOCIETY

THE S. G. & N. R. R. CO
UNLIMITED TICKET

GOOD FOR ONE FIRST-CLASS PASSAGE
WHEN STAMPED ON BACK

Gladstone to Silverton

NO 4413

THE S. G. & N. R. R. CO.
UNLIMITED TICKET

GOOD FOR ONE FIRST-CLASS PASSAGE
WHEN STAMPED ON BACK

Silverton to Gladstone

NO 4413

WILLIAM PLUNKETT WATERCOLOR

The "Columbine Special" on the Silverton Northern stopped at several places along the Rio de las Animas to allow volunteers to pick hundreds of this beautiful State flower of

E. J. DYSON PHOTO —
McNAUGHTON FAMILY COLLECTION

Otto Brendel (left), who owned a group of claims in Maggie Gulch, and James Dyson are shown as they collected Colorado columbines above Howardsville for Columbine Day in 1911.

The Gladstone Branch—the most recent addition to Otto Mears' transportation complex—was, of course, the former Silverton, Gladstone and Northerly Railroad. This segment was 7.17 miles long, with the steepest grade at 5.5 percent, and averaged 3.91 percent over the entire length. Like the extension to Animas Forks, this branch was no straight-line railroad—there were 99 curves, including a reverse curve at milepost 5, composed of two 40-degree curves back-to-back with no transition tangent in between. In number, there were five 40-degreee curves, five of 36 degrees and one of 34 degrees, with the remaining 86 curves all of 30 degrees or less.

Perhaps at this point it is not inconsistent to inject a brief note regarding the measurement of railroad curves. Railroad locating engineers measure curvature by the angle subtended by a 100-foot chord across the curve; the greater the angle, the shorter the radius and the tighter the curve, thus:

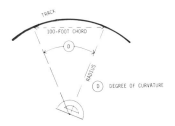

In February, 1910, John C. Woods became the master mechanic of the Silverton Northern, replacing Billy Booker, who had been promoted to general superintendent when Edward Hudson left the

road. Woods later reported that little track maintenance had been done on the road between 1908 and the time of his appointment.

While trackwork might have been somewhat lacking, that was not the case with traffic, for the *Silverton Miner,* in its issue dated July 8, 1910, reported that shipments for the month of June on the now-combined roads had totalled 2,600 tons of concentrate and 862 tons of ore, an increase of 40 percent over May, when concentrates had totalled 1,575 tons and ore had amounted to 375 tons.

A week later, a story in *The Denver Post* of July 14, 1910, shed light on other activities occupying Otto Mears' attention. Mears, John Flaherty and Joseph Bordeleau had leased the Iowa-Tiger mine and were working it with a small crew of very good miners. The men had struck a bonanza vein of gold ore worth $1,200 per ton, one of the richest strikes in the history of the San Juans, and the newspaper was quick to record the happy event.

By July 1, 1911, Silverton Northern locomotive Number 1 had been shoved in ahead of Silverton Number 100 and SG&N Number 33, all stored on the deadline along the SG&N engine-shed in Silverton. Only SN engines, numbers 3 and 4, and SG&N Number 34—none any more than a little over seven years old—were in working order.

In the fore part of the century—even as it does today—Denver held itself out as an attractive place for large conventions, and one such gathering, national in scope, convened in the "Queen City of the Rockies" in the summer of 1911. As part of the decorations for the affair, a great quantity of wild white and lavender Columbines (*Aquilegia cae-*

E. J. DYSON PHOTO —
McNAUGHTON FAMILY COLLECTION

James Dyson (facing away from the camera) and friends are shown at the general store in Howardsville. They were posing with columbines they had picked for Columbine Day, 1911. James Dyson was the construction engineer on the SG&N, and a long-time Silverton resident. He had been a school teacher there during 1879 and 1880, and for many years was the county surveyor.

rulea)—the Colorado State flower—was needed, and Otto Mears donated the use of a train on one of his little roads as a "Columbine Special," with the crew chipping in their services and the townspeople contributing their time. The train consisted of SG&N engine Number 33 (pulled from storage) and SG&N combine Number 1, probably with some flatcars coupled on behind, and was run up to Animas Forks. A local hardware merchant supplied Mears with 12 galvanized-iron washtubs to hold the freshly picked flowers, barely enough to contain the approximately 25,000 Columbines that were gathered on the free excursion. The colorful and showy flowers were shipped out of Silverton on flatcars, then transferred to boxcars at Alamosa. The monstrous bouquets of Nature's lovely handiwork were briefly displayed in front of *The Denver Post* building before being delivered to the convention. As was their custom as proprietors of *The Denver Post*, Harry Tammen and Fred Bonfils grabbed all the credit for the arrangements.

Incidentally, it might be noted that the Columbine now is protected by state law; it is unlawful to pick the flowers or harm the plants on all public lands, and a stunt of the type described above would not be tolerated today — neither on public nor private lands in Colorado.

On August 6, Mears attempted to promote additional business for his roads with a flattering letter to N. R. Bagley. Praising the latter's property above Animas Forks, Mears indicated that if Bagley would build an 800-ton concentrating mill down at Silverton, the railroad could give him a rate of 50 cents per ton on the crude ore. If Bagley were to build the mill near his Frisco tunnel above Animas Forks, Mears quoted a rate of $1.50 per ton from the terminal town. Mears also suggested in his letter that if Bagley would advance the cost of the three-quarter-mile extension—say $20,000— he would be allowed to deduct a portion of the freight charges until he was reimbursed for his costs.

E. J. DYSON PHOTO —
McNAUGHTON FAMILY COLLECTION

Columbine Day in 1911 was a good excuse for everyone to pose for pictures. This one was taken on the engine and tender of SG&N Number 33. From left to right the characters are: Charley Decker, fireman; Edward "Pete" Meyer, engineer; Otto Brendel; Tom Clark, brakeman; and Arthur Hudson, conductor. Standing in front of the tender, from left to right: Tom Dickey; William A. Way, Silverton town attorney until 1966; Sam Wittow; Otto Mears; Al Kramer; and Dr. Henkel. Mears purchased the tubs and took charge of delivering the flowers to Denver, where they were displayed.

A few days later that month, it became known that the management of the Silverton, Gladstone and Northerly had defaulted for the first time on their bond interest coupons. When the Chase National Bank of New York City inquired about the situation, James Pitcher had to explain that he was only the lessee of the road, and that since the Gold King mine at Gladstone was not working, there were no earnings for the road. He referred the bank to John D. Chipman as treasurer of the SG&N.

On August 25, Mears advised Charles H. Graham, the Philadelphia investor who had maintained his position as vice-president of the Silverton Railway after its reorganization, that he had been forced to put considerable sums of money into track maintenance since little had been done along that line for the past three years. Maintenance-of-way had consumed $938, while $787 had been spent on ties. What little production there was from the mines in the Red Mountain area was

being hauled by wagon to Ouray; none was being handled by the railroad, and business—as a result —was dull, except for the Silver Ledge mine at Chattanooga, which was running full force.

It appears that in the late summer of 1911, or at some time not long after, the *Animas Forks* was damaged in an accident for the last time. In Josie Moore Crum's book, *Three Little Lines*, there is an excellent account of the 1906 derailment involving the former Pullman car, as documented in the August 10, 1906, issue of the *Silverton Miner*, but her story purports to describe this accident to the car as having occurred in 1911. Clearly, her source had forgotten when the wrecks had occurred. In any event, after the last accident, the car was returned to the yard in Silverton where it was gradually dismantled, piece by piece.

In August, Mears wrote the Boston officers of the New Gold King Mining Company offering to lease the New Gold King mine, intending to generate business for the Gladstone Branch, and point-

DON STOTT COLLECTION

These two stalwart citizens probably were discussing the affairs of the day in this Eureka saloon at 9:05 a.m., Saturday, December 10, 1910. The saloonkeeper likely had a sizeable number of paying customers that evening, since it was a Saturday. This picture postcard actually was mailed from Eureka three days after the date on the wall calendar.

ing out that he had shown he could operate mines more cheaply than any big corporation. He followed up again in early October, stating that a resolution of problems was necessary before he could put the mine back in operation. He suggested dividing the royalties 50:50, with half going to a local trustee to pay creditors, including the miners, and the other half going to the company for distribution to the bondholders. Money had to be spent on the mill, in any case, since it was in bad shape and recovering only 50 percent of the values in the ore.

On October 5, 1911, the worst floods in Colorado history put all four railroads operating into Silverton out of commission. Winter stocks of food and coal had not yet been laid-in by either the merchants or the residents in the area, and unless the blockades could be lifted, the prospects for famine were frightening. Although estimates of damage to his roads came to $25,000, Mears proceeded as he had after the 1909 floods and quickly repaired the Silverton Northern and the Silverton

Railway. Repairs to the Gladstone Branch, however, were postponed since that line was totally washed out, and reconstruction would involve a job of fairly large dimension.

Inasmuch as his roads were almost useless as matters stood, Mears volunteered his services to the Denver and Rio Grande to clean up the Silverton Branch. The officers of the D&RG accepted his offer with alacrity, President E. T. Jeffery instructing his people as follows on October 15:

Silverton Branch. Mr. Otto Mears to open up from Silverton to Needleton, pursuant to arrangements made with Mr. J. B. Andrews by telephone on October 10th. Division Superintendent Luke to have direct charge and open up line between Needleton and Durango, calling upon Chief Engineer for such advice and engineering assistance as he may need.

Authorized to equip a force of engineers, surveyors and trackmen to work south reconstructing

SAN JUAN COUNTY HISTORICAL SOCIETY

Back in "the good old days," the Fourth of July could hardly go unnoticed in Silverton, as this view clearly shows. You are looking northeast along Greene Street, and apparently the crowd was waiting for the parade to come by. Some of the bandsmen obviously knew where to wet their whistles, as their presence outside the Chicago Saloon seems to indicate.

the roadbed toward Durango, Mears began clearing and rebuilding the track on Friday, the thirteenth, commandeering coal for the construction engine and ditcher from the mines and merchants. Meanwhile, in the absence of the regular service afforded by the Silverton Branch, mail and goods were being freighted by wagon from Ouray to Red Mountain and then brought down on the Silverton Railway. The limited capacity and slowness of the wagon trains was a serious bottleneck, and Silver-

ton residents volunteered to give up their coal and burn wood to hasten the re-establishment of rail transportation.

Using a 50-man crew, and assisted by D&RG Silverton agent, A. S. Hamilton, and Conductor Bondure, Mears cleared the upper four miles of the Silverton Branch the first day; reconstruction of the next six miles to Elk Park required a week's time. By November 10, a month after the arrangements had first been made, Mears reached milepost 480.5 at Needleton. He had employed 428 men to that date, with an average crew size of 235. The D&RG forces during the same period had reached milepost 474.5, six miles below Needleton.

A few days later, the two parties met, finally clearing the nine-week blockade of the area to the great relief of everyone (except possibly for the investors in the Silverton, Gladstone and Northerly, which was still ruined). Contrary to expectations (or perhaps not, depending upon the point of view), the first cars to reach Silverton were loaded not with coal, but rather with beer and caskets!

In mid-October, after the floods had destroyed all the roads and even as he was furiously engaged in rebuilding the upper portions of the Silverton Branch, Mears again wrote the Boston officer of the New Gold King Mining Company, advising that he had 40 men working the mine. He had intended to start the mill by November 1, but the washouts had stopped all progress and if concessions were not made, he would have to close the mine, as well as the SG&N. On November 14, in another letter to the Boston owners, he stated that the members of the Miners Union would strike if not given at least a portion of their pay. The strike threat came about because of a rumor that the proceeds from the New Gold King were to be kept entirely in Boston. There would be no need for such action if the money taken in from the mine— if only in part—were paid out to the miners.

The view below — shot in 1910 — shows the Silver Ledge mill in Chattanooga. The mainline of the Silverton Railway passed in front of the mill, circled around Chattanooga Loop, then climbed the mountainside above the mill, on its way to Red Mountain Pass.

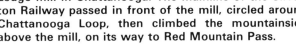

EDITH McNAUGHTON PHOTO —
McNAUGHTON FAMILY COLLECTION

EDITH McNAUGHTON PHOTO —
McNAUGHTON FAMILY COLLECTION

EDITH McNAUGHTON PHOTO —
McNAUGHTON FAMILY COLLECTION

Silverton Northern locomotive Number 1, outfitted with a wedge snowplow, is shown above — and on the opposite page (above) — switching at the Silver Ledge mill. The Chattanooga Loop circled up the hill, in back of the mill. Empty boxcars were spotted under the shed, as they were traded for loaded cars.

Having delivered three cars to the Silver Ledge mill, Silverton Northern locomotive Number 1 turned on Anderson's "kite track" and proceeded downgrade to Silverton with carloads of mine concentrate. The townsite of Chattanooga is to the left, out of view.

EDITH McNAUGHTON PHOTO —
McNAUGHTON FAMILY COLLECTION

CHARLES S. RYLAND COLLECTION

This extremely rare two-shot panoramic view was photographed above Silverton in 1912 — from the side of Kendall Mountain. From left to right, the peaks in the view are: Sultan Mountain, Bear Mountain — then, in the distance beyond the forks of Mineral Creek — Vermillion Peak, Pilot Knob and U. S. Grant Peak. At the center of the photograph, Anvil Mountain looms over the town, while above Cement Creek, Ohio Peak, McMillan Peak and Red Mountain can be seen on the skyline. On the right side of Cement Creek lies the base of Boulder Mountain.

Opposite page, below (left) — Otto Mears' likeness adorned this souvenir spoon, copies of which were given to guests at a banquet in Silverton.

Opposite page, below (right) — in 1935, the Otto Mears house, at Tenth and Reese streets in Silverton, was by no means the "castle" one might expect such a famous person to own. The house still stands today, although the porch and bay window have been removed. Appropriately, the house wore a blanket of snow.

JAMES G. SCHNEIDER PHOTO

DON STOTT COLLECTION

273

CHARLES S. RYLAND COLLECTION

The D&RG enginehouse was the center of attention in this view shot at Silverton. Just behind the enginehouse, the roof of Silverton Northern coach Number 4 can be seen. On the same track (to the right) are Silverton Railway combine Number 11 (the former *Yankee Girl*) and SG&N combine Number 1. In the foreground, the combine, *Red Mountain,* was sitting off the track — and, to the right, was Otto Mears' combination buffet-sleeper, the *Animas Forks,* with its windows boarded up.

Mears was sure he could make a good property of the New Gold King and promised to look after the interests of the Boston people. He planned to incorporate a leasing company with a few of the better miners as partners, since he had access to their secret information, and was sure he could improve the mill. He pointed out that his lease on the Iowa-Tiger two years earlier had netted $15,000 in two months, using only two miners.

On November 19, Mears borrowed $5,000 to partially cover the expenses of repairing the flood damage. Now 71 years old, exhausted by the strenuous exertions of all the work in the preceding weeks, Otto Mears left Silverton for California and semi-retirement. Management of his three little railroads—now a family business—was placed in the hands of his trusted son-in-law, James R. Pitcher, Jr.

274

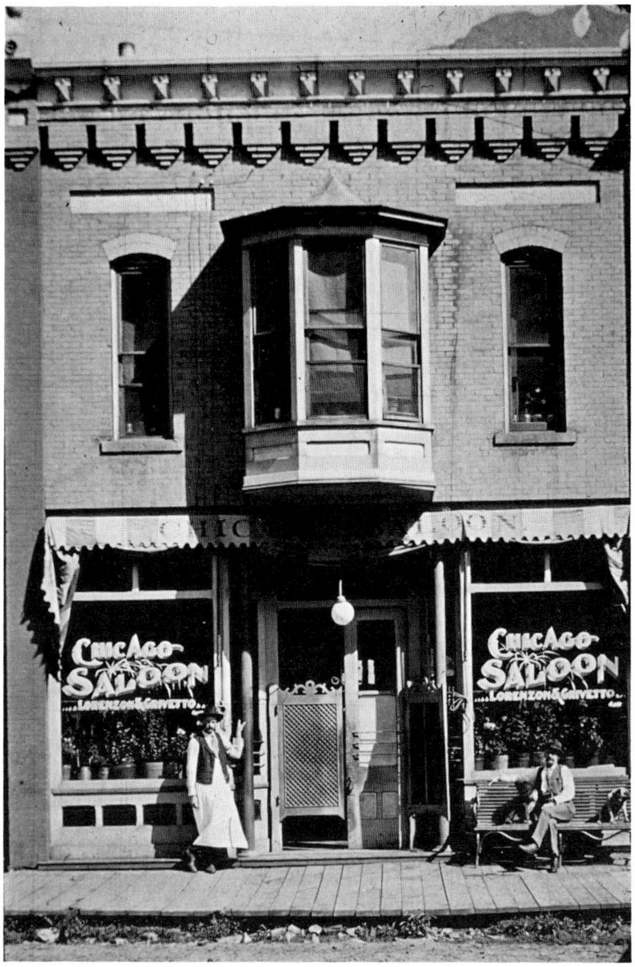

RICHARD A. RONZIO COLLECTION

Mssrs. Lorenzon and Grivetto were proudly standing by their freshly refurnished Chicago Saloon in Silverton when this scene was photographed.

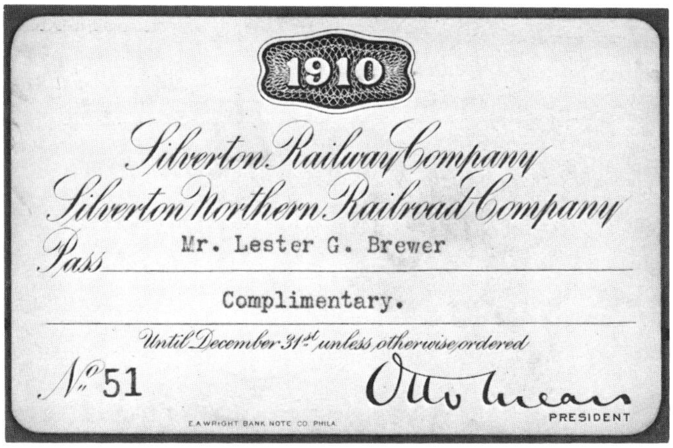
1910
Silverton Railway Company
Silverton Northern Railroad Company
Pass Mr. Lester G. Brewer
Complimentary.
Until December 31st, unless otherwise ordered
No 51
Otto Mears
PRESIDENT
E.A. WRIGHT BANK NOTE CO. PHILA.

SILVERTON

FROM KENDALL MOUNTAIN

A SPECIAL FOUR-PAGE
PICTURE EXTRAVAGANZA

The two 8 x 10-inch glass negatives used to produce the two-page spread on the preceding pages have been enlarged and printed on the next four pages to show greater detail. In *SCENE 1* we see (among other things) Fischer's brewery, located on Mineral Creek (near the left edge and close to the middle of the picture); the North Star (Sultan) mine and mill, upstream from the brewery; the Walsh smelter, to the right of the mine and mill; the second-hand streetcar, which was purchased from Durango, but never used — sitting next to the ties of the Silverton Railway (which curve to the right, at the left edge of the page, heading toward Mineral Creek); the combine, *Red Mountain,* off the track in front of the D&RG yard; the combination buffet-sleeper, *Animas Forks,* on the spur in front of the D&RG roundhouse (at the rear of three 24-foot SN boxcars, in the middle foreground); behind the D&RG roundhouse are four passenger cars — SN coach Number 4, SRy combine Number 11 (the former *Yankee Girl*), SG&N combine Number 1, and (near the D&RG depot) SRR baggage car Number 5; and, beyond the yard, is the newly-built Silverton Northern enginehouse (just above the D&RG roundhouse). *SCENE 2* shows the southern portion of Silverton. Items of interest are: the D&RG passenger depot (near the centerfold, at lower left); the Silverton Northern's office and the superintendent's living quarters, just above the D&RG depot (on Tenth Street). *SCENE 3* reveals the main part of Silverton's business district, with the impressive Grand Imperial Hotel sitting at the corner of Twelfth and Greene streets (near the center of the view); notorious Blair Street, one block east of the hotel (toward the camera), "featuring" numerous saloons and bordellos; while near the bottom of the page, one can plainly see the D&RG bridge over Cement Creek, a short distance downstream from the SN's bridge over the same creek. The two lines crossed each other to the right of these bridges. *SCENE 4* shows the north end of town, where the San Juan County Court House stands out prominently — with the county jail in the same block (just to the right), now used by the San Juan County Historical Society for their museum. Directly below the courthouse — beside Cement Creek — is the Silverton, Gladstone & Northerly enginehouse, while the SG&N's passenger depot is across the track on Mineral Street. The Kendrick-Gelder (or Ross) smelter is on the north edge of town (to the right), on the hillside above Cement Creek. Incidentally, no automobiles can be seen in these four views because at this time (1912) only one — a 1911 one-cylinder Cadillac — could be accounted for in all of Silverton!

GEORGE L. BEAM PHOTO —
JACKSON C. THODE COLLECTION

Silverton was being built to last, as you can see by the many stone and brick buildings on Greene Street in this 1909 photograph. The city hall was new at this time, having been built in 1907 from granite quarried out of the Wyman quarry along Mineral Creek. Sultan Mountain looms above the town, making a beautiful backdrop — and, if you look closely, you can see the Little Dora mill at the far end of the street.

The old Posey & Wingate store in Silverton was taken over by William H. Crooke, who posed with his cronies in front of the relettered store.

RICHARD A. RONZIO COLLECTION

SUNDANCE PHOTO BY DELL A. McCOY

The interior shot below was taken in the main sales-room of the store owned by Joseph Bordeleau, partner of Mears and Slattery in leasing the Iowa-Tiger mines in 1910. Glass cases and clerks to wait on customers certainly discouraged shoplifters.

Sultan Mountain fills the skyline of this view — which looks very much like the scene on the opposite page. The blustery winter winds of a high-pressure system were driving snow clouds east as Silverton awakened on a Sunday morning during early 1975. Many of the buildings along Greene Street look the same today as they did over 60 years ago.

In 1911, Silverton was a very active town, as shown on the following two pages. The camera lens centered on the row of blocks between Blair Street (left) and Greene Street (right). The peaks on the skyline are Grand Turk (on the left) and Sultan Mountain (on the right). To the left of the Rio de las Animas can be seen the foot of Kendall Mountain, with Cement Creek running through the foreground of the view. The new San Juan County Court House, built in 1908, stands out plainly, just beyond Cement Creek — with the jail building appearing to crowd close to it. The SG&N mainline wanders along the near side of Cement Creek and curves to the left to reach its terminal. One block to the left of the SG&N is the Silverton Northern mainline to Animas Forks, and one block farther (to the west) is the D&RG's Silverton Branch, coming from Durango. The Silverton Railway from Red Mountain is in the far distance, wandering across the picture. The D&RG departed from town by way of the canyon of the Rio de las Animas, which can be seen to the far left in this scene.

THE SILVERTON MINER, 1907 —
MORRIS W. ABBOTT COLLECTION

L. C. McCLURE PHOTO —
DENVER PUBLIC LIBRARY WESTERN COLLECTION

281

SUNDANCE PHOTO BY DELL A. McCOY

The second section of the D&RGW's *Silverton* train had just pulled into its namesake town on this early summer day in 1975. The first section of the train had already stopped at Blair Street and the passengers had detrained, as fluffy white clouds drifted by. Anvil Mountain forms part of the backdrop, while the Rio de las Animas spreads across the floodplain in the foreground, flowing through Bakers Park from right to left.

CHAPTER

VI

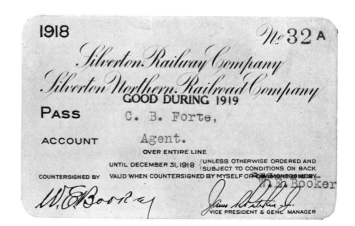

1918   № 32 A
Silverton Railway Company
Silverton Northern Railroad Company
                        GOOD DURING 1919
PASS   C. B. Forte,
ACCOUNT   Agent.
                    OVER ENTIRE LINE
            UNTIL DECEMBER 31, 1918 / UNLESS OTHERWISE ORDERED AND
                                  / SUBJECT TO CONDITIONS ON BACK
COUNTERSIGNED BY   VALID WHEN COUNTERSIGNED BY MYSELF OR C. W. MONTGOMERY
                                                    C. B. Booker
    W. E. Booker   James McLachlan Jr.
                            VICE PRESIDENT & GENL MANAGER

The Pitcher Years
1912 - 1930

WITH THE *PATHFINDER of the San Juan* again gone from the scene, the headaches involved in running and managing the affairs of the Silverton roads now were James Pitcher's as the year, 1912, loomed on the horizon. He had been well-schooled by his close personal and family association with Otto Mears in the five years since they had left New York City together; and, although his father-in-law returned to Colorado from time to time and still had the last word in important decisions, Pitcher showed no hesitation or lack of enthusiasm in tackling the problems before him.

Excepting the brief war boom of 1917, the mining business in the San Juans for the next 12 years was to be fairly slow—with traffic volumes on the Mears roads at such low levels that a paper loss was shown each year after operating expenses, taxes and interest were paid. Since the Mears family owned most of the stock, however, no one really was hurting. A new revival, beginning in 1923, permitted the roads to earn a profit each year until the Great Depression struck in October of 1929.

After Mears left Silverton in November of 1911, one of the first tasks Pitcher undertook was to re-negotiate the proportions paid by his roads to the Denver and Rio Grande for the costs of the car inspector at Durango, shared jointly between the two employers. On November 27, 1911, due to snow up the valley of Mineral Creek, as well as the shortage of fuel and cars resulting from the October flood, he suspended service on the Silverton Railway. In a letter to C. H. Graham of Philadelphia, he stated that the Silver Ledge at Chattanooga would be given train service again when the

D&RG was back in full operation.

The following January, Pitcher tried to clarify the situation concerning the Silverton, Gladstone and Northerly, which had defaulted on its payments for the first time, with the Newtonville Trust Company of Boston, holders of the SG&N mortgage. He pointed out that the Silverton Northern was only the lessor of the SG&N, and that he had no knowledge of what the corporation did with their share of the gross receipts. He also advised the trust company that there would be no revenue from the road that winter due to poor ores and the flood damage that had been incurred the past fall.

The pleasing results enjoyed by Otto Mears in 1909 and 1910 with his lease of the Iowa-Tiger mining complex had subsequently led him to form the Iowa-Tiger Mining Company, with Jack Slattery as partner and co-investor. The new organization leased the properties of the Iowa Gold Mining and Milling Company, and in late January of 1912 they reopened the Iowa company's mill. The first car of ore netted $738.00 for the Mears-Slattery combine.

John H. (Jack) Slattery was a civil engineer who had moved to Silverton from Ironton about 1893, when the Silverton Railroad ran into trouble and cut back service following the Silver Panic. In Silverton, Slattery first bought the Bucket of Blood Saloon, then bought the Hub Saloon in the Grand Hotel—later known as the Grand Imperial. He started a baseball club in Silverton, invited major league players to come and play, became a Colorado state senator, and was second vice-president of the Silverton Railway and the Silverton Northern from 1917 to 1923.

On the ninth of February, 1912, Pitcher wrote to

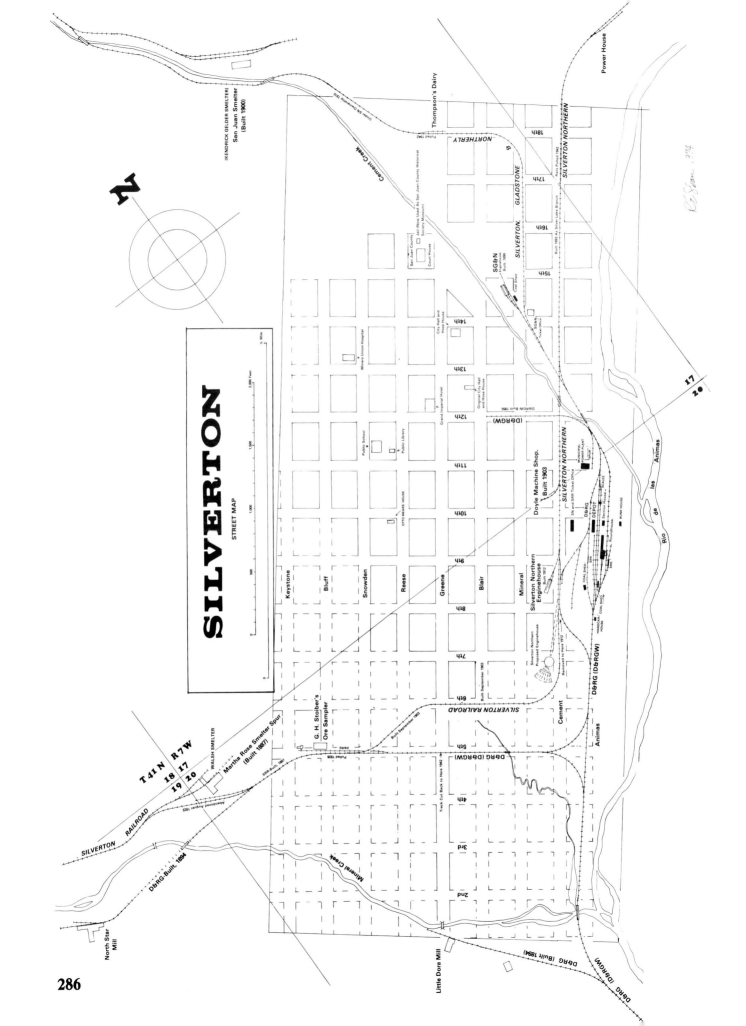

SILVERTON

STREET MAP

0   500   1,000   1,500   2,000 Feet

0   ¼ Mile

N

T 41 N   R 7 W

18 17
19 20

SILVERTON RAILROAD

D&RG-Built 1894

North Star Mill

WALSH SMELTER

Martha Rose Smelter Spur

Martha Rose Smelter (Built 1887)

Abandoned August 1922

SRR-Built 1887

G. H. Stoiber's Ore Sampler

Pulled 1926

D&RG

Built September 1903

Little Dora Mill

Mineral Creek

D&RG (D&RGW)

Track Cut Back to Here 1942

D&RG (Built 1894)

D&RG (D&RGW)

(Kendrick Gelder Smelter)
San Juan Smelter
(Built 1900)

Cement Creek

Under SN Ownership 1910

Thompson's Dairy

Power House

Pulled 1942

Rails Pulled 1942

SILVERTON NORTHERN

Built 1893 As Silver Lake Branch

18th

17th

NORTHERLY

SILVERTON, GLADSTONE, & NORTHERN

16th

15th

SG&N
Enginehouse
Built 1895

SG&N
Coal Shed

SG&N
Ticket Office

San Juan County
Jail (Now Used As San Juan County Historical Society Museum)

Court House

City Hall and Hose House

14th

Miners Union Hospital

13th

Original City Hall and Hose House

Grand Imperial Hotel

12th

D&RGW Built 1906

Keystone

Bluff

Snowden

Reese

Greene

Blair

Mineral

Cement

Animas

417

416

418

7th

6th

5th

4th

3rd

2nd

Public School

Public Library

OTTO MEARS HOUSE

11th

10th

Doyle Machine Shop, Built 1903

SILVERTON NORTHERN

MUNICIPAL POWER PLANT

SN and SRR Ticket Office

D&RG DEPOT

SCALES

SRR

SRR

Section House

BUNK HOUSE

COAL SHED

COAL SHED

Roundhouse

HANDCAR HOUSE

Silverton Northern Enginehouse
Built 1912

Silverton Northern
Proposed Enginehouse
Built September 1903

Removed to Here 1912

D&RG (D&RGW)

SILVERTON RAILROAD

Built September 1903

Rio de las Animas

17
20

286

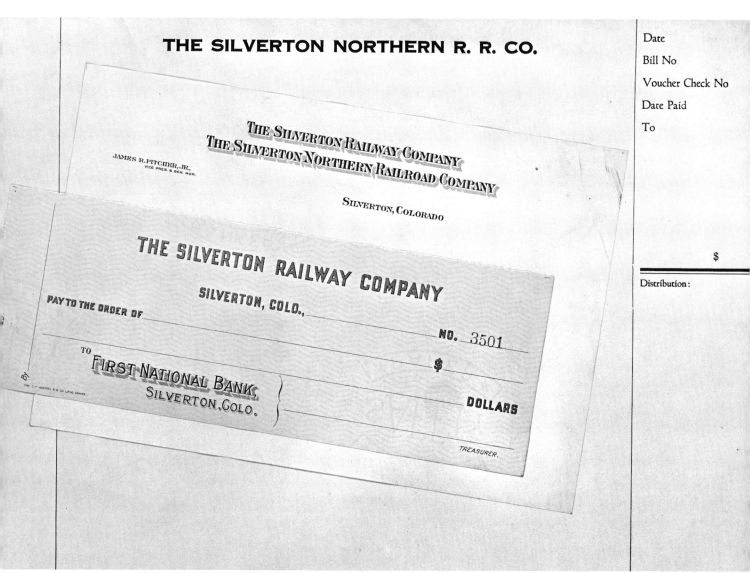

THE SILVERTON NORTHERN R. R. CO.

Date

Bill No

Voucher Check No

Date Paid

To

$

Distribution:

THE SILVERTON RAILWAY COMPANY
THE SILVERTON NORTHERN RAILROAD COMPANY

SILVERTON, COLORADO

JAMES R. PITCHER, JR.,
VICE PRES. & GEN. MGR.

THE SILVERTON RAILWAY COMPANY

SILVERTON, COLO.,

PAY TO THE ORDER OF

NO. 3501

$

TO

FIRST NATIONAL BANK,
SILVERTON, COLO.

DOLLARS

BY

THE C. F. HOECKEL, B. B. CO. LITHO. DENVER.

TREASURER.

SAN JUAN COUNTY HISTORICAL SOCIETY

Examples are shown here of a Silverton Railway blank
check, letterhead and a Silverton Northern billhead.

Mears in Los Angeles, advising him that during January, 75 cars of ore had been shipped on the Silverton Northern, 64 cars on the Silverton Railway and 9 cars on the operating remnant of the Gladstone road. The Iowa mine also had shipped nine cars, but the Silver Ledge was closed temporarily for lack of money. Six carloads of concentrate had been freighted into Silverton from the Gold King mill at Gladstone during the month, and Pitcher planned to have the rest of the branch up Cement Creek rebuilt and reopened by autumn. (Seventeen additional cars of ore would be waiting for loading and transportation at the Gold King when service finally was resumed.) The richest car of concentrate from this wealthy and productive property in 1912 paid $1,474.00.

By May 1, 1912, the Interstate Commerce Commission, in the interest of increased safety, had established rules for locomotive boiler inspection, and Pitcher addressed a letter to Burnham, Williams and Company (the longtime corporate name of the Baldwin Locomotive Works, but no longer applicable since the reorganization of July 1, 1909), asking for blueprints for the boilers of SN engines numbers 3 and 4, and SG&N Number 34. On the thirteenth, Pitcher asked I. H. Luke, the D&RG superintendent in Durango, to move 55 boxcars into Silverton and store them in the yard there so that cars would be available for loading in the event of washouts on the Silverton Branch—so imminently possible each spring.

Later that spring, H. L. Frank, the son of Silverton Northern and Silverton Railway secretary, Jerome B. Frank, became the new auditor and agent in Silverton in place of Harry C. Brown, who had suffered a heart attack in October of 1911.

The 1912 summer passenger schedule of the Silverton Railway showed one passenger train a day

THE SILVERTON MINER, 1907 —
MORRIS W. ABBOTT COLLECTION

Looking down on Silver Lake in 1907, the photographer made an awe-inspiring shot from Little Giant Peak, 13,416 feet above sea level. The summit of Kendall Mountain is on the right, while Snowden Peak is in the notch. More than two-thirds of the lake is visible in this scene. Pollution from the Silver Lake mine (lower right) is quite evident. In fact, tailings (waste minerals) from the Silver Lake mine nearly cut the lake in two. The Iowa-Tiger mining complex caused far less pollution. The Iowa is on the lower left, while the Tiger is near the center. A cableway across the lake connected the two mines.

AFTER 8 DAYS RETURN TO

THE SILVERTON,
GLADSTONE & NORTHERLY
RAILROAD CO.

SILVERTON - COLORADO

DON STOTT COLLECTION

The starting work on a mine required a lot of muscle and luck. This miner was using a pneumatic drill to open a hole for blasting powder, to open up a vein. Candles were still in use in the Iowa-Tiger mine in this 1912 scene.

OSCAR NELSON PHOTO   CARL SKOWRONSKI COLLECTION

THE SILVERTON MINER, 1907 —
MORRIS W. ABBOTT COLLECTION

The reflection in Silver Lake provided a nearly perfect double image in this view, making the origin of the lake's name obvious. The Tiger mine and upper mill are reflected here.

One-quarter mile south of Animas Canyon, Arrastra Gulch suddenly steepens to form this old cirque wall, cut by the head of a glacier more than 10,000 years old. The ore from the Iowa-Tiger and Silver Lake mines was carried down this cliff in ore buckets. The building on the left was the Silver Lake tramway station, where buckets were transferred from the steep upper cableway to the gentler lower line. The building on the right (near the center of the view) was the Iowa-Tiger mill, where the ore was processed and waste discarded before the ore continued its trip down to the lower terminal on the Silverton Northern. In this view, you are looking south; the lake is just over the notch in the head wall of the cirque.

OSCAR NELSON PHOTO — CARL SKOWRONSKI COLLECTION

OSCAR NELSON PHOTO — CARL SKOWRONSKI COLLECTION

This gang was transporting a large gear to the upper terminal of the Iowa-Tiger tramway in 1909.

OSCAR NELSON PHOTO — CARL SKOWRONSKI COLLECTION

The Iowa-Tiger mill, on the side of Little Giant Peak in Arrastra Gulch, is shown here as it appeared in 1912. The tramway buckets, which operated on the line to Silver Lake, entered the mill at the two open doors (upper right). If you look closely, you can see a bucket just outside one of the doors. The lean ore was fed to the stamps in the left half of the mill and worked downhill by gravity. Rich ore and concentrate then was trammed on down to the Silverton Northern for ship-ment to one or more smelters for further processing.

Looking southeast at the same mill shown above — still called the Iowa mill when the view below was made in 1903 — one can see both of the cableways that served the Silver Lake mines. Buckets running on the lower line came in and went out of the mill from the doors in the tower-like structure.

THE SILVERTON MINER, GOLDEN SAN JUAN EDITION — MORRIS W. ABBOTT COLLECTION

OSCAR NELSON PHOTO — CARL SKOWRONSKI COLLECTION

In this scene you are looking east, across Arrastra Gulch, at the Iowa-Tiger mill (on the lower right), and the Silver Lake tramway station (above and to the left).The ore entered these buildings from the upper right and went downhill to the Silverton Northern, to the left. Concentrate was moved from the mill down to the SN by wagon.

from Silverton to Red Mountain, requiring 1 hour and 30 minutes in each direction. Since service no longer was offered beyond Red Mountain, it would appear that the Joker tunnel, where loadings from the Guston, Yankee Girl and Genessee-Vanderbilt were handled, had been closed. Most of the other Red Mountain mines also must have shut down about that time, for 1912 was the last year to show any noticeable passenger revenues for the road.

In May, the little Stover railway motorcar, which had achieved so much popularity during its trial runs after delivery in August of 1908, finally broke down. Stover had gone out of business and transferred the plans and patterns for his machines to the Buda Foundry and Manufacturing Company of Chicago. On June 8, the parts necessary to repair the little railcar were ordered by the Silverton Northern from Buda; however, the manufacturer shipped the wrong items. Pitcher followed up by writing again on June 18, 28 and 29 over the foul-up—each time more indignantly. At last, on July 1,

OSCAR NELSON PHOTO — CARL SKOWRONSKI COLLECTION

This was the carrier cable used for the Iowa-Tiger tramway. The tow cable was lighter.

OSCAR NELSON PHOTO — CARL SKOWRONSKI COLLECTION

These tramway towers and maintainence shacks belonged to the Iowa-Tiger, shown here in 1905, in Arrastra Gulch.

he sent the manufacturer drawings of the parts required, the correct parts were received and the car was returned to service once again.

On June 30, 1913, boiler inspection reports for Silverton Northern engines, numbers 1, 3 and 4; and for SG&N Number 33, were finally submitted to the ICC. Although it was undoubtedly passed also, the record for SG&N engine Number 34 has not survived. Silverton, Gladstone and Northerly Number 32 had been scrapped and the boiler now was at Mears' sawmill at Tefft; Silverton Railway Number 100 was sitting on the deadline in Silverton. Silverton Northern Number 1 had not seen any service since July 1, 1911; however, during the brief 1917 boom, it was to be resurrected, parts cannibalized from engines 32 and 100 being used to keep it going at that time.

The Silverton Northern's employees, doing their part as dutiful citizens of the community, gained the thanks of the people of Silverton for their efforts in support of the Miners Union hospital. The railroad crews held benefit dances at the Miners Union hall in February, 1912, and again in March, 1913, bringing in a total of $350.00, which was turned over to the hospital.

In mid-January of 1914, there occurred another of those by-now-expected winter blizzards that blocked all the roads. On Tuesday, January 22, the Silverton Northern crews reached Gladstone, and by Wednesday afternoon the entire line was clear; only one slide had been encountered and that was bucked out with the pilot plow on the engines. Thankfully, no shoveling had been necessary and business on the branch was resumed with little loss of time. Passengers outbound on the D&RG were able to leave Silverton that Tuesday only through the kindness of James Pitcher; the big road had no coaches in Silverton and the only train in town was the work outfit up from Durango, which had just finished clearing the line. Pitcher loaned one of the Silverton Northern's coaches to go back with the work train, thus saving an extra day's layover for the travelers.

During the next week, a larger storm dropped its snows on the area, and the D&RG spent the entire first week of February clearing the Silverton

This view was shot inside the Iowa-Tiger tramway terminal in 1910, showing workers standing beside one of the ore buckets. These buckets were made to rotate at the points where the yoke fastens on.

OSCAR NELSON PHOTO — CARL SKOWRONSKI COLLECTION

Branch once again. By February 6, the work train from Durango had reached a point a mile south of Elk Park—seven and one-half miles down the cañon from Silverton. The local newspapers quoted the road's representatives as saying, "The first train will be here when it arrives."

With the aid of about 50 shovelers, the Silverton Northern crew of "snowbuckers" broke through the slides on their line between Silverton and Eureka much more quickly than expected, and trains between the two towns had already resumed their schedules. Pitcher then took the railroad's American Railroad Ditcher steam shovel; and, with a crew of 25 men, proceeded to work south, clearing the D&RG tracks until he met the big road's outfit from Durango.

In 1914, Otto and Mary Mears decided to settle permanently in California, and bought into the Hotel Maryland in Pasadena to provide themselves with a home and a source of regular income. Back east, in Colorado, the Guggenheim's Silver Lake mine failed to make expenses; and, with a less than favorable outlook for the future, it was promptly closed. Although portions of the property later would be turned over to small lessees, this pre-World War I closure marked the end of large-scale operations for this mine as a separate entity. It was later incorporated into the Shenandoah—Dives operation from 1930 to 1952. Total production from the Silver Lake mine, under the Guggenheims, had amounted to $7,790,000—nearly as remunerative to that ownership as the property earlier had been to Ed and Lena Stoiber.

Another mining complex of worthwhile scope was the Bagley, or Frisco, tunnel above Animas Forks. In the two-year period encompassing 1913 and 1914, this operation produced 7,166 tons of ore, with a value approaching $100,000. Otto Mears had shown his usual uncanny perception in his appraisal of the holdings of Bagley in 1911, when he had urged the owner to consider construction of a mill.

In 1913, 1914 and 1915, the Silverton, Gladstone and Northerly conducted operations on a tri-weekly basis, running a mixed train on Mondays, Wednesdays and Fridays. The outbound train left Silverton at 1:00 p.m., arriving at Gladstone at 1:45 p.m., while the return journey was scheduled to leave Gladstone at 2:15 p.m. and arrive back in Silverton at 3:00 p.m. But on February 6, 1915, a snowslide blocked the track, and operation of the seven-and-one-half-mile line was brought to a halt for the remainder of that spring.

On July 10, 1915, the owners of the SG&N finally lost their railroad through foreclosure, after defaulting on the mortgage interest requirements.

OSCAR NELSON PHOTO — CARL SKOWRONSKI COLLECTION

These miners rode ore buckets to work, rather than use the narrow, steep trail.

OSCAR NELSON PHOTO — CARL SKOWRONSKI COLLECTION

This was a temporary cable tramway station used during construction of the Iowa-Tiger line. The small gasoline engine (center) was noted for the amount of noise it could make.

OSCAR NELSON PHOTO — CARL SKOWRONSKI COLLECTION

The riffle tables in the Iowa-Tiger's upper mill suffered damage when the roof caved in at Silver Lake because of a snowslide.

GROUT PHOTO — DON STOTT COLLECTION

This was the Little Dora mill (or Hercules Consolidated Mining Company) at the base of Sultan Mountain, one mile southwest of the Imperial Hotel in Silverton. The road in the foreground — with the bridge spanning

Mineral Creek — is Greene Street. The mill was served by the D&RG from a spur coming off the Silverton Branch, down by the Rio de las Animas (to the left). The mill received its water from about half a mile up

Mineral Creek, in the flume above the D&RG boxcars. Incidentally, these cars were among the type that forced Alex Anderson to rebuild all the bridges on the SN and SRR in 1904. They were twice as heavy (when loaded) as the older type — with each one of the new cars having a capacity of 25 tons. The Needleton Peaks appear in the Animas Canyon (behind the boilerhouse smokestacks).

RICHARD A. RONZIO COLLECTION

Blair Street in Silverton was infamous for its many saloons and "girls of the night." The Tremount Saloon was one of the "finest" night spots in town back around the turn of the century — and attracted many of the hard-working miners who were seeking to quench their thirst and satisfy their lustful desires. Notice the girls gazing "longingly" out of the upstairs windows.

Opposite page, above — this American Smelting & Refining Company receipt and bill were made out to Otto Mears, lessee of the Gold King mine.

Opposite page, below — the Pitcher family enjoyed a picnic one summer day in 1912, with Silverton Northern railbus Number 1, the Stover vehicle. From left to right: James R. Pitcher Jr., J. R. Pitcher III, Otto M. Pitcher, Robertson M. Pitcher, an unnamed friend, Cora M. Pitcher and another friend.

THE SILVERTON MINER —
GOLDEN SAN JUAN EDITION, 1907

To counteract evil in Silverton, the more pure of soul constructed this and other churches in Silverton. This one was the Congregational Church as it looked in 1907.

DUPLICATE

rm 1. 10m.

ORE SETTLEMENT
AMERICAN SMELTING AND REFINING CO.
DURANGO PLANT

No. *187*

MONTH *Feb* 1913

ought of *Otto Mears, Lee*
Gladstone, Colo

Durango, Colo., *Feb 5* 1913

NO.	LOT NO. Smelter	LOT NO. Mine	NAME OF ORE	GROSS POUNDS	Moisture Per Cent.	NET POUNDS	ASSAY Ounces Gold	Ounces Silver	% Lead	% Copper Dry	% Silica	% Iron	% Zinc	%	BASIS OF SETTLEMENT Per Oz. Gold	Per Cent. Silver	Per Unit Lead	Per Unit Copper	Treatment Per Ton	Net Value Per Ton	TOTAL VALUE
49	6044	16-129	Gold King	429001 1³		380520	97⁵	7 4⁵	4 0⁵	0 ¹⁰	√	33 ¹			$79-95	21⁵			186	21128	404 87
72	6045	16-130	" "	417208 ⁸		380501 ¹⁰	7 ¹⁵	3 ¹⁵	0 ²⁰	√	9 33 ⁵				√ √		√		236	23320	441 38

W YORK QUOTATIONS - DATE OF *Settlement*

Silver ... 62 3/8 ... Per Oz.

Lead ... " Cwt.

Copper ... 15775 ... " Lb.

DEDUCTIONS

Lot 6044 ... 85.81
Freight ... 6045 ... 83.44
Switching ... 2.06

846 25

117 12 5

$ 675 00

t Proceeds

AMERICAN SMELTING AND REFINING CO.

SAN JUAN COUNTY HISTORICAL SOCIETY

Received from Otto Mears Loma Dollars

Durango, Colo. February 5th 1913

Sixteen & 87 ...

For Royalty on shipments from Gold King Mines

Lots 6044 lb. 129
6045 lb. 130
credit to account of Otto King Mine Co.

American Smelting & Refining Co.
Durango, Colo.
Fred Hagen

$ 16 87/100

COLORADO RAILROAD MUSEUM COLLECTION

On the following two pages — recess time at the Silverton school provided an unknown photographer the perfect opportunity to capture the town's young folk at play in 1910. This building has since been replaced with a more sound structure. All grades were taught in the same school.

A. PAYNE COLLECTION — COURTESY DON STOTT

A locomotive, with snowplow blade attached, had just arrived in Silverton, C. 1912. You are looking northeast, up the D&RG track beside the Silverton depot. Silverton Railway baggage car Number 5 — sitting on the house track next to the depot — was nearly buried in snow. The building to the right was the D&RG two-stall roundhouse, rebuilt in 1903, and torn down during the Great Depression.

The troubled road had been no joy to its owners in recent years, and history—paralleling the situation of five years previously—was about to repeat itself. To Otto Mears and his Silverton Northern, the adversity afflicting this little road was opportunity knocking at the door once again, and the SN board of directors decided to make an offer for purchase of the trackage and equipment, allowing $40,000 for the purpose. Ever mindful of the dollar, Mears succeeded in buying the SG&N for $14,600 at the foreclosure sale on July 23, and then transferred the title to the Silverton Northern by deed.

Meanwhile, on Mears' other roads that spring, the Silver Ledge resumed work, and by May 6 was shipping again on the Silverton Railway. The *Silverton Standard,* on June 19, reported that the Silverton Northern had opened up for the new season.

An article in the July 10, 1915, issue of the same paper is the first record found regarding the new railbus—nicknamed *Casey Jones*—reporting that *Casey* had jumped the track at the Green Mountain switch while running on the reopened Silverton Northern. Clyde Jones had designed and built *Casey Jones* the previous winter in the machine

shops of the Sunnyside mine at Eureka, using a Maxwell motor and what were reported as junk parts. It is likely that the former Stover railbus was part of the junk.

The original and primary purpose of the new railbus was to serve as an ambulance in cases of emergency, although the mine yard foreman, Henry Gray, used it to make all his lodge meetings in Silverton, as well as for other social occasions. The eight miles to Silverton from Eureka normally took 20 minutes.

Casey seated 11 passengers, had a four-wheel pilot truck and a chain drive to the single rear axle, with brakes operated by turning the steering wheel. The car had a special jack built-in for setting it on the rails and for turning it around, while brooms were mounted just behind the pilot to clean the rails ahead of the car.

In 1918, after another misfortune, *Casey* was rebuilt again at a cost of $1,000; a Cadillac engine, transmission, drive shaft and differential were substituted for the old parts in the running gear. Old *Casey Jones* now is a prime exhibit among the displays at the museum of the San Juan County Historical Society in Silverton.

300

DR. JAMES R. JACKSON PHOTO

Casey Jones looked like this near the end of operations. She was spotted at the Sunnyside mill on July 2, 1940, where this picture was shot.

The Silverton Northern enginehouse, which was built in 1912 at Ninth and Cement streets, is shown here as it appeared in 1972.

301

THE SILVERTON NORTHERN RAILROAD COMPANY

FREIGHT TARIFF NO. 4

CANCELS FREIGHT TARIFF No. 2

OF

LOCAL RATES

ON

ORE

BETWEEN

SILVERTON, COLORADO

AND

STATIONS IN COLORADO

ISSUED JULY 25, 1915 EFFECTIVE SEPTEMBER 5, 1915

Between SILVERTON, COLORADO, And	RATES IN DOLLARS PER TON OF 2,000 POUNDS Car Lots Minimum Weight 30,000 lbs.	
	Valuation Over $15 00	Valuation Under $15.00
Robin.....................Colo.	0.60	0.60
Collins................."	0.60	0 60
Howardsville............."	1.00	0.75
Old Hundred............."	1.25	0 75
Green Mountain..........."	1 25	0 75
Hamlet..................."	1.10	0.75
Middleton..............."	1.10	0.75
Kittimac................"	1.25	0 75
Minnie.................."	1.25	0.75
Eureka.................."	1.25	0.75

Between SILVERTON, COLORADO And	RATES IN DOLLARS PER TON OF 2,000 POUNDS Car Lots Minimum Weight 30,000 lbs.	
	Valuation Over $15.00	Valuation Under $15.00
Tom Moore.............Colo.	2.00	1.25
Silver Wing............."	2.25	1.50
Astor..................."	2.25	1.50
Lion Tunnel............."	2.50	1.75
	Valuation Over $25.00	Valuation Under $25.00
Waldheim..............Colo.	0.40	0.40
Animas Forks..........."	2.50	1.75

JAMES R. PITCHER, JR.,
Vice-President and General Manager,
Silverton, Colorado.

SAN JUAN COUNTY HISTORICAL SOCIETY

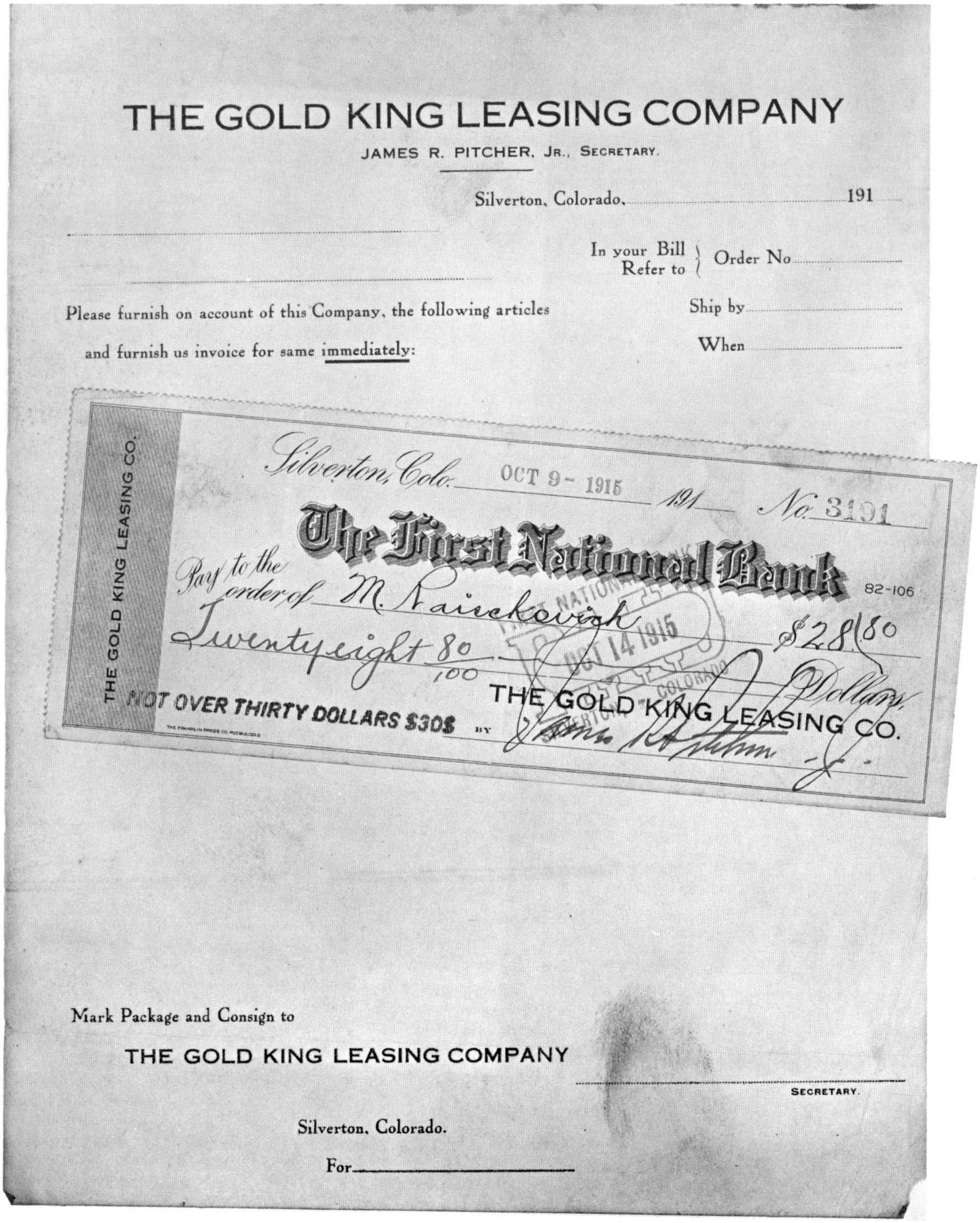

THE GOLD KING LEASING COMPANY

JAMES R. PITCHER, Jr., Secretary.

Silverton, Colorado, ... 191

In your Bill Refer to } Order No.

Please furnish on account of this Company, the following articles and furnish us invoice for same immediately:

Ship by

When

THE GOLD KING LEASING CO.

Silverton, Colo. OCT 9 - 1915 191 No. 3191

The First National Bank

82-106

Pay to the order of M. Naiickovich

Twentyeight 80/100 Dollars $28.80

NOT OVER THIRTY DOLLARS 30

THE GOLD KING LEASING CO.

BY James R. Pitcher Jr.

FIRST NATIONAL BANK OCT 14 1915 SILVERTON, COLORADO

Mark Package and Consign to

THE GOLD KING LEASING COMPANY

Secretary.

Silverton, Colorado.

For

SAN JUAN COUNTY HISTORICAL SOCIETY

An example of a Gold King Leasing Company bill and check in 1915.

THE SILVERTON RAILWAY COMPANY

THE SILVERTON NORTHERN RAILROAD COMPANY

JAMES R. PITCHER, JR.,
VICE PRES. & GEN. MGR.

SILVERTON, COLORADO

SUNDANCE PHOTO BY DELL A. McCOY

This azure-blue pond above timberline is Lake Emma, at an elevation of 12,300 feet. The Sunnyside mine and boarding house stood on the vacant foundations in the foreground. The ridge of Bonita Peak, as well as Hurricane Peak, cradle the lake. Directly below Lake Emma, the current operations of the Standard Metals Corporation continue to dig ore out of the old Sunnyside mine.

304

SUNDANCE PHOTO BY DELL A. McCOY

Broken "fuel containers" of the miners lie beside the pithead of the Sunnyside mine, in silent witness to the rigors of life above timberline. It has been written that a month's production from the mines of the San Juans could have paid the national debt — provided that the good miners did not carry too much ore away in their dinner pails.

MORRIS W. ABBOTT COLLECTION

SAN JUAN COUNTY HISTORICAL SOCIETY

FREIGHT BILL   FORM 1-10M-7-15

Gold King Lsg. Co.

Silverton, Station, _7-28-16_ 19____

TO THE SILVERTON NORTHERN RAILROAD CO. DR.

For Transportation and Advanced Charges, from_____ Via_____

BILLING REFERENCE	DESCRIPTION OF ARTICLES	WEIGHT	RATE	AMOUNT
W. B. No.	Car spotted loaded coal 6-29-16			
Car No.. 9539	" released empty 7-27-16			
Consignor	From 6-29-16 to 7-27-16 = 37 days			
	Allowed 7 days to unload 7			
	" 4 Sundays 30 "	demurage	1.00	20 00
	" 1 Holiday			
	" 7 days free			

Advanced Charges,

Total

JUL 31 1916

Received Payment_____ Jos. E. Iresback _____ 19___   Agent.

MORRIS W. ABBOTT COLLECTION

Opposite page — the entire Pitcher family turned out to watch Silverton Northern Number 3 and the ditcher plow through the North Star slide in 1915. James R. Pitcher Jr., vice-president and general manager, was standing on the pilot. Two of the Pitcher boys were perched on the engine and Cora M. Pitcher was watching from the wagon road. The American Railroad Ditcher (serial number 578) was purchased in 1910, sold to the D&RG in 1920 as ditcher OW, and finally went to the White Pass & Yukon Route in World War II.

Cora Mears Pitcher was watching Silverton Northern Number 3 and the ditcher open up the branch to Animas Forks. The North Star slide on the north side of the Rio de las Animas — opposite Arrastra Gulch — was always a problem when snow conditions were unstable.

Examples of SN freight bills issued in 1916 are shown below and on the opposite page.

SAN JUAN COUNTY HISTORICAL SOCIETY

FREIGHT BILL

FORM 1-10M-7-15

A. S. & R. Co. (Dgo)

Silverton, Station, 7-26-16 19___

TO **THE SILVERTON NORTHERN RAILROAD CO.** DR.

For Transportation and Advanced Charges, from _____ Via _____

BILLING REFERENCE	DESCRIPTION OF ARTICLES	WEIGHT	RATE	AMOUNT
W. B. No. 30.				
Car No.. 3345	13 sacks Ore	1454	25	3 38
Consignor Gold King Sg Co 7/8	2 sacks Ore	190	35	67
WD	Advanced Charges,			
	Total			4 05

Received Payment_____ JUL 31 1916 ____ 19___

Jos. E. Dresback _____ Agent.

RAYMOND F. SPENCER WATERCOLOR

Silverton Northern Number **4** is shown above as it rounded the curve at the Sunnyside mill in Eureka, with a passenger train in tow. The train consisted of Otto Mears' special "Pullman," the *Animas Forks,* and Silverton Northern coach Number 4 (on the rear).

Silverton Northern locomotive Number **1** had been resurrected from the rip track for the World War I boom in zinc concentrate. Here, at Porphyry Gulch, she had derailed while backing downgrade on the Silverton Railway during 1916.

MORRIS W. ABBOTT COLLECTION

SILVERTON NORTHERN R. R. CO.

GOOD FOR ONE PASSAGE

ANAMAS FORKS
—TO—
SILVERTON

FIRST CLASS. *Otto Mears*
President.

591

SILVERTON NORTHERN R. R. CO.

GOOD FOR ONE PASSAGE

SILVER LAKE
—TO—
SILVERTON

FIRST CLASS. *Otto Mears*
President.

729

SILVERTON NORTHERN R. R. CO.

GOOD FOR ONE PASSAGE

SILVERTON
—TO—
EUREKA

FIRST CLASS *Otto Mears*
President.

6090

SILVERTON NORTHERN R. R. CO.

GOOD FOR ONE PASSAGE

MIDDLETON
—TO—
SILVERTON

FIRST CLASS. *Otto Mears*
President.

582

531

1681

3849

Examples of SN tickets.

MORRIS W. ABBOTT COLLECTION

The bell, alligator crossheads and guides had been removed from Silverton Northern Number 1 when this view was shot beside the SN enginehouse.

MORRIS W. ABBOTT COLLECTION

By 1915, only the three newest locomotives were in use, Silverton Northern's numbers 3, 4 and 34. The rip track was the scene of these dead engines (left to right): Number 1, Number 100 and Number 33.

MORRIS W. ABBOTT COLLECTION

Old Number 100, the *Ouray* of fond hopes, sat here as a moribund derelict, its parts having seen further service in Number 1 and Number 33. The cylinder heads, crossheads and guides were on Number 1; the cab was on Number 33. The pilot and smokebox front were gone, as was the boiler jacket. It continued to serve as a source for spare parts until 1923.

THE SILVERTON NORTHERN RAILROAD CO.
Gladstone Branch.
UNLIMITED TICKET

GOOD FOR ONE FIRST CLASS PASSAGE
WHEN STAMPED ON BACK
SILVERTON TO GLADSTONE

NO. 11614

THE SILVERTON NORTHERN RAILROAD CO
Gladstone Branch
UNLIMITED TICKET

GOOD FOR ONE FIRST CLASS PASSAGE
WHEN STAMPED ON BACK.
Gladstone to Silverton

NO. 11611

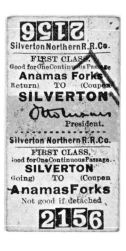

2156
Silverton Northern R.R.Co.
FIRST CLASS.
Good for One Continuous Passage
Anamas Forks
Return) TO (Coupon
SILVERTON
President.
Silverton Northern R.R.Co.
FIRST CLASS.
Good for One Continuous Passage.
SILVERTON
Going) TO (Coupon
Anamas Forks
Not good if detached
2156

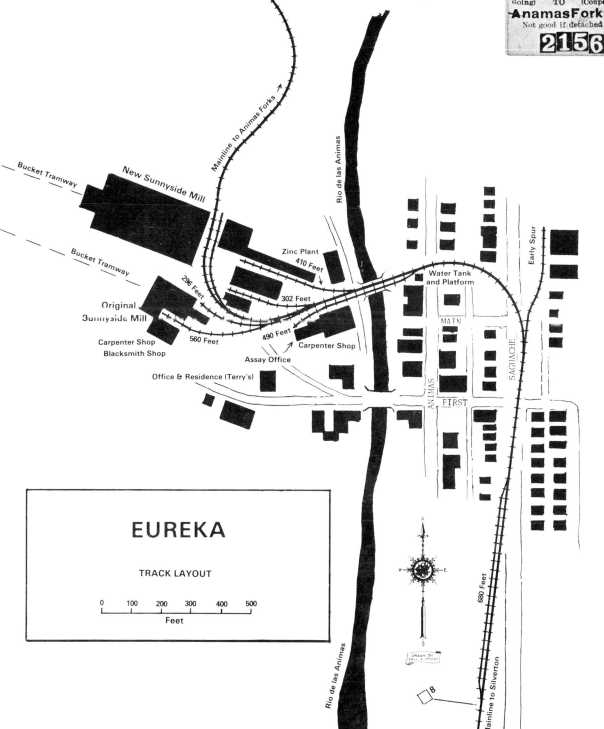

Bucket Tramway

New Sunnyside Mill

Mainline to Animas Forks

Rio de las Animas

Bucket Tramway

Zinc Plant
410 Feet

Early Spur

Water Tank
and Platform

296 Feet

302 Feet

Original
Sunnyside Mill

490 Feet

560 Feet

Carpenter Shop

MAIN

Carpenter Shop
Blacksmith Shop

Assay Office

SAGUACHE

Office & Residence (Terry's)

ANIMAS

FIRST

EUREKA

TRACK LAYOUT

0   100   200   300   400   500

Feet

680 Feet

DRAWN BY
DELL A McCOY

Rio de las Animas

8

Mainline to Silverton

ROBERT E. SLOAN COLLECTION

The old and new Sunnyside mills sat side-by-side after completion of the mill structure on the right in 1917. Materials came from the Gold Prince mill at Animas Forks. The original mill, on the left, was built in 1899. With the completion of the new mill, 500 tons of concentrate could be produced per day.

By mid-August of 1915, the Sunnyside mill at Eureka was shipping carloads of high-grade zinc concentrate. World War I had begun in Europe the preceding fall, and demand for the metal had zoomed because of its vital importance in the manufacture of cartridge brass. Throughout the war years, a train of 10 cars of rich zinc concentrate moved down the Silverton Northern about once a week from the Sunnyside mill to Silverton, where it was picked up by the D&RG and rushed to delivery at the smelter in Pueblo within 48 hours.

On September 4, 1915, the newspaper at Silverton reported an accident involving a pushcar on the Gladstone Branch; nothing serious had occurred, but the item made a good space filler, in addition to demonstrating to the paper's readers (and to future historians, as well) just how complete its coverage was of happenings in the San Juans. Nine months later, illustrating yet again the esteem in which he still was held by his former neighbors, Otto Mears was made president of the Silverton Motor Club on July 21, 1916. That season also was to see the opening of the Animas Forks Branch for the last time—inaugurating the final year of operation of the trackage which had involved so much painful effort by Alexander Anderson, Thomas Wigglesworth, Marshall Smith

311

Form 3756.

Uniform Bill of Lading—Standard Form of Straight Bill of Lading approved by the Interstate Commerce Commission by Order No. 787 of June 27, 1908.

THE DENVER & RIO GRANDE RAILROAD COMPANY

STRAIGHT BILL OF LADING—ORIGINAL—NOT NEGOTIABLE.

Shippers No. _____

Agents No. _____

RECEIVED, subject to the classifications and tariffs in effect on the date of issue of this Original Bill of Lading.

at ___Silverton Colo._____ July 19, 1916_____ 191____,

from _____Gold King Leasing Co.___ *Otto Mears*_____

the property described below, in apparent good order, except as noted (contents and condition of contents of packages unknown), marked, consigned, and destined as indicated below, which said Company agrees to carry to its usual place of delivery at said destination, if on its road, otherwise to deliver to another carrier on the route to said destination. It is mutually agreed, as to each carrier of all or any of said property over all or any portion of said route to destination, and as to each party at any time interested in all or any of said property, that every service to be performed hereunder shall be subject to all the conditions, whether printed or written, herein contained (including conditions on back hereof) and which are agreed to by the shipper and accepted for himself and assigns.

The Rate of Freight from _____

to _____ is in Cents per 100 Lbs.

												IF Special	IF Special
IF—Times 1st	IF 1st Class	IF 2d Class	IF 3d Class	IF 4th Class	IF 5th Class	IF Class A	IF Class B	IF Class C	IF Class D	IF Class E		per_____	per_____

(Mail Address—Not for purposes of Delivery.)

Consigned to _____A. S. & R. Co._____

Destination, ____Durango_____ State of __Colo._____ County of _____

Route, _____ Car Initial ____R. G._____ Car No. _____

No. Packages	DESCRIPTION OF ARTICLES AND SPECIAL MARKS	WEIGHT (Subject to Correction)	Class or Rate	Check Column	
					If charges are to be prepaid, write or stamp here, "To be Prepaid."
					Prepaid
					2.70
13 Sks Ore		1454			Received $_____ to apply in prepayment of the charges on the property described hereon.
	Lot 131-A				*Canning*
					Agent or Cashier.
	Value $ 100.00				Per _____ (The signature here acknowledges only the amount prepaid.)
					Charges Advanced:
					$ _____

_____*Otto Mears*_____
____Gold King Leasing Co._____ Shipper. _____ Agent.

Per_____WMB._____ Per _____

(This Bill of Lading is to be signed by the Shipper and agent of the carrier issuing same.)

NOTICE—The clauses shown on reverse side hereof must be signed by shippers who desire to avail themselves of lower ratings based on declared or invoice value.

SAN JUAN COUNTY HISTORICAL SOCIETY

The D&RG issued this bill of lading to Otto Mears for
Gold King ore sent to the Durango smelter.

MORRIS W. ABBOTT COLLECTION

One of the Class 56 engines was pulling Silverton, Gladstone & Northerly combine Number 1 upgrade toward Gladstone when this view was photographed in 1912. You are looking southwest, down Cement Creek.

A portion of Dome Mountain dominates this view of Eureka in 1915. Former Silverton, Gladstone & Northerly combine Number 2 had been spotted on a siding at the main street in town, as Silverton Northern locomotive Number 1 switched cars in the Sunnyside yard. The square water tank was the last building to survive in Eureka.

RICHARD A. RONZIO COLLECTION

and Arthur Ridgway some 10 years before.

On July 28, uncertain *Casey Jones* jumped the tracks again, this time up at Gladstone. Schedules for the Silverton Northern in that summer of 1916 called for one mixed train daily, and an additional freight on Tuesdays, Thursdays and Saturdays, to and from Eureka.

Despite the rather limited scheduling shown in the timetables, wartime prosperity had definitely come to the San Juan mining districts. As an example of the business being handled, September of 1916 saw 6 cars of ore shipped over the old SG&N, 158 on the Silverton Railway and 185 from mines along the Silverton Northern line, and 110 more carloads were shipped during the first 20 days of the following month.

In November and December, the old wooden 64-foot Howe "pony" truss bridge, number 496-A, on the mainline of the D&RG's Silverton Branch— where it crossed Mineral Creek as it entered the south limits of Silverton was replaced. Last renewed in 1893, the old timber span was dismantled by a bridge gang under foreman J. T. Walsh and replaced with a second-hand 64-foot through girder bridge retrieved from the little narrow-gauge Florence and Cripple Creek Railroad at Cañon City when that line was abandoned. The D&RG also replaced its antique, worn-out 29-foot, 40-ton track scale (originally installed at Silverton in 1890) with a used 44-foot, 60-ton scale formerly located at Colorado Springs.

In January of 1917, the Terry family, owners of the Sunnyside mine and mill at Eureka, the largest shipper over the Silverton Northern, were endeavoring to sell their property to the United States Smelting and Refining Company. The Terrys chartered a special train of D&RG narrow-gauge business cars to bring seven of the smelting company's directors to Eureka, in company with a retinue of mining engineers, clerks and attendants. The train, consisting of one of the D&RG's Class 47 (later T-12) ten-wheel passenger engines handling kitchen-provision car B-3 and office cars B-1 and B-2, was known popularly as the "Million Dollar Special."

An apocryphal tale has come down through the years about the journey of the special from Silverton to Eureka. The crew is rumored to have skirted the provisions of Rule "G" by accepting a few hospitable invitations to enjoy some of the elegant liquid refreshment aboard. As the procession passed the north end of town, the couplers between the engine tender and the B-3 parted, and the little Ten-Wheeler proceeded several miles by itself before the engineer and fireman realized their train no longer was trailing along behind. The engineer, thinking quickly, plowed the track on to Eureka; and, upon returning to his train, he told everyone the snow was so deep that he had thought

it better to go ahead and clear the line before returning to pick up the cars.

The three business cars were parked for a week on a siding at the Sunnyside mill in Eureka while the property was being investigated. Then—after safe passage through the deep snow on the Silverton Northern—on the way back to Durango early in the morning of January 21, 1917, the train derailed on ice which had clogged the frog of the switch to Bell's Spur at milepost 468.15, about a mile south of Rockwood, turning the engine and all three cars over the embankment. The B-2, rear car on the train, slid 50 feet down the side of the mountain, while the B-3 and B-1 were completely destroyed in the fire that resulted.

After the wreckage was salvaged, the badly damaged B-2 was put through the Burnham car shop and rebuilt as an officers' sleeping and observation car, renumbered B-3. The plush little car still exists—in much-altered form, complete with air conditioning—as the privately owned *Nomad*, headquartered in Durango.

RICHARD A. RONZIO COLLECTION

The enlarged Sunnyside mill was a profitable operation, taking low-grade ore, figured at $10 to $30 per ton, and milling it into ore worth $50 to $100 per ton. Silverton Northern Number 1 was switching boxcars adjacent to the Animas Forks Branch — which circled around the mill and headed upgrade to the right.

Silverton Northern Number 1 was pulling a 10-car train of Sunnyside zinc into Silverton, in this 1917 photograph. She had been rebuilt for the boom at this time, with old spoked pilot wheels from an early incarnation of SN Number 3 or Number 4, and Laird crossheads and guides, plus the tender from SN Number 32. The master mechanic had certainly been prowling through the junk piles. The boxcars were 25-ton (3,000 series) and 20-ton (4,000 series) D&RG cars.

SAN JUAN COUNTY HISTORICAL SOCIETY

Evidently nothing discouraging developed as a result of the unfortunate accident, for two months later the Terry family sold the major portion of their shares to the "Sunnyside Mining and Milling Company" for $500,000 in cash and a promise of future loans for development. The first of these loans was used later that spring to buy the huge mill of the Gold Prince Mining Company at Animas Forks. The mill's machinery was dismantled and hauled down the hill to Eureka—the last revenue trips made over the Animas Forks Branch by the Silverton Northern. Henceforth, the fortunes of Mears' and Pitcher's railroad would be bound up almost entirely with the welfare of the Sunnyside mill.

In March of 1917, at the time the Sunnyside Mining and Milling Company acquired the Terry family holdings, it also expended an additional $677,000 to purchase title to the mining claims covering the Gold Prince, Sunnyside and Washington mines, together with parts of the Spur and Belle Creole veins. By the end of the year, the new

RICHARD KINDIG COLLECTION

Silverton Northern locomotive Number 3 was pulling a train of boxcars upgrade, as shown here about 1915. This scene was photographed where the bridge crossed the Rio de las Animas at the edge of Howardsville.

Most of the miners rode the buckets to and from the Silver Lake mine, some of which are shown here arriving at the halfway station, high above Arrastra Gulch.

OSCAR NELSON PHOTO — CARL SKOWRONSKI COLLECTION

VAUGHAN JONES PHOTO —
RICHARD A. RONZIO COLLECTION

Silverton Northern Number 1 and Silverton Northern Number 33 were plowing out the Chattanooga Loop in 1917 when the 33 suddenly derailed. The flanger was ahead of Number 1.

In this view, SN Number 33 leaned over on the grade after derailing. The Silver Ledge mill is in the background. Notice the dog atop the air tank on the tender and another one at the front end of the tender.

MORRIS W. ABBOTT COLLECTION

company had shut down all the existing mills except its own big plant at Eureka; the latter installation was used as the test bed for developing a flow sheet for a new 500-ton capacity mill, also located in Eureka.

When the new mill—very advanced technologically—opened in April of 1918, it was one of the first flotation mills in the country; production far exceeded expectations, with 500 to as much as 1,000 tons of ore being processed each day. However, in April of 1919—after a full year's successful operation of the new installation—everything at the associated mine, except the tramway terminal and transformer house, was destroyed in a disastrous fire. The Sunnyside began rebuilding immediately and the Silverton Northern was kept busy bringing supplies up to Eureka for repairing the damage. The work of reconstruction finally was completed by September of that year.

But the boom for the railroad was followed by a bust; no sooner had the repair work at the mine been completed than the big new Sunnyside mill itself caught fire and burned to the ground. With the expenditure of more thousands of dollars, the mill was rebuilt by the U.S. Smelting and Refining Company and operated until December of 1921, when a drop in market prices—following World War I—forced it to close. Since this was the principal source of traffic to the Silverton Northern, the railroad was very seriously affected, but the Sunnyside was able to reopen in 1922, to the great relief of Otto Mears and James Pitcher.

Effective with the new year starting January 1, 1918, the Federal government took over the management of the railroads of the United States. William G. McAdoo was appointed director general of railroads and the U.S. Railroad Administration was assigned the awesome responsibility of operating all the roads for the duration of World

War I and for 21 months thereafter. [Under government control, expenses and confusion ballooned in proportion—largely because the USRA was an inefficient bureaucracy rather than a management corporation — Ed.] The railroads were returned to private management on March 1, 1920, somewhat short of the date originally proposed in the authorizing legislation.

Deterioration from under-maintenance and fearful wear and tear from the immense volumes of traffic during the war had occurred, and Congress authorized payments to the railroads as compensation. In order to determine the amounts to be paid, and also to establish an equitable investment base for fixing rates of return for each railroad, the Interstate Commerce Commission organized its Bureau of Valuation immediately following the end

RICHARD A. RONZIO COLLECTION

Three unknown Silvertonites posed in front of the Silverton Northern depot for this view. The Silverton Railway still existed in principle at this time, if not in actual fact.

of the European conflict. The plan was to allow each railroad to earn no more than six-percent of its valuation each year, freight and passenger tariffs being adjusted to avoid excess profits, and for the several years following, much effort was devoted to making a complete physical inventory and calculating attendant investment costs for each individual property.

After inventorying the Silverton Northern's property, the ICC settled on a valuation of $214,446 as the basic investment for the road. Otto Mears protested vigorously that the evaluation of his little railroad was understated, and to a degree, his protests were effective; Valuation Document Number 568, dated February 25, 1927, in Volume 121 of the ICC Reports, set a final valuation of $222,645 for the road.

The years 1917 and 1918 also witnessed other events—significant or otherwise—to southwestern Colorado. Charles W. Montgomery was appointed

RICHARD A. RONZIO COLLECTION

An accident has provided us with this detail shot of the SN ditcher (later, D&RGW OW). The ditcher had taken a spill on the Silverton Railway, a mile or so west of Silverton during World War I. SN Number 1, with an extra tender, had come to the rescue and the wrecking crew was about to see what could be done to set things right.

auditor of the Mears roads in 1917, replacing H. L. Frank; while in 1918, the dreadful influenza epidemic fatally afflicted one-third of the population of Silverton.

During these two years, too, the Rio Grande Southern was plagued with constant trouble from the Ames slide, and on several occasions leased the Silverton Northern's ditcher for use in keeping their line open. When they requested the machine again in April of 1919, Pitcher refused, saying he would need it on his own roads for a period of at least 60 days, starting late that same month. The RGS then turned to its parent, the Denver and Rio Grande, and leased the big road's narrow-gauge steam excavator OQ—in 1919 and again in 1920. Finally, in August of the latter year, the D&RG paid out $9,000 to buy the Silverton Northern's ditcher, adding it to its roster of equipment with the designation OW—and, after shuffling parts, sent the RGS ditcher 030.

The postwar period on Otto Mears' old Silverton Railway found things going from bad to worse. In 1919 only 49 trips were made over the line, with 10 of the runs being accounted for by work trains. Operations in 1920 were even lower, with 32 trips being run over only part of the line, work trains accounting for one-half of the total. The road accumulated a net deficit of $8,877 during the calendar years 1916 to 1920.

Only one mine along the entire route had worked more-or-less continuously since 1912, and it had supplied only about 15 cars of ore a year. During the preceding few years, the ore from that mine had been hauled nine miles to Ouray by wagon and carried away by the D&RG.

In 1920, Joseph E. Dresback replaced C. W. Montgomery as auditor of the Silverton and the Silverton Northern companies, and four years later, Dresback took the place of William E. "Billy" Booker as general manager of the latter line when that long-time, faithful pioneer employee finally retired.

No operations at all were conducted over the Silverton Railway in 1921, nor was there any traffic

J. D. SEARS PHOTO —
U.S. GEOLOGICAL SURVEY

A survey party was on Red Mountain Pass during the summer of 1921, when the camera recorded their field car. This was the site of Sheridan Junction, where 45-pound rail was still in place. But in two more short years all the rail was gone, leaving only a few spikes and rotten ties. The sign read, "Railroad Crossing — Danger — Look out for the Cars," which was rather unlikely at this time. In this view, you are looking toward the south.

in sight for 1922—automobiles and light trucks had supplanted the railroad for both passenger and freight service. Ancient locomotive Number 100, the only engine owned by the company, although still in existence, had been condemned and none of the equipment owned was suitable for use under the safety appliance laws. Other than in Silverton, only 20 people lived along the route. The Silverton Northern had been furnishing crews, equipment and maintenance to the Silverton Railway at cost for many years.

Under such depressing circumstances, the joint management of the Silverton and the Silverton Northern filed a petition with the Interstate Commerce Commission on August 9, 1921, for permission to abandon the Silverton Railway. The usual public hearings were scheduled, but before the time set for the hearings, the Colorado Public Utilities Commission filed a motion to dismiss the proceedings—on the ground that the railroad was located wholly within the State of Colorado, and therefore, the ICC was without jurisdiction.

With this action by the PUC, the abandonment

proceedings were placed in limbo, until a decision by the United States Supreme Court on March 13, 1922, in the case of the State of Texas vs. Eastern Texas Railroad Company renewed Mears' hopes of putting the Silverton Railway to final rest. A new application for permission to abandon again was filed with the Colorado PUC, and on June 13, 1922, Mears refiled the petition with the ICC. Four days later—on June 17, 1922—the Interstate Commerce Commission gave its permission for abandonment.

And so the little narrow-gauge Silverton Railway was quietly allowed to die—writing *fine* for the old familiar "Silverton and Red Mountain" line, once so vital to the existence and welfare of the people and the mines of the San Juans—route of the precious white buckskin and the solid silver passes, the rare and lovely watchfob medallion, and the intricate and beautiful silver filigree passes—a monument to the skills of civil engineer Charles Wingate Gibbs, and to the unconquerable spirit and unflagging energy of the indomitable Otto Mears, *Pathfinder of the San Juan.*

This spectacular panoramic view of Eureka was taken in 1921, looking toward the southwest. The town had changed very little, except that the original Sunnyside mill — built in 1899 — now was gone, as a result of the 1920 fire. The steel of the Gold Prince mill had been used to build this new Sunnyside mill. The rails were still in place on the steep Animas Forks branch (to the right), on the half-mile-long fill where Otto Mears and the Navajos had their last fight. Nothing had moved over these rails since 1917.

The surviving rolling stock was transferred to the Silverton Northern, and on November 22, 1923, at a meeting of the board of trustees, a quitclaim deed conveying the right-of-way, but not the structures or materials, of the Silverton Railway was signed, and turned over to San Juan County and the Colorado Highway Department. Most of the rail was finally removed in 1926, save the spur

RICHARD A. RONZIO COLLECTION

to the North Star Sultan mine on the edge of Silverton, which lasted until 1942. The right-of-way in Ouray County reverted to the owners of the adjoining mining claims.

Today's famed "Million Dollar Highway," U.S. Route 550, follows very closely along the roadbed of the old Silverton Railway in San Juan County, between Silverton and the summit of Red Moun-

tain Pass, as old Sheridan Pass now is named. From the summit north to Ironton, most of the old roadbed can be traced only by rotted, buried crossties and forgotten track spikes as it winds its way along the side of Red Mountain—through occasional cuts and over eroding fills—to Corkscrew Gulch, and then switchbacks down into Ironton Park. Tourists driving along the highway between

MORRIS W. ABBOTT COLLECTION

Silverton Northern Number 3 was bucking snow on the mainline leading to the D&RG depot in Silverton in 1926. The building at right was the office of one of Silverton's lumber and coal dealers. You are looking toward the northeast.

the summit and Ironton are not even aware of the old Silverton Railway grade over on the opposite, or east, side of the valley—for the highway snakes down the hillside along the route of Otto Mears' old toll road.

* * * * *

Starting in 1920, Otto Mears and James Pitcher began concentrating their efforts on strengthening the Silverton Northern financially—weeding out unnecessary equipment and cutting expenses. Since engine Number 1 had broken down again, it was summarily scrapped, along with rusty old Silverton Railway Number 100 and unserviceable SG&N Number 33, both of which had been cannibalized over the years for parts to keep the "One-Spot" running.

From the period just before World War I, the Silverton Northern's yard in Silverton had been a collection point for derelict rolling stock, including the ex-Pullman, *Animas Forks,* which never again turned a wheel after its last wreck in 1911. The bad order cars were gathered together, shoved out of town, rolled over and burned, and the metal sorrowfully salvaged from the ashes of former aspirations and prosperity.

In the fall of 1922, the Gold King mine closed its portals, eliminating the main reason for operating and maintaining the Gladstone Branch. The seven-and-one-half-mile line was kept intact, however, in order to maintain the Silverton Northern's valuation base for return-on-investment purposes. Production of the Gold King during its lifetime had totalled 711,144 tons of ore, with a value of $8,385,407, contributing its share to the aggregate value of mineral production from all the mines in San Juan County, which, in the half-century from 1873 to 1923, came to $70,381,891.

The *Silverton Standard,* in one of its last issues for 1922, reported on December 7 that, ". . . S.N. engine number 34 was returned during the week by the D.&R.G.W. Railroad after use since early in the year. . . ." The outside-frame 2-8-0 with the fancy capped stack, originally purchased by the Silverton, Gladstone and Northerly, was considerably heavier than any of the narrow-gauge Consolidations on the big road; and, in a twist reversed from proceedings of earlier times, had been leased to the Denver and Rio Grande Western by James Pitcher's little road. It was of substantial help in handling traffic on the narrow-gauge lines between Alamosa and Durango, being used until delivery of the new American Locomotive Company "sports model" Class K-28 outside-frame 2-8-2's was assured.

The prosperity burgeoning throughout the nation during the mid-1920's gradually filtered down even to the remote San Juan region of Colorado, and on January 10, 1925, Pitcher inaugurated a second train each Saturday over the Silverton Northern to Eureka. Its single purpose was to supply the Sunnyside operations with enough empty cars to keep the mine and mill working on Sundays.

In the spring of 1926, having disposed of its own machine to the D&RG five and one-half years previously, the Silverton Northern asked the Rio Grande Southern for the temporary loan of that road's steam ditcher, number 030. Hand labor would be too expensive and too inefficient in clearing the right-of-way of all the rock and other natural debris that had accumulated along the line.

WILLIAM PLUNKETT WATERCOLOR

SN Number 3 and the ditcher were working together in the scene above — clearing a snowslide at the Pinnacles. This was along the Rio de las Animas, just below the Silver Lake mill.

During the summer runoff, the Rio de las Animas is a brilliant blue-green. This view was photographed looking downgrade beside the Silver Lake mill site. The Silverton Northern curved to the right in the distance at the Pinnacles, as it headed into Silverton.

SUNDANCE PHOTO BY RUSS COLLMAN

325

RICHARD A. RONZIO COLLECTION

When this photograph was taken, Silverton Northern Number 4 was being rerailed after a spill on the line above Howardsville.

On the night of February 12, 1927, a dance was held in Eureka, and a free special excursion train was advertised for the affair. The train would leave Silverton at 8:00 p.m. and was scheduled to depart from Eureka on the return journey at 1:30 a.m. Free sandwiches and coffee also would be available on the special, but parents were cautioned that children under 14 years of age would not be allowed to participate in the festivities.

Two weeks after that happy jaunt, a major winter storm hit the area on February 25, 1927, leaving a foot of snow on the level in Silverton. The King Solomon slide near Howardsville came down and covered the Silverton Northern's track to a depth of 10 to 20 feet over a distance of 1,600 feet; slides down the cañon of the Rio de las Animas below Silverton left the D&RGW in even worse shape. Joe Dresback and his crew, used to fighting snow, dug their railroad out rapidly.

On January 7, 1928, the *Silverton Standard* reported that the passenger train on the Silverton Northern to Eureka would be running on Saturdays, in addition to its regular weekday schedule. Another special excursion train, this time from the upper end of the line, was run on February 11, departing Eureka at 7:15 a.m. and arriving at Silverton at 8:00 a.m., giving everyone a day on the town before the Firemen's Ball that night. A second special that month was run to Eureka for a dance on February 29, the extra day of Leap Year being a fine excuse for the celebration.

In the years just before the Depression hit, the mines and railroads were earning money hand over

MORRIS W. ABBOTT COLLECTION

Joe Dresback and his crew were bucking snow on the Silverton Northern with SN Number 4 when this shot was made.

Silverton Northern locomotive Number 3 had suffered a delay at the Rio del las Animas bridge leading into Howardsville. D&RGW boxcar 3379 had derailed. This was at milepost 6 in 1926.

STEVEN R. WESTRUM COLLECTION

RICHARD A. RONZIO COLLECTION

The Pride of the West team — with a scraper — met the Silverton Northern train at the main road crossing in Howardsville, just after the train had bucked its way through a snowslide. SN combine Number 2 (ex-SG&N Number 2) brought up the rear of the train.

fist. The Sunnyside mill shipped 156 carloads of ore by May 1, and another 140 carloads in July of 1928, while the combined Shenandoah and Dives outfits moved 12 carloads and the Lackawanna shipped 10 more. On the Eureka train in October, 1928, Ralph Plantz moved over to the engineer's side of the cab in the temporary absence of Edward "Pete" Meyer.

Early in February of 1929, the Silverton Northern was snowed-in and the D&RGW was blocked by a snowslide above Needleton. The big road hired five snow-shovelers to help the regular men clean out the Silverton Branch, but the extra men considered their pay of 31 cents an hour too low and called a strike. Joe Dresback and his crew went down from Silverton and had the slide cleared away by February 23, but in the process, Silverton Northern engine Number 4 derailed on hard ice in the track, five miles south of Silverton, and toppled over. "Pete" Meyer was at the

Silverton Northern snow-bucking train, composed of engines 34 (in front) and either 3 or 4 (following), was making the snow fly in this action shot.

RICHARD A. RONZIO COLLECTION

D. E. ROGERS PHOTO

RICHARD A. RONZIO COLLECTION

On an autumn day in 1951, the late afternoon sun began to cast long shadows across the townsite of Eureka. At this time, a fair number of railroad souvenirs could be found in this area since tourists had not yet discovered this remote area. Galena Mountain forms one wall of the valley — shown here in the distance.

Silverton Northern Number 4 was charging up the line with its wedge plow when recorded in this view on February 27, 1927.

Opposite page, below — this view was taken at the Silver Lake powerhouse, at Waldheim, in the 1920's. Silverton Northern Number 4, with a wedge plow, was pulling a gondola and two boxcars — followed by SN Number 3 — as they opened the line after a heavy snowfall.

328

MORRIS W. ABBOTT COLLECTION

Tom Lonergan (left), conductor, and Edward (Pete) Meyer, engineer, posed with Silverton Northern locomotive Number 4, with plow attached.

MORRIS W. ABBOTT COLLECTION

The King Solomon slide near Howardsville covered the Silverton Northern mainline with 10 to 20 feet of snow, as shown here in 1927. SN Number 3 could not handle this slide, so miners were called in to hand shovel the line open.

MORRIS W. ABBOTT COLLECTION

329

MORRIS W. ABBOTT COLLECTION

The day after the view printed on the preceding page was taken, a persistant photographer recorded another action picture at the same spot. Silverton Northern locomotive Number 3 was taking the curve at the Silver Lake powerhouse, followed by six boxcars and a chaircar or combine.

A spring flood in 1927 washed out parts of the Silverton Northern mainline. The missing bridge originally carried rail into the Silver Lake mill, and still had a whistle post in place. The road up Arrastra Gulch to the Silver Lake mines can be seen just above the bridge abutment to the left.

ROBERT E. SLOAN COLLECTION

Opposite page — in 1927, a flood made short work of the south bridge that led into the Silver Lake mill. The bridge never was replaced until the mill was scrapped.

throttle, W. W. Taylor was firing, and Thomas Lonergren was the conductor, while Meyer's son, Lloyd, was along as the supplyman and clerk. Joe Manzanares was with Meyer and Taylor in the cab at the time of the derailment and had three ribs broken. Pete was trapped in the cab when the engine overturned—narrowly escaping with his life—and had to be hospitalized following his rescue. Meyer was away from his job until March 3. Engine Number 4 had to be sent to the D&RGW shop at Alamosa for repairs, which required three weeks.

A snowslide below Howardsville on March 9 buried 1,100 feet of track, and on the following April 6, A. S. Berkey, master mechanic of the SN, told the local newspapers that both his road and the D&RGW were completely blocked by snow.

That summer, a new mining combine, the Shenandoah-Dives Company, was formed to operate the North Star, Terrible, Mayflower, Shenandoah and Dives mines, all located on King Solomon Mountain. Shenandoah-Dives opened their mill in 1933—despite the Depression, which had collapsed the national economy. This consolidated mining operation was to produce $29-million in ore by 1948. The Shenandoah-Dives later incorporated the Silver Lake and Iowa-Tiger mines and operated until 1952.

MORRIS W. ABBOTT COLLECTION

DENVER PUBLIC LIBRARY WESTERN COLLECTION

The view above and on the opposite page was taken in the early 1920's from the top of the Sunnyside mill in Eureka, looking out across the settlement. *Casey Jones* was on the track in the center foreground, and 23 boxcars were scattered about on sidings and spurs.

ROBERTSON MEARS PITCHER COLLECTION

James Robertson Pitcher Jr., as he appeared in 1928, the third president of the Silverton Northern Railroad; born, 1879; died, 1933.

The railbus, *Casey Jones,* was rebuilt again in the summer of 1929, reaching its present form. The new 12-seat body—hardly a "body by Fisher" —was built by Hans Tanstad of the Eureka Carpenter Shop.

At the Silverton Northern's annual meeting of stockholders and directors in October of 1929, the management of the road was realigned. Otto Mears at last relinquished the presidency, being replaced by his son-in-law, James R. Pitcher, Jr., while Pitcher's wife, Cora, became the vice-president. Joseph E. Dresback was replaced as auditor by Norman F. Bawden of Silverton, and Edward "Pete" Meyer was elevated to the job of superintendent. James R. Pitcher, III, replaced Jerome B. Frank as the treasurer.

The Silverton Northern now was exclusively a one-family operation, overseen by James Robertson Pitcher, Jr.

JACKSON C. THODE COLLECTION

JACKSON C. THODE COLLECTION

While clearing a snowslide above Needleton, on the Silverton Branch of the D&RGW — on February 23, 1929 — Pete Meyer ran Silverton Northern Number 4 up on solid ice that had completely covered the rails. The locomotive toppled over in the ditch with Pete and Joe Manzanares in the cab, injuring both men. As a result, the engine had to be sent to Alamosa for repairs.

In the view at left, the tender of Number 4 had been re-railed and the engine itself was back on its wheels, ready to be pulled back onto the rails after being righted with block and tackle.

JACKSON C. THODE COLLECTION

CHAPTER VII

--- REPORT OF ABANDONMENT OF THE ---
SILVERTON NORTHERN RAILROAD
as reported in the *ICC Reports*, Vol. 252, issued for the months of December, 1941, through October, 1942.

Under: "Cases disposed of without printed report," page 807:

F.D. No. 13738, Silverton Northern Railroad Company Abandonment. Decided August 31, 1942. Certificate issued permitting abandonment, as to interstate and foreign commerce, by the Silverton Northern Railroad Company of its lines of railroad in San Juan County, Colo.

The End of the Line
1930 - 1942

IN OCTOBER, 1929, the stock market crashed and the first shuddering throes of the Great Depression began to shake the economy. Total train mileage on the Silverton Northern that year was 6,296 miles; in 1930, after the Sunnyside closed, Pitcher shut down operation of the railroad in October, bringing about a reduction to 5,323 miles run by trains for that operating season.

Earlier in the summer, an irate taxpayer wrote a letter to the editor of the *Silverton Standard* to the effect that railroads were guaranteed huge profits and were seeking to raise rates during hard times. To set the matter straight, Pitcher responded with a scathing rebuttal, published in the *Standard* for August 9, 1930:

Silverton Standard
Silverton, Colo.
Dear Sirs:
Reference is made to an article in your last issue under the heading "Metal Prices—Freight."

We take exception to the statements of Albert E. Hayes and especially to the one which reads "Railroads are guaranteed a fixed profit on what everyone knows is inflated valuation."

Had Mr. Hayes taken the trouble to acquaint himself with the provisions of the Interstate Commerce Act, he would have learned that the railroads are guaranteed nothing but that they are permitted to retain, as a fair return, up to 6 per cent of their valuation as determined by the Interstate Commerce Commission. The rate which the carriers are permitted to thus retain, up to 6 per cent, is variable, is fixed by the Commission from time to time and at present is 5¼ per cent.

The commission spent ten years, at a cost of approximately one hundred million dollars to the government and carriers, in arriving at a valuation of the railroads, and surely this valuation by the Commission as a result of intensive examination of railroad properties is worth more than the offhand statement, "what every one knows is inflated valuation."

Mr. Hayes also states that: "They (the railroads) are besieging the Interstate Commerce Commission for permission to increase rates on ore shipments from western states." As a matter of fact, the recent hearing in Denver held by a Commissioner and some Examiners was held for the purpose of determining the fairness of rates on products of mines in relation to rates on other commodities and does not necessarily presage a change in rates, either upwards or downwards and moreover, this hearing, and others held in western mining centers, were on the initiative of the Interstate Commerce Commission and not of the railroads.

In view of the facts as stated above which are all a matter of record, it would seem that Mr. Hayes is grossly ignorant of the subject on which he writes, and we will thank you to publish this letter so that his misstatements may be corrected.

Very truly yours
J. R. Pitcher

To add injury to insult, on March 26, 1931, the Federal government made preliminary plans to confiscate $42,700 from the management of the Silverton Northern under the provisions of the Transportation Act of 1920 and its amendments. This legislation provided ". . . that one-half the net operating income of a railroad in excess of six-percent of its valuation shall be recapturable to the government." The railroad had reduced its trackage in operation from 20 miles in 1923 to 12 miles in 1926 by not running any trains on the Gladstone Branch, thereby reducing its value for rate-making and return-on-investment purposes from $240,000 to $150,000. In so making the little railroad profitable, the Pitchers and the Silverton Northern now were about to be penalized.

The *Silverton Standard,* in support of the local enterprise, editorialized that this was unfair treatment of a railroad whose earnings were based on the booms and busts in mining.

In late 1930, the State Public Utilities Commission of Colorado authorized the Silverton Northern to suspend operations from December 3 to the following June 30; since 98 percent of the traffic was the business from the Sunnyside Mining and Milling Company—which had closed—the remaining two-percent did not justify keeping the road open. In 1931, as a consequence, no passenger service was offered at all, and only 501 miles of freight service were produced during the whole year.

During the summer, on June 24, 1931, at the age of 91, Otto Mears died at the family home in Pasadena, California. His railroad was not doing much better—the guiding hand of the Silverton Northern could help it no more. Newspapers all over the state of Colorado mourned the passing of the *Pathfinder of the San Juan,* and even the prestigious *New York Times* noted his death on its front page. His wife, Mary, had died in Pasadena earlier—in 1924—four years after the couple celebrated their Golden Wedding Anniversary. In August, 1931, the ashes of Otto and Mary Mears were scattered on Engineer Mountain above Silverton, returning the remains of the two pioneers for the last time to the land they loved.

Railroad service was suspended on January 1, 1932, with an understanding between the company and shippers served by the Silverton Northern that any freight offered would be handled during the temporary suspension. On January 30, the Silverton water tank of the D&RGW, also used by the little road, was disconnected by the owner; after additional months of inactivity, on June 25, the railroad hauled into Silverton what was left of a bridge that had been wrecked by slides during the winter on the Gladstone Branch.

At the annual meeting of the Silverton Northern on June 28, 1932, the board of directors voted in favor of requesting a loan from the Interstate Commerce Commission and the Reconstruction Finance Corporation for about $15,000 to pay half of an earlier bank loan, as well as taxes, wages and salaries, and to provide for maintenance-of-way and equipment. After the auditor checked the books, the figure requested in the July loan appli-

cation came to $12,945, but the loan was denied in August, the commission stating that it was unable to find that such an amount, loaned to the Silverton Northern, would be adequately secured.

The senior Pitchers left Silverton in mid-September of 1932—moving to the family hotel in Pasadena—and three months later, on the day after Christmas, James R. Pitcher, Jr., died in that California city at the age of 53.

At a special meeting of the family and the board of directors in Pasadena on January 2, 1933—sorrowful in its implications—Cora Mears Pitcher was elected president; James R. Pitcher, III, became vice-president, treasurer and general manager; and Robertson Mears Pitcher became the secretary.

GERALD M. BEST PHOTO

At this spot on the Million Dollar Highway, a splendid view of Silverton is provided for tourists traveling north from Durango. In this scene, Silverton was slumbering shortly after the end of World War II. By this time, the Silverton Railway had been gone for several years. A D&RGW freight train was pulling out of the wye, heading for Durango.

No trains were operated over the Silverton Northern in 1933 or 1934. When California railroad enthusiast, Gerald M. Best, first visited Silverton in the latter year, the little railroad was dormant—the locomotives were locked inside the enginehouse and it was apparent that no operations had been conducted for some time.

The settlement of Animas Forks, high up on the headwaters of the Rio de las Animas, had been abandoned in the early 1920's when it became evi-

dent that the famed Gold Prince mine finally had closed its workings for the last time. Never again would the need exist for trains to traverse the steep branch above Eureka; and, in 1936, the Silverton Northern directors offered the grade of the Animas Forks extension to San Juan County if the county would pay the cost of removing the rails. When the county authorities accepted the proposition, Pete Meyer fired up Number 3 once again, after four years of idleness, and used it to

HAROLD K. VOLLRATH COLLECTION

Silverton Northern Number 34 was switching empty cars at the northeast edge of Silverton when this picture was taken, during April of 1930. The 34 was an outside-frame 2-8-0 built by Baldwin in 1904.

haul in the scrap.

In mid-November of 1936, after 30 years of existence, the right-of-way of the railroad from the Tom Moore bridge and Lion tunnel to the upper end of the line was reverting to its original status as a road. Engineer Pete Meyer returned old engine Number 3 to rest in the rickety engine-shed, and sadly locked the doors again.

During the late 30's, the Shenandoah-Dives and the Pride of the West mines trucked their ore to Silverton, where it was loaded and shipped out by the D&RGW. This system was hardly beneficial to the Silverton Northern; 584 cars of ore were shipped out by the D&RGW in 1936, none of which originated on the Silverton Northern.

The Pitchers were no longer concerned about maintaining the long unused Gladstone and Green Mountain branches since they served no useful purpose and were a tax liability. The Gold King mine and mill were still involved in litigation and the mill was in extremely bad repair. The Pitchers filed for abandonment of these two branches during the summer and the Colorado Public Utilities Commission scheduled a hearing on abandonment, purely a formality at that point, for November 17, 1937. The branches were removed from the San Juan County tax base in 1938.

By June of 1937, the nation was beginning to hasten its pace of recovery from the dismal days of the Great Depression. In the San Juans, joyful rumors started: the Sunnyside mill at Eureka intended to reopen after being at a standstill for the past six and one-half years! The stories even went so far as to suggest that the D&RGW would operate the Silverton Northern!

How great it was to have the rumors become reality when repairs to the long-unused tracks were taken in hand after Mrs. Pitcher returned to Silverton on August 27. In the middle of September, 1937, only two weeks later, the Silverton Northern's first revenue train in seven years was run to Eureka; and, during the early weeks of the following month, 40 empty boxcars for the Sunnyside's operations were brought up to Silverton by the D&RGW.

The sudden and unexpected revival of business caught the Silverton Northern without a useable caboose for the train crew. The former SG&N car was a thing of the past, while the SN's old four-wheel "bobber," number 1005—which had been caboose number 17 on the Silverton Railroad back in ancient times—was too far gone for use without a major rebuilding. Quick action was required, and in November, 1937, the railroad bought

GERALD M. BEST PHOTO

The Silverton, Gladstone & Northerly enginehouse at Fourteenth and Mineral streets in Silverton was beginning to show its age when this picture was taken on July 3, 1937. The county courthouse is in back of the wedge plow, which was used for snow removal. The flanger and a work flat head the line on the rip track.

JAMES D. OSBORN PHOTO — GERALD M. BEST COLLECTION

This is Silverton Northern boxcar 2006, previously Silverton, Gladstone & Northerly 1006, illustrated here on the SG&N mainline in Silverton.

JAMES D. OSBORN PHOTO —
MORRIS W. ABBOTT COLLECTION

Silverton Northern locomotive Number 3 posed at Eureka — on the bridge over the Animas — for this classic view, produced on August 15, 1938. The Sunnyside mill yard was in the background.

RICHARD H. KINDIG PHOTO

Casey Jones, the railbus owned by the Sunnyside mine, was caught resting in the yard at Eureka, July 2, 1940. The Sunnyside mill buildings surrounded the bus — with the square water tank visible in the distance, across the Rio de las Animas.

D&RGW caboose number 0556 off the rip track in Durango. This short, old eight-wheeled waycar with a square cupola had been built in 1885, and had seen better days to be sure, but it would provide the train crew with a workable office and the expense certainly was less than the cost of rebuilding either the railroad's own caboose, or the coach or combination cars which had not turned a wheel for so many years.

On the last day of 1937, the *Silverton Standard* reported that over 1,000 cars of concentrate had been shipped out of Silverton over the D&RGW during 1937 and that about 400 of them had originated on the Silverton Northern.

By the end of 1937, locomotive Number 3, the track and the equipment all were repaired and ready for the winter's work; and, in Februrary, March and April of 1938, the Silverton Northern was put back into service. About $2,400 a month was being received for loading and bringing out zinc concentrate for shipment via the Denver and Rio Grande Western, and the Colorado and Southern lines to the AS&R smelter at Amarillo, Texas. The D&RGW was handling 165 carloads of zinc concentrate a month.

The usual slides began running in February; slides at Porcupine Gulch and Hamlet closed the Silverton Northern for 10 days. Then, on April 29, 1938, a major slide came down on the Silverton Northern track at Hematite, near the Howardsville bridge and the railroad was blocked.

Two months later, on July 1, the Sunnyside mill closed down for the last time. The blame is often laid to a strike by the mill workers, but there was no strike at the Sunnyside. (The Shenandoah-Dives was struck at that time by the local CIO union.) Instead, the Sunnyside closed for the usual reason, an adverse metal market. This was the "last straw" for the SN, and operations came to a quick end.

Railfan James D. Osborn visited Silverton on August 15, 1938; and, after talking to Pete Meyer,

JAMES D. OSBORN PHOTO
GERALD M. BEST COLLECTION

Silverton Northern Number 3 had picked up the eight-wheel caboose to tack her onto the end of a freight train being prepared for a trip to Eureka. This was August 15, 1938, and you are in Silverton, looking north toward the SG&N enginehouse.

got to ride in the cab of SN Number 3 on a cleanup run to Eureka to bring in cars. His photographs were the last ones taken of the Silverton Northern in operation. The final curtain had fallen for the Silverton Northern; the road would never run again except to haul in the scrap from dismantling.

In an attempt to reduce transportation costs, the Sunnyside started to drive a tunnel from the mill at Eureka northwest some three miles to get under the workings at Lake Emma. This tunnel would have permitted mining the remaining ore from the bottom upward by "stoping," or caving, the ore directly into ore cars and tramming them out to the mill. This would have eliminated most of the surface working up at Lake Emma and would have greatly reduced the cost of mining. This Sunnyside tunnel project was stopped by December 9, and the Silverton Northern did not operate at all in 1939. The purpose of the Sunnyside tunnel was finally fulfilled when—in 1959—the American tunnel project was started at Gladstone; and, in the '60's, the tunnel connected the workings of the Gold King, Sunnyside and Gold Prince mines.

During the 15 years of operation under the management of the United States Smelting, Refining and Mining Company, the Sunnyside mine and mill had produced two and one-half million tons of

The sunlight warmed the smokebox and pilot of Silverton Northern Number 3, resting inside the SG&N enginehouse on June 4, 1940.

JOHN W. MAXWELL PHOTO

JOHN W. MAXWELL PHOTO

In 1940, the Silverton Northern enginehouse had the fine aroma of grease, oil and coal.
SN locomotive Number 4 was in for repairs at the time.

ore worth $50-million, all of which was transported from the area by the Silverton Northern Railroad. Total mineral production of the mines in San Juan County from 1873 to 1948 came to $123-million — almost half of which came just from the Gold King — Sunnyside — Gold Prince properties. Production from the mines remaining after the ill-fated year of 1938 was all hauled away by motor trucks.

In 1938, the few remaining pieces of Silverton Northern rolling stock—the chaircar, a combine, the caboose purchased in 1937, five ex-SG&N boxcars and one ancient snow-flanger—were ready for the boneyard. Engines numbers 3, 4 and 34, together with miscellaneous parts, plows and shop machinery, however, still had some potential utility and the Silverton Northern's management never

gave up hope that their little railroad would revive yet again in times to come. Optimistic to the bitter end, for the next four years they waited and watched while their railroad rusted away.

The litigation over the Gold King finally had been settled during 1938 so General Manager R. M. Pitcher had been holding off removing the rail from the Gladstone and Green Mountain branches even after abandonment had been approved because of persistent rumors that the Gold King and Old Hundred mines would reopen. However the promised boom did not pay off and so early in September, 1938, Pitcher started selling rail from the Gladstone Branch to the Shenandoah-Dives Mining Company. One-hundred tons were sold at $17.50 per ton, in place, beginning at Gladstone and working south toward Silverton. Pitcher

343

E. F. WHITMORE PHOTO — JACKSON C. THODE COLLECTION

Silverton Northern Number 34 posed for this parting shot at the time she was ready for shipment from Silverton in 1943 — her main rods dropped for movement over the D&RG.

cautioned Norm Bawden to make sure that no rail was lifted between the SG&N enginehouse and the smelter. Truckers salvaging the Silver Lake mill, two miles out of town on the Silverton Northern, asked permission to drive along the railroad's right-of-way, but Pitcher refused. The track was in such poor shape that any removal of rail and ties could only result in extraordinary expense for new ties to put the railroad back in condition, he told the truckers, and covering the ends of the ties with

dirt would result in considerable damage to the good ties already in the track.

The D&RGW, in need of repair rail for use at Moffat and Villa Grove, over in the San Luis Valley, arranged to buy 50 lengths of 45-pound rail from the SN. They would pay $24.00 a ton for the material, which Pitcher made available from the SN's rail pile. On September 19, 1940, the big road offered to sell the Silverton Northern three narrow-gauge ditchers, numbers OW, OX and 030 (the

JAMES D. OSBORN PHOTO —
GERALD M. BEST COLLECTION

SN Number 3 had just pulled a trainload of loaded boxcars down into Silverton, and was photographed in front of the D&RG passenger depot on August 15, 1938. The cars were about to be spotted on a siding for the D&RG to pick up.

344

RONALD F. RUHOFF PHOTO

The Mayflower mine was still being worked in 1963 — as this lighted entryway indicates. A powered scoop-shovel and trailer flatcar had been sidetracked. This view was photographed inside the shed which had been built in front of the entrance tunnel to the mine.

OSCAR NELSON PHOTO — CARL SKOWRONSKI COLLECTION

The Mayflower mine was high on the side of Little Giant Peak in Arrastra Gulch. The mine machinery was cabled to the pithead, as shown here, lashed between buckets. The Mayflower mine became part of the Shenandoah-Dives group in 1928.

JAMES D. OSBORN PHOTO — GERALD M. BEST COLLECTION

Silverton Northern locomotive Number 3 sizzled to herself in the early morning sunlight of a summer day in 1938. She was waiting for the run to Eureka.

RICHARD H. KINDIG PHOTO

The schoolhouse at Eureka was near the Silverton Northern track, as shown here in July of 1940. The Sunnyside mill sat on Eureka Mountain. Many of the houses, including the school, later were removed to Silverton. Several houses went as far away as the Idarado mine on Red Mountain Pass, where they are still in use.

This view (at right) shows the massive machinery inside the Sunnyside mill at Eureka.

MRS. MARVIN GREGORY COLLECTION

OW was the machine first purchased by Otto Mears for the SN in 1910; number 030 was the former RGS machine received during September of 1939 in exchange for engine Number 455), but for some "unfathomable" reason, Pitcher and his little railroad were not buying.

By February 8, 1941, the last of the company's stationery was gone; on February 15, the last index to tariffs of the Silverton Northern was published.

Although there was an undercurrent of hatred among the striking workers, the labor situation at the Shenandoah-Dives was quiet. The CIO labor union was confident it would win the lawsuits, but the National Labor Relations Board still had made no decision by March 13, and Manager Chase of the big mine, likewise confident of his company's position in the controversy, was still trucking ore from his reserves.

In late March of 1941, the D&RGW picked up the rail and joint bars it ordered, paying $281.00 for the lot. Norm Bawden was scouting around for a purchaser for the rest of the Gladstone Branch rail, meanwhile.

In September of 1941, with no real prospects any longer in sight for reopening the Sunnyside operation at Eureka, R. M. Pitcher offered the Silverton Northern's remaining three locomotives for sale. Number 3 was in good operating condition and the asking price was $2,400, but numbers 4 and 34, needing overhaul, could be had for $2,000 and $2,250, respectively. Pitcher estimated that to put Number 34 in first-class condition in the shop at Alamosa would cost $1,000, while $1,500 would be required for repairs to Number 4. The Colorado Tax Commission set an assessed valuation of $40,000 for the railroad that year.

That fateful Sunday, December 7, 1941, saw the beginning of the epilog for the little railroad. The United States suddenly was at war with Japan, and

JAMES D. OSBORN PHOTO — GERALD M. BEST COLLECTION

scrap metal became a needed commodity. The Silverton Northern's board of directors now consisted of Otto Mears' daughter, Cora Pitcher, and her two sons, James R. Pitcher, III, and Robertson Mears Pitcher, and following the stockholders' meeting on May 11, 1942, Mrs. Pitcher offered the railroad's property for sale for $17,000 to pay off delinquent taxes.

The end of the road was the tax sale held on August 7, 1942, to obtain the money for the back taxes. Winning bidder was the Dullen Steel Products Company of Seattle.

On August 31, 1942, the ICC finally gave permission for abandonment of the entire Silverton Northern line and the Dullen company could begin pulling rail. The first scrap shipments of the Silverton Northern's shop equipment, rails and rolling stock were made in October of 1942.

About this time, the United States government was searching frantically for three-foot-gauge equipment to use on the narrow-gauge White Pass and Yukon Route, running between Skagway, Alaska, and Whitehorse, in the Yukon Territory of Canada. This was a vital link in supplying construction materials for the Alcan Highway— now called the Alaska Highway—then being built

A stub three-way switch is in the foreground in this view of the Sunnyside mill yards at Eureka in 1938. Notice the building to the right with the sloping bin for coal to be shoveled into.

SAN JUAN COUNTY HISTORICAL SOCIETY

Judge J. L Terry's house is on the left side of this view, while the Sunnyside mill — as it appeared in the 1930's — was the main subject. The railbus, *Casey Jones,* is in the foreground.

347

SUNDANCE PHOTO BY DELL A. McCOY

The buckets of the Mayflower mine's aerial tramway rode this elevated rail inside the mine building, where they were turned for a return trip to the mill, two miles away on the Rio de las Animas. This overhead rail was used to move buckets off the cableway for repair or storage. When buckets were put back in service, they were moved out on the rail, where they were locked onto the cable to the left. The track ran back into the mine — around the curve to the right — for loading ore.

348

JAMES D. OSBORN PHOTO — GERALD M. BEST COLLECTION

In 1938, the entire consist of Silverton Northern boxcars and the road's single caboose, was parked on the SG&N mainline. Sultan Mountain is in the background.

through Canada to Alaska by the U.S. Army Corps of Engineers. The three locomotives from the Silverton Northern were requisitioned by the U.S. Army Transportation Corps in October, 1942, and they were shipped to the WP&Y in May, 1943, as part of the major expansion of that road due to its critically needed character. SN Number 3 became WP&Y Number 22; SN Number 4 became WP&Y Number 23; and SN Number 34 (originally built for the SG&N) became WP&Y Number 24.

After hard wartime use, WP&Y numbers 22 and 23—ex-SN 3 and 4, respectively—were returned to "the States" in late 1945 to the General Army Depot at Auburn, Washington, where they were offered for sale by the War Assets Administration on December 7, purchased by M. Bloch and Company of Seattle, and dismantled that same month. WP&Y Number 24—ex-SN 34—gave up the ghost and was retired in 1944, finally being dismantled at Skagway, Alaska, in 1951.

The fireman of Silverton Northern Number 3 enjoyed this view from the cab as the locomotive hauled a train downgrade along the Rio de las Animas during 1938. This view was photographed across the river from Waldheim, as the train headed toward Silverton.

JAMES D. OSBORN PHOTO — GERALD M. BEST COLLECTION

E. F. WHITMORE PHOTO — | JACKSON C. THODE COLLECTION

This photograph shows Silverton Northern Number 34 after she had been pulled out of the SG&N enginehouse in Silverton for the last time, with Number 3 coupled to her pilot.

When this view was photographed, the SG&N enginehouse sheltered Silverton Northern Number 34 at Silverton. Notice the wall construction compared with the SN enginehouse.

RICHARD H. KINDIG PHOTO

Opposite page — on June 4, 1940, during a railfan trip, Silverton Northern Number 3 and Number 34 were found slumbering in the old rickety SG&N enginehouse in north Silverton.

E. F. WHITMORE PHOTO — D. E. ROGERS COLLECTION

In April of 1943, Silverton Northern Number 4 was pulled out of the SN enginehouse for the last time, and was pushed down to the mainline by D&RGW Number 319. Later, she was reconditioned in Alamosa for the White Pass & Yukon railroad. In this view you are looking northeast, at the south end of the Silverton yard, with Kendall Mountain in the background. Incidentally, it is common to see snow on the ground in Silverton in April.

RICHARD H. KINDIG PHOTO

JOHN W. MAXWELL PHOTO

This Silverton, Gladstone & Northerly pushcar is at the Colorado Railroad Museum at Golden, Colorado.

The tattered remains of Silverton Railroad baggage car Number 5 rested in a backyard in Silverton as of 1973.

JERRY B. HOFFER PHOTO

Silverton Northern caboose Number 1005 (previously Silverton Railroad Number 17) was originally D&RG Number 0516, built in 1880 as Denver & Rio Grande Railway caboose Number 17. The body of this car was used for years as a storage shed — as shown at left, behind the Western Colorado Power Company office, northeast of Silverton.

JOHN W. MAXWELL PHOTO

The remains of a work train, consisting of several flatcars, a flanger and a boxcar, sat beside the SG&N enginehouse in 1937.

RICHARD A. RONZIO COLLECTION

NATE FLESNESS PHOTO

The SRR combine, *Red Mountain,* and SRy combine Number 11 at Tefft Spur.

NATE FLESNESS PHOTO

This is the end door on the baggage end of Silverton Railroad combine, *Red Mountain,* as it looked in 1972.

The combine, *Red Mountain,* was photographed at the passenger end, December, 1972, at Tefft Spur.

NATE FLESNESS PHOTO

One of the clerestory windows of the *Yankee Girl* was photographed to show the beauty of the design. The glass was burgundy red with frosted white trim. The wooden frame was painted green. From the typical Pennsylvania Dutch appearance of the design, it is believed the car was constructed by Billmeyer & Small of York, Pennsylvania.

RON PECK COLLECTION

353

E. F. WHITMORE PHOTO — D. E. ROGERS COLLECTION

The last photograph of Silverton Northern's 2-8-0's, Number 3 and Number 34, coupled together on SN trackage, was taken during April of 1943. The two were being towed down to the D&RGW mainline beside the depot.

RICHARD H. KINDIG PHOTO

Two Silverton Northern boxcars, numbers 2003 and 2007—ex-SG&N 1003 and 1007—still survived as of 1975 at the Texaco bulk oil distribution plant near the former D&RGW depot in Silverton. SN coach number 4 is now part of the Pioneer diner in Durango, while Silverton Railroad caboose number 17—later SN number 1005—serves as a tourist booth for the Silverton Chamber of Commerce.

The Silverton Railroad's 1888 baggage car still survives in Silverton, while remnants of the 1888 combine, *Red Mountain,* and the combination baggage-chaircar, Number 3, *Yankee Girl,* still exist (as of this writing) at the old sawmill site at Tefft Spur. The boiler of SG&N Number 32 also

(Text continued page 372)

E. F. WHITMORE PHOTO — JACKSON C. THODE COLLECTION

In April, 1943, Silverton Northern Number 4 was about to awaken from her long slumber so she could go to Skagway, Alaska, to take part in the war effort.

This whistle formerly echoed off the mountainsides around Silverton when it was on Silverton Railroad locomotive Number 100.

RII L TIEGS COLLECTION —
SAN JUAN COUNTY HISTORICAL SOCIETY

Opposite page, below — when Richard Kindig photographed the SN enginehouse on June 30, 1939, only the tender of SN engine Number 4 was resting outside the doors. You are looking southwest in this view, toward Sultan Mountain. Harp switchstands and stub switches lasted until the bitter end of the railroad.

HAROLD K. VOLLRATH COLLECTION

ERNEST S. PEYTON PHOTO

The Silverton depot of the D&RGW railroad was in working order in June of 1946. Later — in 1969 — the railroad donated the depot to the San Juan County Historical Society.

Originally built for the Silverton Railroad, this building was used both as a depot and office building. This 1945 view was taken looking west, at Tenth and Cement streets in Silverton.

Ready for shipment to Durango, Silverton Northern Number 34 was resting behind a string of boxcars. The D&RG section house was beyond the boxcars in this view — looking south toward the Silverton depot.

RICHARD A. RONZIO COLLECTION

JAMES D. OSBORN — MORRIS W. ABBOTT COLLECTION

In 1938, the Silverton, Gladstone & Northerly depot at Fourteenth and Mineral streets in Silverton was but a ghost, boarded up and weathering away.

In June, 1945, the old Silverton, Gladstone & Northerly grade in Silverton had been deprived of its track, and all that could be seen of the railroad at this point were two SN boxcars, tipped over on their sides.

ERNEST S. PEYTON PHOTO

This stub switch in Silverton served Thomson's Dairy, which was located off the Silverton, Gladstone & Northerly mainline, heading up Cement Creek.

JOHN W. MAXWELL PHOTO

357

JOHN W. MAXWELL PHOTO

The tender of Silverton Northern Number 4 was sitting outside the SN enginehouse in Silverton on June 4, 1940.

Fittingly, it was snowing when the last Silverton photograph of Silverton Northern Number 3 was taken in 1943.

E. F. WHITMORE PHOTO — JACKSON C. THODE COLLECTION

HAROLD K. VOLLRATH COLLECTION

The D&RGW mixed train to Silverton is shown above as it pulled out for Durango in 1946. The D&RGW's handcar shed is on the left while the SN's handcar shed is on the right.

The old mainline grade of the Silverton Northern looked like this in 1945. This view was photographed at Eighth Street, adjacent to the D&RGW depot.

ERNEST S. PEYTON PHOTO

RICHARD H. KINDIG PHOTO

The North Star Sultan mill at the southwest corner of Silverton — on Mineral Creek — was served by the Silverton Railway. The mine was falling into decay in 1940 when this photograph was taken. Today, the mill is little more than a pile of rubble, having been abandoned for many years.

Not much remained of what had been an SG&N boxcar when this photograph was made in 1940. The scene was the old Walsh smelter siding on the southwest edge of Silverton. A portion of Silverton is visible in the background of this view, at the base of Kendall Mountain.

RICHARD H. KINDIG PHOTO

SUNDANCE PHOTO BY DELL A. McCOY

It is only a matter of time before the effects of winter snows and spring rains will reduce what is left of the North Star mill to its natural state. This view was shot in 1975 at the southwest edge of Silverton, just off the old grade of the Silverton Railway.

JAMES D. OSBORN PHOTO — GERALD M. BEST COLLECTION

JAMES D. OSBORN PHOTO — GERALD M. BEST COLLECTION

A Silverton Northern combine — old SG&N Number 2 — was parked on the rip track at the SG&N enginehouse in this 1938 photograph.

This second view of old SG&N Number 2 shows a work flat made from an old SG&N gondola (behind the combine) and the corner of an SG&N handcar.

The third photograph of the old SG&N combine presents a straight-on side view.

JAMES D. OSBORN PHOTO — MORRIS W. ABBOTT COLLECTION

SAN JUAN COUNTY HISTORICAL SOCIETY

Silverton Northern coach Number 4 was photographed as a derelict in Silverton during 1947. The coach is now a diner in Durango.

SUNDANCE PHOTO BY DELL A. McCOY

A rail brace — such as this one — as well as spikes, splice bars and other items, were left behind when rail was salvaged from the abandoned Silverton, Gladstone & Northerly right-of-way.

Here, you are looking north at the SN balloon loop of 30-degree curvature (194-foot radius), one-half mile south of Eureka.

SUNDANCE PHOTO BY DELL A. McCOY

DR. JAMES R. JACKSON PHOTO

DR. JAMES R. JACKSON PHOTO

SUNDANCE PHOTO BY DELL A. McCOY

Opposite page, above — rusted and weathered, the Silver Lake mill presented this appearance in July of 1940. At this time, the track of the Silverton Northern was still in place in the canyon of the Rio de las Animas.

Opposite page, below — Silverton Northern coach Number 4 showed what was left of her color scheme in this view, photographed in Silverton on July 7, 1940.

Having arrived in the San Juans with high hopes, man often departed sadder but wiser — for only a handful of men were destined to make large sums of money from the region's mineral resources. This high mountain valley once boasted of a thriving mining town — Eureka. Today, little remains of the community. Here and there you can find weathered railroad ties, and the crumbling foundation of the giant Sunnyside mill is easy to find. But nearly everything else is gone. In the distance, Galena Mountain's snow-capped peak tops out at 13,278 feet. The SN's branch to Animas Forks once passed in front of the derelict water tank, crossed over the Rio de las Animas and curved sharply to the right, through the mill yard.

365

BILL TIEGS COLLECTION —
SAN JUAN COUNTY HISTORICAL SOCIETY

This is the number plate of the Silverton Railroad's locomotive, *Ouray.* It was found in the Silverton yard during the 1960's by Bill Tiegs, who was one of the last D&RGW station agents to work in Silverton.

GERALD M. BEST COLLECTION

After serving two years with the White Pass & Yukon Route, U.S.A. 22 (ex-SN 3) and U.S.A. 23 (ex-SN 4) were shipped down to Auburn, Washington, to be scrapped. There, they were photographed for the last time, on March 29, 1945.

RICHARD B. JACKSON PHOTO

D&RGW ditcher OW — the old Silverton Northern ditcher — which had acquired the boom of D&RGW ditcher OX (including the pile-driver attachment), was photographed in Alamosa on August 1, 1938.

366

SUNDANCE PHOTO BY DELL A. McCOY

The Old Hundred mill above Howardsville — shown on this page — was a magnificent ruin by 1960. By then it had been stripped of all workable machinery and the winter snows had taken their toll. The upper photographs show the exterior walls, while the lower photographs show the cableway entrance into the mill, at the rear. The interior was constructed of heavy timbers.

SUNDANCE PHOTO BY DELL A. McCOY

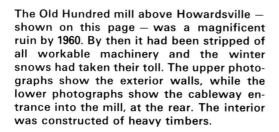

SUNDANCE PHOTO BY DELL A. McCOY

SUNDANCE PHOTO BY DELL A. McCOY

367

SUNDANCE PHOTO BY DELL A. McCOY

A boarding house that was never used stands today near the Rio de las Animas, a short distance above the townsite of Eureka. This striking view was taken from the old grade of the Silverton Northern Railroad.

SUNDANCE PHOTO BY DELL A. McCOY

One puffy little cloud was floating across the Colorado sky in front of Storm Peak when this color view was shot. The Big Giant mine's pithead was at the back of this pond on King Solomon Mountain. The wooden tower (to the right) is one of several that were used to support the cableway, which transported ore down to the small mill owned by this operation in the Animas Canyon. This area is near the site of the Little Giant mine — one of the first major producers of gold in the San Juans — discovered in 1871. Bullion City was in this locale, also.

SUNDANCE PHOTO BY DELL A. McCOY

SUNDANCE PHOTO BY DELL A. McCOY

The Little Nation mill — shown above — is located at Howardsville, and remains standing today as one of the last survivors of mining during Silverton Northern Railroad days. This mill was built in the 1920's. Notice the old ties of the Green Mountain Branch circling around the mill in the righthand photograph. The camera lens was pointed toward the northwest.

370

D. E. ROGERS PHOTO

Opposite page — *Casey Jones* rested for a time at the south end of Silverton (as shown on the preceding page) after being moved from Eureka. The steering wheel operated the brakes, and the chassis came from a four-door touring sedan.

In the 1960's, *Casey Jones* was spotted beside a motel in Silverton for the enjoyment of wanderers in the San Juans. Note the absence of windshield wipers.

ERIC W. JOHNSON PHOTO

SUNDANCE PHOTO BY DELL A. McCOY

SUNDANCE PHOTO BY DELL A. McCOY

The Buffalo Boy cable tramway house is a short distance above the Old Hundred mill in Cunningham Gulch. It now has been rebuilt into an apartment and office building and is owned by the Stone Silver Corporation. This firm also owns the Buffalo Boy mine. Exploration leading to the possible reopening of the mine was undertaken during 1974. The mill at this site burned down in the late 1930's.

SUNDANCE PHOTO BY DELL A. McCOY

Red Mountain Number 2 and the ghost town of Ironton — as well as the abandoned grade of the Silverton Railway (above the townsite) — were slumbering under a blanket of powder snow when this photograph was produced.

is at Tefft, while relics of the Silverton Railroad's original locomotive, Number 100, and the Silverton Northern's railbus, *Casey Jones,* are at the San Juan County Historical Society museum in Silverton. The depot, caboose and baggage car are now owned by the San Juan County Historical Society. The Silverton Northern office, depot and enginehouse buildings in the town still are recognizable.

Thus ended 55 years of flamboyant and spectacular Rocky Mountain railroading in Colorado. Some of the once-famous mines are again producing valuable ore, but highways, motor trucks and automobiles have taken the place in the hearts and minds of most men—the majority of whom do not even know about the far more interesting and colorful . . .

* * * * *

RAINBOW ROUTE

SUNDANCE PHOTO BY DELL A. McCOY

Looking straight at *the Knob* (the small domed hill at the side of the ghost town of Red Mountain), this view reveals the remains of the National Belle mine's shafthouse. The Yankee Girl mine building is in the foreground — adjacent to the rotting ties that formerly supported the rails of the spur which served as a coal-delivery track for the mine. The mainline of the Silverton Railway climbed upgrade to Red Mountain town (to the left) where the upper switchback and wye were located. From this settlement, the line came out and circled around *the Knob,* continued uphill to the right, and then curved out of sight over Red Mountain Pass (called Sheridan Pass when the Rainbow Route was in operation).

FINANCIAL TABLE

Fiscal Year Ended	Passenger Earnings	Freight Earnings	Total Revenues	Operating Expenses	Net Earnings	Interest	Taxes	Dividends	Surplus or Loss
THE SILVERTON RAILROAD									
1888				NO DATA					
1889	$	$	$ 80,882	$34,285	$46,597	$25,500	$		$21,096
1890	12,144	93,529	105,673	51,127	54,546	25,500			29,046
1891	13,084	108,527	121,611	57,548	64,063	25,500			38,563
1892	9,891	94,942	104,833	59,145	45,688	25,500			20,187
1893			100,037	62,822	37,215	25,500			11,715
1894			56,715	31,696	25,019	25,500			-681
1895	3,065	54,131	77,139	33,928	43,211	25,500			17,711
1896	3,016	69,311	52,259	32,349	19,910	25,500			-5,590
1897	2,202	37,928	37,855	24,920	12,935	25,500			-12,565
1898	1,817	28,022	34,785	22,679	12,106	25,500	1,938		-8,275
1899	1,681	5,504	10,885	8,986	1,899	25,500	1,564		-17,662
RECEIVERSHIP									
1900	1,800	10,055	16,256	12,593	3,663	25,500	1,598		-26,526
1901	2,214	7,922	14,192	14,241	-49	25,500	1,100		-26,649
1902	2,818	8,777	15,121	16,326	-1,205	25,500	1,738		-28,443
1903	2,707	7,649	14,008	14,012	-4	25,500	802		-26,306
1904	3,213	8,839	12,986	11,793	1,193	25,500	1,010		-25,363
REORGANIZED AS SILVERTON RAILWAY									
1905	816	8,432	9,242	5,802	3,440	25,000	1,062		-17,161
1906	NO DATA, LEASED TO RED MOUNTAIN RAILROAD, MINING AND SMELTING COMPANY								
1907				NO DATA					
1908	2,516	18,557	21,072	19,571	1,501	25,075	1,062		-24,635
1909				NO DATA					
1910	2,464	13,424	15,888	14,898	990	25,040	1,153		-25,203
1911	1,265	11,876	13,205	14,158	953	25,103	763		-26,819
1912	1,366	12,230	13,600	17,119	3,519	25,219	300		-29,034
1913	70	9,415	9,488	9,773	285	25,119	387		-25,791
1914	43	9,292	9,367	7,634	1,733	25,096	439		-23,802
1915	52	1,683	1,765	3,939	2,174	25,234	138		-27,546
1916	0	16,447	16,657	15,634	1,018	26,352	1.		-25,334
1917	0	22,805	23,308	20,853	2,455	27,696			-25,241
1918	0	6,934	6,934	6,973	-45	25,702			-25,747
1919	0	4,186	4,186	4,919	-733	25,499			-26,232
1920	0	1,398	1,423	7,867	-6,444	26,012			-32,457
1921	0	0	0	496	-479	25,000			-25,479
END OF OPERATIONS									
THE SILVERTON, GLADSTONE & NORTHERLY RAILROAD									
1900				NO DATA					35,366
1901	$ 1,197	$ 31,507	$ 36,997	$20,289	$16,708	$ 6,000	$	$3,630 (3%)	$10,708
1902	3,387	27,019	33,605	20,052	13,553	6,000	711	7,260 (6%)	6,822
1903	4,493	38,564	43,378	23,883	19,495	6,000		3,630 (3%)	13,495
1904	3,708	49,889	53,939	31,807	22,132	6,000	1,410	3,630 (3%)	9,682
1905	12,456	29,071	55,357	32,681	22,676	6,000		7,260 (6%)	9,416
1906	8,541	57,580	66,549	44,113	22,535	6,000		7,260 (6%)	9,275
1907	6,541	57,789	64,414	37,943	26,471	6,000		7,260 (6%)	11,779
1908	5,762	44,744	50,542	42,909	7,633	6,000			1,633
1909	2,271	26,187	29,350	29,129	221	6,000	1,358		-7,692
LEASED BY SILVERTON NORTHERN RAILROAD, JANUARY 1, 1910									
THE SILVERTON NORTHERN RAILROAD									
1896	$	$	$ 2,494	$ 655	$ 1,839	$ 1,000			-829
1897	440	17,135	17,576	9,071	8,505	9,000	186		-681
1898	227	18,691	18,918	8,711	10,207	9,000	991		216
1899	317	18,535	18,906	7,475	11,431	9,000	473		1,958
1900	276	18,767	19,084	7,959	11,125	9,000	452		753
1901	584	28,562	29,146	9,922	19,224	9,000	318		9,305
1902	1,137	28,723	29,860	15,161	14,692	9,000	851	15,000 (10%)	-10,302
1903	1,094	28,312	29,757	12,288	17,469	9,000	479		7,990
1904	5,323	31,707	39,707	24,304		9,000	994		5,712
1905	6,713	37,982	45,131	26,066	19,064	11,889	1,473		-2,209
1906	6,713	47,981	54,819	34,788	20,031	13,000	1,100		5,931
1907	14,558	66,929	85,890	43,713	42,177	14,072	1,070		26,858
1908	11,232	59,636	78,509	32,229	46,280	13,288	1,399		31,593
1909	4,509	36,369	42,496	27,782	14,714	13,136	1,178		400
1910	6,645	53,668	60,993	44,075	16,858	13,000	1,965		1,893
1911	4,544	43,209	48,483	35,753	12,730	13,708	1,121		-2,099
1912	2,083	34,948	37,460	34,501	2,959	13,859	1,142		-12,043
1913	1,971	45,556	52,842	36,272	16,570	13,303	1,196		843
1914	1,749	49,870	57,443	40,521	16,922	13,524	1,258		-1,995
1915	2,557	46,432	54,601	35,085	19,516	13,351	801		-1,863
1916	2,452	55,100	59,321	48,168	11,153	13,513	1.		-759
1917	2,575	74,746	82,623	52,307	30,316	16,730			15,630
1918	2,184	52,177	56,166	55,673	493	13,418			-11,865
1919	2,013	42,753	45,753	48,859	-3,106	13,629			-16,741
1920	1,770	70,542	73,110	58,982	14,128	19,000			-2,509
1921	113	11,117	11,395	22,238	-10,843	13,684			-23,998
1922	192	8,760	8,985	16,464	-11,879	14,082	4,400		-3,403
1923	1,495	53,798	55,503	41,862	16,480	15,036	1,783		1,444

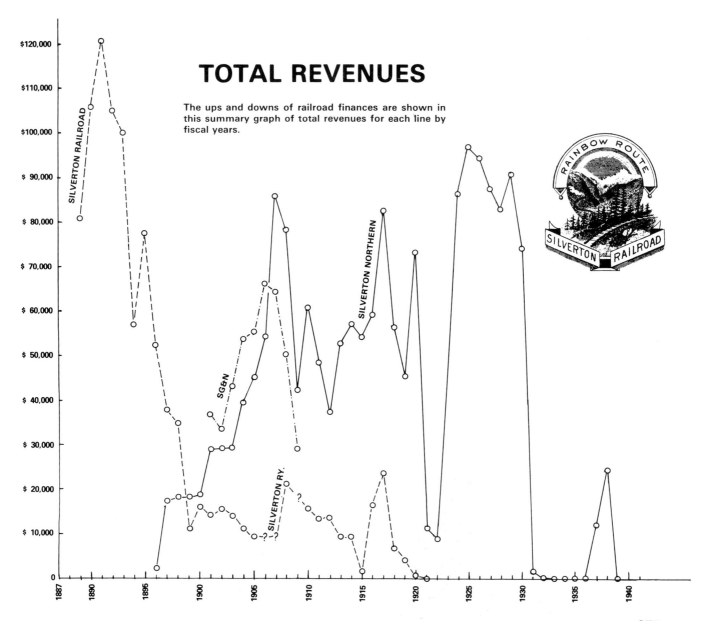

2.

Year									
1924	1,397	84,489	86,099	59,845	26,254	14,107	2,809		9,369
1925	1,431	94,666	96,467	61,531	34,936	13,981	2,307		18,916
1926	1,476	92,427	94,107	51,036	43,071	14,396	3,486		25,192
1927	1,178	85,715	87,372	76,999	10,373	14,271	4,090		-7,828
1928	1,018	81,150	83,061	65,393	17,668	14,442	3,794		-568
1929	880	88,344	91,532	67,326	24,206	15,152	4,022		5,012
1930	188	73,264	74,282	50,099	24,183	15,122	5,196		3,852
1931	0	1,512	1,628	18,844	-17,216	19,976	4,276		-41,190
1932	0	37	52	15,733	-15,681	16,500	3,319		-35,400
1933	0	0	2	12,624	-12,622	16,302	2,147		-31,065
1934	0	0	0	522	-522	15,362	2,356		-18,240
1935	0	0	0	510	-510	15,092	2,214		-17,816
1936	0	0	0	259	-259	15,000	1,688		-17,921
1937	0	12,356	12,356	12,344	12	15,000	3,240		-18,681
1938	0	24,537	24,537	17,497	7,040	15,000	3,907		-13,163
1939	0	0	0	384	-384	15,000	1,632		-17,134
1940	NO OPERATIONS					15,000	1,513		
1941	NO OPERATIONS								
1942	ROAD ABANDONED, OCTOBER 1942								

Data from *Poor's Manual of Railroads* and *ICC Annual Reports* on the statistics of railways.

1. From 1916 to 1921, taxes are included in operating expenses.
2. Period of tabulation changes from fiscal year to calendar year in 1924.

TOTAL REVENUES

The ups and downs of railroad finances are shown in this summary graph of total revenues for each line by fiscal years.

SUNDANCE PHOTO BY DELL A. McCOY

Along this rock-strewn flat — just south of Eureka — can be found several highly untypical stretches of abandoned tangent grade. The SN's balloon loop was straight ahead and to the left, hidden by the undergrowth.

This Silverton Railroad 30-pound rail was used to shore up the railroad embankment near Guston.

WILLIAM PLUNKETT PHOTO

Geologic History Appendix

Since the routes of all three of Otto Mears' Silverton railroads and the locations of all the mines which form the primary subject of this book were determined by the geology of the San Juan Mountains, a brief review of the geologic history is an important part of the story. While the oldest rocks in the area are about two-billion years old, the part of the geology important to these railroads and their supporting industry begins near the close of the age of dinosaurs.

About 80-million to 65-million years ago, the San Juans did not yet exist. A major sea—actually an extension of the Gulf of Mexico—reached from Texas to the Arctic Ocean, and from western Colorado to Minnesota. The vegetation in southwestern Colorado was tropical and included such plants as breadfruit, palms, magnolia and redwoods. These plants grew in swamps on the southwest shore of that sea. The dinosaurs living on these plants were duckbill dinosaurs, horned dinosaurs and the last of the huge sauropods, 70-foot-long *Alamosaurus*. Carnivorous dinosaurs such as *Gorgosaurus* preyed on them. As these ancient plants died, they became buried, and eventually produced the rich coal beds found south and west of the San Juans [Figure 1]. This low-sulfur coal is particularly high in quality and easy to get at in the area that was served by the southern end of the Rio Grande Southern.

Plankton—tiny floating plants and animals that grew in the surface waters of the sea—sank to the bottom after death and were buried in the sea bottom mud. Their bodies were converted to oil and natural gas over a long period of time. The oil and gas migrated into the beach and delta sands deposited at the edge of the sea, resulting in the oil fields of the San Juan Basin in northern New Mexico, originally marketed with the assistance of the Farmington Branch of the Denver & Rio Grande Western.

At the very end of the age of dinosaurs (the end of the Cretaceous period), about 65-million years ago, there was an early episode of volcanic activity in the San Juans, and the sea retreated from the region for the last time. There were four main volcanic centers, each more-or-less similar to Mount Vesuvius in Italy today. These centers were at La Plata, Rico and Ouray, in Colorado, and the nearby Carrizo Mountains in Arizona. The La Plata and Rico volcanoes injected large amounts of hot molten granite into cracks in the older rocks— heating, baking, spreading them apart and bulging them up into mountains. These volcanoes gave off large amounts of superheated water and steam containing metal sulfides in solution. These metal sulfides crystallized in cracks and fractures in the rocks to produce the La Plata and Rico ore bodies which provided revenue for the Rio Grande Southern.

At the end of this volcanic episode, the Needle Mountains and the rest of the San Juan Range as well were uplifted for the first time [Figure 2]. These mountains were very high at first, but gradually were worn down to their present size by the constant erosion caused by rain, snow, ice, rivers and streams. The sand and clay that were eroded from these mountains were deposited in the San Juan Basin to the south—in the area between Durango, Santa Fe, Farmington and Chama. These rocks are Eocene in age and have fossils of the small four-toed horse, *Eohippus,* buried in them. Growing on top of these rocks are the forests that were logged by the New Mexico Lumber Company and others, and that were the source of lumber, bridge timbers and ties for all the railroads in the area.

Then, about 35-million years ago—during the Oligocene epoch—something major happened approximately 160 miles deep, down under the San Juans. As a result of continental drift and plate tectonics, the Atlantic Ocean was growing wider and the floor of the east Pacific was forced under the western edge of North America, as the continent moved westward, away from the center of the Atlantic. As the former floor of the Pacific Ocean sank deeper and deeper, it grew hotter and hotter, finally melting under southwestern Colorado, among other places. Within the next five-million years, at least 8,000 *cubic miles* of basaltic lava erupted from at least seven major volcanoes in the area, extending from Silverton to Lake City, Creede, Wagon Wheel Gap, south to Chama and northeast to Bonanza. About 1,000 cubic miles of these dark gray ropy and blocky lavas—similar to those of Mount Fuji in Japan, or Hawaiian volcanoes—came from the Silverton and Lake City craters [Figures 3 and 4]. The San Juan tuffs and flows are these earliest lavas. These early lavas

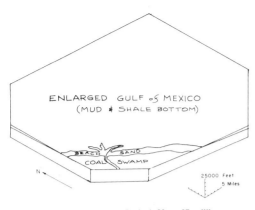

Figure 1. Late Cretaceous Period, 80 to 65-million years ago. Formation of coal and oil on the edge of a much expanded Gulf of Mexico.

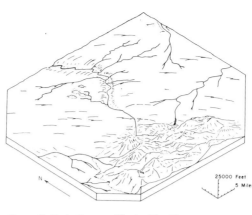

Figure 2. Early Eocene Epoch, 50-million years ago. Time of the first uplift of the Needle Mountains.

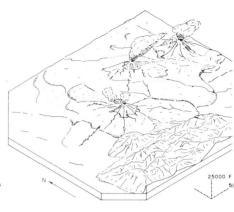

Figure 3. Early Oligocene Epoch, 35-million years a Eruption of the San Juan Tuff.

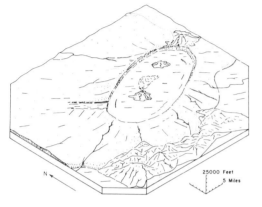

Figure 4. Early Oligocene Epoch, 30-million years ago. Formation of the San Juan volcanic depression by the sagging of the crust under the weight of the lava flows.

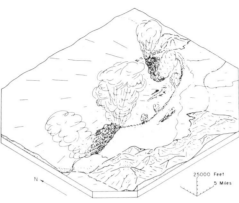

Figure 5. Middle Oligocene Epoch, 29-million years ago. Ash flow volcanic eruptions of the Silverton Volcanic Group.

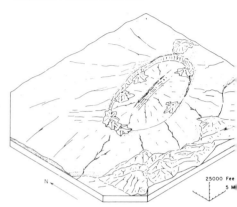

Figure 6. Middle Oligocene Epoch, 28-million years a Resurgence of volcanoes, doming of the San Juan v canic depression, formation of radial fractures of 1 Telluride, Ouray and South Silverton areas, and forr tion of the Gold King - Sunnyside - Gold Prir fractures.

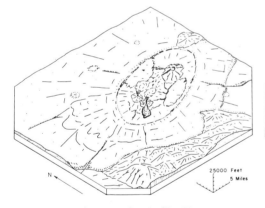

Figure 7. Late Oligocene Epoch, 27-million years ago. Crater lakes formed in the margin of the San Juan volcanic depression near the present sites of Ouray and Pole Creek Mountain.

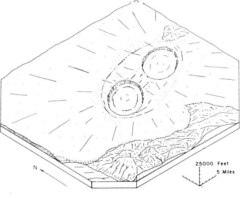

Figure 8. Late Oligocene Epoch, 26-million years ago. Sinking of the Silverton and Lake City Calderas from the weight of the lavas in them.

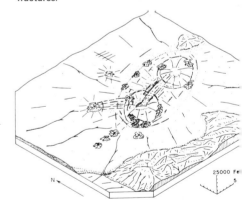

Figure 9. Late Oligocene Epoch, 25-million years a Injection of the granites of Stony Mountain, Mou Wilson, Ophir, Red Mountain, Sultan Mountain a Galena Mountain, and the formation of metal ores old fractures.

Perspective block diagrams, looking northeast at an area 50 miles in east-west width and 45 miles wide from north to south. The area shown extends from Rico in the southwest (near) corner to 5 miles east of Lake City and to 10 miles north of Ridgway. Drawings from Colorado School of Mines Quarterly, *volume 63.*

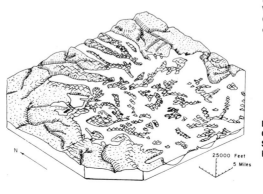

Figure 10. Late Pleistocene Epoch, 10,000 years ag Glaciers cover all but the highest peaks of the centr San Juan Mountains and extend downstream Ridgway, Cimarron, Creede and Durango.

378

generally eroded to form cliffs, such as Lizard Head, the peak that became the symbol of the Rio Grande Southern.

These volcanoes were major peaks, with lava flows extending as far north as Anthracite and Cripple Creek, extending east under the San Luis Valley, west as far as Lizard Head and south as far as Dulce, New Mexico. The main vent for the Silverton volcanoes shifted from time to time, but was usually somewhere near Gladstone. This mountain stood about 10,000 feet higher than the countryside at Durango or at Gunnison. Another of these volcanoes was located about 15 miles northeast of Lake City and 6 to 10 miles north of Cannibal Plateau (where Alferd [sic] Packer ate most of the Democrats in Hinsdale County during the winter of 1873).

About 30-million years ago, the chemical composition of the lavas deep down in the melting pot (or magma chamber) changed. As the magma beneath the crust cooled, only lower-temperature melting rocks were still molten lava, and these had more silica and water in them. The character of the activity in all seven of the major volcanic centers changed from fluid, runny *basalts* like those of Mount Fuji, Japan, or Hawaii, to explosive *rhyolites,* like those of Vesuvius, near Pompeii in Italy. The large amount of water, combined with the molten lava under pressure at great depth, flashed into steam when those lavas reached the low pressure at the surface. This steam literally blew those lavas apart and into the air [Figure 5].

As a result, a large amount of volcanic ash, dust and "bombs" were thrown into the air, most of which fell back to the ground near the crater from which they erupted. The fine dust and ash was blown downwind for great distances. The brightly colored rocks now being eroded in the Big Badlands of South Dakota came from volcanoes in the San Juan Mountains and from Yellowstone National Park. These rocks are 600 feet thick and are 1,200 miles downwind from the volcanoes from which they came.

The color of these rocks is different than the earlier lavas. The earlier basalts are dark gray and weather to a dark purplish gray, while the later rhyolites are tan or light gray and weather to a pink or red color. Set against a clear blue autumn sky—contrasted with the golden tones of quaking aspen—these rocks probably were the inspiration for the name, "Rainbow Route."

The total volume of these later rocks, the *rhyolites,* is about 4,000 cubic miles. In the Silverton - Lake City area, they are known as the Silverton and Potosi volcanics [Figures 6, 7]. They make up—among others—Red Mountain and Storm

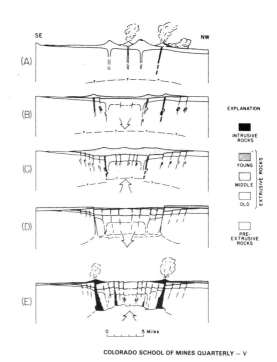

Figure 11

Cross section through the Silverton Caldera the individual sections are: A—35 million B—30 to 29 million years ago; C—28 million , D—26 million years ago and E represents the stages of volcanism about 25 million years ago.

Peak. The magma chamber, or melting pot, under the Silverton volcano probably extended under the Lake City volcano as well, and was about 40 miles in diameter. As lavas would surge up and spew out over the countryside, the pressure under the volcano would be released and the volcano would settle back down on top of the magma below, not leaving any empty space. The collapse took place along circular faults, or fractures, about 10 miles in diameter. These collapse craters, or *calderas,* were much larger than the craters of the volcanoes themselves. During the 3-million years of rhyolite ash flows and falls, the central part of the Silverton caldera sank 3,000 feet, so the same lavas that are on top of the mountains at Camp Bird or Telluride are down at river level at Silverton. In addition, with each surge, all the surrounding rocks would be strained and broken along regular fracture lines [Figures 8, 12, 13].

As the Silverton and Potosi volcanic rocks were being deposited, other minor volcanoes in the area were formed at Ophir, Sneffels, Camp Bird, Sultan Mountain, Bear Mountain, Galena Mountain and Mount Wilson [Figure 9]. The ore bodies associated with these minor volcanoes were the source of the many mines in these areas.

The last lavas to come out of the magma chambers included enough water to be more water

Figure 12
Side scanning radar photograph of the Silverton Caldera and the southern part of the Lake City Caldera, each outlined by dashed lines. Silverton is located at the letter 'S,' the scale is 1 inch equals 4 miles.

than rock. The water contained much dissolved ore minerals, mostly sulfides of iron, copper and lead, with small amounts of silver and gold. This super-heated water came boiling up to the surface through the cracks and fractures in the older rocks. As the water rose, it cooled and the pressure was reduced so the minerals could no longer be kept in solution. The minerals were deposited in the walls of the old fractures and cracks in the rocks, in exactly the same fashion as minerals in water form boiler scale and crusts inside water pipes. Most of this took place along vertical cylinders called pipes, and the pulverized rocks in those pipes were leached and altered and replaced with ore by the hot water. In the process, the pipes were cemented to much harder rocks than those around them. As a result, they stand out as slightly higher hills. *The Knob* at Red Mountain is an example of such a pipe. All the major ore bodies of the Red Mountain mining district were such pipes and went more-or-less straight down. All the ore bodies of the San Juan Range mining districts, from Creede to Bonanza to Silverton, were deposited by these late, hot waters, although not all in pipes. The original ores, deposited in the cracks and crevasses of the older rocks, consisted of pyrite (iron sulfide, or "fool's gold"), galena (lead sulfide) and various copper sulfides, all containing gold and silver in small amounts.

As long as these minerals were buried deeply, with no oxygen available, they were stable. However, since most of the ores were in the areas of major fractures where the rocks had been weakened by crushing and crumbling, especially the ring fractures of the big calderas, they were in the areas where the major streams and valleys of the San Juans developed. So, for example, the faults along which the Silverton caldera sank are marked and outlined by Red Mountain Creek on the northwest, Mineral Creek on the southwest, and

the Rio de las Animas from Animas Forks to Silverton. If you look at the accompanying maps, you will see that these creeks outline a more-or-less circular area about 10 miles in diameter.

The Lake City caldera is about the same size and is bounded on the north and northwest by Henson Creek, and on the east and south by the Lake Fork of the Gunnison River. The area between the Silverton and the Lake City calderas was thoroughly fractured, collapsed and mineralized in a dumbbell pattern with the Silverton and Lake City calderas being the two circular ends, and the Gold King - Sunnyside - Gold Prince vein the narrow connecting link.

There are seven other major collapse calderas in the San Juan Range, in addition to the Silverton and Lake City calderas. Two were important for their impact on the railroads. These were the Creede and the Platoro calderas. The Creede caldera is located between Wagon Wheel Gap and a point 10 miles west. The Rio Grande del Norte makes a semicircular loop around the north rim of the caldera, while Wagon Wheel Gap itself is the valley excavated in the ring-shaped fault around the caldera. The southern rim is marked by the Roaring Fork of the Rio Grande and by Lime Creek.

The Platoro caldera is southwest of Summitville and is bounded by the Rio Conejos and by the South Fork of the Rio Conejos. This caldera is located about 20 miles north of Chama, New Mexico, and 20 miles east of Pagosa Springs, Colorado. This caldera is the source of the ashy mudflows that posed landslide problems on the Antonito to Chama run of the Denver and Rio Grande Railroad.

This volcanic episode came to an end about 24-million years ago. Since that time, the rain and snow falling on the region formed rivers which carved away the original volcano shape and gave the San Juan Mountains their present rugged form.

As these valleys were carved out of the rocks, the original sulfide ores reacted with air and water at the surface. As a result, sulfuric acid was released, the rocks were leached and the metals were left behind as richer lead and copper carbonate ores close to the surface. The gold was released as little flakes that were washed downstream to form the placer deposits in the stream sands and gravels. As a result, the first ores mined close to the surface were the rich bonanza ores.

Finally, in the last 2-million years, mountain glaciers [Figure 10] deepened the valleys to their present shape and carved the many needle-shaped peaks and glacial amphitheatres, called *cirques*

NASA-ERTS Satellite photograph of the San Juan Mountains and adjoining areas in Colorado and New Mexico, taken on June 5, 1973. The white areas are snow in the mountains or bare ground in the deserts of New Mexico or to the northwest of Montrose. The Silverton Railroad right-of-way north of Chattanooga and the Silverton Northern right-of-way north of Eureka are still snowed-in, explaining why Mears did not operate these portions of his roads from January to late May or early June each year.

GUNNISON

MONTROSE

RIDGWAY

LAKE CITY

CREEDE

OURAY

TELLURIDE

OPHIR

SILVERTON

N

RICO

PAGOSA SPRINGS

DURANGO

ORES

CORTEZ

GATO

LUMBERTON

MESAVERDE
CLIFF HOUSES

COLORADO

NEW MEXICO

FARMINGTON

0   10   20   30   40   50   MILES

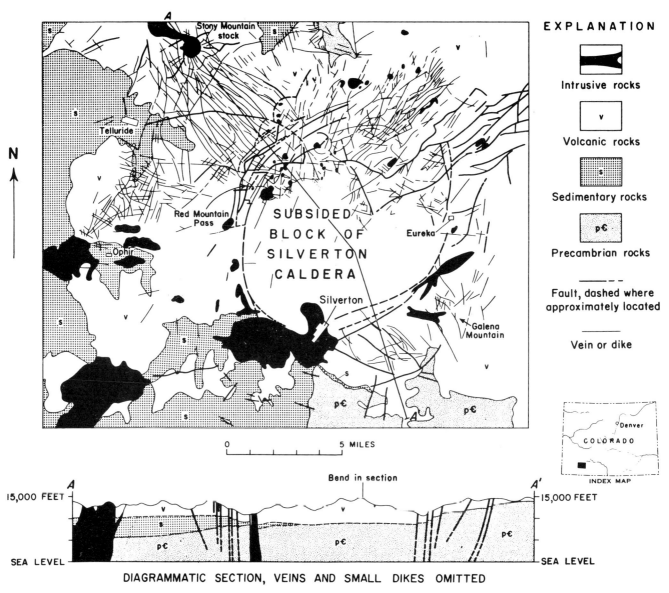

EXPLANATION

Intrusive rocks

v — Volcanic rocks

s — Sedimentary rocks

p€ — Precambrian rocks

— — — Fault, dashed where approximately located

——— Vein or dike

INDEX MAP

COLORADO — Denver

DIAGRAMMATIC SECTION, VEINS AND SMALL DIKES OMITTED

DAVID G. VARNES, U.S. GEOLOGICAL SURVEY PROFESSIONAL PAPER 378 — A

Figure 13

Generalized geologic map of the Silverton Caldera.

(pronounced "sirks"). These cirques are present at the heads of most valleys in the region and their near vertical walls posed the biggest problems to crossing passes. The Highland Mary, Gold Prince and Silver Lake mines are all in cirques.

After the ice retreated—about 10,000 years ago —the valley walls were all too steep, resulting in landsliding, which was a major problem along all the routes of the mountain railroads of the area.

This **NASA-ERTS** satellite photograph of the central San Juan Mountains was taken on **September 27, 1972,** to show the lack of snow, typical of the local climate up until early winter. Compare this view with the one taken in June. (See page 245.) Scale: 1 inch = 8 miles.

Equipping the Silverton Railroads

The three little narrow-gauge railroads headquartered in Silverton, Colorado, could — in some respects — be considered more fortunate than many of their contemporary brethren. While their location and construction through the rugged San Juan Range of the Rocky Mountains imposed continuing challenges, hardships, and heavy expenses in maintenance and operation, the problems and costs of equipping their lines were eased by the ready accessibility of large and varied quantities of motive power and rolling stock, maintained by the neighboring Denver and Rio Grande Railroad, and its associated lines, the Rio Grande Western, and Rio Grande Southern companies.

More than three-fifths of the grand total of 79 items of rolling equipment ultimately owned by the three Silverton lines were acquired second-hand; only 4 locomotives and 26 pieces of rolling stock ever were purchased new.

Otto Mears started his Silverton Railroad in 1887 with a used locomotive—Number 100, the *Ouray*—purchased from the Denver and Rio Grande, together with an arch-roof combination baggage-chaircar, which he named, *Red Mountain,* and a matching baggage car, later numbered 5, both purchased new. Three years later, in 1890, he purchased his first new locomotive, a two-truck Shay-geared engine—Number 269, named *Guston* —but within two years he disposed of the Shay, offering it to the Rio Grande Southern in exchange for second-hand RGS Number 34, a regular narrow-gauge rod engine, which then became Silverton Number 101. Also in 1890, he bought a used coach, presumably from the D&RG, giving it the name, *Yankee Girl.* Subsequently, this car carried numbers 3 and 11, and ended its life as a combination baggage-chaircar, having been converted by 1896.

In the spring of 1891, Mears purchased a snow-flanging car, giving it the number, "3," probably acquiring it from the D&RG, although whether new or used has not been determined. The following year, he added 37 third-hand 24-foot, 10-ton capacity boxcars of D&RG-RGW ancestry to the Silverton roster, and finally, in September of 1895, he purchased a used four-wheeled "bobber," the Silverton Railroad's caboose Number 17, from the D&RG, where it had been Number 0516.

Thus, in its lifetime, the Silverton Railroad accounted for 3 locomotives, 2 combines, 1 baggage car, 37 boxcars, 1 flanger, and 1 caboose, only 2 of these items being purchased new.

* * * * * *

After organizing his Silverton Northern Railroad in 1895, Otto Mears arranged to stock the new line initially with used equipment from his Silverton Railroad. The latter road's engine Number 101 was transferred to the Silverton Northern and designated Number 1, along with 10 of the Silverton's little boxcars, renumbered as Silverton Northern 100 through 109. Then, in 1901—after several years of fighting the San Juan's snowstorms with inadequate means—Mears purchased a flanger, probably second-hand from the D&RG, and assigned number "1" to this snowfighter.

Three years later, in May of 1904, the second locomotive purchased new by Otto Mears put in its appearance as Silverton Northern Number 3. This was followed in 1906 with yet another new engine—Silverton Northern Number 4—a duplicate of the "Three-spot." No record has appeared as to what Silverton Northern engine Number 2 might have been; no reference to such a locomotive is found anywhere in the voluminous correspondence of Alexander Anderson, although the number may have been reserved for the results of his inquiries regarding additional used motive power in 1903.

In the years that followed, a variety of equipment was acquired by the Silverton Northern. During 1906, a second-hand, narrow-gauge 48-foot-long Pullman buffet - sleeping car was purchased from the Pullman Company; rebuilt for service on the Mears' road, it was given the name, *Animas Forks.* Two years later, the railroad bought new a 12-seat gasoline-powered motor railbus, built by Stover in Freeport, Illinois. Several years earlier, the road had contracted and partially paid for—but had never received—a 28-seat motorcar, built by the Mack Brothers Motor Car Company in Pennsylvania.

January, 1909, saw the acquisition of yet another second-hand passenger car from the Denver and Rio Grande, built originally by Jackson and Sharp at Wilmington, Delaware, in 1882, as D&RG coach Number 90, renumbered 314 in 1885, and given the number, "4," when purchased by the Silverton Northern. During the following year—

1910—Otto Mears, ever intrigued with the workings of mechanical equipment, ordered a brand new, steam-driven, 30 horsepower, "J" model, self-propelled railroad ditcher, built by the American Hoist and Derrick Company in St. Paul, Minnesota. Number designation of this machine in the Silverton Northern equipment roster has not been found, but in a twist from the usual course of equipment affairs on the Mears roads, the ditcher eventually was bought by the D&RG from the SN.

The last piece of rolling stock to be purchased by the Silverton Northern came many years later, when the road bought used D&RGW caboose Number 0556 in November, 1937, in time to serve for the reopening of the Sunnyside mine and mill at Eureka. The old lettering on the car was painted over, but the car was not renumbered by the railroad.

Discounting the equipment received from its sister Mears road, included in the roster of the Silverton Railroad, the Silverton Northern—over the span of its existence—was responsible for two locomotives, two coaches, one passenger railbus, one flanger, one ditcher and one caboose, four of these items having been acquired new.

* * * * * * *

The little Silverton, Gladstone and Northerly Railroad—which was financed and built independently of Otto Mears, but which ultimately came under his control and subsequent ownership—followed much the same pattern as the other two Silverton roads in equipping its line with rolling stock and motive power. Starting in 1899, the road bought a used locomotive from the Rio Grande Southern, carrying the number, "32," on both lines, supplementing this engine with a new combination baggage-chaircar, numbered "1," 10 new boxcars, numbered from 1000 through 1009, and an otherwise unidentified "service" car (perhaps a used flanger or caboose). In 1900, another used locomotive, Number 33, was acquired from the RGS, where it had carried the same number, and the supply of rolling stock was further augmented by 10 new open-top gondolas, numbered from 2000 through 2009.

Four years later, business on the SG&N justified additional motive power, and a new outside-frame capped-stack, narrow-gauge 2-8-0, numbered "34," was added to the roster. The next year, the final addition to the equipment of the road was made when a new and larger combination baggage-chaircar, numbered "2," was purchased.

Thus, the short seven-mile-long Silverton, Gladstone and Northerly—smallest of the three little

roads operating out Silverton—equalled, or even surpassed, its two neighbors in the matter of equipment, accounting for 3 locomotives, 2 combines, 10 boxcars, 10 gondolas and 1 "service" car, with 23 pieces of this equipment entering service in new condition.

* * * * * * *

The items that remained of all the engines and equipment just discussed, ultimately came into the possession of the Silverton Northern, as the surviving company of the three little railroads. Of the 37 original 24-foot boxcars on the Silverton Railroad, one was in such poor condition when the cars were received in 1892 that it had been struck from the roster by 1895; the remaining 36 were carried on the combined rosters of the Silverton, and Silverton Northern lines until 1906, when all were struck since they were unable to satisfy the Interstate Commerce Commission's requirements for safety appliances on cars in interstate commerce.

Five of the Silverton, Gladstone and Northerly gondolas, and all 10 boxcars survived to be leased to the Silverton Northern in 1910. However, by 1915, when Otto Mears purchased the road and its equipment for the Silverton Northern, the remaining gondolas were gone and the boxcars were renumbered 2000 through 2009 for the SN. Within two years, only two of the boxcars remained fit for revenue service and these were dropped from the roster in 1924. Notwithstanding the deletions from the records, however, five of the ex-SG&N 32-foot boxcars survived on the line until the end of operations, including numbers 2003, 2004, 2006, 2007 and 2008. The carbodies of 2003 and 2007 still exist as a storage shed in Silverton.

The two Silverton Railroad combination passenger cars, *Red Mountain* and *Yankee Girl*, along with ex-SG&N locomotive Number 32, were scrapped between 1911 and 1915, and the carbodies and engine boiler were shipped to Mears' new sawmill at Cascade Creek (Tefft Spur) on the Rio de las Animas, south of Silverton. In 1920, the Silverton Northern's American Railroad ditcher was sold for $9,000 to the Denver and Rio Grande, where it became Number OW.

By 1923, two more locomotives—Mears' original Silverton Railroad Number 100 and ex-SG&N Number 33—finally had been cleared off the scrap line in Silverton, and the next year, Silverton Northern engine Number 1 followed them into oblivion. Only three locomotives—Silverton Northern engines 3 and 4, and ex-SG&N Number 34—all purchased new in the opening decade of the Twentieth Century—now remained on hand.

The final roster included the three locomotives, the original Silverton Railroad arch-roof baggage car, ex-SG&N combine Number 2, Silverton Northern passenger coach Number 4, one caboose —ex-D&RGW Number 0556—an old flanger and five bad order ex-SG&N boxcars.

From earth to earth . . . dust to dust.

*   *   *   *   *   *   *

Motive Power History and Specifications

Silverton Railroad Number 100, the *Ouray,* the first locomotive acquired by Otto Mears, was purchased second-hand from the D&RG for $6,500, in November of 1887. Fresh from overhaul by the D&RG's Burnham shops in Denver, the engine consisted of the frame and running gear of the third Class 60 locomotive received by the big railroad—road number 42, the *Anglo Saxon* (Baldwin serial number 4938, built in 1880), in service February 27, 1880, upon which was mounted the boiler of Class 60, Number 283 (Baldwin serial number 6057, built in 1882), in service March 11, 1882. The boilers on the two engines were exchanged (for reasons unknown) during the shopping process prior to Mears' purchase.

These two Class 60 locomotives were part of a group of 59 engines designed and built by Baldwin for the Denver and Rio Grande. The first engine in Class 60—road number 22, the *Alamosa* (Baldwin serial number 4076, built in 1877), placed in service May 25, 1877, and later renumbered 228—was the heaviest narrow-gauge power built up until that time, and was an experimental and test engine which introduced the eight-coupled wheel arrangement to Colorado's narrow-gauge lines. It was the only Class 60 engine with a wagon-top boiler.

The second and third locomotives in the class—road number 41, the *Grand Cañon* (later Number 229), and Number 42, the *Anglo Saxon*—were built early in 1880 and entered service in February of that year. Numbers 240 through 255 were built in 1881, the first being placed in service June 24, 1881, and the balance built in 1882. Augmenting this supply, 28 additional members of Class 60 were built to the Baldwin design by the Grant Locomotive Works at Paterson, New Jersey—23 of the engines in 1881 and the remaining 5 in 1882. The first of these entered service on May 20, 1881.

The 87 locomotives in Class 60, together with 53 similar, but somewhat lighter, Baldwin engines in Class 56, formed the bulk of the D&RG's narrow-gauge freight motive power until 1903, and were widely leased and sold to other lines. By the early 1920's, when the D&RGW changed its locomotive classification system from a weight to a tractive-effort basis, all the Class 56 engines had been disposed of, and those Class 60 locomotives remaining at the time were redesignated Class C-16.

The Class 60 engines were 30-ton Consolidation-type (2-8-0) locomotives, intended primarily for freight service. Cylinders were 15 x 20 inches; total wheelbase was 17 feet, 10 inches, with a driving wheelbase of 11 feet, 4 inches; and the main rod was connected to the second pair of drivers. The driving wheels were 36 inches in diameter, with 31-inch centers; only the front and rear pairs were flanged. The two center pairs were blind, i.e., without flanges; the second pair had tires 6½ inches wide, while the third pair had tires 6 inches wide. Pilot wheels in the pony truck were 24 inches in diameter. Although actual weight of these engines ranged in the neighborhood of 58,600 pounds, the planned weight had been 60,000 pounds, hence the designation as "Class 60." Weight on driving wheels was 52,000 pounds and tractive effort was 14,474 pounds.

The boiler was straight, 50 inches in diameter at the smokebox, and contained 153 flues 2 inches in diameter by 9 feet, 7-3/4 inches in length. The firebox, located inside the frame side pieces, was 6 feet 11-15/16 inches long by 25-1/8 inches wide inside. Each boiler was tested hydrostatically to 180 pounds pressure per square inch at the time of manufacture, but had no other specified limit on it as delivered. At first, these boilers were listed by the railroad with 145 pounds working steam pressure, but later—with no modification—sometimes were listed as 160-pound boilers.

Tenders of the Class 60 engines, carried on two four-wheel archbar trucks, had a capacity of 2,500 gallons of water and 6 tons of coal.

The Class 56 locomotives, with a weight of about 56,000 pounds (hence, the class designation), were the lighter of the two classes, the first of these being engine Number 24, the *Mosca* (Baldwin serial number 4191, built in 1877), placed in service on the D&RG in November of 1877. Most dimensions of the two classes were similar, but the boiler diameter on Class 56 engines was 48 inches at the smokebox, while the cylinders were 15 x 18 inches. The total wheelbase was 17 feet, 7½ inches, and the domes were spaced differently on the boiler. Class 56 engine tenders, slightly lower in height than those on the Class 60 locomotives, had a capacity of 1,500 gallons of water and 6 tons of coal.

In those busy, happy, prosperous years preceding the Silver Panic of 1893—when the mines and their associated facilities, located along the Silverton Railroad, were increasing production to unheard of dimensions—frugal Otto Mears found it much less expensive to supplement his single locomotive with rented power than to purchase and maintain another engine. At least 11 "foreign line" locomotives enhanced the scenery along the Rainbow Route during those years, as follows:

D&RG Number 65, *San Cristoval*	Class 56	January, 1889, to July, 1889; January 1, 1890, to January 23, 1890
D&RG Number 38, *Mancos*	Class 56	January 24, 1890, to ? , 1890
D&RG Number 61, *La Jara*	Class 56	October 22, 1890, to November 16, 1890
D&RG Number 67, *Weminuche*	Class 56	October 17, 1890, to November 26, 1890
D&RG Number 203, *Navajo*	Class 60	June 1, 1891, to April 1, 1892
D&RG Number 55, *Tomichi*	Class 56	August 27, 1891, to November 17, 1891
RGS Number 8 (ex-D&RG Number 248, *Comanche*)	Class 60	January 1, 1892, to April 12, 1892
RGS Number 5 (ex-D&RG Number 245, *Frying Pan*)	Class 60	July 7, 1892, to November 19, 1892
RGS Number 7 (ex-D&RG Number 247, *Pawnee*)	Class 60	August 14, 1892, to September 2, 1892
RGS Number 6 (ex-D&RG Number 246, *Otterbees*)	Class 60	September 2, 1892, to October 10, 1892
RGS Number 34	Class 56	November 27, 1892, to December 31, 1892

The last locomotive listed—RGS Number 34—was kept by the Silverton Railroad and was renumbered 101. This engine was obtained in exchange for Shay Number 269. Number 34 originally had been D&RG Class 56 engine, Number 79, the *La Plata* (Baldwin serial number 5226, built in 1880). This locomotive, as well as Silverton, Gladstone and Northerly engines 32 and 33 (Baldwin serial numbers 5185 and 5225 respectively, both built in 1880), were sequentially-numbered sister locomotives with similar histories, all having been transferred from the D&RG to the Denver and Rio Grande Western Railway (the Utah lines) as part of the settlement ending the disastrous feud between the Colorado and Utah portions of the Rio Grande system in July of 1886. The original D&RGW changed its name to Rio Grande Western in 1889 without changing the road numbers of these locomotives.

By November of 1891, when the RGW had completed the rebuilding of its lines to standard-gauge, the narrow-gauge locomotives were rendered surplus and these three were sold to the Rio Grande Southern. The RGS, in turn, subsequently disposed of the engines—one by trade to the Silverton Railroad in 1892—the other two, no longer required after the Silver Panic took place, were sold to the Silverton, Gladstone and Northerly in 1899 and 1900.

During the period of mining recovery in Colorado — after the 1893 debacle — the Silverton Northern, as had the Silverton Railroad more than a decade before, found itself short of motive power. Pending delivery of its new locomotive, Number 3

(then on order), it arranged to rent an engine from the D&RG during the fall of 1903. After putting up with the irritating problems induced by four badly worn and thoroughly unreliable engines—as related earlier—the road finally found success with a D&RG Class 60 engine, Number 281, using this locomotive from October 25, 1903, until the end of that year's operating season. The next year, the road leased Grant-built D&RG Class 60 engine, Number 208, for construction work; the engine was in this service from early May until June 2, 1904.

New Motive Power and Equipment

The first locomotive purchased new by Otto Mears for his burgeoning little railroad empire in the Silverton area was Shay-geared locomotive Number 269 for the Silverton Railroad. As the first engine of its kind in southwestern Colorado, this three-foot-gauge engine was ordered personally by Mears—in early 1890—at the Lima Machine Works, Lima, Ohio. He had stopped off there while on a trip back East to arrange financing for his Rio Grande Southern Railroad, which had been incorporated on October 2, 1889. (Two small two-foot-gauge locomotives of the Gilpin Tramway at Central were the first Shays to operate in Colorado.)

After reaching Durango on April 19, 1890, the Shay spent nine years in the San Juans before being sold, but during only 11 months of that time was it in use on the Silverton Railroad. During the remainder of that period, it was located on the RGS, spending many more years in storage than in use. Lettered, "SILVERTON R.R. CO.," with the name, "GUSTON," on the side panels of the cab, and the builder's serial number—269—painted on the sand dome as the road number, the Shay was a Lima Class 37-2, with a weight of 37 tons. Each of the two trucks held four 29½-inch driving wheels, all powered through bevel gears and crank and jackshafts by three 10 x 12-inch cylinders; the tank held about 1,800 gallons of water and nearly 1¾ tons of coal. On level track, the engine's tractive effort approximated 17,000 pounds—about the same as a D&RG Class 70 (later, Class C-19) 2-8-0 —but on a four-percent grade it could pull five or six boxcars, about three times as much as the Silverton Railroad's other engine, the second-hand Class 60 2-8-0, Number 100. While the Shay's tractive effort was high, its speed over the road was very low and its utility to the Mears roads thus was found—no doubt with considerable disappointment—to be at a minimum.

Upon first appearing at Durango in the spring of 1890, the Shay immediately was pressed into service on the south end of the Rio Grande Southern, under construction engineer Thomas Wigglesworth. It was assigned both to handling coal traffic and to work train service, building the railroad. Upon completion of the RGS, on December 19, 1891, the Shay was at last turned over to the Silverton Railroad. However, about November 27, 1892—less than a year later—it was sent back to the RGS (perhaps intended for use on the Enterprise Branch out of Rico) in trade for that road's Class 56 engine, Number 34.

The RGS finally sold the Shay, which it had renumbered second Number 34, but supposedly never used, in July, 1899, to the Siskiwit and Iron River Railroad at Ashland, Wisconsin. From there it went to Doucette, Texas, where it was located first on the line of the Thompson Brothers Lumber Company, and then with the Fidelity Lumber Company. The latter, in turn, sold it to the Turkey Creek Lumber Company at Waynesboro, Mississippi, where it was acquired in 1928 by the neighboring Stark and Oldham Brothers Lumber Company, who subsequently dismantled it for scrap, at the end of a long, widely-travelled and varied career.

In May of 1904, the Silverton Northern Railroad took delivery of the second engine to be purchased new by Otto Mears. Carrying road number, "3," and Baldwin serial number, "24109," the locomotive was a three-foot-gauge, inside-frame 2-8-0, Baldwin Class 10-26-E-315, with 37-inch drivers (the center two pair blind), two 24-inch pilot wheels, and 16 x 20-inch cylinders. Weighing in at 72,000 pounds, it had 18,819 pounds of tractive

effort. The boiler, 52 inches in diameter, was straight; flues were 11 feet, 7¾ inches in length, and the firebox was 83-15/16 inches long by 24-1/8 inches wide. The tender, loaded, weighed 60,000 pounds, and had a capacity for 3,000 gallons of water and 5 tons of coal.

The engine was delivered with two 3-inch safety valves and a whistle on the steam dome; two injectors; a capped, straight stack, mounted on an extended smokebox; alligator crossheads; Stephenson valve gear; wooden pilot and cab; a 16-inch, round-case, oil-burning headlight; Westinghouse airbrakes, with one 9½-inch airpump on the right side; and Master Car Builder (MCB) automatic couplers. Number 3 originally was painted olive green and aluminum, with the tank lettered, "SILVERTON NORTHERN," and the number, "3," on the front plate, sand dome and rear of the tender tank. Meant to be the closest approximation of the Class 60 narrow-gauge freight engine— exemplified by Silverton Railroad Number 100, then being manufactured by Baldwin—it actually was much closer to an updated, modernized version of a D&RG Class 70 (or Class C-19) engine, first produced in 1881.

The original cost of Silverton Northern locomotive Number 3 was $8,648.75.

During that same month of May, 1904, the Silverton, Gladstone and Northerly also took delivery of a new Consolidation (2-8-0) locomotive—this one with an outside-frame—Baldwin Class 10-26-E-316, serial number 24130, numbered SG&N 34. Like Silverton Northern Number 3, this new SG&N engine had 37-inch drivers (with the center two pair blind), two 24-inch pony-truck wheels, and 16 x 20-inch cylinders. With a weight of 88,100 pounds, it was somewhat heftier than the new power on the Silverton Northern, but the tractive effort of 18,000 pounds was no greater than that of the neighboring locomotive.

The 54-inch diameter boiler on SG&N Number 34 was straight, with flues 14 feet, 11¾ inches in length, and was riveted to a firebox 50-7/16 inches long by 45-3/4 inches wide. The tender weighed 54,000 pounds when fully loaded, and held 2,400 gallons of water and 5 tons of coal. The total weight of engine and tender was 142,100 pounds.

The locomotive was delivered with two 3-inch safety valves and a whistle on the steam dome; two injectors; an extended smokebox, graced by a capped, straight stack; Laird crossheads; Stephenson valve gear; cast steel frame; a wooden pilot braced with steel; a wooden cab; a 16-inch oil-burning headlight; Westinghouse airbrakes, with one 9½-inch pump on the left side; and Master Car Builder (Janney style) automatic couplers.

Painted olive green and aluminum when delivered, it was lettered with the name, "GOLD PRINCE," on each side of the cab, with "S.G.& (34) N.R.R." on the sides of the tender tank, and the number, "34," on the front plate, sand dome and rear of the tender.

After the Silverton, Gladstone and Northerly was bought by Otto Mears' Silverton Northern in 1915, SG&N engine Number 34 was relettered for the new owner, but was not renumbered, as shown in the plan. An electric generator was added and the oil headlight was electrified. A snowplow pilot also was added, but is not shown in the plan.

The last of the locomotives purchased new by Otto Mears was Silverton Northern engine Number 4, shipped to Colorado from Philadelphia by the Baldwin Locomotive Works, on April 26, 1906. A Baldwin Class 10-26-E-325, with serial number 27977, the new narrow-gauge Consolidation was an almost exact duplicate of its two-year-old sister, SN Number 3, the principle difference being in the tender, which had high sides, and a capacity of 2,000 gallons of water and 5 tons of coal. At some later date, the capacity of the tender was increased to 3,000 gallons of water.

In those "ancient times," predating galloping inflation, Mears paid $8,375.00 for Silverton Northern Number 4, a price that was $273.75 *less* than he had paid for SN Number 3, two years before!

*   *   *   *   *   *   *

When the Silverton Northern was forced to shut down in 1938, due to the strike at the Sunnyside mill, engines 3, 4 and 34 were put away in the dilapidated little enginehouse in Silverton, perhaps never again to see active service on any railroad. But then, in 1942—with the advent of World War II—the three locomotives were commandeered by the U.S. Army and shipped off to the White Pass and Yukon Route in Alaska, where Number 3 became WP&Y Number 22; Number 4 became WP&Y Number 23; and Number 34 became WP&Y Number 24. After the war, engines 3 and 4 were returned to Seattle and scrapped; Number 34, damaged while in service on the WP&Y, was held at Skagway—finally being dismantled there in 1951.

The last piece of equipment purchased new by Otto Mears for any of his railroads came in 1910, when he bought an American Railroad ditcher, serial number 578, from the American Hoist and Derrick Company of St. Paul, Minnesota, for the Silverton Northern. Rather than the usual style— self-propelled on its own track laid on the deck of a flatcar—the new machine was a "J" model, originally developed for logging roads, built on a

riveted-steel underframe and fitted with a 5/8-cubic-yard bucket. A center jackshaft, working through bevel gears and universal joints, drove the inside axles on both 4-foot, 6-inch-wheelbase, four-wheel Master Car Builder trucks.

Wheel size was 24 inches and automatic couplers were installed at the factory. The airbrake piping for train operation went straight through under the car, without interruption, the brakes on the ditcher being operated independently by steam. The upright boiler, 91 inches tall, was 43 inches in diameter, and contained 120 flues 2 inches in diameter; the two-cylinder steam engine, 7-inch bore by 8-inch stroke, was rated at 30 horsepower. Total weight of the whole rig was 34,000 pounds when the bunkers were filled to their capacity of 400 gallons of water and 1,200 pounds of coal.

Except for minor differences in underframe and boom construction, the Silverton Northern ditcher was nearly identical with RGS Number 030 (serial number 1005), built in November, 1919; D&RG Number OX (serial number 1087), built in December, 1920; and a similar machine on the Uintah Railway (serial number 1216), built in May, 1924, all by the American Hoist and Derrick Company.

The Silverton Northern ditcher was rented by the Rio Grande Southern at intervals during the years 1916, 1917 and 1918. In August, 1920, the D&RG bought the machine for $9,000, and assigned it the identifying symbol, OW.

Apparently, in 1920 the booms on the narrow-gauge ditchers were shuffled around by the D&RGW. The boom and pile-driver attachment from D&RGW Number OX was installed on the OW, the original boom from the ex-SN ditcher becoming part of RGS Number 030. Presumably, the boom from the RGS ditcher was transferred to D&RGW Number OX.

In 1939, the Rio Grande Southern's ditcher Number 030 was accepted in trade by the D&RGW for used narrow-gauge 2-8-2 locomotive, Class K-27, Number 455. And the next year, the big road turned around and offered the three ditchers—OW, OX and 030—for sale to the Silverton Northern. With its own property completely shut down, the little Mears road had no interest in any such acquisition.

Two years later, D&RGW Number OW was commandeered by the U.S. Army during World War II, and accompanied the Silverton Northern engines to the White Pass and Yukon Route, who scrapped it in 1944. D&RGW ditcher Number OX went to the Southern Pacific's narrow-gauge line and was converted to gasoline operation in 1946. The final history of RGS (D&RGW) Number 030 is not yet known.

Consolidated Roster of Officers

THE SILVERTON RAILROADS
1887 — 1942

Alexander Anderson
Auditor	SRR	1892-1896
Secretary	SRR	1893-1904
Director	SRR	1894-1898
Director	SN	1895-1907
Treasurer	SN	1895-1907
General Manager	SRR	1898-1904
Auditor	SN	1899
Receiver	SRR	1899-1904
General Manager	SN	1900-1904
Director	SRy	1905-1907
Treasurer	SRy	1905-1906
Treasurer	SRy	1906-1907

J. A. Atkinson
Agent, Red Mountain and Ironton	SRR	1889
Agent, Silverton	SRR	1891-1892

George H. Barnes
Director	SG&N	1899
Secretary	SG&N	1899-1913

Martin F. Bartlett
Director	SG&N	1909-1915

W. D. Batchelor
Auditor	SRy	1907-1908
Auditor	SN	1907-1908

Norman F. Bawden
Auditor	SN	1929-1942

A. S. Berkey
Master Mechanic	SN	1929

Charles E. Bibber
Director	SG&N	1899

John Blackman
Director	SG&N	1899

William E. Booker
Master Mechanic	SRR	1889-1904
Master Mechanic	SN	1895-1910
Superintendent	SN	1908-1923
Superintendent	SRy	1920-1923

Harry C. Brown
Agent	SRR	1904
Agent, Silverton	SRR	1904
Agent, Silverton	SN	1904-1912
Agent, Silverton	SRy	1905-1912
Auditor	SRy	1909-1912
Auditor	SN	1911-1913

E. D. Carmichael
Agent, Silverton	SG&N	1909-1912

William Chaifaut, Jr.
Director	RMRRMS	1902-1908

John D. Chipman
President	SG&N	1899-1908
Director	SG&N	1900-1915
Treasurer	SG&N	1910-1915

J. W. Christman
Director	RMRRMS	1902-1908

George Crawford
Vice-President	SRR	1887
Director	SRR	1887-1893
Director	RMRRMS	1902-1908
Gen. Manager	RMRRMS	1902-1908
Director	SRy	1905-1917

Cyrus W. Davis
Director	SG&N	1899-1909
Vice-President	SG&N	1899-1909

J. Walter Davis
Director	SG&N	1899-1908

W. H. Dixon
Agnt, Silverton	SRR	1895-1896

Joseph E. Dresback
Agent, Silverton		1916-1920
Auditor	SRy	1920-1923
Auditor	SN	1920-1928
Superintendent	SN	1924-1928
Assistant Treasurer	SN	1926-1927

John A. Ewing
Director	SRy	1905-1917
Secretary	SRy	1908-1918

E. T. Fraim
Director	RMRRMS	1902-1908

E. L. France
Agent, Silverton	SG&N	1900

H. L. Frank
Auditor	SRy	1912-1916-
Agent, Silverton	SRy	1912-1916
Agent, Silverton	SN	1912-1916
Auditor	SN	1914-1916
Auditor	SG&N	1914-1915

Jerome B. Frank
Director	SN	1895-1898
Director	SN	1908-1930
Secretary	SN	1908-1929
Auditor	SN	1909-1910
Director	SRy	1917-1923
Secretary	SRy	1919-1923

Mark Gallert
Director	SG&N	1904-1915
President	SG&N	1909-1915

J. A. George
Agent, Silverton	SG&N	1901-1908

Charles W. Gibbs
Chief Engineer	SG&N	1888-1891

Charles H. Graham
Director	SRR	1897-1904
Vice-President	SRR	1897-1904
Director	RMRRMS	1902-1908
President	RMRRMS	1902-1908

Director	SRy	1905-1913
Vice-President	SRy	1905-1913

Louis G. Green
Director	SG&N	1904-1915

S. M. Green
Vice-President	SRR	1893-1897
Director	SRR	1894-1904

Ernest Griel
Roadmaster	SRR	1888-1889

Simon Guggenheim
Director	SN	1903-1905

A. W. Harrison
Chief Engineer	SN	1920-1929
Director	SN	1931-1942

D. M. Haynes
Superintendent	SG&N	1909

Charles L. Hill
Director	SRR	1897

James H. Houston
Director	SG&N	1910-1915

Edward H. Hudson
General Manager	SN	1906
Superintendent	SN	1906-1908
Superintendent	SRy	1906-1908

Nathan Hunter
Roadmaster	SRR	1890-1891

J. M. Johnson
Director	SG&N	1910-1915
Vice-President	SG&N	1910-1915
General Manager	SG&N	1910-1915
Director	SN	1922-1928

Charles F. Jones
Director	RMRRMS	1902-1908
Vice-President	RMRRMS	1902-1908

Fred A. Jones
Director	SG&N	1899-1915

W. P. Kellogg
Director	RMRRMS	1902-1908

J. V. Kilbourn
Agent, Silverton	SRR	1889

W. Z. Kinney
Director	SG&N	1899-1908
Superintendent	SG&N	1899-1908

E. J. Lawrence
Director	SG&N	1899-1915

Moses Liverman
General Manager	SRR	1888-1896
Director	SRR	1891-1896
Secretary	SRR	1892-1893
Director	SN	1895-1897

George C. Logan
Roadmaster	SRR	1891-1897

T. J. McKelvey
Agent, Red Mountain and Ironton	SRR	1892-1898
Agent, Silverton	SN	1898-1904
Agent, Silverton	SRR	1899-1904
Auditor	SRR	1903-1904
Auditor	SN	1903-1904

John L. McNeil
Director	SRR	1889-1904
Treasurer	SRR	1890-1904
General Manager	SRR	1897

Mary Mears
Director	SRy	1922-1923

Otto Mears
Director	SRR	1887-1904
President	SRR	1887-1904
Director	SN	1895-1930
Vice-President	SN	1895-1899
General Manager	SN	1895-1899
President	SN	1900-1929
Director	SRy	1905-1923
President	SRy	1905-1923

Edward "Pete" Meyer
Superintendent	SN	1929-1942

C. William Montgomery
Auditor	SRy	1917-1919
Auditor	SN	1917-1919
Director	SRy	1918

J. H. Morris
Agent, Red Mountain and Ironton	SRR	1891

F. L. Newhouse
Director	SN	1903-1905

A. B. Page
Director	SG&N	1909

Cora Mears Pitcher
Director	SRy	1920
Director	SN	1920-1942
Vice-President	SN	1930-1933
Treasurer	SN	1931-1942
President	SN	1934-1942

James R. Pitcher, Jr.
Director	SN	1906-1934
Vice-President	SN	1907-1929
Treasurer	SN	1907-1930
General Manager	SN	1907-1933
Treasurer	SRy	1907-1923
Director	SRy	1908-1923
General Manager	SRy	1908-1923
Secretary	SG&N	1914-1915
Vice-President	SRy	1918-1923
Asst. Secretary	SN	1923-1924
President	SN	1930-1933

James R. Pitcher, III
Secretary	SN	1930-1937
Director	SN	1931-1942
Vice-President	SN	1934-1935
General Manager	SN	1934-1935

Otto Mears Pitcher
Director	SN	1935-1942

Robertson Mears Pitcher
Vice-President	SN	1936-1942
General Manager		1936-1942

Director	SN	1938-1942
Secretary	SN	1938-1942

John A. Porter
Director	SRR	1887-1893
Vice-President	SRR	1888-1892

Oliver P. Posey
Director	SRR	1887
Second Vice-Pres.	SRR	1892-1893

W. H. W. Quick
Director	RMRRMS	1902-1908

Harvey Riddle
Attorney	SRy	1905
Director	SN	1906-1919
Attorney	SN	1907-1919
Director	SRy	1917-1919

Arthur O. Ridgway
Superintendent	SRy	1905
General Manager	SN	1905
Superintendent	SN	1905

Fred O. Roof
Director	SN	1898-1902

Frank L. Ross
Attorney	SN	1919-1933

Herbert L. Ross
Director	SRR	1897

Ben B. Russell
Attorney	SRR	1900-1904

J. W. Schofield
Director	SRR	1898-1904

E. Cooper Shapley
Director	RMRRMS	1902-1908

W. M. Shoemaker
Agent, Silverton	SRR	1897-1898
Agent, Silverton	SN	1897-1898

John H. Slattery
Director	SRy	1916-1920
Second Vice-Pres.	SRy	1918-1922
Director	SN	1920
Asst. Vice-President	SN	1910-1923
Director	SRy	1922-1923

Marshall D. Smith
Director	SN	1906-1919
Director	SRy	1917

Henry M. Soule
Director	SG&N	1899-1909
Treasurer	SG&N	1904-1909

James B. Staley
Director	RMRRMS	1902-1908
Sec.-Treas.	RMRRMS	1902-1908

F. B. Stevenson
Agent, Silverton	SRR	1893

Albert Thompson
Director	RMRRMS	1902-1908

F. P. Thornton
Auditor	SRR	1897-1899

Fred Walsen, Sr.
Director	SRR	1887-1891
Treasurer	SRR	1887-1889
Director	SRR	1894-1904

Director	SN	1895-1905
President	SN	1895-1899
Vice-President	SN	1900-1906

Fred Walsen, Jr.
Secretary	SN	1897-1905
Director	SN	1898-1902
Auditor	SRR	1901-1902

E. S. Warner
Agent, Gladstone	SG&N	

J. H. Ernest Waters
Chief Engineer	SRR	1887
Director	SRR	1888-1893
Chief Engineer	SRR	1892

W. G. Weaver
Agent, Silverton	SRR	1892-1893

John C. Welty
Director	SRR	1897-1904

G. Whetmore
Director	SG&N	1899

Adair Wilson
Attorney	SRR	1887-1899
Director	SRR	1891-1896

John W. Wingate
Director	SRR	1887-1891
Secretary	SRR	1887-1891

John C. Wood
Master Mechanic	SN	1910-1913

Samuel N. Wood
Director	SRR	1887

C. W. Young
Director	SG&N	1910-1915

LEGEND

RMRRMS — Red Mountain Railroad, Mining and Smelting Company

SRR — Silverton Railroad

SRy — Silverton Railway

SG&N — Silverton, Gladstone and Northerly Railroad

SN — Silverton Northern Railroad

LOCOMOTIVE ROSTER

ROAD NUMBER	BUILDER'S NO. AND DATE	NAME	TYPE	CYLINDERS	DRIVERS	ENGINE WEIGHT	TRACTIVE EFFORT	REMARKS (See Below)
SRR No. 100	Baldwin No. 4938, 1880 and No. 6057, 1882	*Ouray*	2-8-0	15"x 20"	36"	58,600	14,474	1.
SRR No. 269	Lima No. 269 April, 1890	*Guston*	Shay 0-4-4-0T	3-10"x 12"	29½"	74,000	16,900	2.
SRR No. 101	Baldwin No. 5226, 1880		2-8-0	15"x 18"	36"	56,200	13,025	3.
SG&N No. 32	Baldwin No. 5185, 1880	*Gold King*	2-8-0	15"x 18"	36"	56,200	13,025	4.
SG&N No. 33	Baldwin No. 5225, 1880		2-8-0	15"x 18"	36"	56,200	13,025	5.
SG&N No. 34	Baldwin No. 24130, May, 1904	*Gold Prince*	2-8-0	16"x 20"	37"	88,100	18,800	6.
SN No. 1	Baldwin No. 5226, 1880		2-8-0	See SRR No. 101 above				7.
SN No. 2	——		——	——	——	——	——	8.
SN No. 3	Baldwin No. 24109, May, 1904		2-8-0	16"x 20"	37"	72,000	18,819	9.
SN No. 4	Baldwin No. 27977, April, 1906		2-8-0	16"x 20"	37"	72,000	18,819	10.
SN No. 34	Baldwin No. 24130, May, 1904		2-8-0	See SG&N No. 34 above				11.

———— REMARKS ————

1. Originally D&RG Class 60, Number 42, the *Anglo Saxon*, purchased second-hand November, 1887, for $6,500. Received with boiler of D&RG Class 60 engine, Number 283, Baldwin serial number 6057. Scrapped Silverton 1923.

2. Purchased new by Otto Mears from Lima Machine Works, Lima, Ohio; Lima Class 37-2. In service on RGS April, 1890, to December, 1891; on SRR December, 1891, to November, 1892. Traded to RGS in exchange for RGS Number 34 November 1892. Sold by RGS July, 1899.

3. Originally D&RG Class 56, Number 79, the *La Plata*, valued at $4,383.53 in transfer to D&RGW Railway, Number 79, July, 1886. Sold to RGS, RGS Number 34, November, 1891, for $1,200. Received by SRR (Number 101) December, 1892, in exchange for Shay Number 269. Transferred to SN Number 1, December, 1896.

4. Originally D&RG Class 56, Number 77, the *Rinconida*, valued at $4,744.72 in transfer to D&RGW Railway Number 77, July, 1886. Sold to RGS

Number 32, November, 1891, for $1,200. Purchased second-hand by SG&N (Number 32) August, 1899, for $3,252. Scrapped in Silverton about 1911 and boiler shipped to sawmill at Tefft Spur.

5. Originally D&RG Class 56, Number 78, the *Sandia*, valued at $4,383.53 in transfer to D&RGW Railway, Number 78, July, 1886. Sold to RGS Number 33, November, 1891, for $3,000. Sold by RGS to G. M. Dilley & Son, Palestine, Texas, September, 1899; returned by Dilley and purchased second-hand by SG&N (Number 33) October, 1900, for $3,200. Scrapped in Silverton in 1923.

6. Purchased new; Baldwin Class 10-26-E-316. Originally painted olive green and aluminum. Acquired second-hand by SN (No. 34) January, 1915, when entire railroad was sold to Otto Mears.

7. Transferred to SN Number 1 from SRR Number 101, December, 1896. Rebuilt with larger airpump and extended smokebox in 1904. Scrapped in Silver-

ton in 1924.

8. No data. Engine may not have existed, or the number was reserved for leased engine or planned purchase of used locomotive.

9. Purchased new at cost of $8,648.75; Baldwin Class 10-26-E-315. Originally painted olive green and aluminum. Sold to White Pass & Yukon, Number 22, October, 1942; returned to Seattle, Washington, 1944. Scrapped in Seattle in 1944.

10. Purchased new at cost of $8,375.00; Baldwin Class 10-26-E-325. Originally painted olive green and aluminum. Sold to White Pass & Yukon, Number 23, October, 1942; returned to Seattle, Washington, 1944. Scrapped in Seattle in 1944.

11. Originally SG&N Number 34, acquired second-hand by SN (Number 34) January, 1915, when SG&N was purchased by Otto Mears. Sold to White Pass & Yukon, Number 24, October, 1942; stored unserviceable at Skagway, Alaska, 1944. Scrapped in Skagway in 1951.

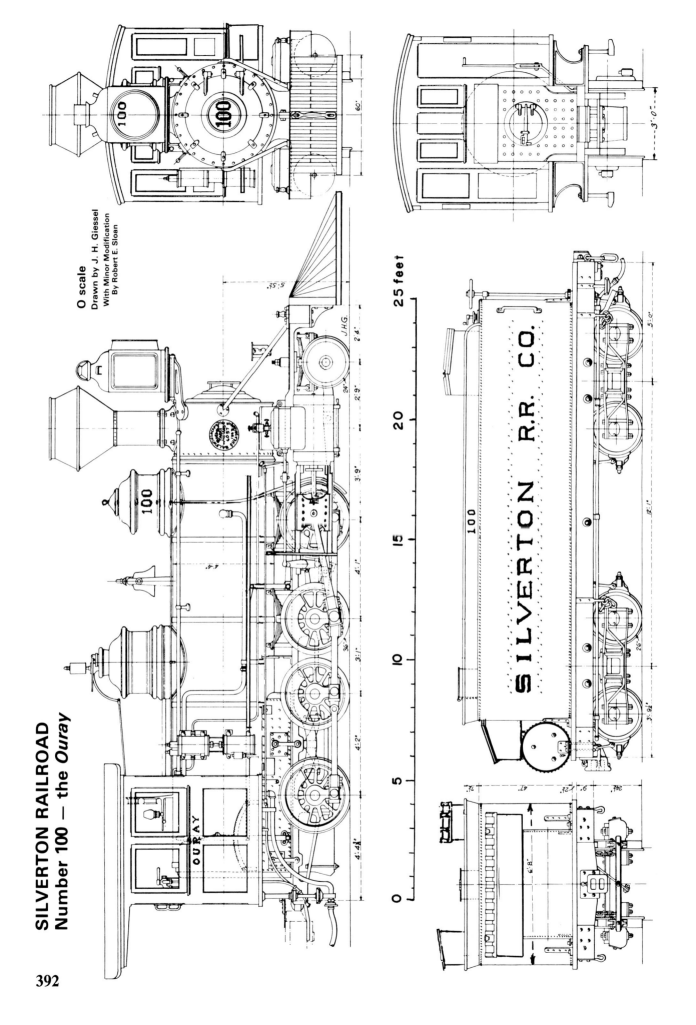

SILVERTON RAILROAD
Number 100 — the *Ouray*

O scale
Drawn by J. H. Giessel
With Minor Modification
By Robert E. Sloan

SILVERTON R.R. CO.

25 feet

392

SG&N Locomotive Number 32
Gold King

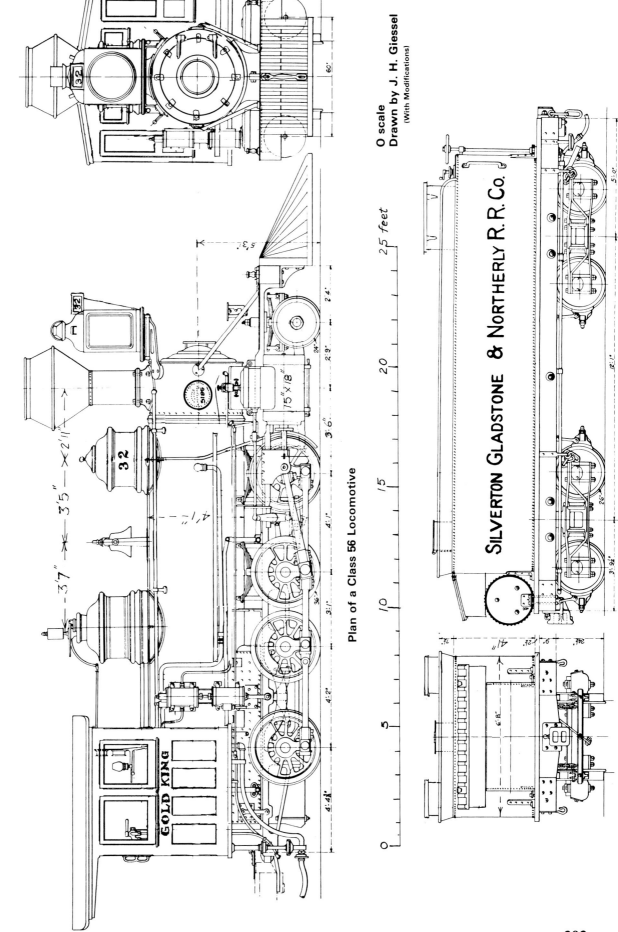

Plan of a Class 56 Locomotive

O scale
Drawn by J. H. Giessel
(With Modifications)

SILVERTON GLADSTONE & NORTHERLY R. R. Co.

393

SILVERTON NORTHERN
Locomotive Number 4

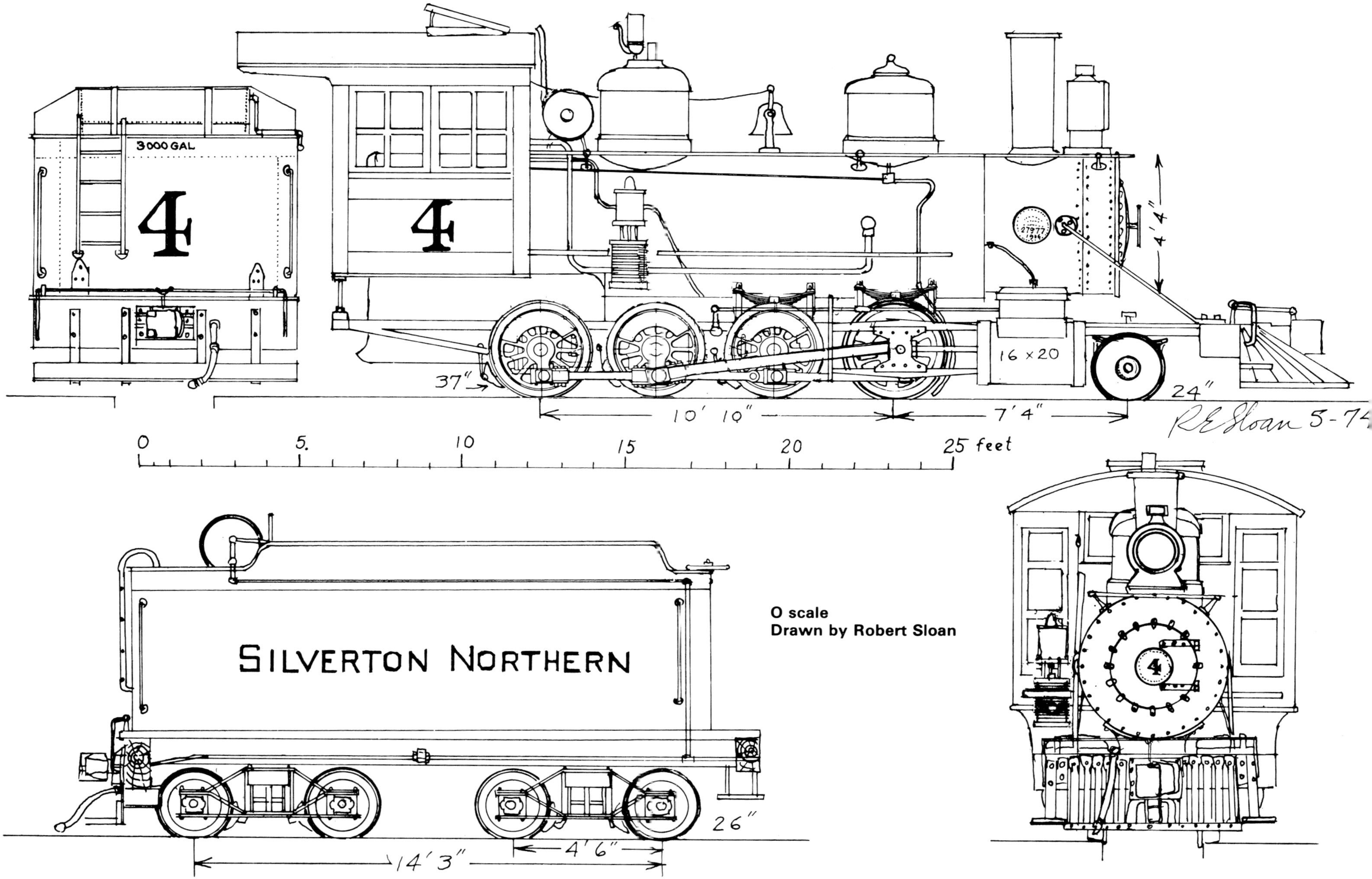

24"

R.E. Sloan 5-74

16 × 20

7'4"

25 feet

20

10'10"

15

37"

10

5.

0

3000 GAL

4

4

O scale
Drawn by Robert Sloan

SILVERTON NORTHERN

26"

4'6"

14'3"

394

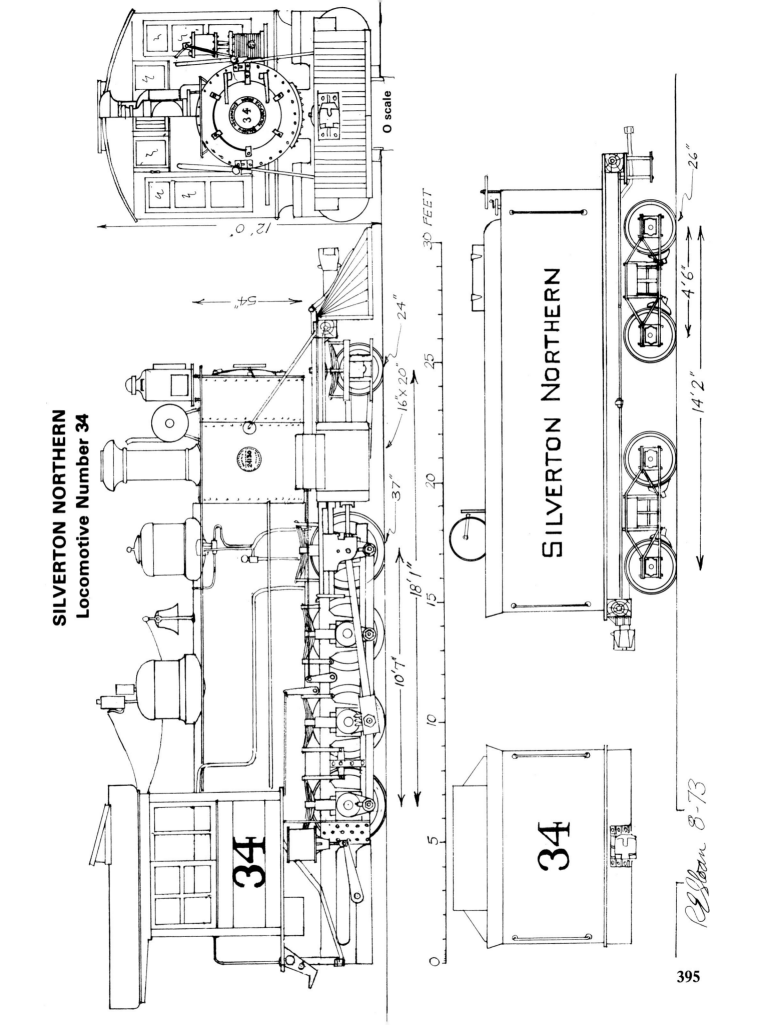

SILVERTON NORTHERN
Locomotive Number 34

SILVERTON NORTHERN

O scale

30 FEET

395

SILVERTON NORTHERN RAILBUS

Casey Jones

O scale

Drawn by Ken Pruitt

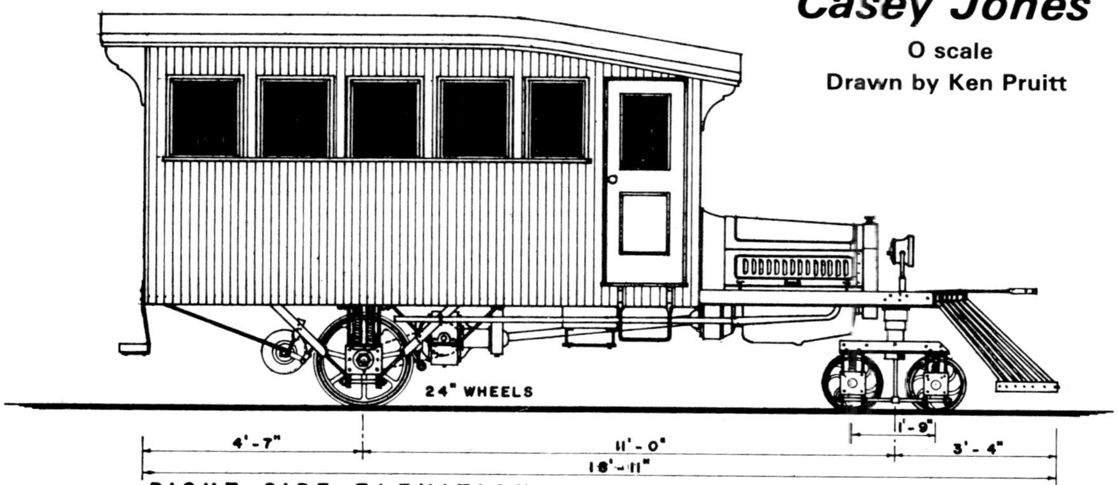

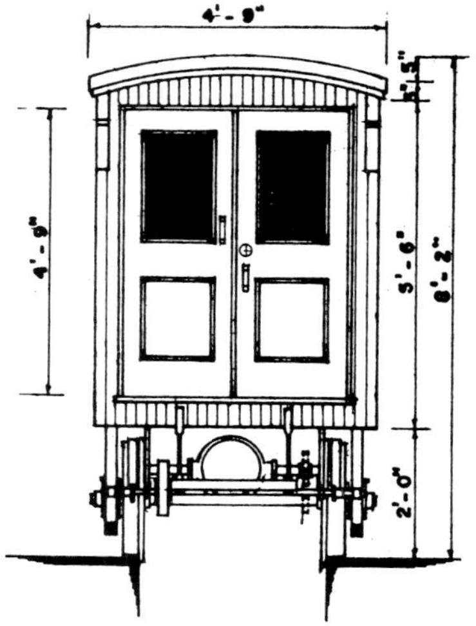

REAR ELEVATION

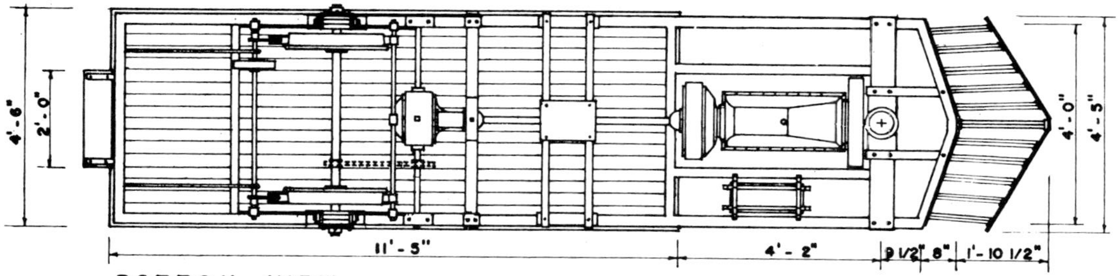

4'-9"

9'-2"

3'-6"

2'-0"

9'-8"

FRONT ELEVATION

END

BOTTOM
13" PILOT
WHEELS

3'-0"

1'-9"

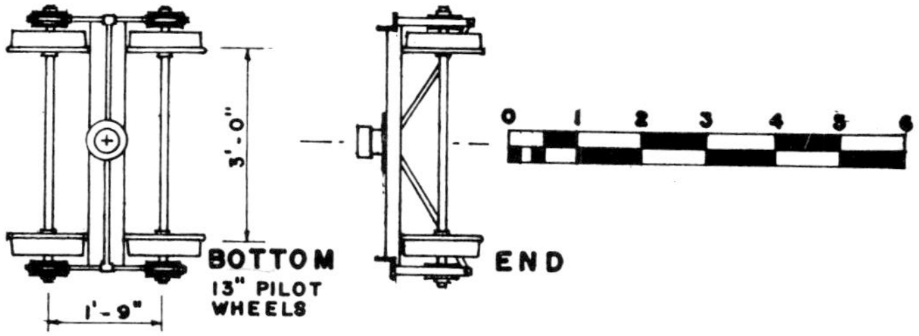

PILOT TRUCK

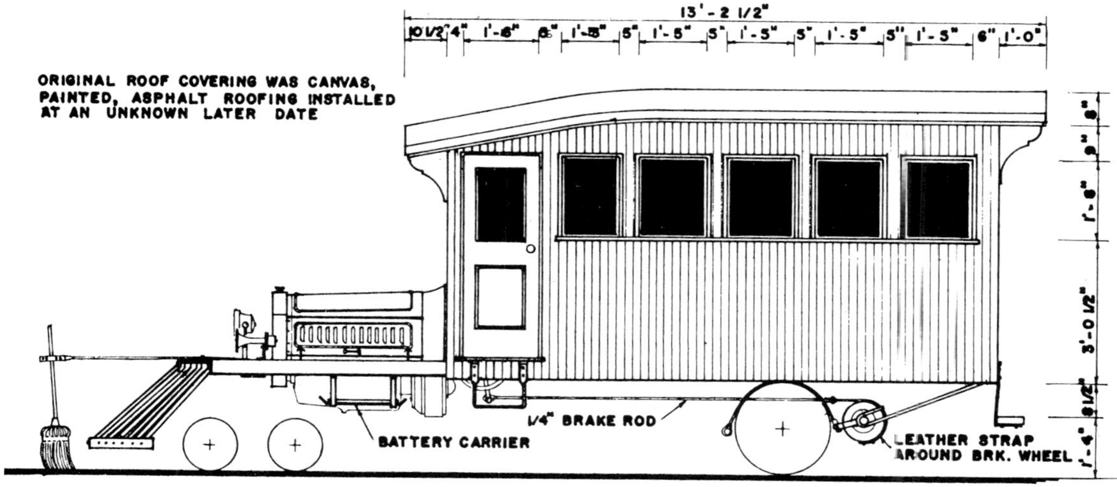

Casey Jones, the SN railbus, was designed by Clyde Jones and was built in the shops of the Sunnyside mine in 1918.

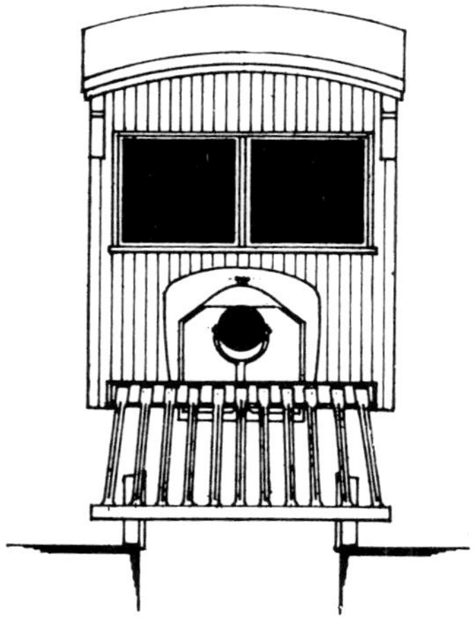

RIGHT SIDE ELEVATION

24" WHEELS

3'-4"

1'-9"

11'-0"

18'-11"

4'-7"

BOTTOM VIEW

4'-5"

4'-0"

1'-10 1/2"

2 1/2" 8"

4'-2"

11'-5"

2'-0"

4'-6"

LEFT SIDE ELEVATION

LEATHER STRAP
AROUND BRK. WHEEL

1/4" BRAKE ROD

BATTERY CARRIER

6"

1'-6"

3'-0 1/2"

2 1/8"

13'-2 1/2"

1'-0"

6"

1'-5"

5"

1'-5"

5"

1'-5"

6"

1'-5"

6"

1'-5"

1'-6"

10 1/2"

4"

ORIGINAL ROOF COVERING WAS CANVAS,
PAINTED, ASPHALT ROOFING INSTALLED
AT AN UNKNOWN LATER DATE

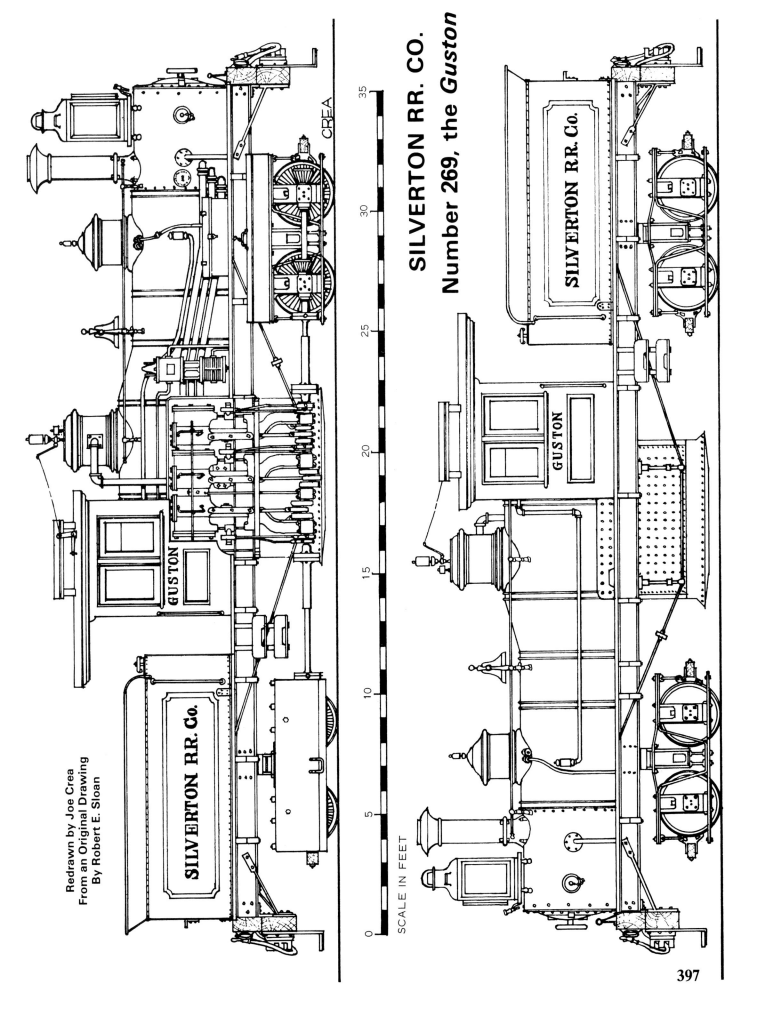

SILVERTON RR. CO.
Number 269, the *Guston*

Redrawn by Joe Crea
From an Original Drawing
By Robert E. Sloan

SCALE IN FEET

SILVERTON R.R. Co.

GUSTON

CREA

SILVERTON NORTHERN DITCHER

Serial Number 578, built in 1910 — sold to D&RGW OW in 1920.
Received original boom of Number 1087, D&RGW OX;
boom of Number 578 went to RGS 030;
boom of SN 1005 went to the OX.
D&RGW OW was shipped to WP&Y in 1942;
scrapped in 1945.

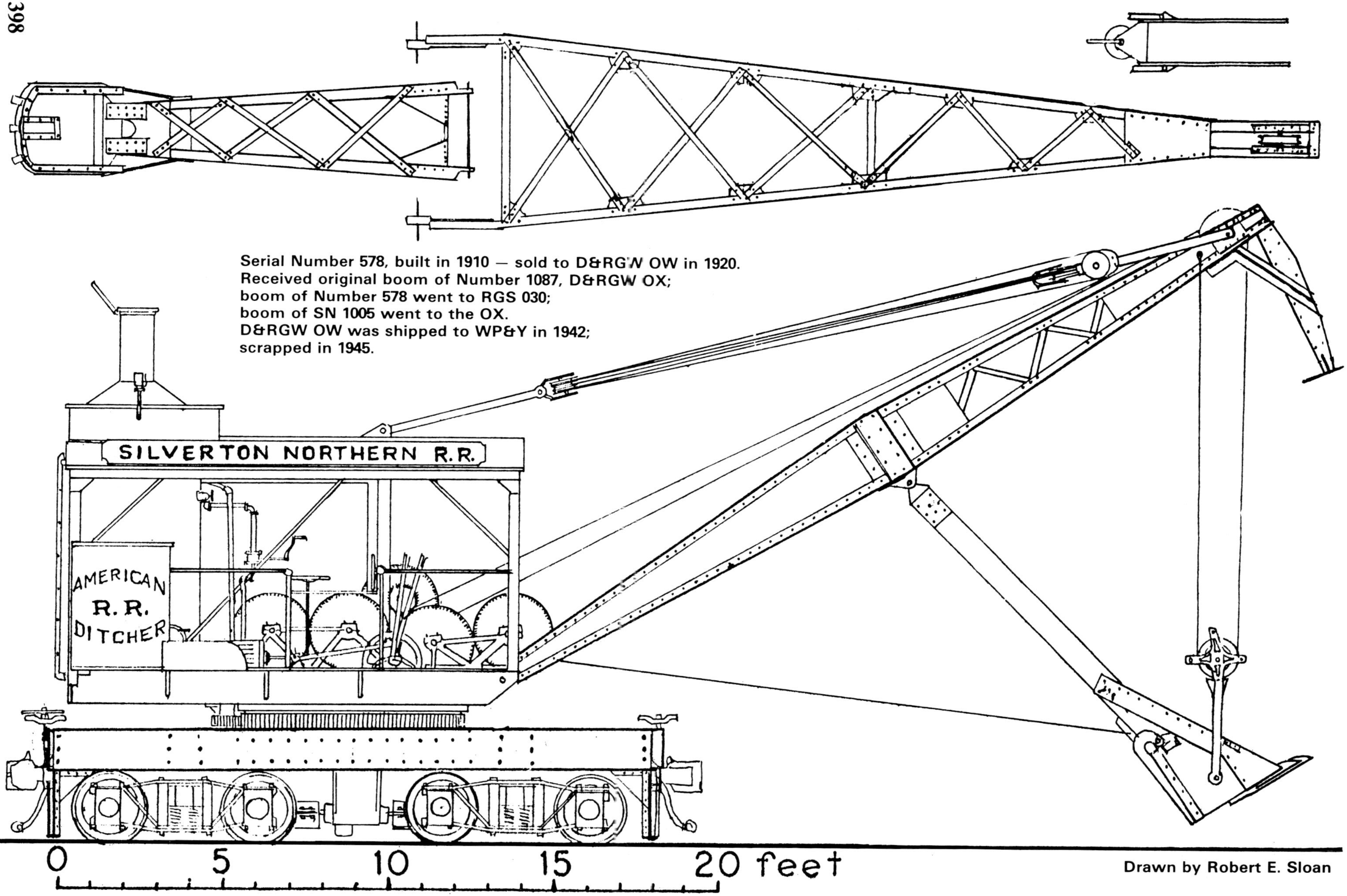

SILVERTON NORTHERN R.R.

AMERICAN R.R. DITCHER

20 feet

Drawn by Robert E. Sloan

398

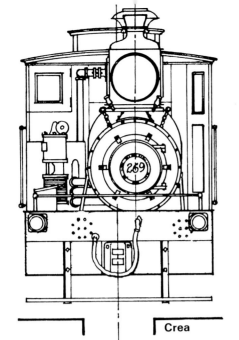

Crea

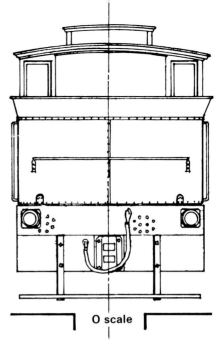

O scale

SILVERTON RAILROAD
SHAY NUMBER 269

0   5   10   15

SCALE IN FEET

SRR COMBINE
RED MOUNTAIN

SILVERTON RAILROAD
BAGGAGE-EXPRESS
NUMBER 5

O scale

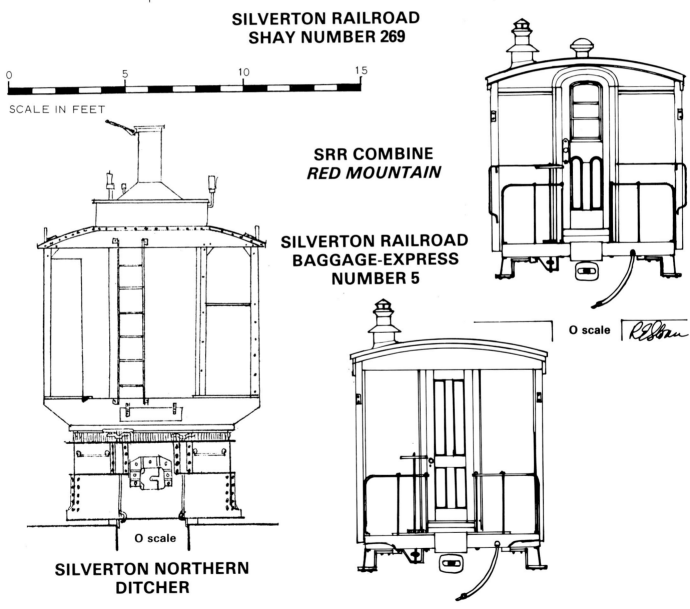

SILVERTON NORTHERN
DITCHER

O scale

SILVERTON RAILROAD COMPANY COMBINE
Red Mountain

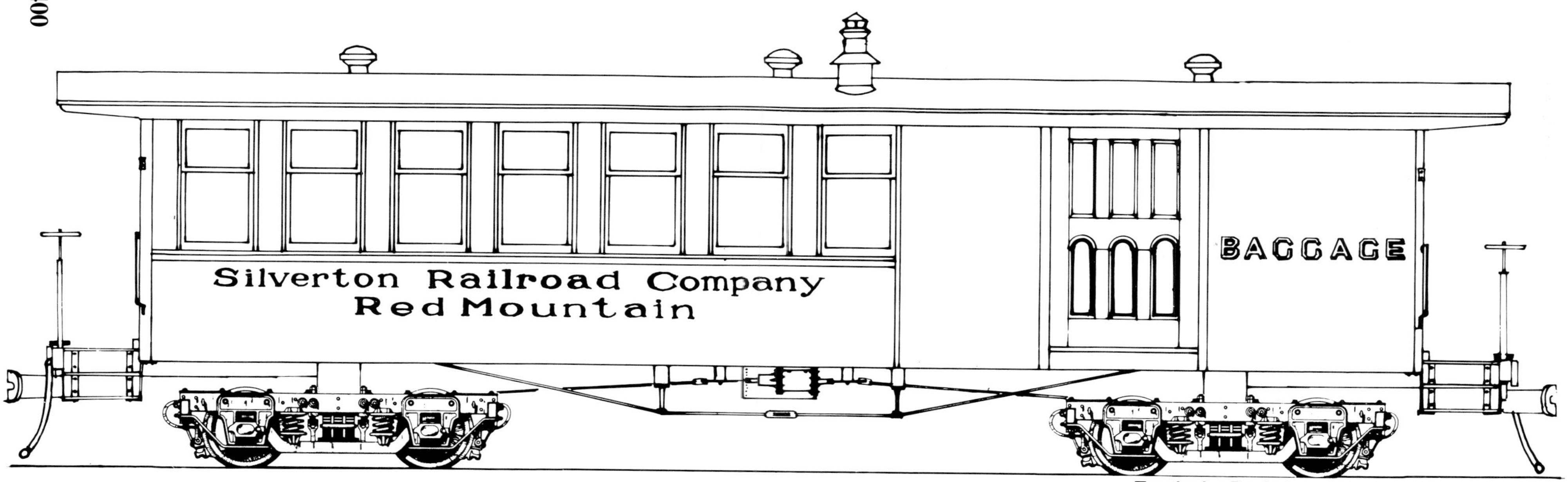

BAGGAGE

Silverton Railroad Company
Red Mountain

Trucks by Backshop

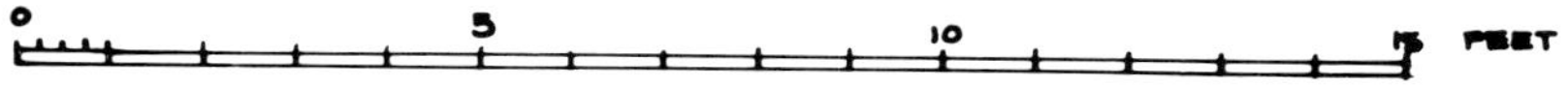

O scale

FEET

SILVERTON RAILROAD COMPANY
Baggage Express Car Number 5

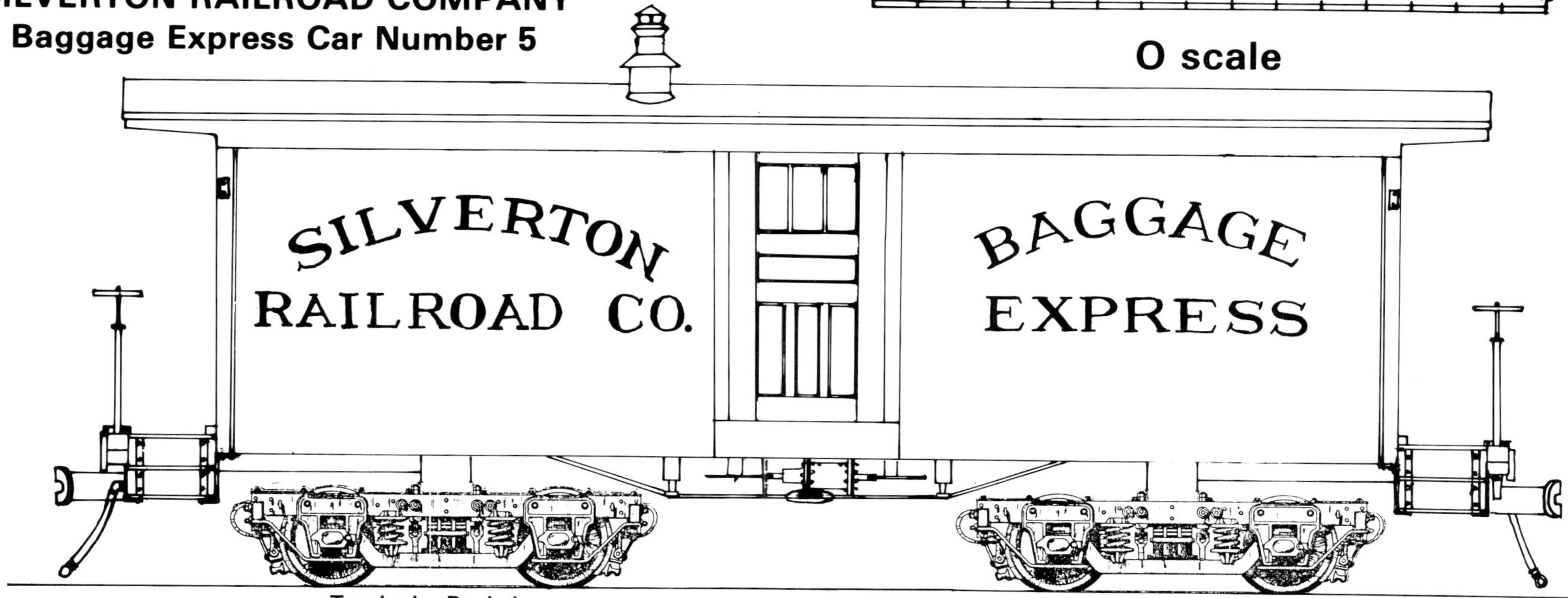

BAGGAGE EXPRESS

SILVERTON RAILROAD CO.

Trucks by Backshop

R E Sloan

400

SILVERTON NORTHERN PULLMAN CAR
ANIMAS FORKS

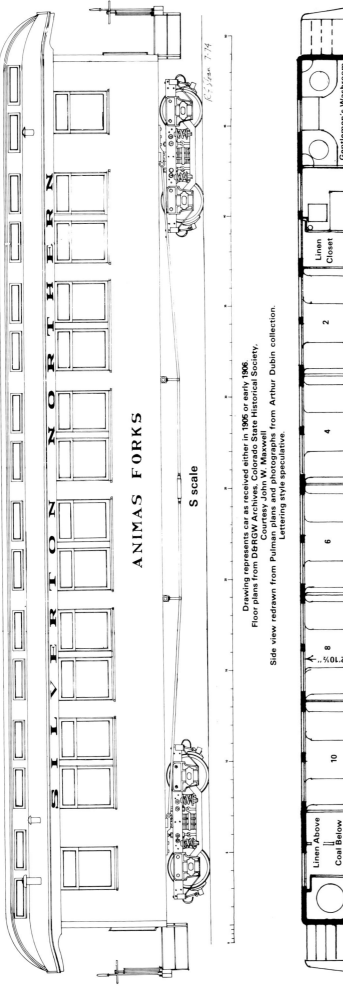

ANIMAS FORKS

S scale

Drawing represents car as received either in 1905 or early 1906.
Floor plans from D&RGW Archives, Colorado State Historical Society,
Courtesy John W. Maxwell
Side view redrawn from Pullman plans and photographs from Arthur Dubin collection.
Lettering style speculative.

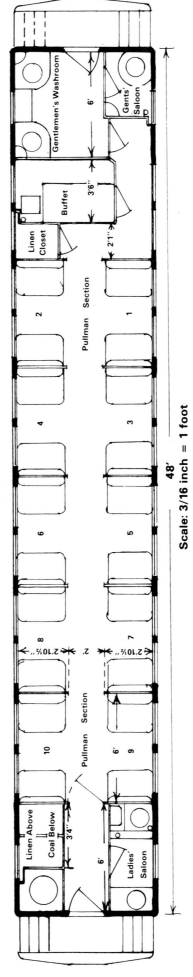

Gentlemen's Washroom

Gents'
Saloon

6'

3'6"

Buffet

Linen
Closet

2'1"

Pullman Section

2

1

4

3

6

5

8

7

2'10½"

2'

2'10½"

10

9

6'

Linen Above
Coal Below

3'4"

Ladies'
Saloon

6'

48'

Scale: 3/16 inch = 1 foot

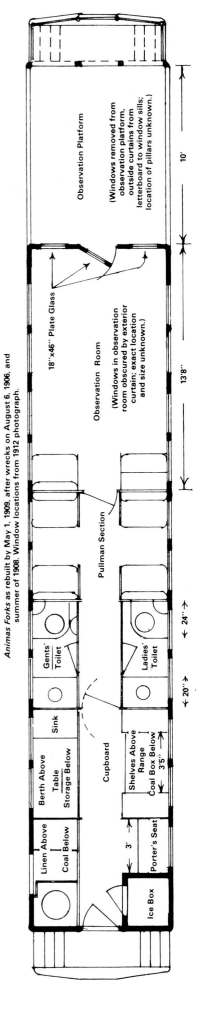

Observation Platform

(Windows removed from
observation platform,
outside curtains from
letterboard to window sills;
location of pillars unknown.)

10'

18"x46" Plate Glass

Observation Room

(Windows in observation
room obscured by exterior
curtain; exact location
and size unknown.)

13'8"

Pullman Section

Gents'
Toilet

Ladies'
Toilet

24'

Sink

Cupboard

Shelves Above
Range

Coal Box Below

3'5"

20'

Berth Above
Table

Storage Below

Linen Above
Coal Below

Porter's Seat

3'

Ice Box

Animas Forks as rebuilt by May 1, 1909, after wrecks on August 6, 1906, and
summer of 1908. Window locations from 1912 photograph.

DENVER.&. RIO GRANDE. RAILWAY.
STANDARD BOX CAR
DENVER SHOPS
3-26-81

D&RG Ry. plan for the standard 10-ton 1881 boxcar. SRR boxcars 500 to 544 and SN boxcars 100 to 109 were this type of car.

D&RGW Collection — Courtesy of Jackson C. Thode

O Scale: 1/4 inch = 1 foot

SG&N BOXCAR
O scale

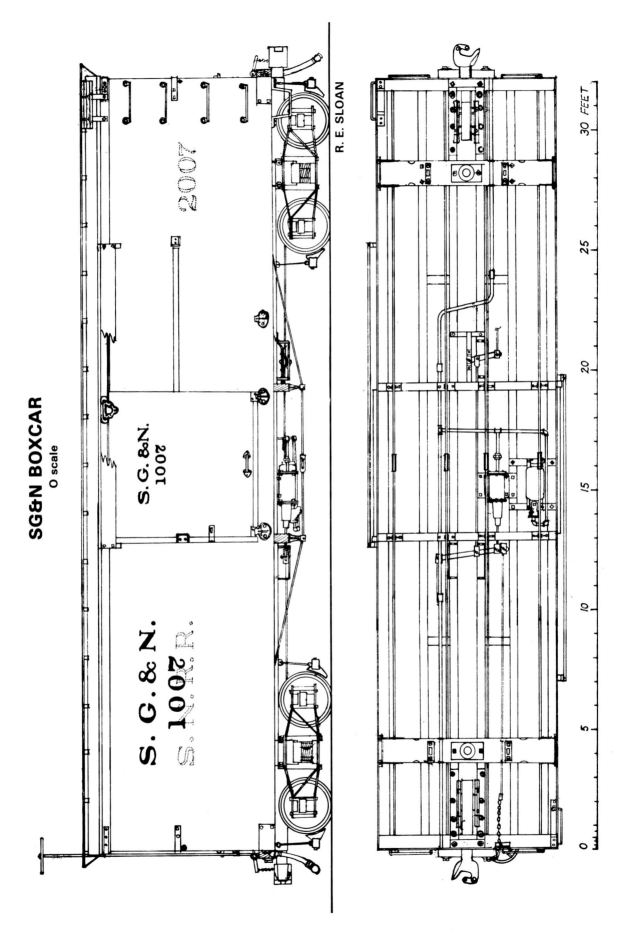

R. E. SLOAN

S. G. &N.
1001

S. G. & N.
2001

30 FEET
25
20
15
10
5
0

DENVER & RIO GRANDE FLANGER

Flanger Scale 1/4" = 1ft. D&RG Shops Durham, Denver Colo.
Designed September 1885. Flanger No.1 put in service November 14th '85

The Silverton shortlines had at least two of these cars

Courtesy Jackson Thode

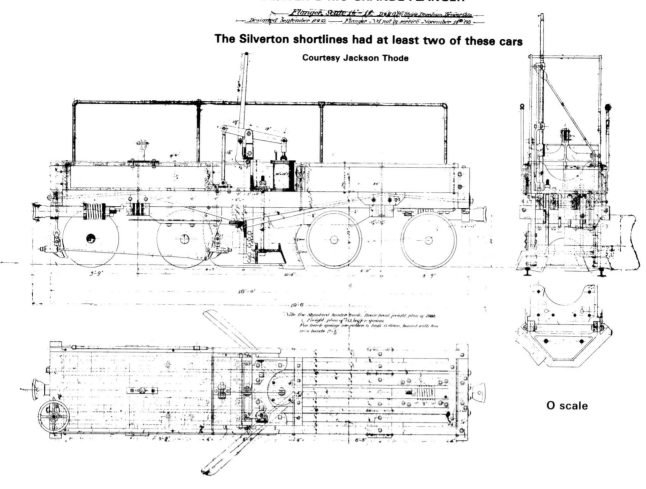

O scale

DENVER & RIO GRANDE RAILWAY
STANDARD BOXCAR — August 26, 1881.

As lettered for cars used by the
Silverton Railroad and the
Silverton Northern Railroad.

HO scale

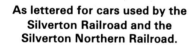

SG&N BOXCAR
O scale

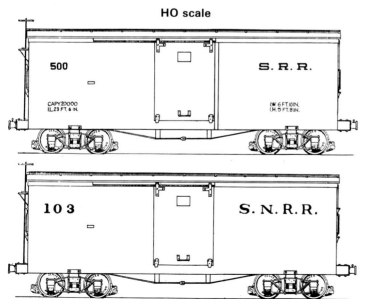

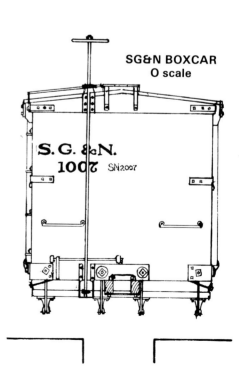

STANDARD "CABOOSE CAR" D.&R.G.RR.
DENVER SHOPS

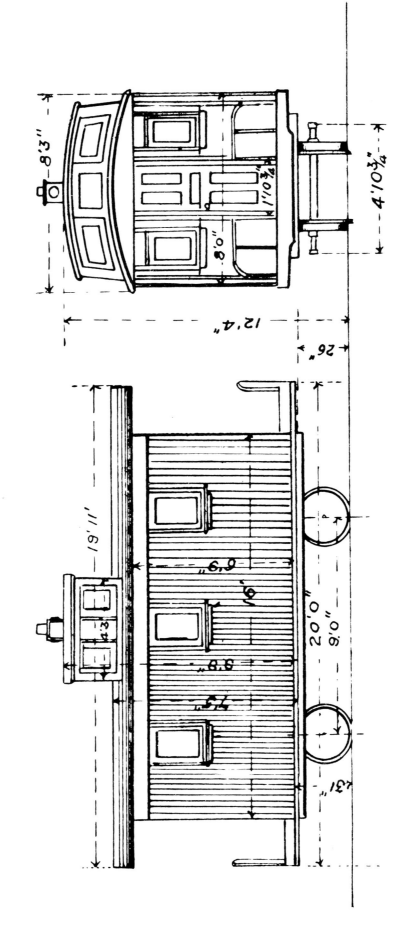

SILVERTON NORTHERN CABOOSE
Number 1005

SILVERTON RAILWAY CABOOSE
Number 17

O Scale: 1/4 inch = 1 foot

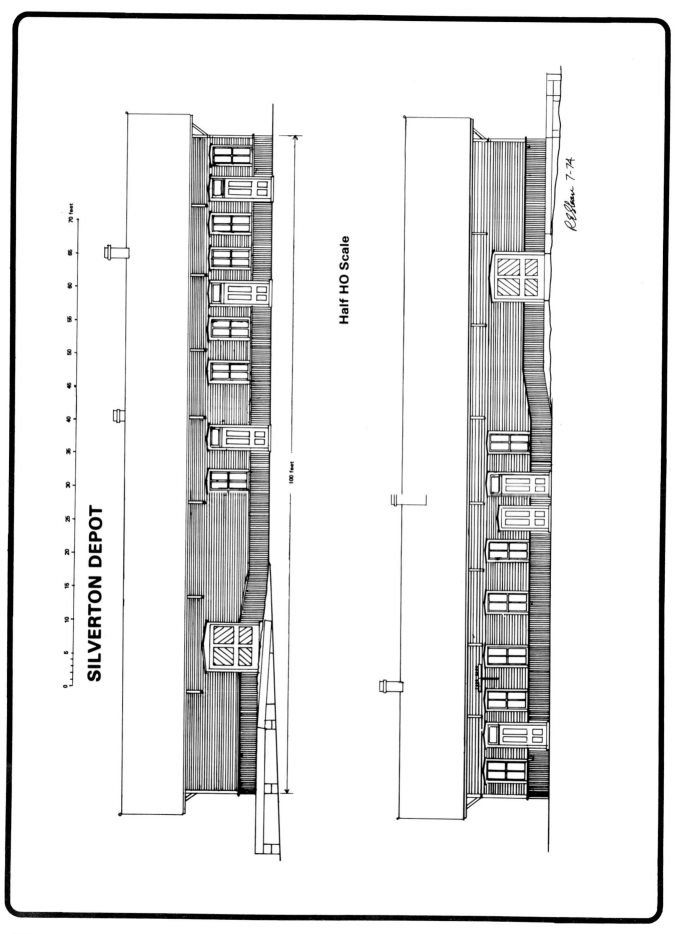

SILVERTON DEPOT

Half HO Scale

R.E.Sloan 7-74

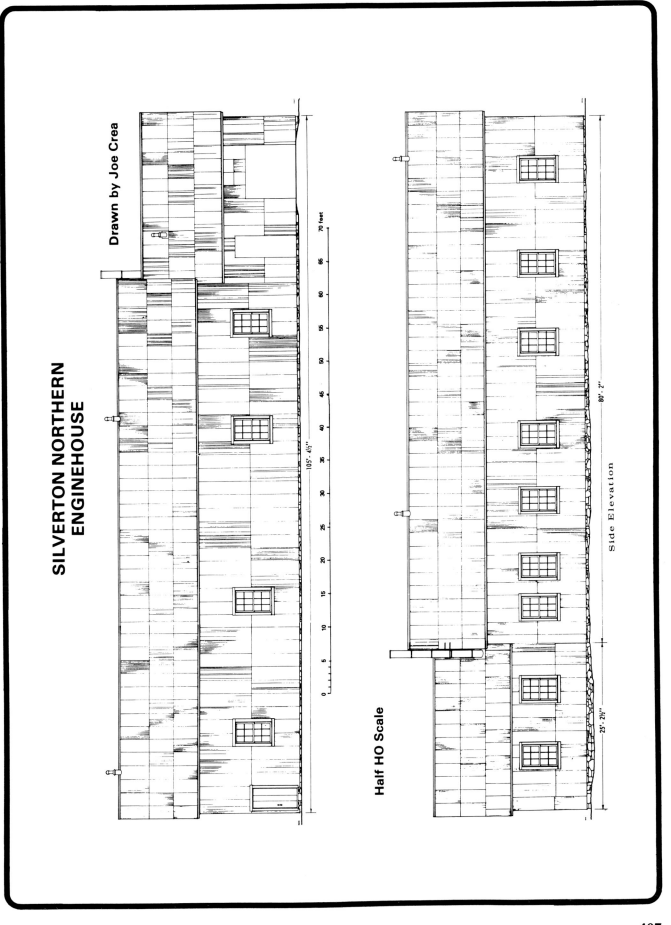

SILVERTON NORTHERN
ENGINEHOUSE

Drawn by Joe Crea

Half HO Scale

Side Elevation

105' - 4½"

80' - 2"

25' - 2½"

0   5   10   15   20   25   30   35   40   45   50   55   60   65   70 feet

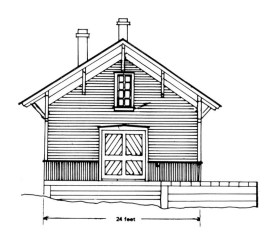

24 feet

R.E. Sloan 7-74

END PLANS
DEPOT &
ENGINEHOUSE

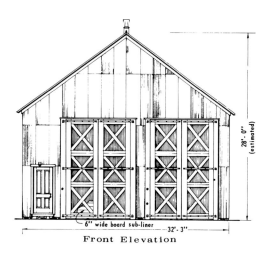

28'- 0" (estimated)

6" wide board sub-liner

32'- 3"

Front Elevation

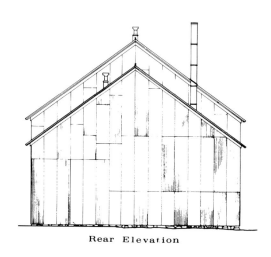

Rear Elevation

Half HO Scale

0   5   10   15   20   25 feet

RED MOUNTAIN DEPOT
HO scale
Drawn by Randall Williams

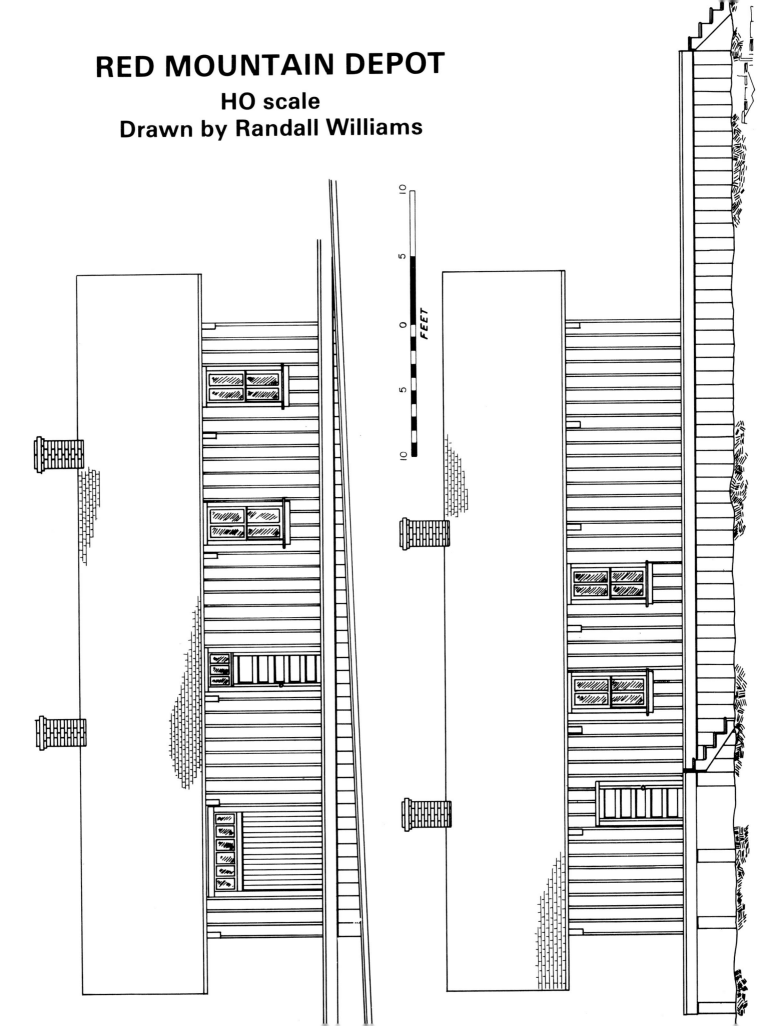

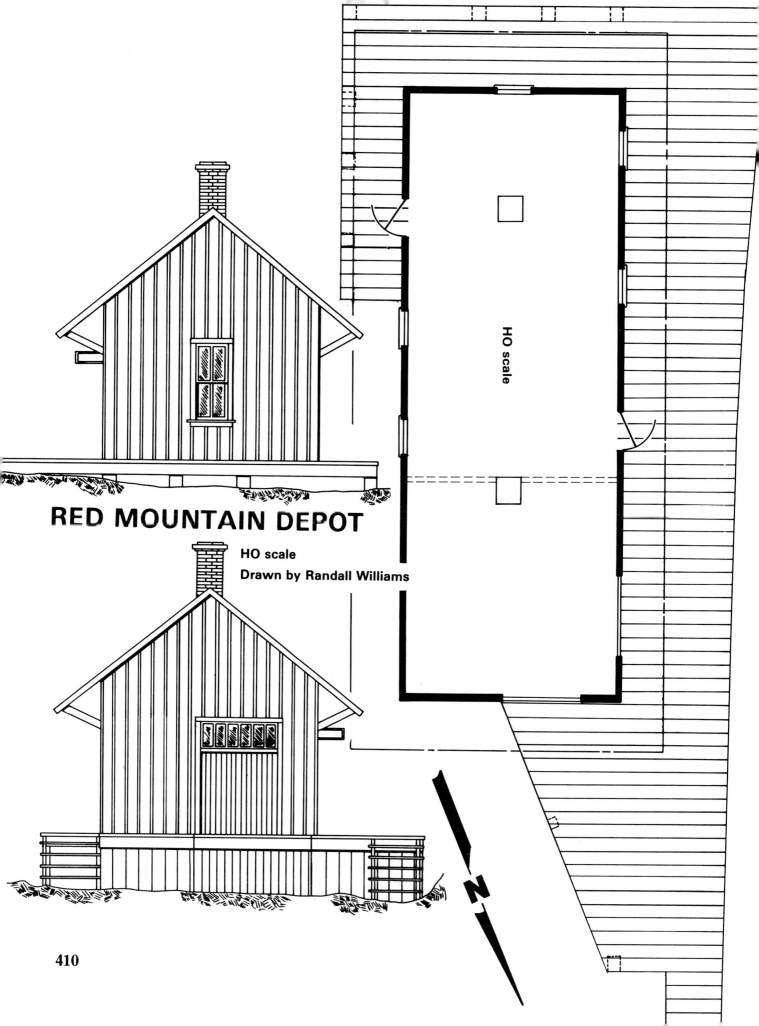

RED MOUNTAIN DEPOT

HO scale
Drawn by Randall Williams

HO scale

N

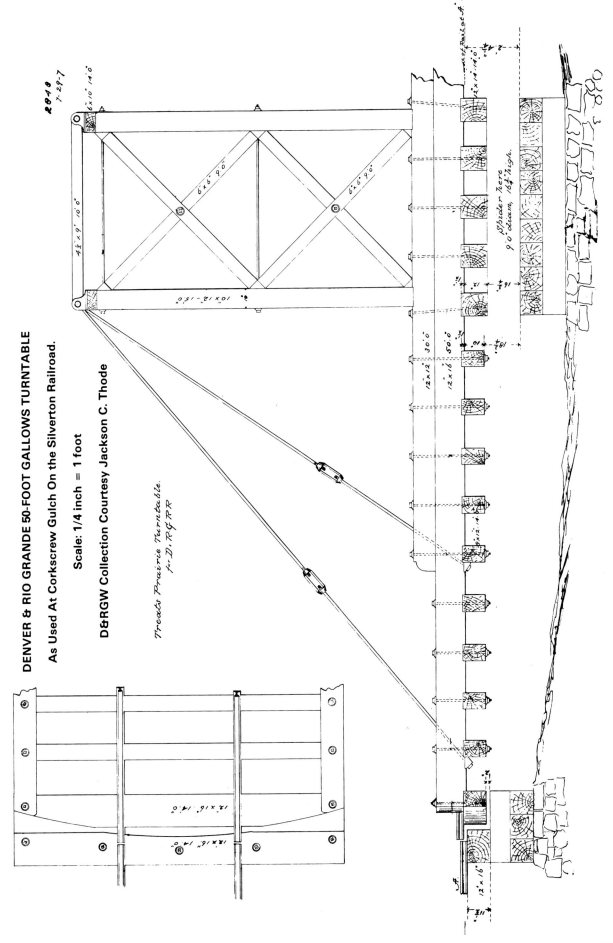

DENVER & RIO GRANDE 50-FOOT GALLOWS TURNTABLE

As Used At Corkscrew Gulch On the Silverton Railroad.

Scale: 1/4 inch = 1 foot

D&RGW Collection Courtesy Jackson C. Thode

D&RG 50-FOOT GIRDER TURNTABLE

Originally used at Marshall Pass and transferred to Animas Forks on the Silverton Northern in 1904

Courtesy of Jackson Thode

Scale: 3/16 inch = 1 foot

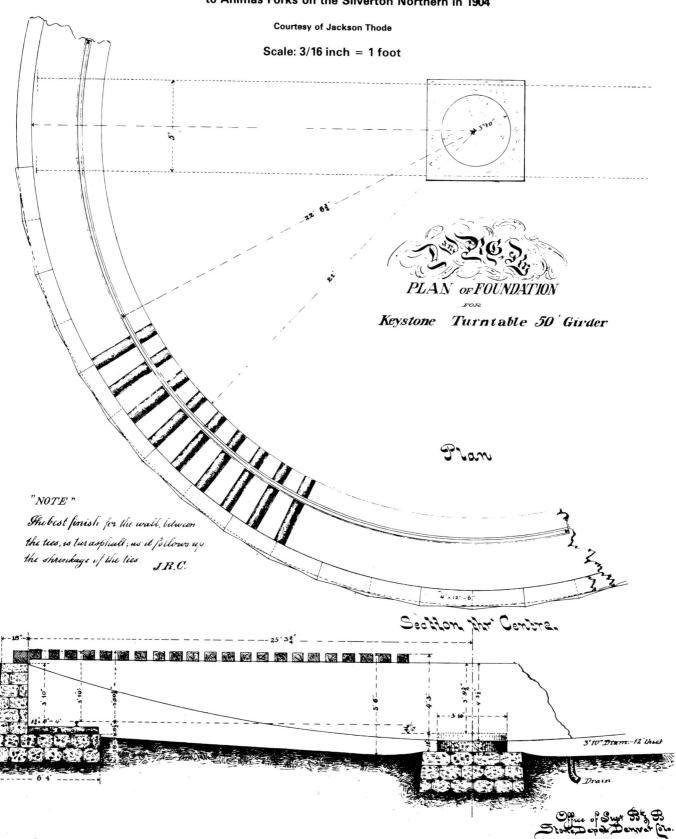

D&RG

PLAN of FOUNDATION

FOR

Keystone   Turntable 50' Girder

Plan

"NOTE"

The best finish for the wall, between the ties, is tar asphalt; as it follows up the shrinkage of the ties.   J.R.C.

Section thr' Centre.

Office of Supt B & B
Stone Depot Denver Colo.

Bibliography

The bulk of the unpublished archival material on the three Silverton shortline railroads is in the Mears collection of the State Historical Society of Colorado at the Colorado State Museum, Denver. These consist of personal letters and the surviving files of the Silverton Northern Railroad.

The letter book of the Silverton Northern, covering the period from May 1, 1896, to July of 1900, is in the files of the Colorado Railroad Museum at Golden, Colorado. The cash book, ledger and journal of the Silverton Railroad, for the period from April 1, 1889, to December 31, 1891, are in the files of the San Juan County Historical Society at Silverton. The original survey books of the Silverton Railroad, together with those of the Ouray and Ironton Electric Railway, Light and Power Company, likewise are in the custody of the San Juan County Historical Society.

No archival material for the Silverton, Gladstone and Northerly Railroad has been found in Colorado. Some may yet exist in New England, although it did not come to light in our research.

NEWSPAPER FILES CONSULTED INCLUDE:

The Silverton Weekly Miner (Silverton, Colo.), in particular, the special 65-page issue of September 27, 1907, entitled, *The Golden San Juan Edition,* which reviewed in detail much of the mining and railroad history of the region to that date.
The Silverton Standard (Silverton, Colorado).
The Denver Post (Denver, Colorado).

BOOKS AND PAMPHLETS INCLUDE:

Anonymous, 1899, reprinted 196(?), *San Juan County,* 44-pages, The Silverton Standard, Silverton, Colorado.
Athearn, Robert G., 1962, *Rebel of the Rockies: A History of the Denver and Rio Grande Western Railroad,* 395 pages, Yale University Press, New Haven, Connecticut.
Bauer, W. H.; Ozment, J. L.; and Willard, J. H.; 1971, *Colorado Postal History: The Post Offices,* J-B Publishing Company, Crete, Nebraska.
Beebe, Lucius; and Clegg, Charles; 1958, *Narrow Gauge in the Rockies,* 224 pages, Howell-North Books, Berkeley, California.
Brown, Robert L., 1965, *An Empire of Silver,* 334 pages, Caxton Printers, Ltd., Caldwell, Idaho.
Burbank, Wilbur S.; and Luedke, Robert G.; 1969, *Geology and Ore Deposits of the Eureka and Adjoining Districts, San Juan Mountains, Colorado,* U.S. Geological Survey Professional Paper 535, 75 pages.
Burbank, W. S., et al, 1941, *Preliminary Geologic Map of the Red Mountain, Sneffels, and Telluride Districts of the Silverton Caldera, Ouray and San Miguel Counties, Colorado,* U.S. Geological Survey, Washington, D.C.
Chappell, Gordon S., 1971, *Logging Along the Denver and Rio Grande,* 190 pages, Colorado Railroad Museum, Golden, Colorado.
Crofutt, George A., 1885, reprinted 1966, *Grip Sack Guide of Colorado,* 264 pages, Cubar Associates, Golden, Colorado.
Cross, Whitman; Howe, Ernest; and Ransome, F. L.; *Silverton Folio,* U.S. Geological Survey Folio 120, Washington, D.C.
Crum, Josie Moore, 1960, *Three Little Lines,* 78 pages, Durango Herald-News, Durango, Colorado.
Crum, Josie Moore, 1961, *The Rio Grande Southern Railroad,* 431 pages, San Juan History, Durango, Colorado.
Denver and Rio Grande Railroad, *Official Roster,* Number 20, June 1, 1891, to Number 37, January 1, 1901; Number 1, April 1, 1902, to Number 10, April 1, 1916.
Denver and Rio Grande Western Railroad, *Official Roster,* Number 11, April 1, 1923.
Eberhart, Perry, 1969, *Guide to the Colorado Ghost Towns and Mining Camps,* fourth edition, revised, 496 pages, Sage Books, Chicago, Illinois.
Ferrell, Mallory H., 1973, *Silver San Juan: The Rio Grande Southern Railroad,* 643 pages, Pruett Publishing Company, Boulder, Colorado.
Hauck, Cornelius; and Richardson, Robert; 1963, *Steam in the Rockies, A Steam Locomotive Roster of the Denver and Rio Grande,* 32 pages, Colorado Railroad Museum, Golden, Colorado.
Kaplan, Michael, 1971, "Otto Mears and the Silverton Northern Railroad," *Colorado Maga-*

zine, Volume XLVIII, Number 3, pp 235-254 Denver, Colorado.

Koch, Michael, 1971, *The Shay Locomotive: Titan of the Timber,* 500 pages, World Press, Denver, Colorado.

Kulp, Randolph L., editor, 1959, *History of Mack Rail Motor Cars and Locomotives,* Lehigh Valley Chapter, National Railroad Historical Society, Allentown, Pennsylvania.

Kushner, Ervan F., 1973, *A Guide to Mineral Collecting at Ouray, Colorado, with Notes as to the History and Geology,* second edition, enlarged, 80 pages, published by the author, 5 Colt Street, Paterson, New Jersey.

Interstate Commerce Commission, 1922, *Finance Docket Number 1549, Abandonment of Line by Silverton Railway,* Reports, Volume 72, pages 13 to 16, Washington, D.C.

Interstate Commerce Commission, *Annual Reports on the Statistics of Railways,* 1887 to 1909, Washington, D.C.

Interstate Commerce Commission, 1927, *Valuation Docket Number 568, Silverton Northern Railroad Company,* Reports, Volume 121, pp 635-655, Washington, D.C.

Interstate Commerce Commission, 1942, *Finance Docket number 13738, Silverton Northern Railroad Company Abandonment.* Reports, volume 252, p. 807.

LeMassena, Robert A., 1963-1965, *Colorado's Mountain Railroads,* Volumes I-III, Smoking Stack Press, Golden, Colorado.

Lima Locomotive Works, 1925, *Shay Geared Locomotives, Catalogue Number S-4,* 30 pages, reprinted 1971 by Old Line Publishers, Milwaukee, Wisconsin.

Lipman, P. W., et al, 1970, *Volcanic History of the San Juan Mountains,* Geological Society of America Bulletin, Volume 81, pp 2329-2352.

Luedke, Robert G.; and Burbank, Wilbur S.; 1968, *Volcanism and Cauldron Development in the Western San Juan Mountains, Colorado,* Colorado School of Mines Quarterly, Volume 63, Number 3, pp 175-208.

Morley, Jim, " 'Oh Hell' Albertson, Engineer,"

Trains magazine, November, 1942, pp 4-15, Kalmbach Publishing Company, Milwaukee, Wisconsin.

Osborn, James D., "He Built Narrow-Gauge Roads," *Railroad Magazine,* February, 1941, pp. 76-85.

Osterwald, Doris B., 1965, *Cinders & Smoke,* 96 pages, Western Guideways, Lakewood, Colorado.

Poor's Manual of Railroads, 1887-1940.

Portrait and Biographical Record of the State of Colorado, 1899, pp 1253-1254, Chapman Publishing Company, Chicago, Illinois.

Railroad Gazette, 1887-1908, *Railway Age Gazette,* 1902-1913, *Railway Gazette,* 1914-1938, Simmons-Boardman Publishing Company.

Ransome, F. L., 1901, *Economic Geology of the Silverton Quadrangle,* U.S. Geological Survey Bulletin 182, 265 pages, Washington, D.C.

Ranger, Dan Jr., 1964, *Pacific Coast Shay,* 112 Pages, Golden West Books, San Marino, California.

Ronzio, Richard A., 1967, *Colorado Smelting and Reduction Works,* 1966 Brand Book, Volume XXII, pp 109-145, Denver Westerners, Denver, Colorado.

Schneider, James G., 1975, *Otto Mears — Pathfinder of the San Juan.* The Westerners Brand Book, Chicago, volume 31, pp. 81-88.

Searcy, Helen M., et al, editors, 1942-1961, *Pioneers of the San Juan Country,* Volumes I-IV, 792 pages, Sarah Platt Decker Chapter, National Society of the Daughters of the American Republic, Durango, Colorado.

Smith, Duane A., 1970, *Ho for the San Juans,* 20 pages, privately published, Durango, Colorado.

Varnes, David J., 1963, *Geology and Ore Deposits of the South Silverton District, San Juan Mountains, Colorado,* U.S. Geological Survey Professional Paper 378-A.

Wolle, Muriel S., 1949, *Stampede to Timberline, The Ghost Towns and Mining Camps of Colorado,* 544 pages, published by the author, Boulder, Colorado.

INDEX

Index Continued

ADDITIONAL REFERENCES —

For additional reading, you may wish to refer to the following books:

LeMassena, Robert A. *Rio Grande . . . to the Pacific!* Sundance Publications, Ltd., Denver, Colorado, 1974.

McCoy, Dell A. and Russ Collman. *The Rio Grande Pictorial.* Sundance Publications, Ltd., Denver, Colorado, 1971.

Williams, Ames W. *Otto Mears Goes East — The Chesapeake Beach Railway.* Meridian Sun Press, Alexandria, Virginia, 1975.